LAURA MAY TODD

How to Get Away

Cabins, cottages, hideouts and the design of retreat

Lannoo

Table of Contents

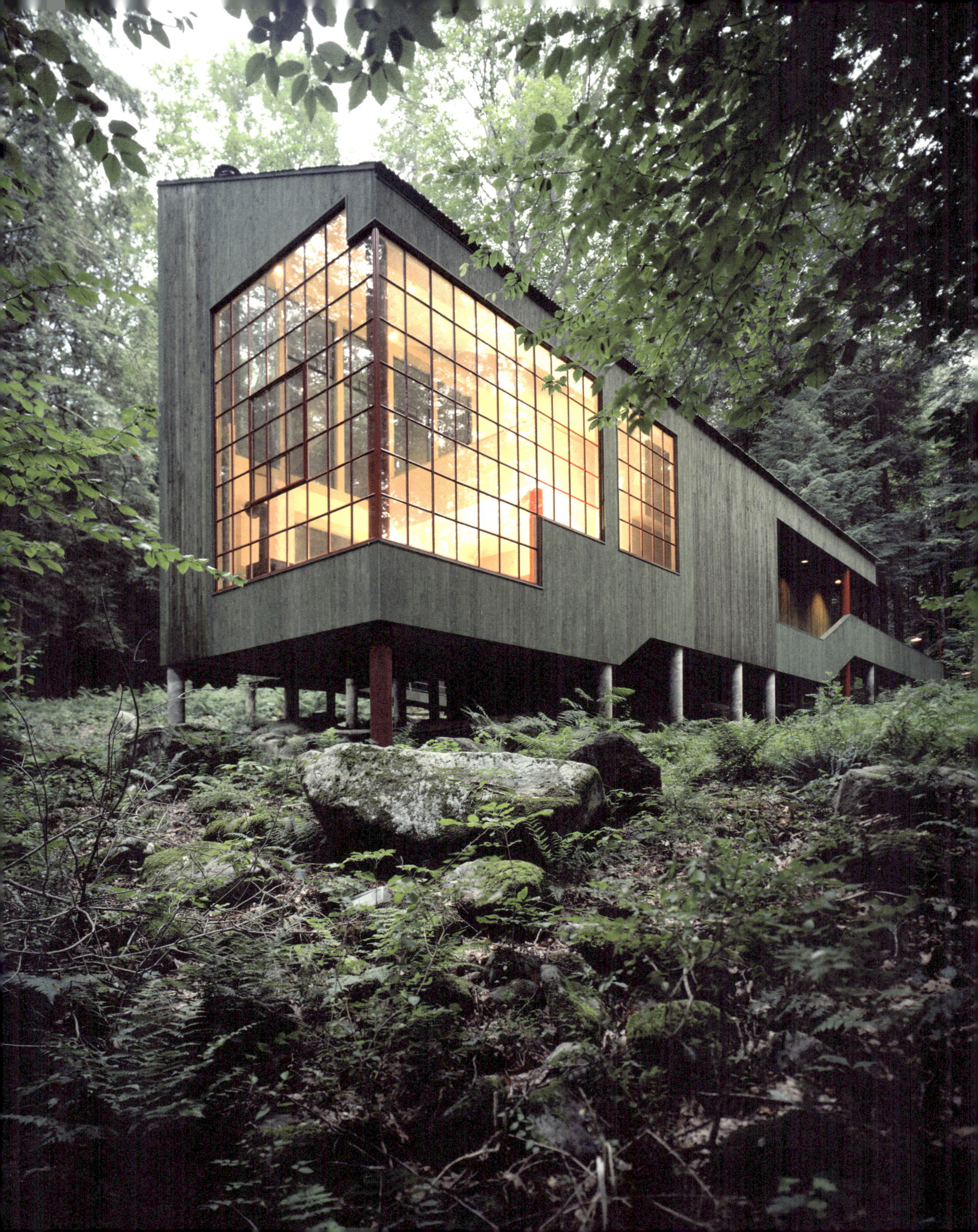

Introduction

The Design of Retreat

The Design of Retreat

When I was a child, I spent most of my weekends at a small cottage my family owned in the forested wilds of British Columbia, Canada. Most Friday afternoons, both in the hot, dry summer and the harsh deep freeze that is a Prairie winter (we lived in Calgary, Alberta, just past the foothills of the Rocky Mountains, roughly a four-hour drive away), my parents would pack my sister and me into our Windstar minivan and set out westward. There was nothing beautiful about the small house we would arrive at after hours spent weaving through mountain roads. Set in a quiet, remote valley in the Kootenay region, its exterior was clad with cheap aluminium siding, its floors were covered with peeling and yellowed linoleum, and the walls were made of plywood boards printed with a faux timber grain – a classic 1980s look. They were so thin I could hear my sister in the next room breathing as she slept. But it looked out over fluffy juniper bushes and a tangle of crab apple trees – spindly, grey-trunked figures – where we would watch white-tailed deer in the evenings teetering on their back legs to snatch the bitter-tasting fruit, or, if we were lucky, an ambling black bear sniffing for food on its way to or from its winter rest. Just beyond the trees was a field of tall grass scattered with wildflowers, where all day long you could hear the droning of bees, drowned out only by the chorus of crickets that would rise at dusk. If you kept going, the field abruptly stopped at the crest of a hill, where you would enter a pine forest that led down to a lake, a reservoir that meandered all the way to the American border a few hours south.

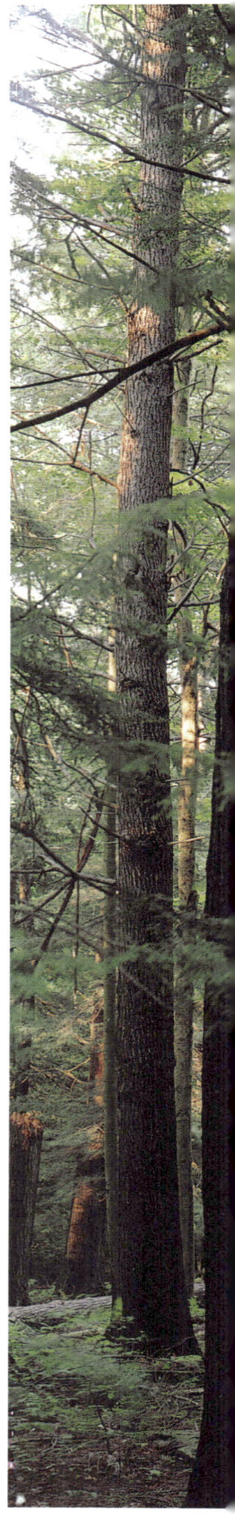

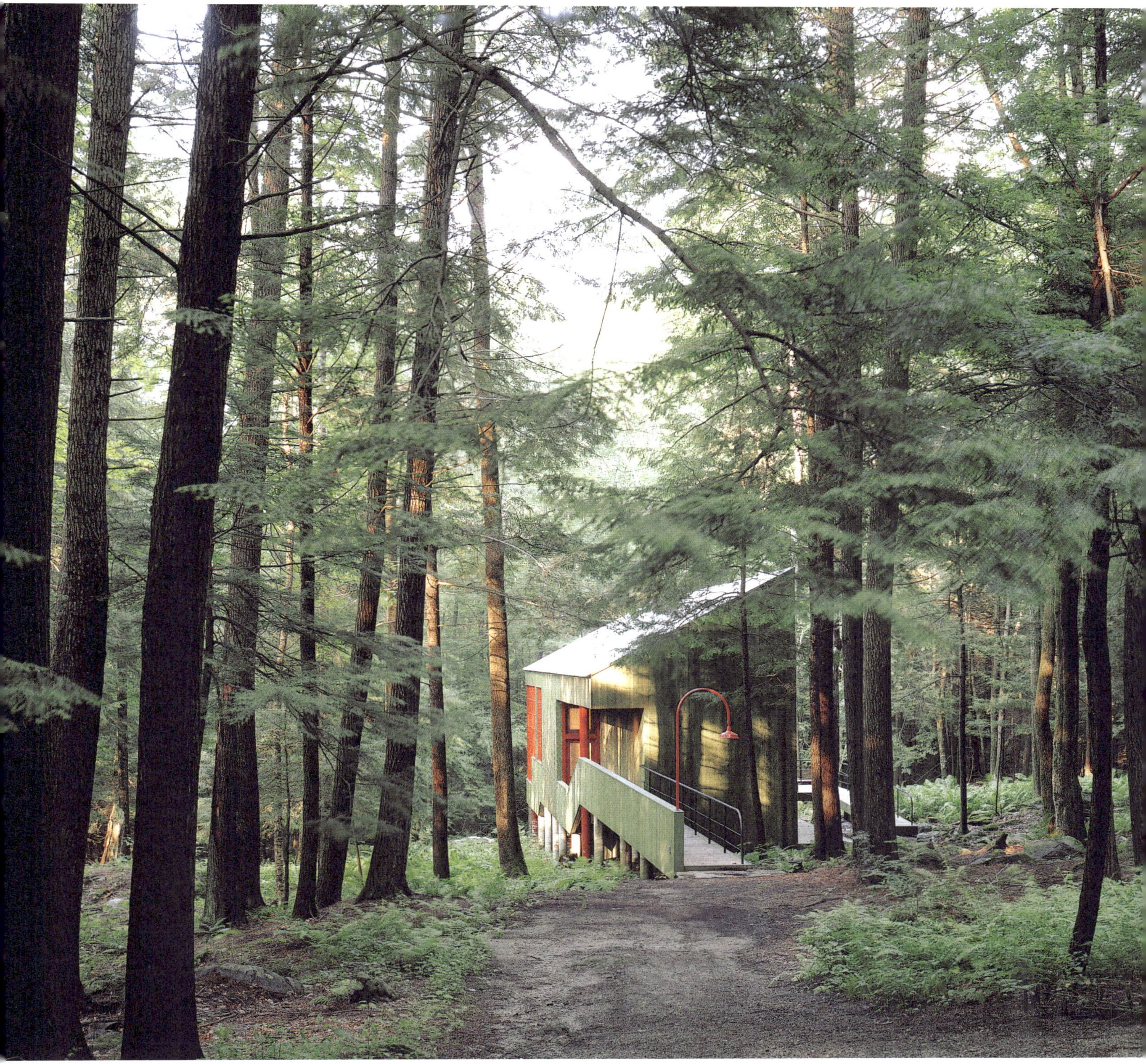

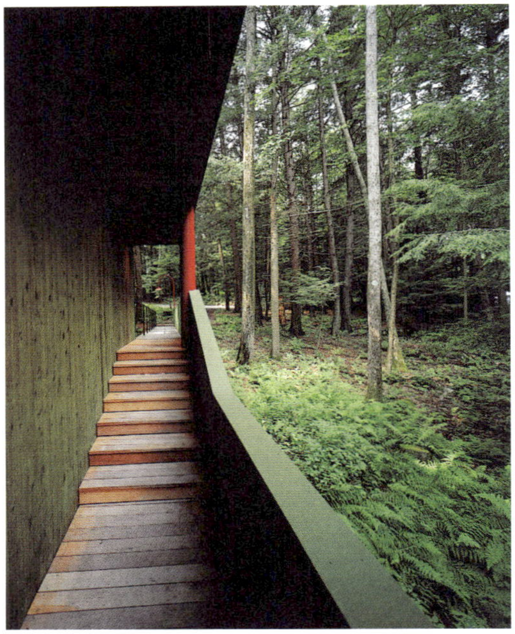

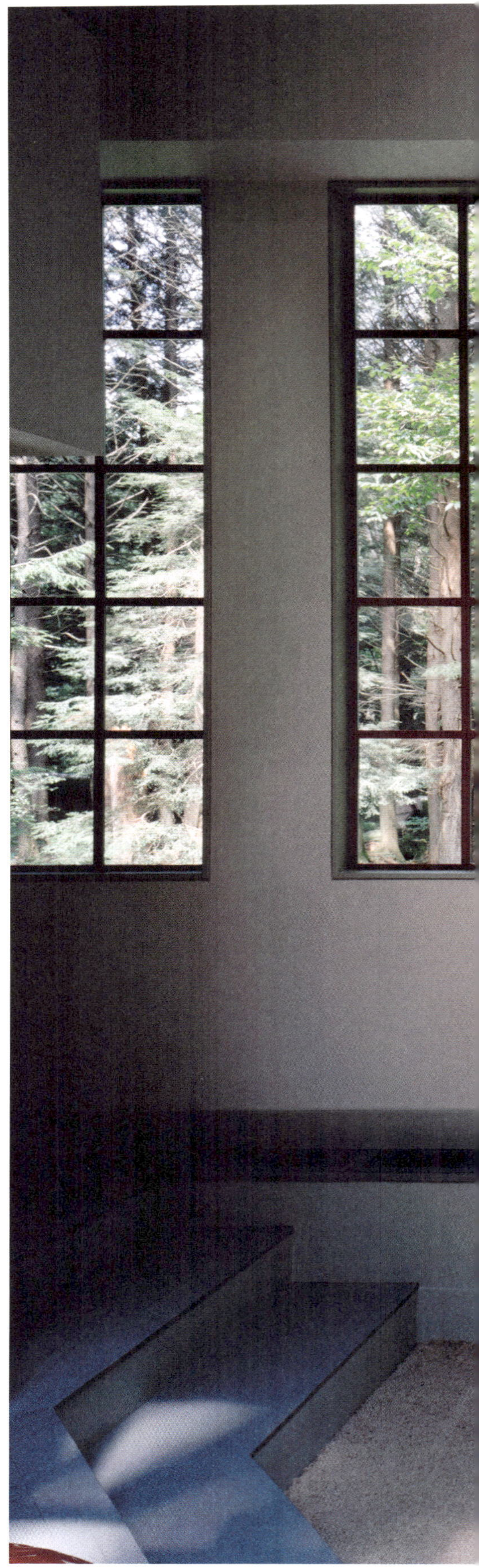

There was nothing special about the house's simple bones, but it was filled with the kind of quotidian souvenirs that give a family home its soul. On the shelves in the small living room, we had arranged our collection of misshapen rocks painted to resemble cars or flowers or frogs. There was a six-point deer antler proudly hung on a wall, which had been shed by one of the stags that frequented the apple trees, a trophy we had found on a walk in the forest one day in late fall. Beside it, there were taxonomic posters of the local fish that my father would pull from the network of rivers that ran nearby: rainbow trout, perch, Dolly Varden (a red-bellied cold water trout inexplicably named for a Dickens character). This is the landscape and its attendant bounty that imprinted on me at an early age, providing the mementoes that shaped my own idea of escape.

As an adult, when I imagine the perfect sanctuary where I would like to disconnect and disappear, my mind conjures a place similar to Forest House in West Cornwall, Connecticut by Peter Bohlin, co-founder of architecture firm Bohlin Cywinski Jackson. The house, a modest family refuge in the middle of a pine forest, was built in 1975 for Bohlin's parents. At the time, it was a quietly impressive architectural statement, a modernist reimagining of the forest cabin, a typology as old as colonial America itself. Rather than playing into the Davy Crockett-esque tropes one may associate with a cabin in the woods, Bohlin worked within the architectural language of his time, masterfully melding the strict tenets of modernism with what is clearly a keen devotion to the surrounding nature and its preservation.

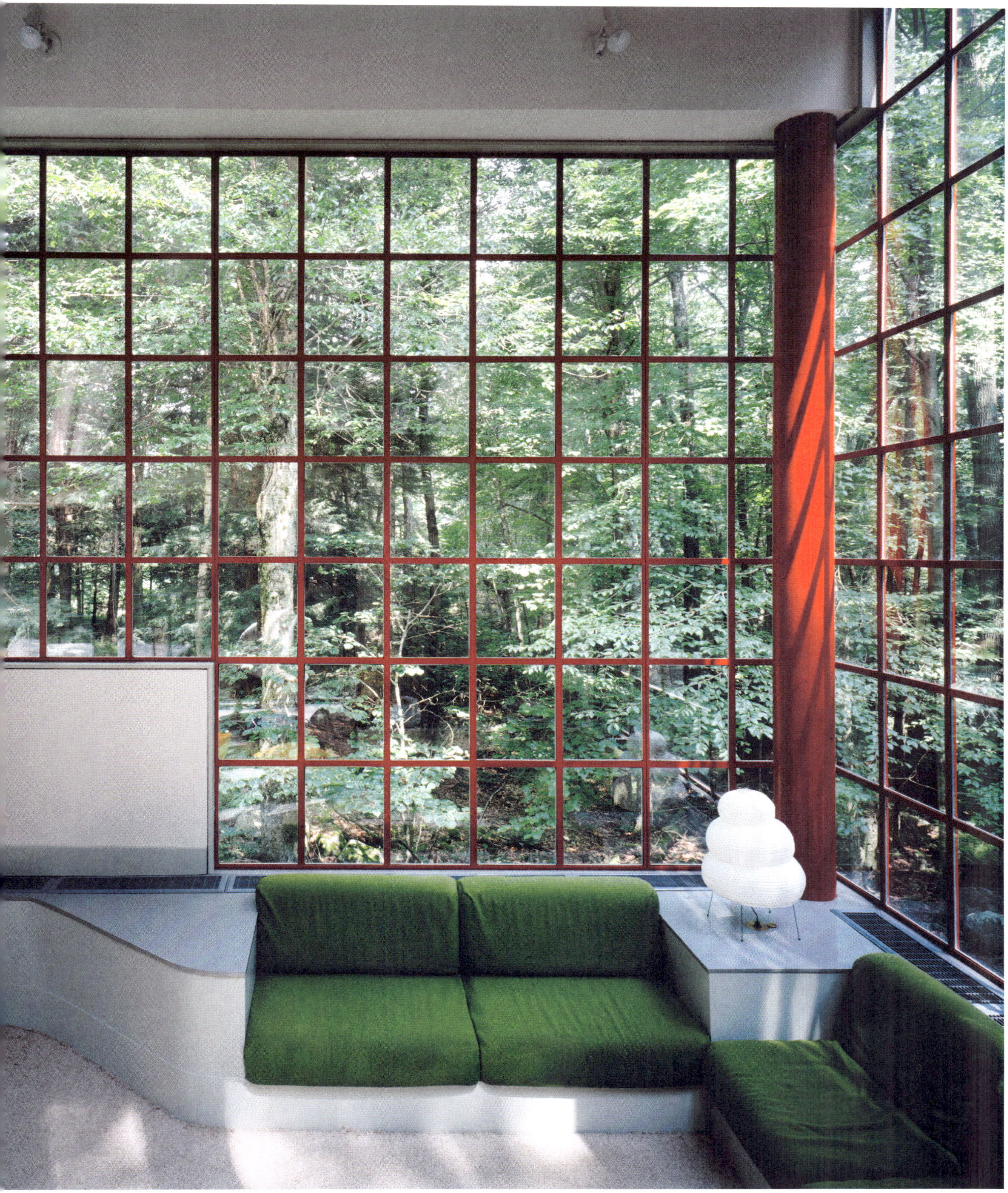

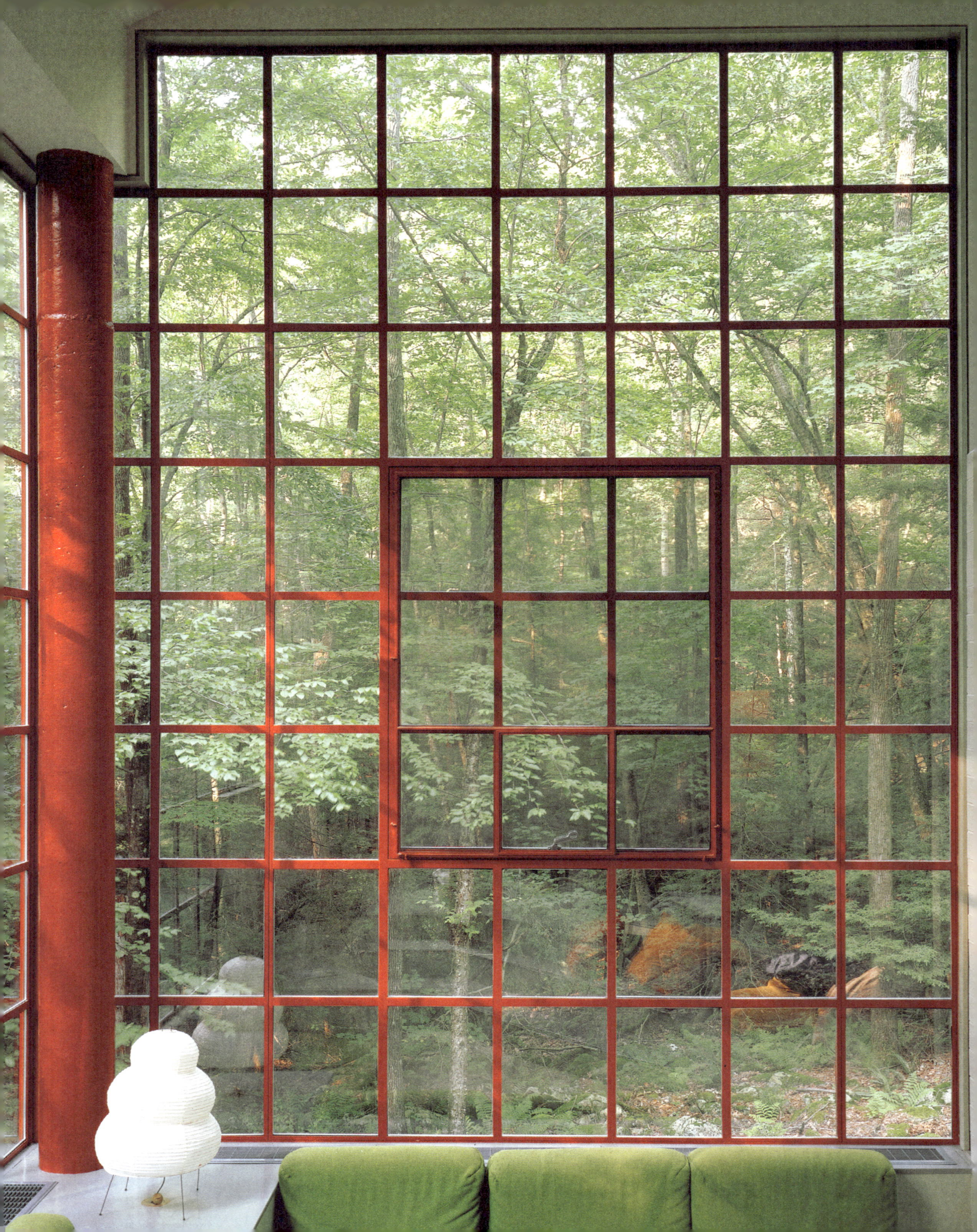

When I first came across pictures of the Forest House, it stirred something within me. It is seductive in a way that only the simplest of designs can be. Slender pilotis hoist the structure aloft, making the home seem as if it's floating above the mossy ground like a ship gliding through the forest – the walkway leading to the front door playing the role of the gangplank. Inside, clean white surfaces and sharp lines guide the eye to the natural treasures outdoors, a sea of pristine pine trees framed by tall industrial-style red-gridded windows. Aesthetically, it is worlds away from the simple cottage I grew up visiting on the weekends, but at its core, it speaks to the same desire to retreat: to completely lose oneself in the depths of nature. I can easily picture myself in the evening sitting on the sofa built into the wall next to the window, the yellow glow of the lights illuminating the house like a celestial orb hovering in the darkness, obscuring the swampy darkness of the woods beyond.

The motivation behind this book, *How To Get Away*, was to discover what exactly that vision of retreat is for some of the most creative and prolific artists and designers working today. Whether that may be their own hideout, or a space they have designed for a client or, in the case of Forest House, for a member of their own family, the notion of escape looks different for everybody. There is something fundamentally out of the ordinary about designing a home for escape. Unlike a primary residence, there is room for flights of fancy: to explore less conventional ways of living that wouldn't fly in the day-to-day.

In these pages, we will travel across the globe to see how those impulses play out. In the Namib Desert in Namibia, we visit an artist-designed house that mimics the local wildlife; in the south of France we peak into a chateau-retreat dreamed up by a prolific designer, while in Lebanon we wander round a stone house built into a mountain. Meanwhile, on both coasts of the United States, we encounter artists who have built their own worlds in wildly different ways.

Whether your idea of retreat is a mud-walled hut in the desert or, like me, a simple cabin in the forest, each designer, artist or homeowner has something in common: once planted, the desire to escape is, put simply, inescapable.

LAURA MAY TODD

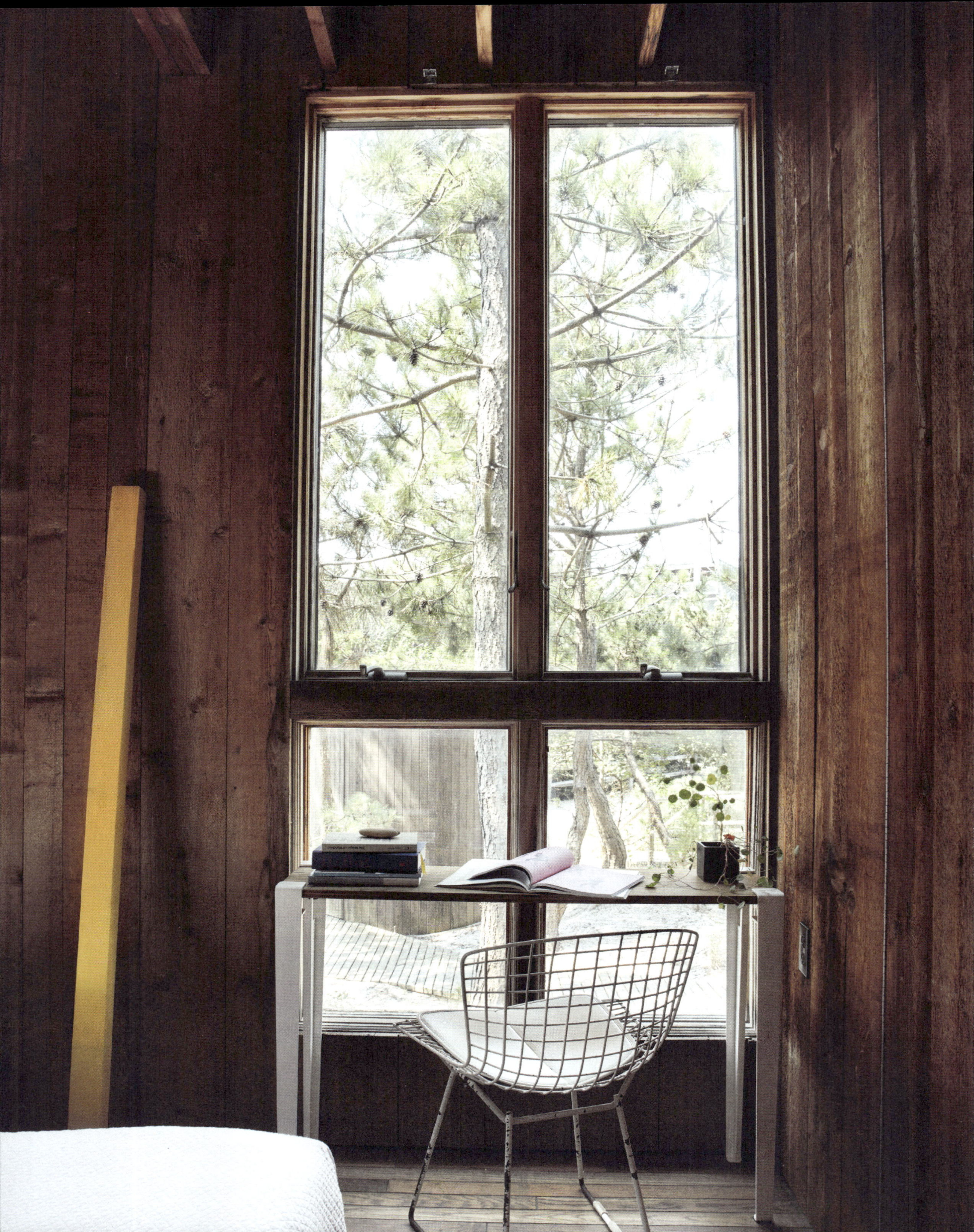

CHAPTER 01

Cabins & Cottages

When we conjure up the idea of a getaway house, it is often a rustic little abode, set deep within the forest, that is the first thing to come to mind. Perhaps an A-frame log cabin overlooking a waterfall, or a quaint lakeside cottage with no neighbours for miles. These homes, scattered across countries with vast areas of untamed wilderness like the United States and Sweden, encapsulate our innate desire to disappear into the landscape, interpreted through the creative lens of the architects, artists and designers who have realised them.

A Creative Couple's Rustic Refuge from the City

CARMEL, NEW YORK (US) **KEVIN RYAN & ROB ASHFORD**

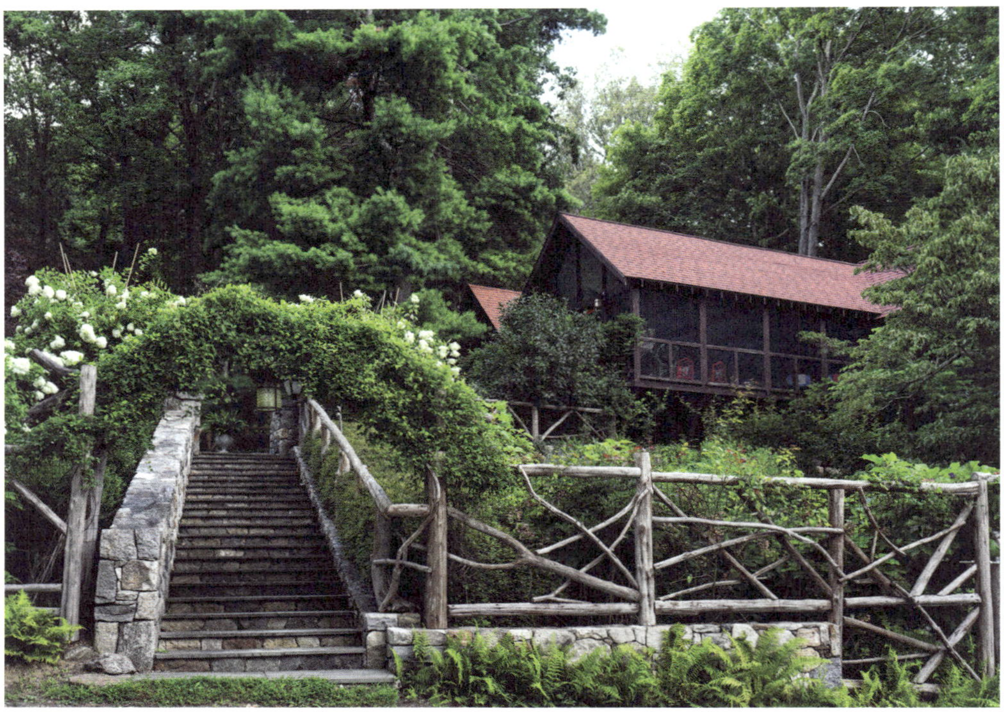

In the early 20th century, the wooded expanses of upstate New York were a popular retreat destination, where city dwellers would spend their summer months in rustic wooden bungalows, just large enough to fit a single family. These communities formed constellations around lakes or golf courses and often centred around a communal hall where holidaymakers would meet for meals and entertainment. However, by the 1960s, as international travel became more accessible, many of these retreats were rendered defunct. In recent years, though, their charm is being rediscovered.

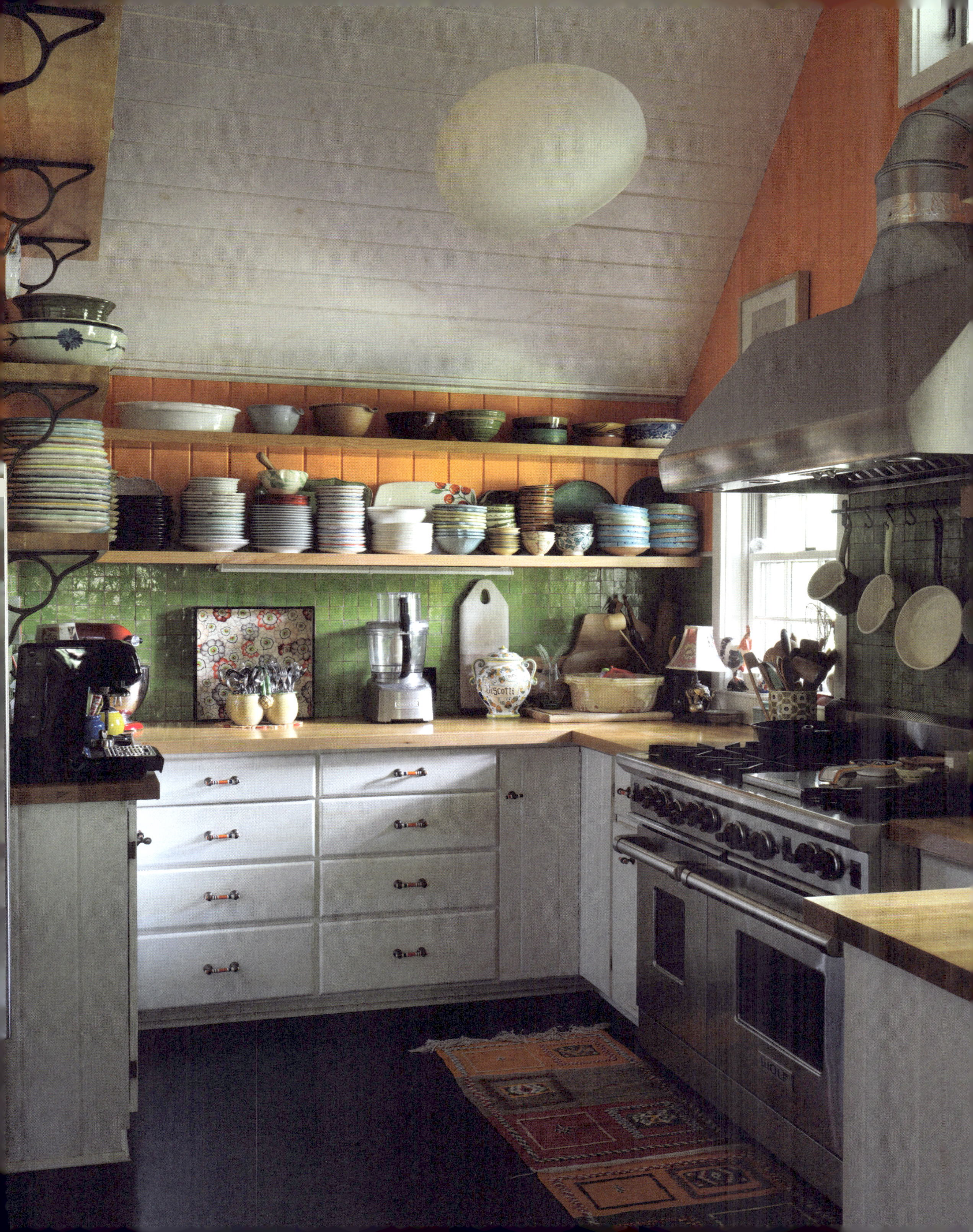

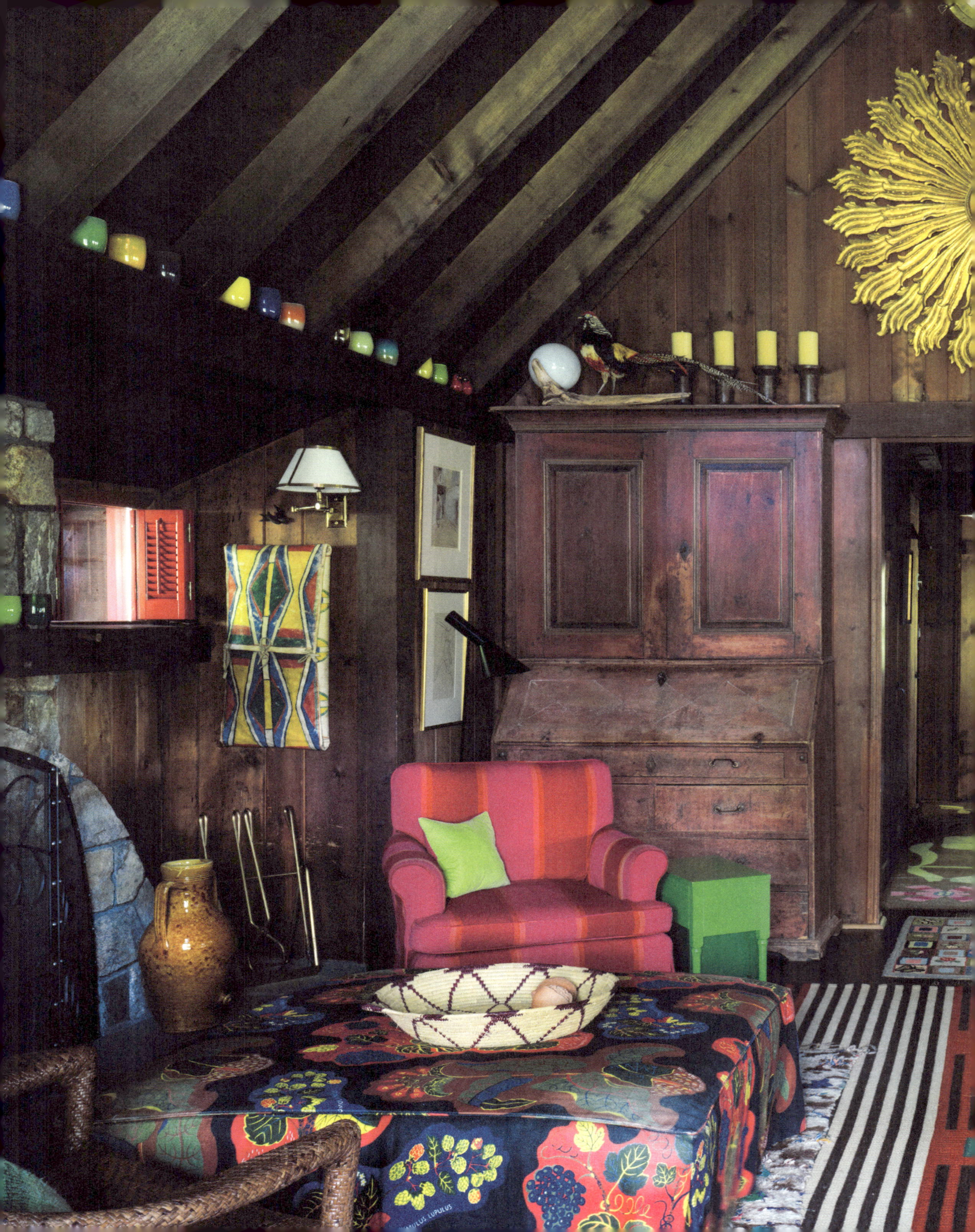

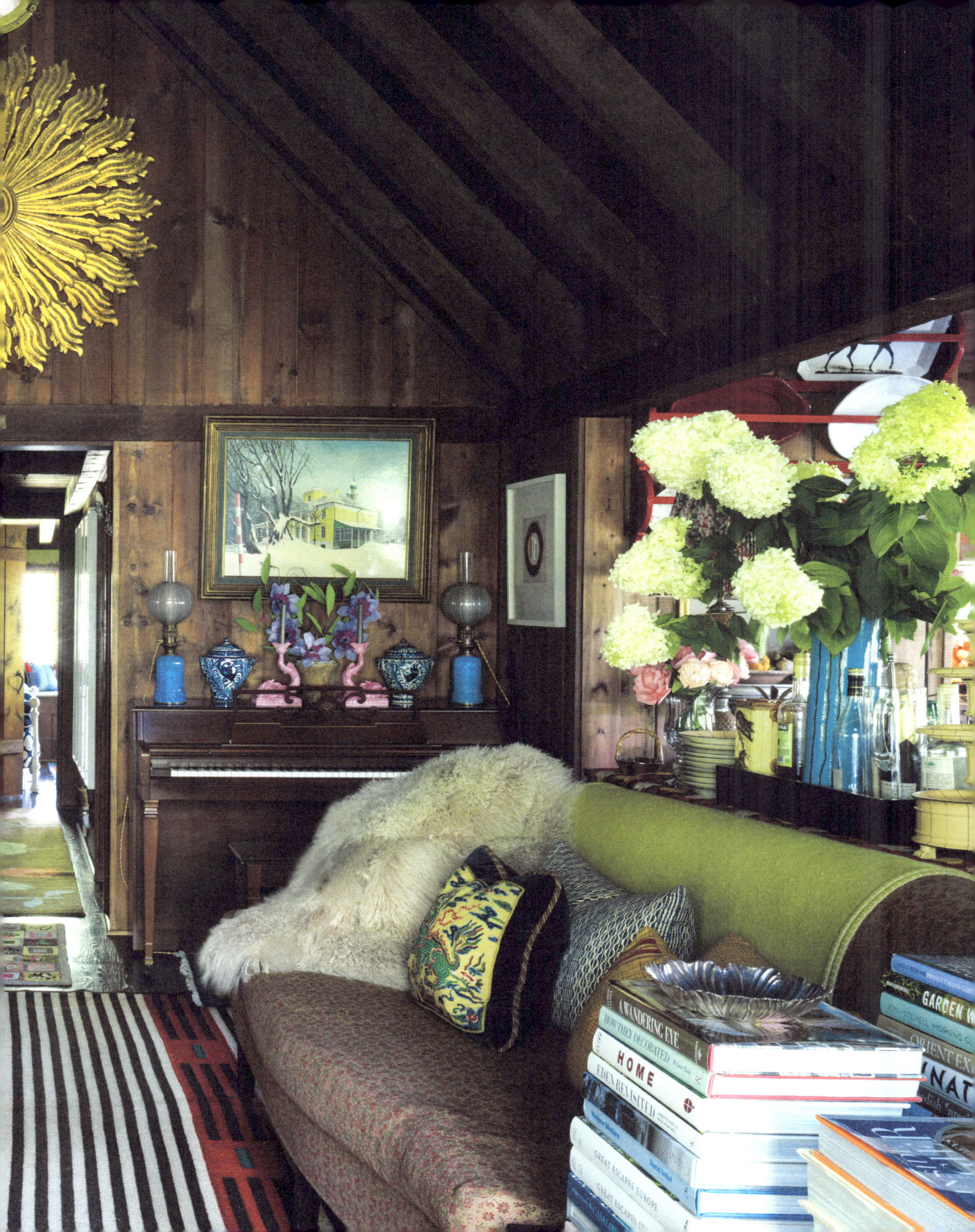
A WANDERING EYE
HOW THEY DECORATED
HOME
EDEN REVISITED

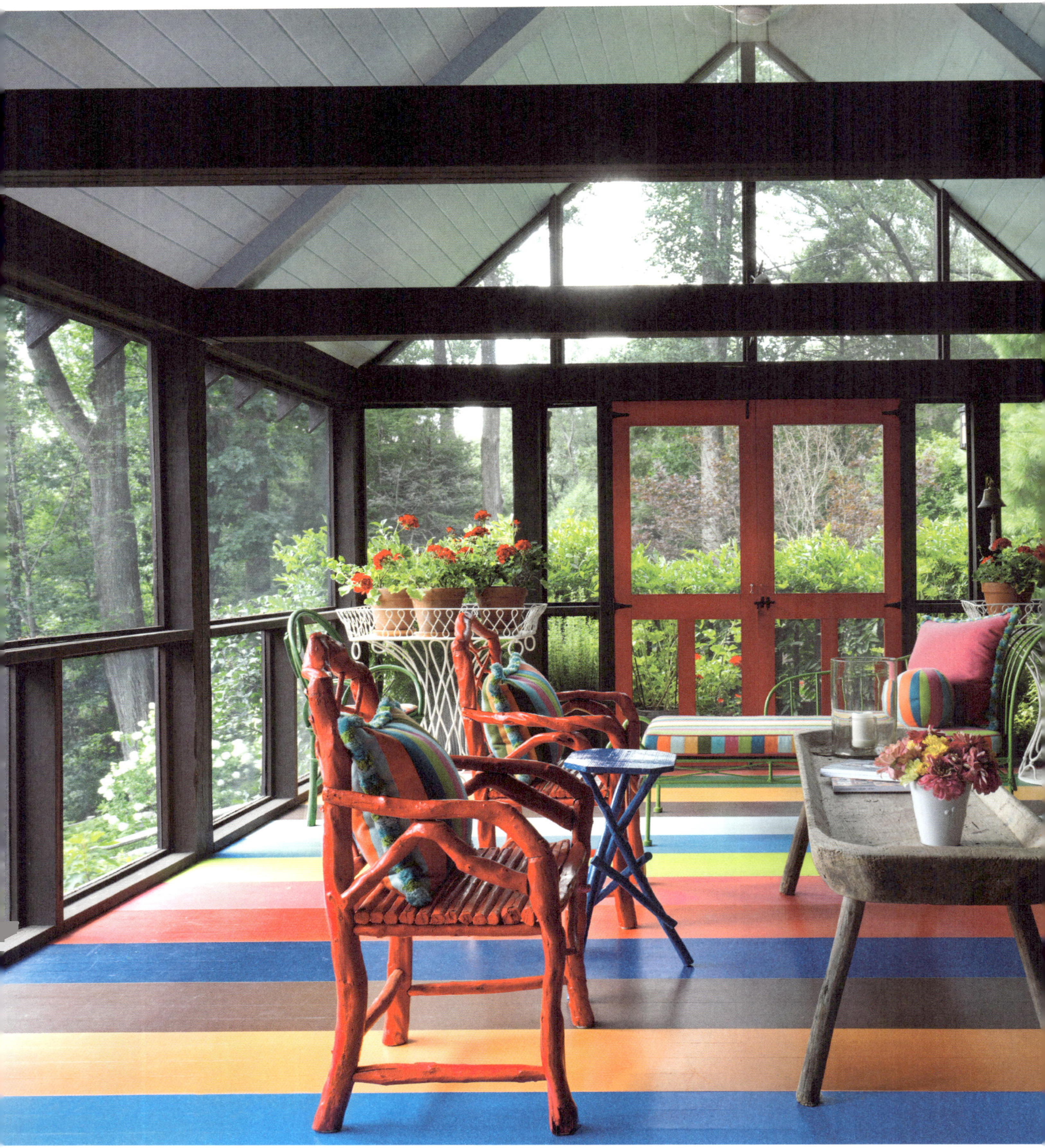

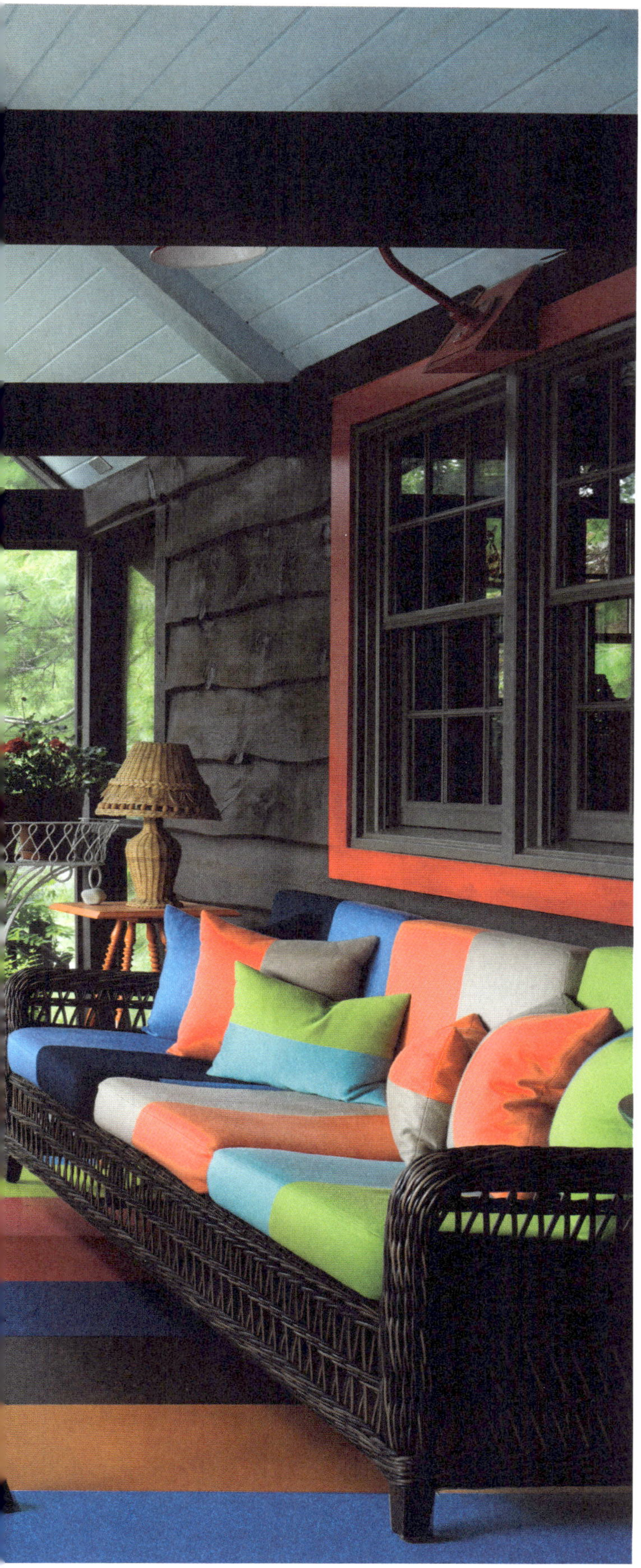

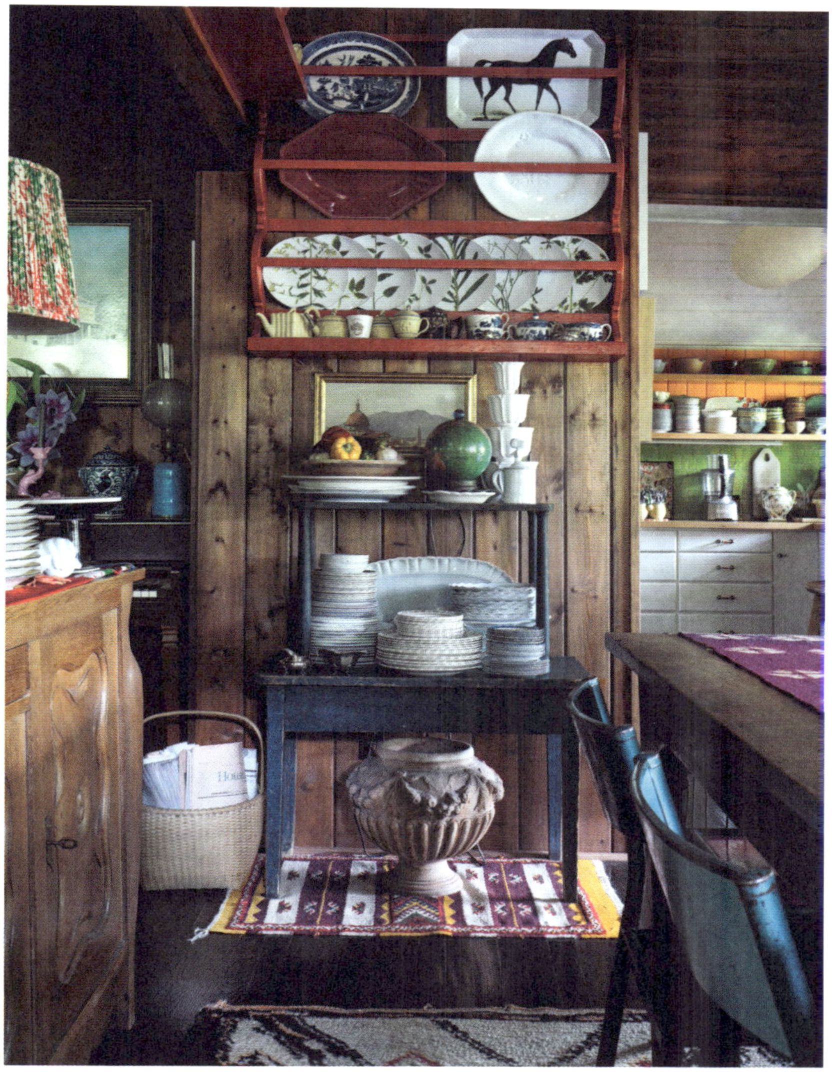

Rob Ashford, a Tony and Emmy Award-winning director and choreographer, and his husband, Kevin Ryan, a senior managing partner at an architecture and design firm, have vacationed in Putnam County for over 20 years. This particular community, the Sedgewood Club, broke ground in 1928, and the cabin's rustic charm still owes much to its original design. Though the pair has slightly tweaked the layout – for example, enlarging the kitchen, which they painted in vibrant shades of orange and lime – its historic spirit remains.

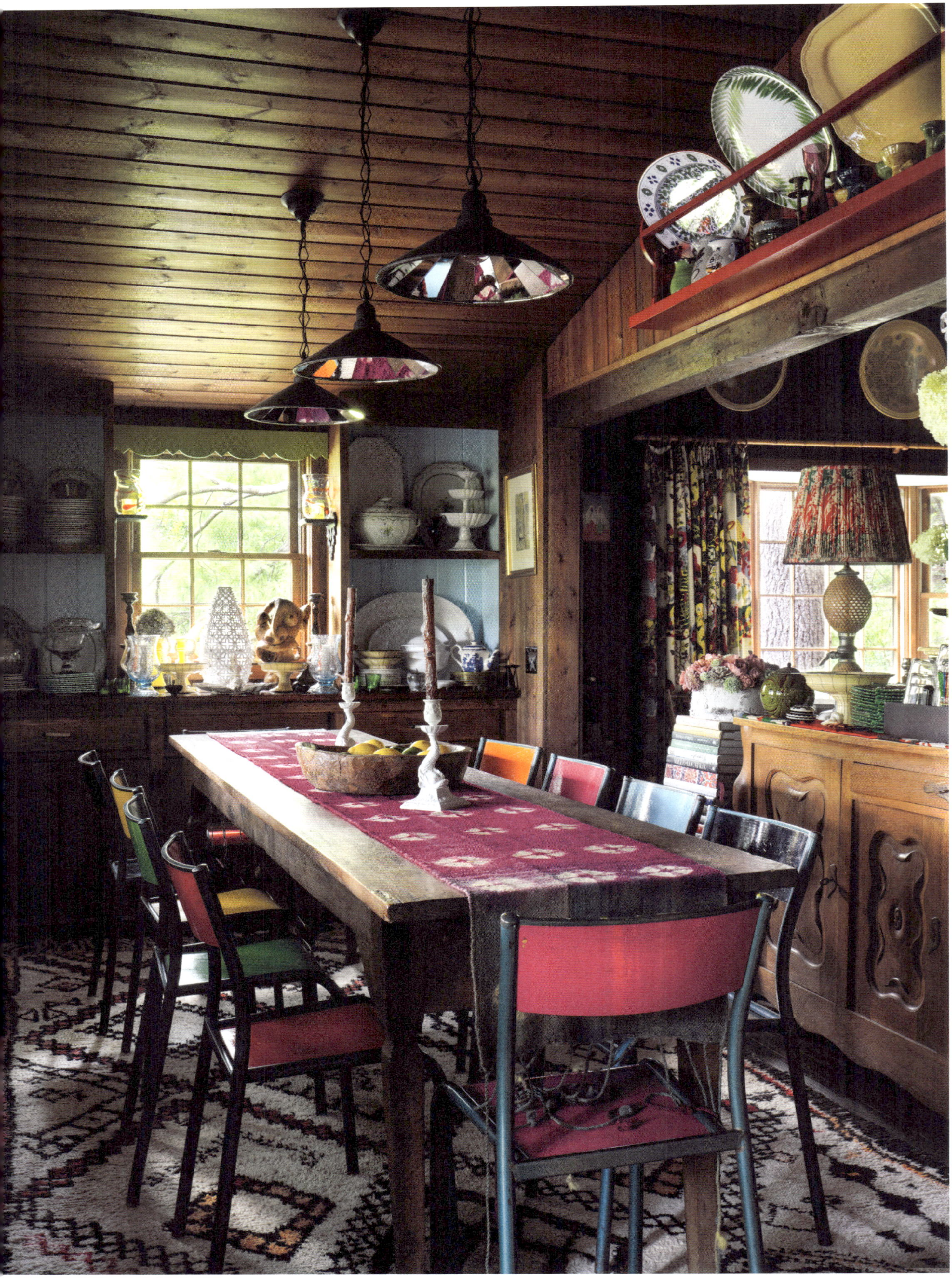

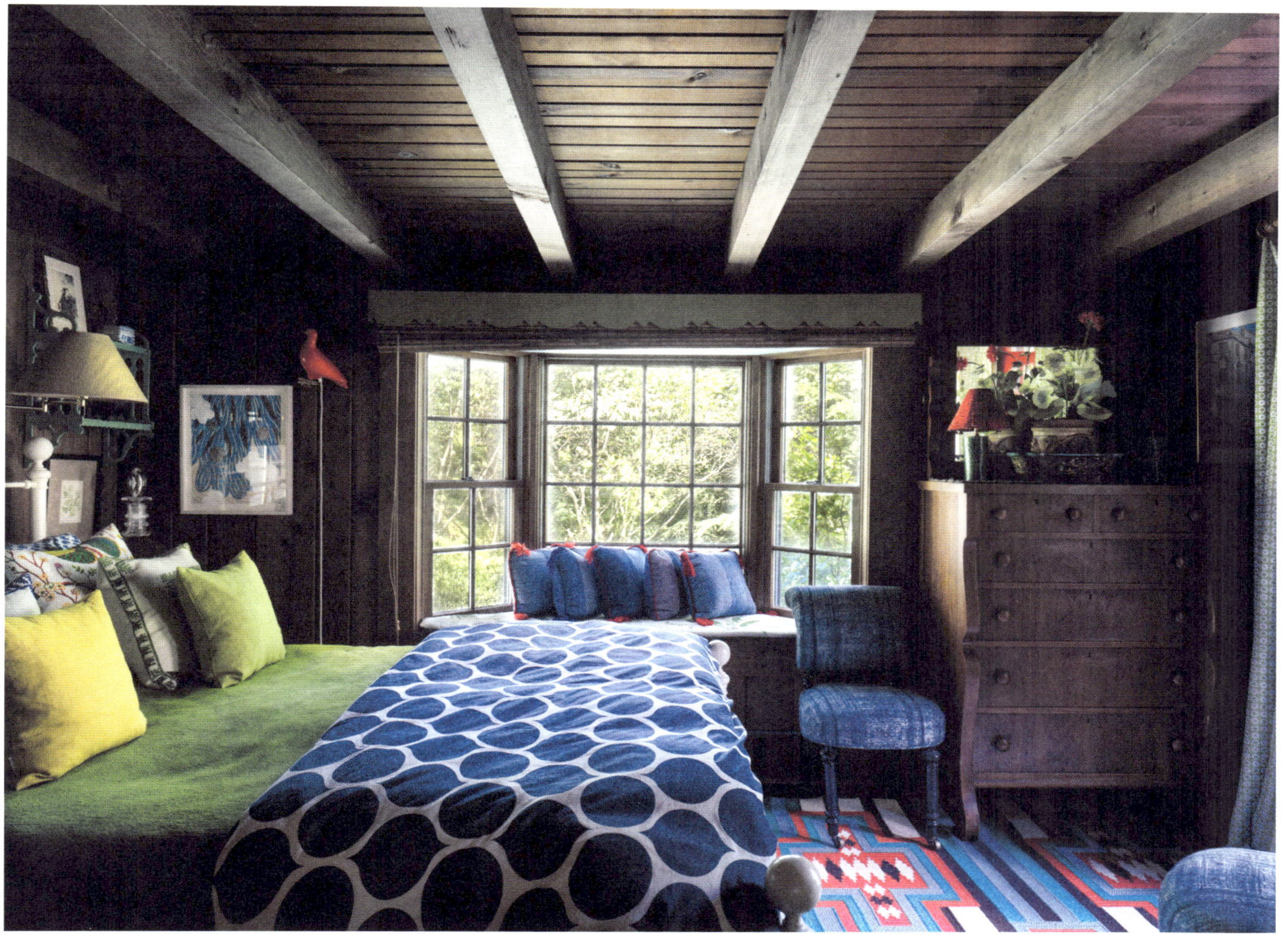

Every available surface and walls of the quaint A-frame cabin is charmingly cluttered with Ashford and Ryan's eclectic mix of contemporary art, modernist design pieces and vintage scores. An antique farm bed dominates the primary bedroom, above which is hung a mountain scene by contemporary artist Clemens Kois, alongside photographs by Paolo Ventura, portraits of the couple by painter Gene Meyer and a slender column-shaped lantern by mid-century artist and designer Isamu Noguchi.

Where there once was an open-air porch overlooking a tranquil forest, the couple created a glassed-in sitting room with a brightly, Technicolor palette. Inspired by a home they came across on holiday in Uruguay, they hand-painted solid-coloured stripes on the patio floor, which they matched with a rainbow-hued sofa and chaise longue – the perfect playful contrast to the cabin's heavy hand-hewn wooden architecture.

A Forest Cabin Built from Scratch by a Sculptor

INVERNESS, CALIFORNIA (US) **IDO YOSHIMOTO**

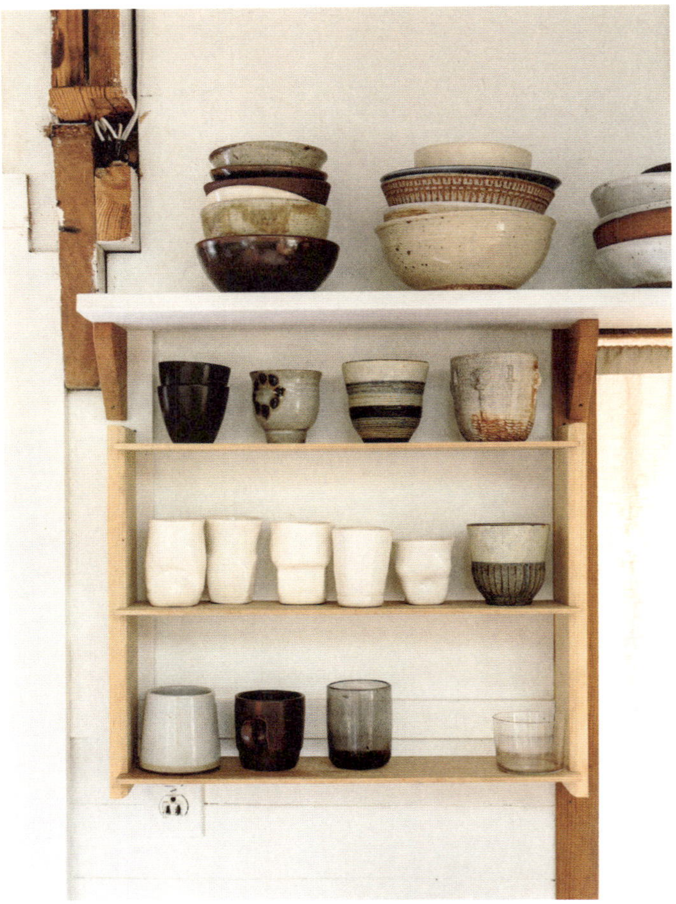

Collectives of artists and bohemians have long been drawn to the picturesque forested wilds of Northern California. Its pristine landscapes and abundant space provide the ideal backdrop for creative exploration. Woodworker and artist Ido Yoshimoto was raised within one of these communities in the pine forests outside Inverness, Marin County. Following in the footsteps of his godfather, the renowned sculptor JB Blunk, and artist father, Rick Yoshimoto, he has settled in a wild stretch of land at the end of a long dirt road within a verdant natural reserve.

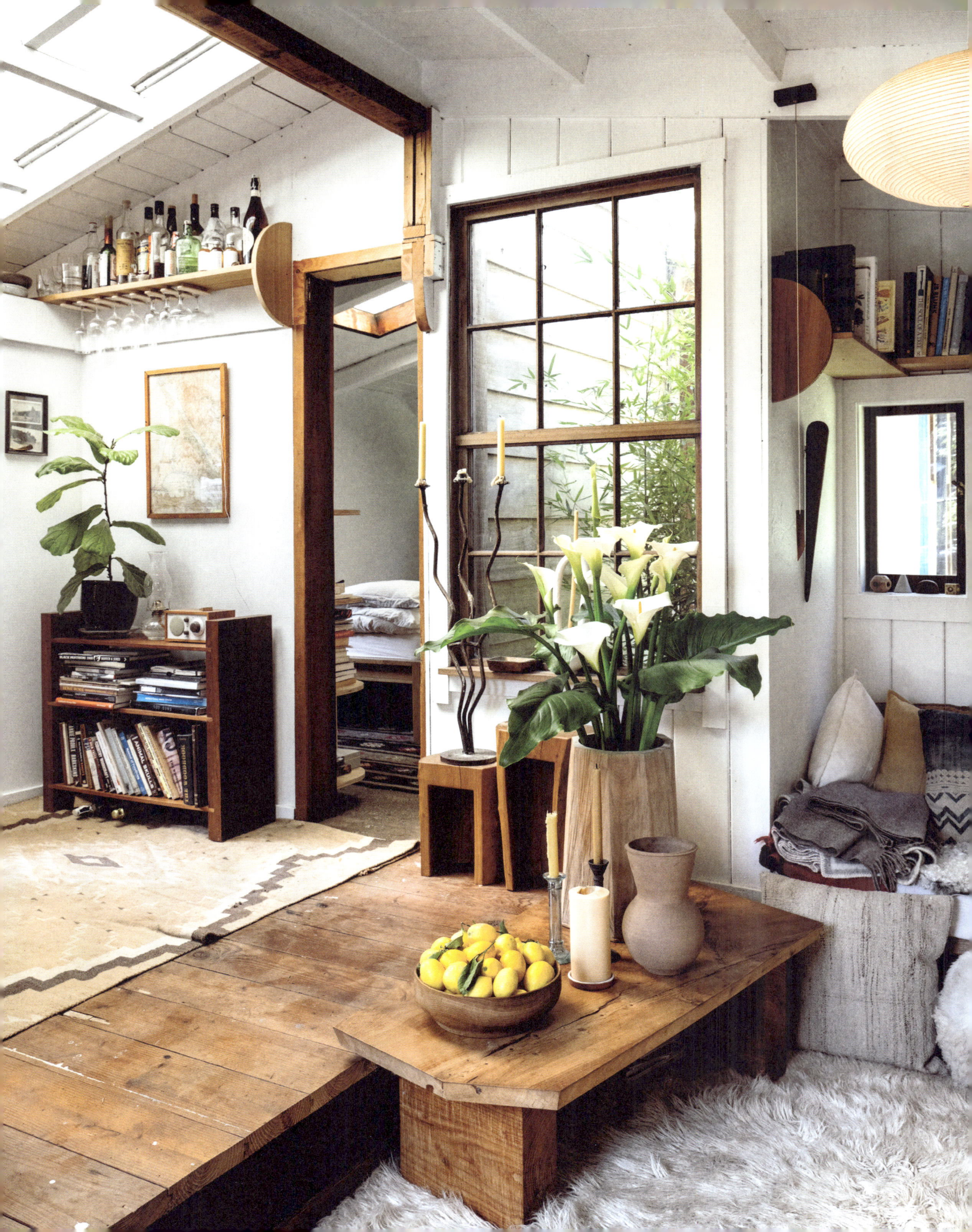

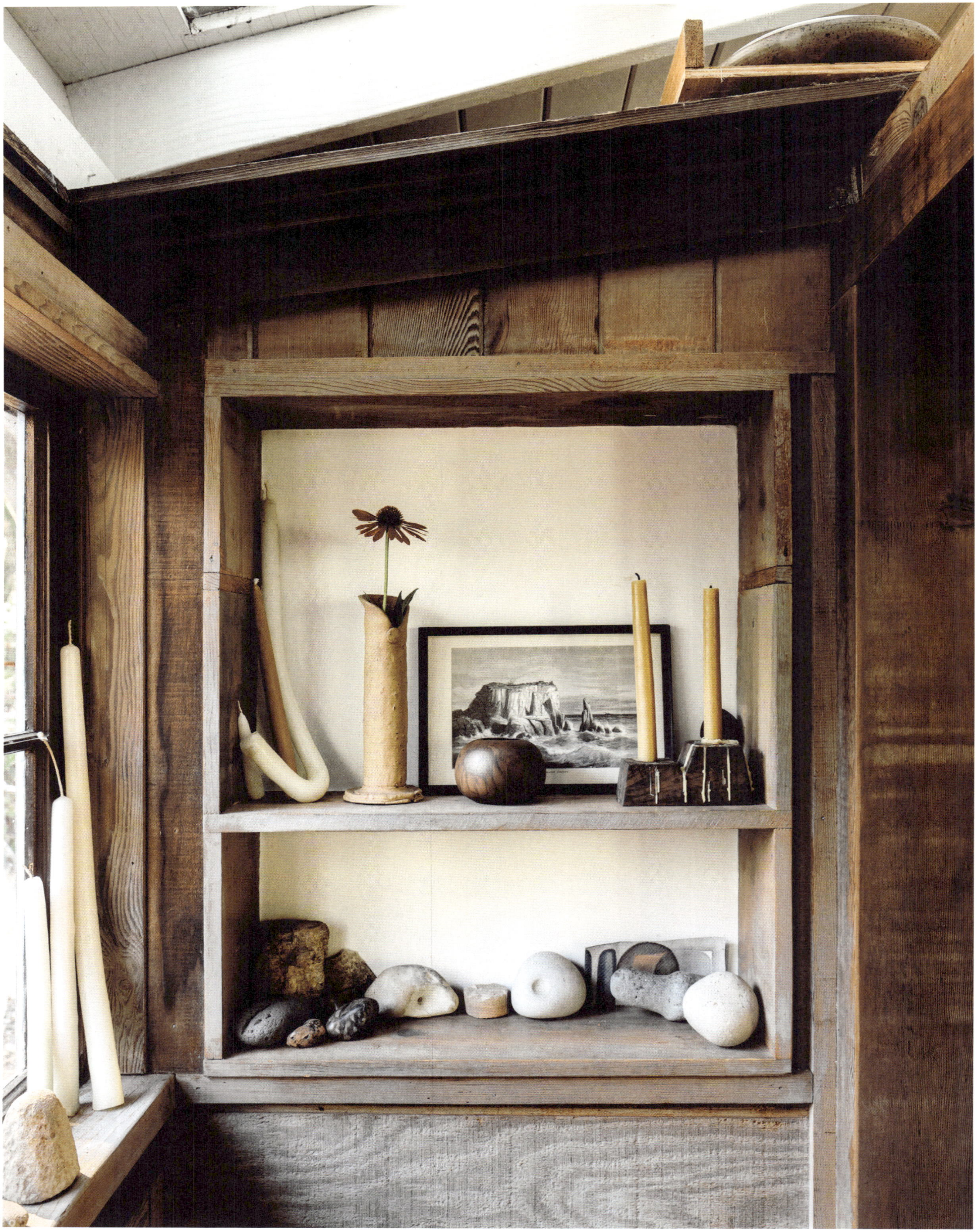

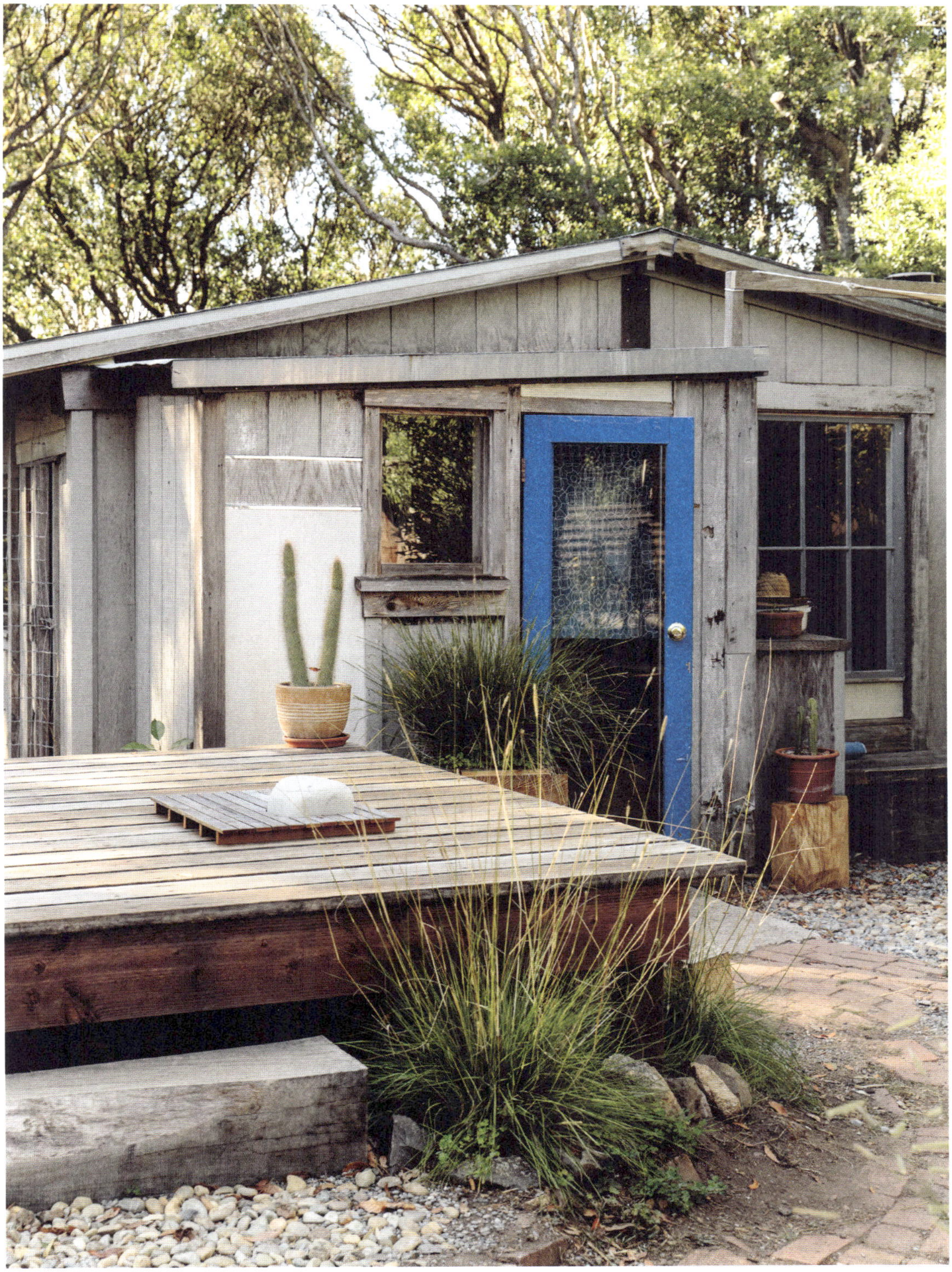

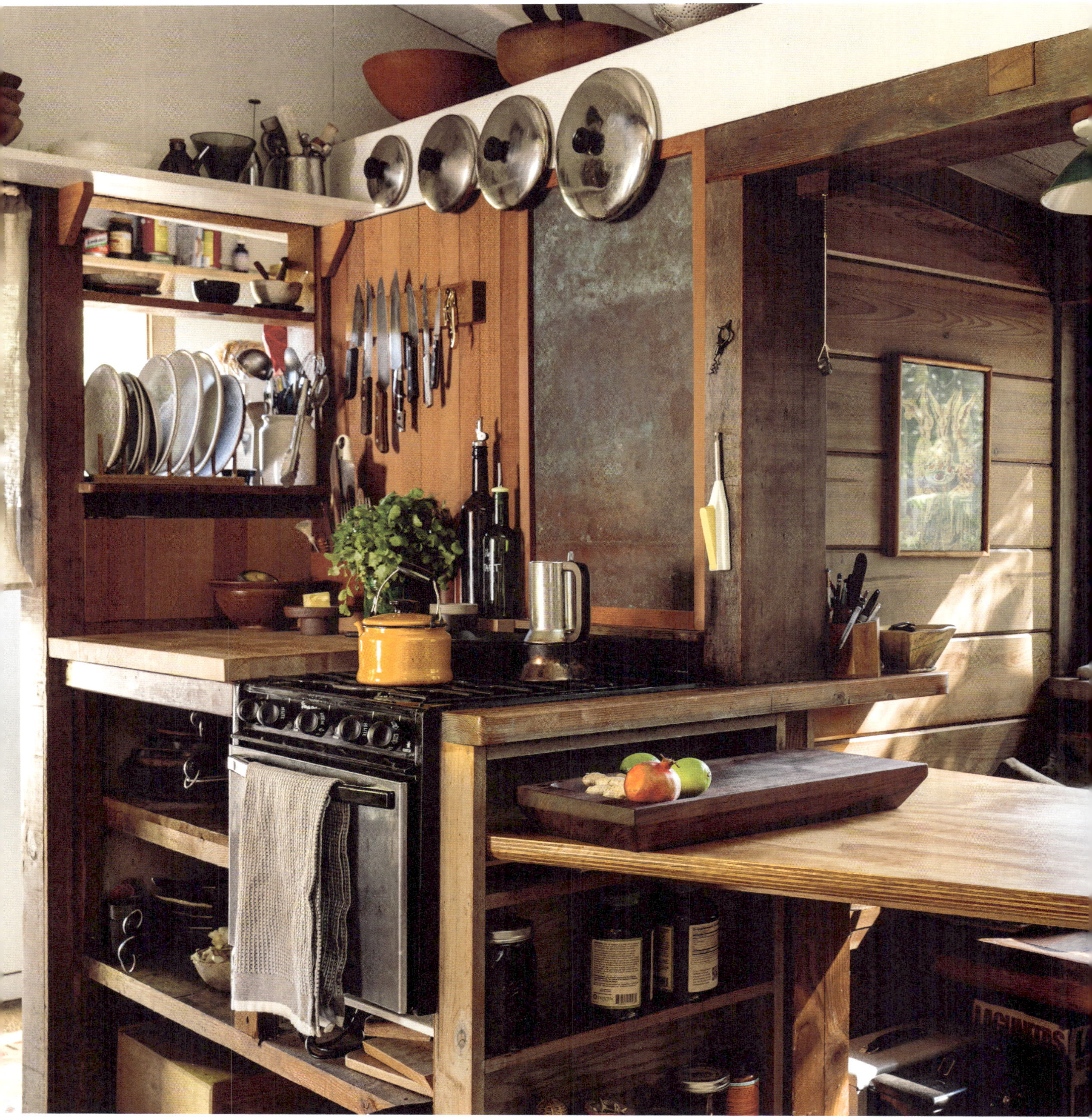

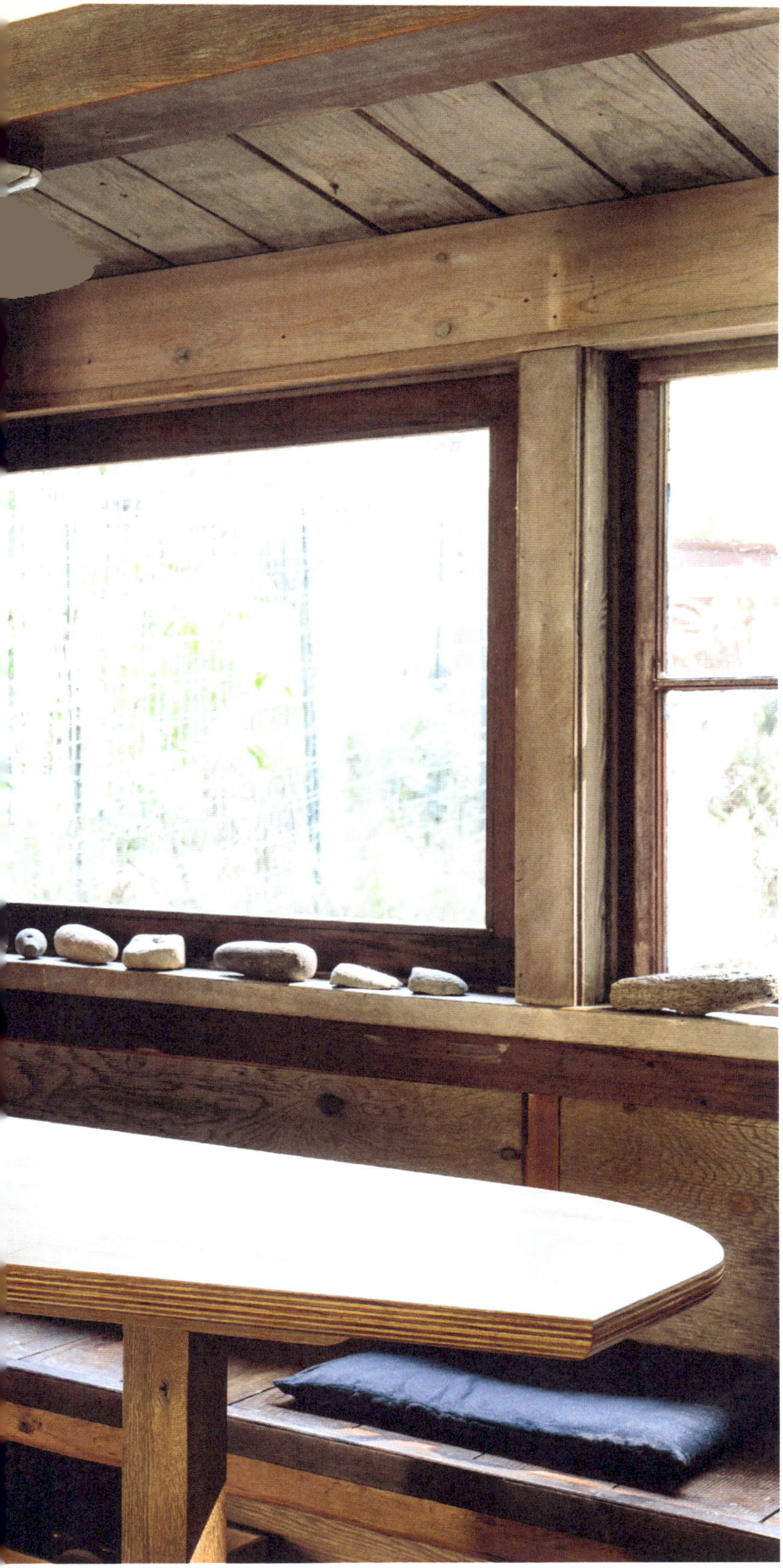

'When I took over, the building was uninhabited for many years and the forest had encroached onto the property,' Yoshimoto says of the existing structure, which was built in the 1980s. 'There have been multiple residents and each has added on or modified the design.' The original construction project saw him slowly building up the home entirely by himself, fashioning the shelves, lights, tables and stools for the humble cabin in his nearby workshop. 'My goal was to create something comfortable and liveable while applying my aesthetic and using the materials available, most of which were reused and reclaimed scraps from my art studio,' says Yoshimoto, whose artwork – which resembles monolithic, totem-like sculptures carved from solid blocks of wood – has been shown in galleries as far-flung as San Francisco and Tokyo. 'Because it is a small space, most everything is built-in.'

In furnishing the home, Yoshimoto turned to his community to source the domestic tools that would populate his day-to-day life. 'Every plate, cup and bowl has been made by an artist that I know or collected from travels,' he says of the hand-hewn objects that include ceramic pieces made by his father, art by his godfather Blunk, as well as paintings by friend Jessica Niello and Californian artist Raymond Yelland. 'I really enjoy having a personal collection. To let things curate themselves by way of connection.'

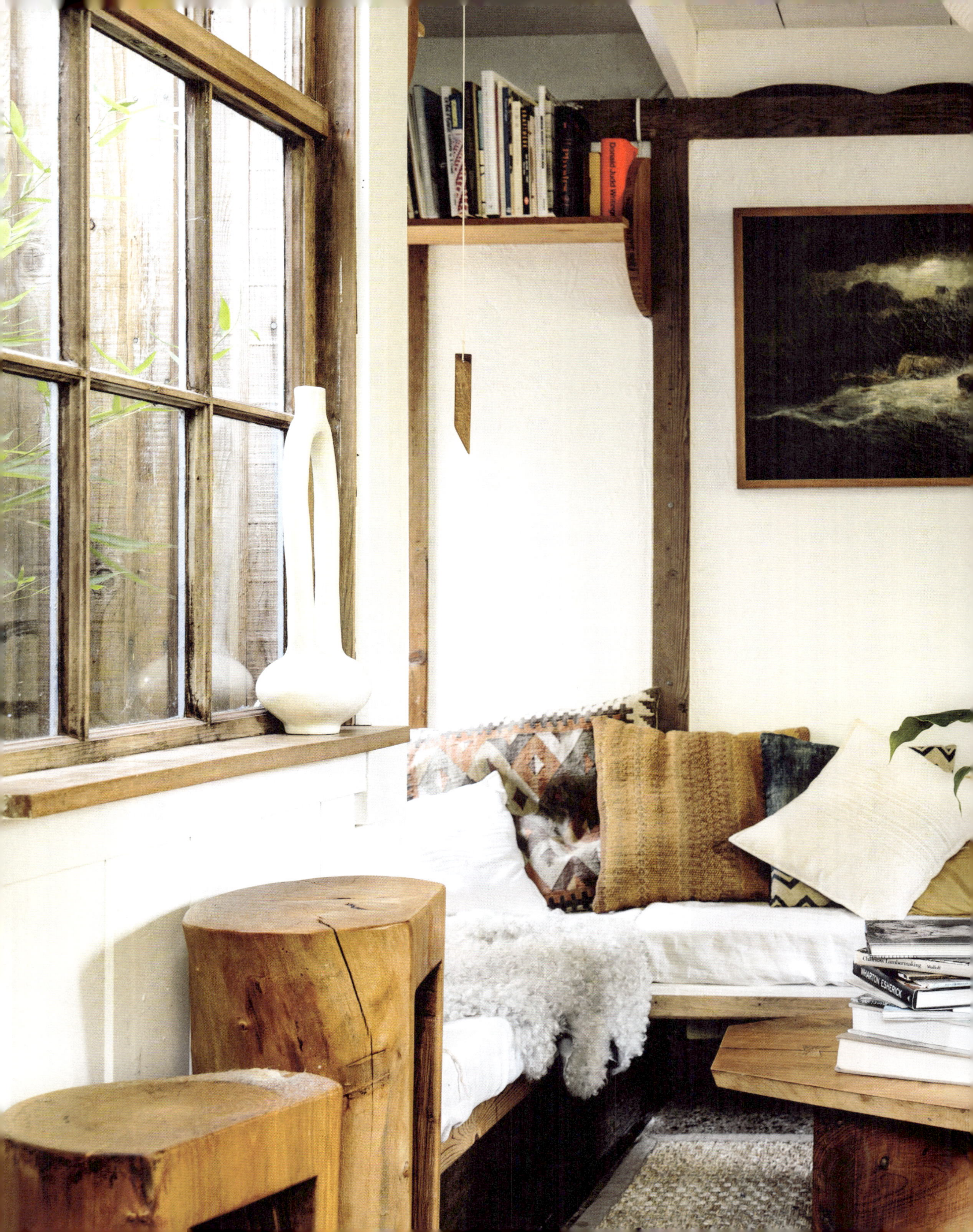
WHARTON ESHERICK

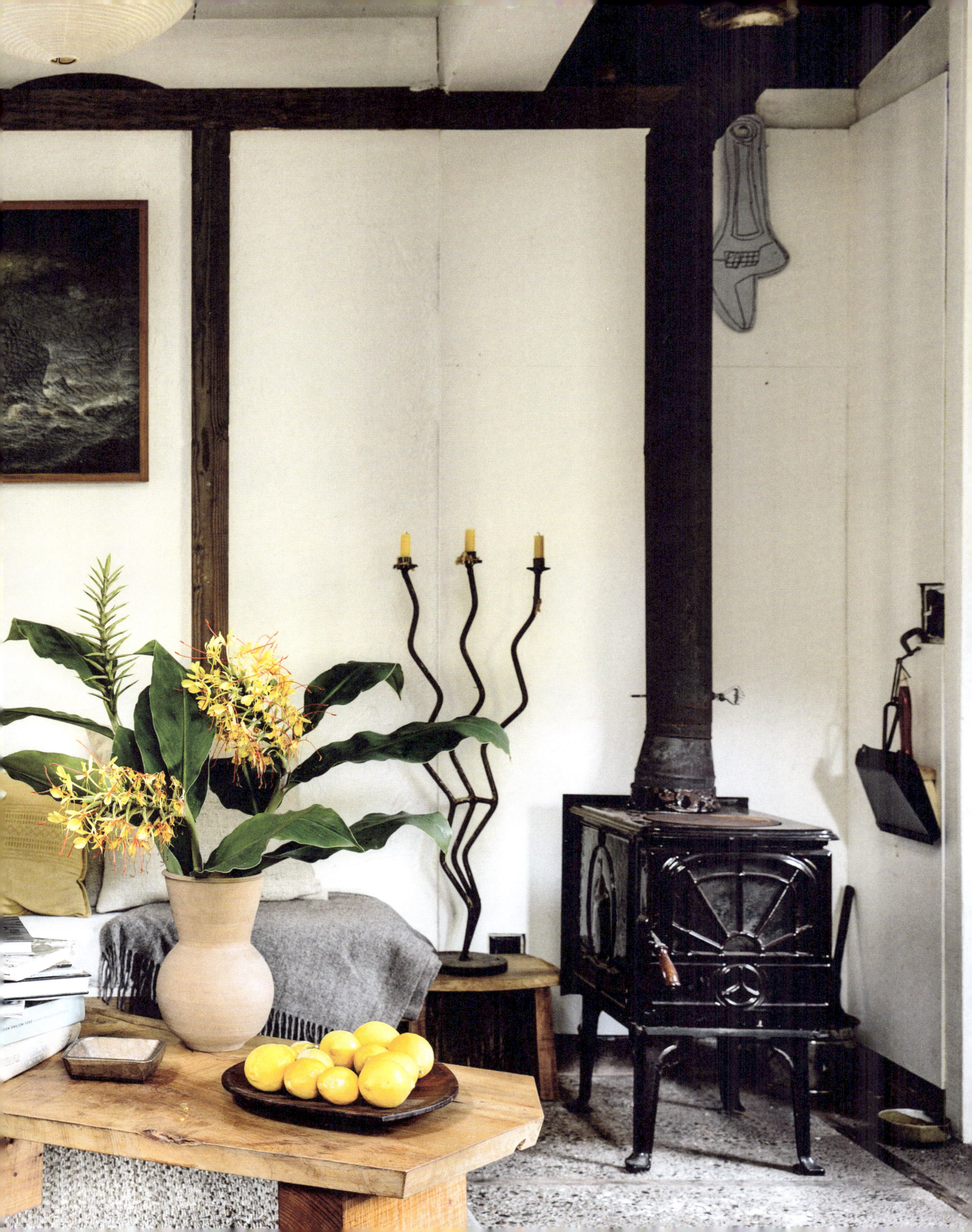

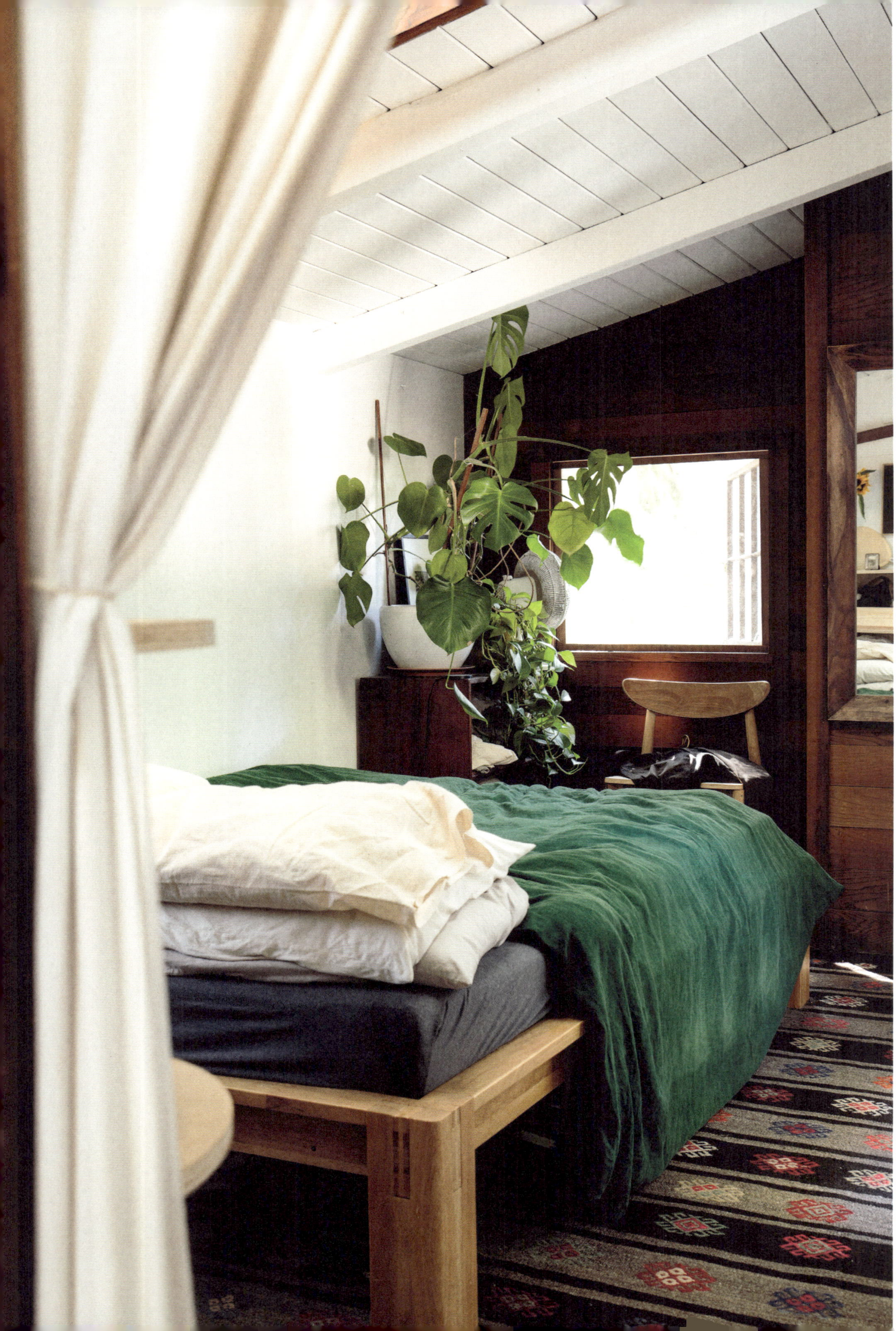

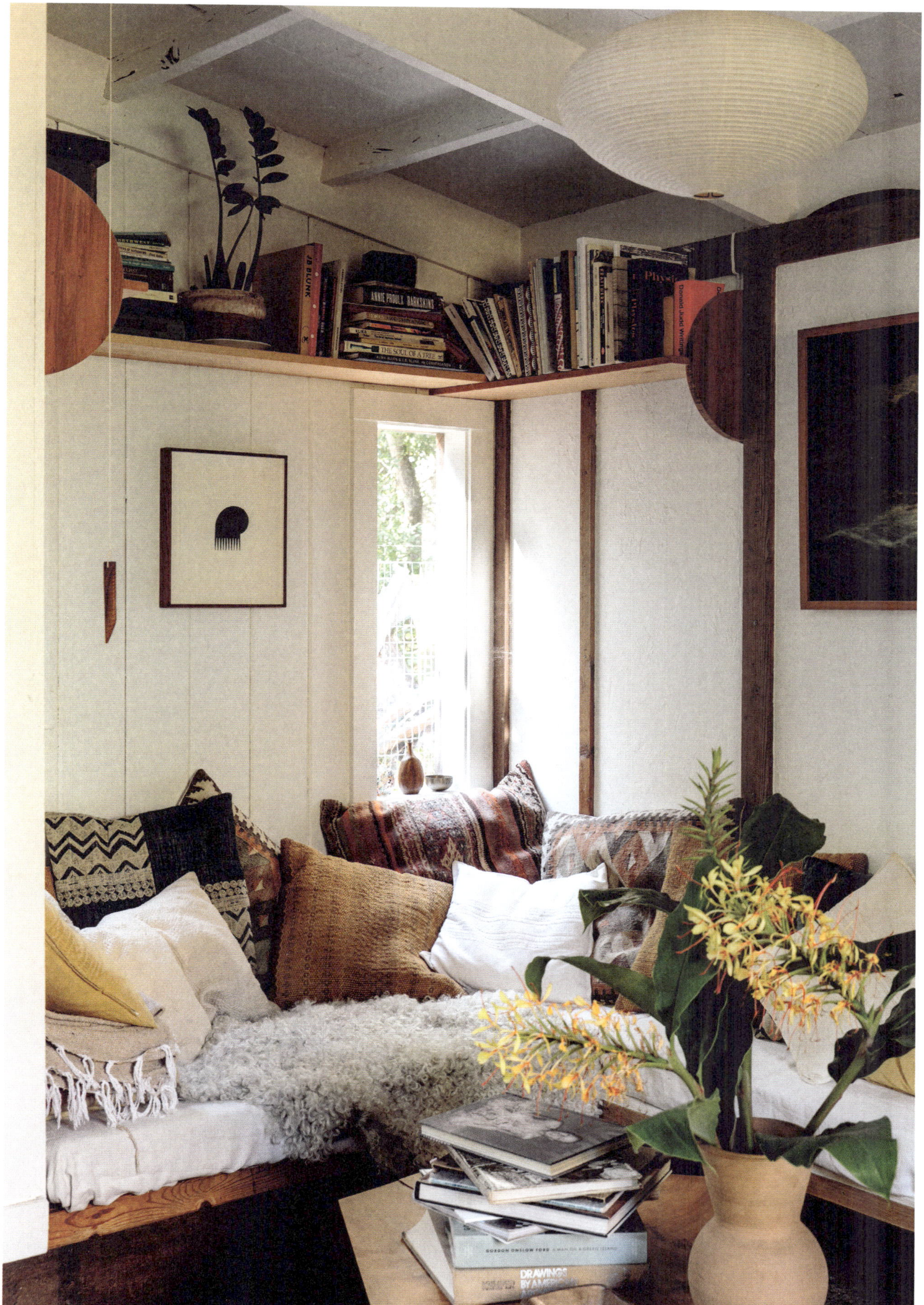
JB BLUNK
ANNIE PROULX BARKSKINS
THE SOUL OF A TREE
Donald Judd Writings
GORDON ONSLOW FORD

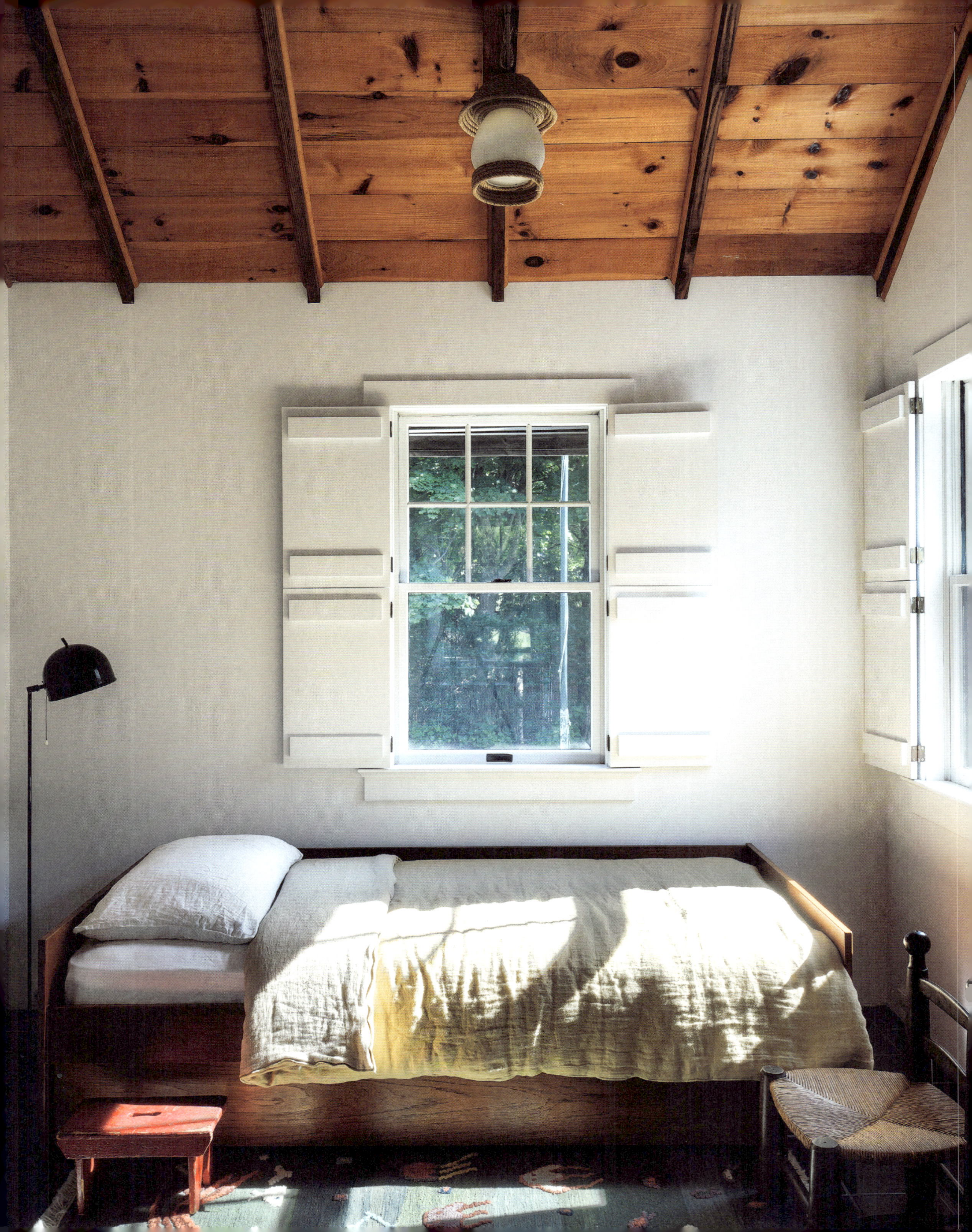

A Young Family's Updated Island Cottage

SHELTER ISLAND, NEW YORK (US) **WORKSTEAD**

Drive a few hours north-east from Manhattan, through the suburbs of Long Island, almost to its very tip, then hop on a ferry across the softly lapping Peconic River and you will arrive on Shelter Island, a quiet wetland paradise in New York's Gardiners Bay. A slightly slower and less flashy alternative to the nearby Hamptons, the bucolic charms of the island are what convinced real estate entrepreneur Nick Gavin to purchase a simple cedar-shingled one-room cottage a short walk from the beach.

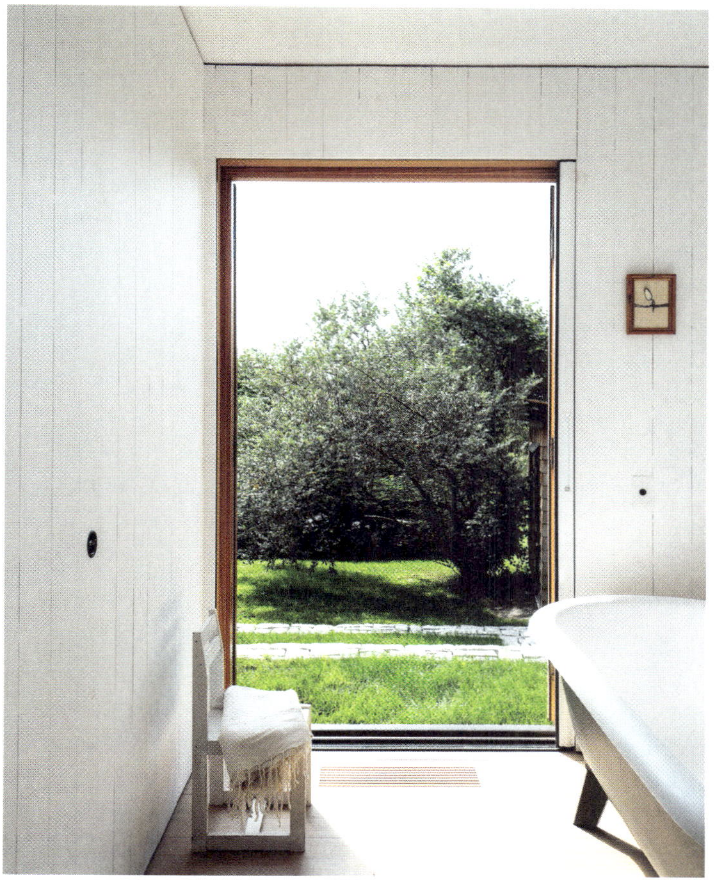

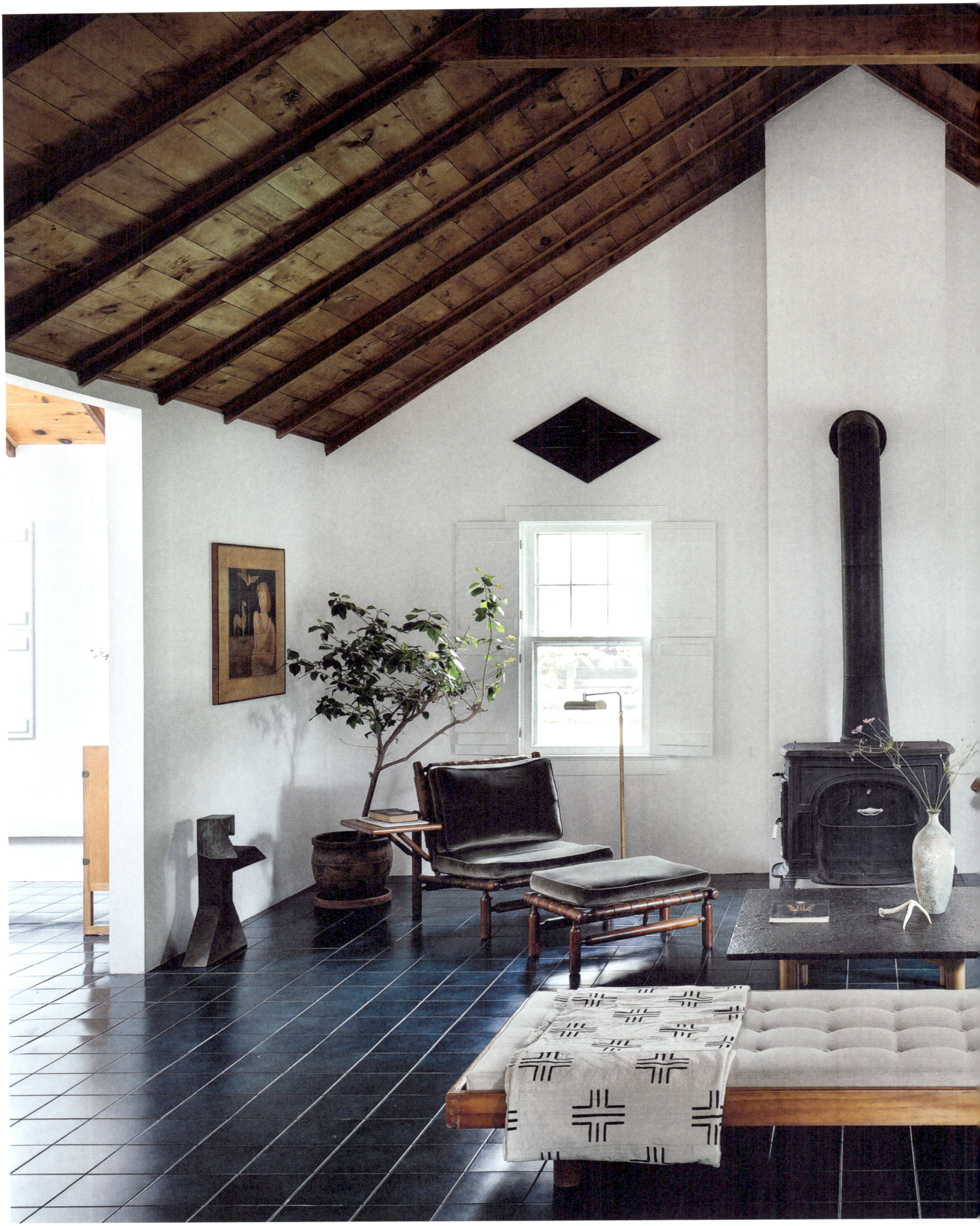

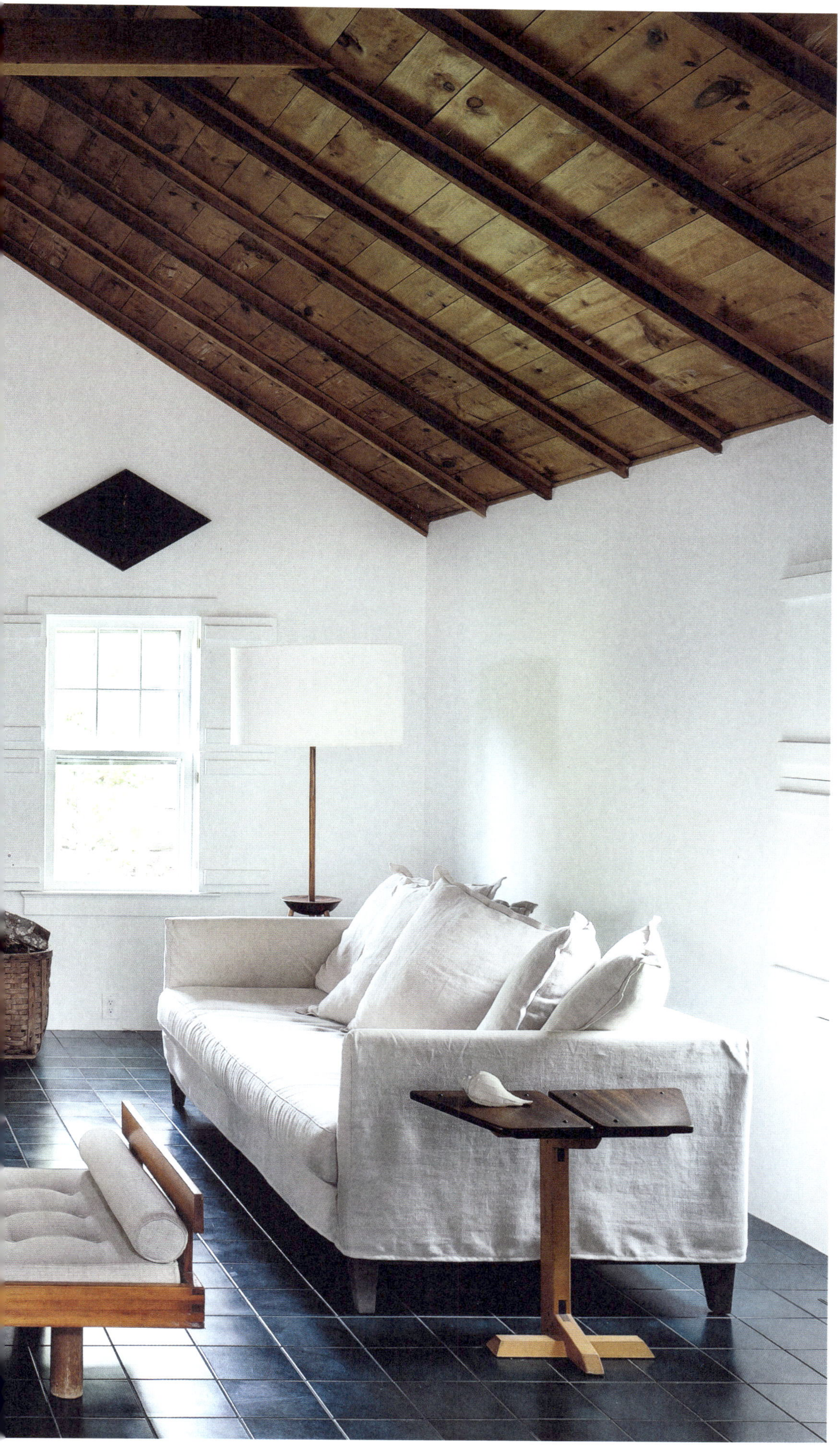

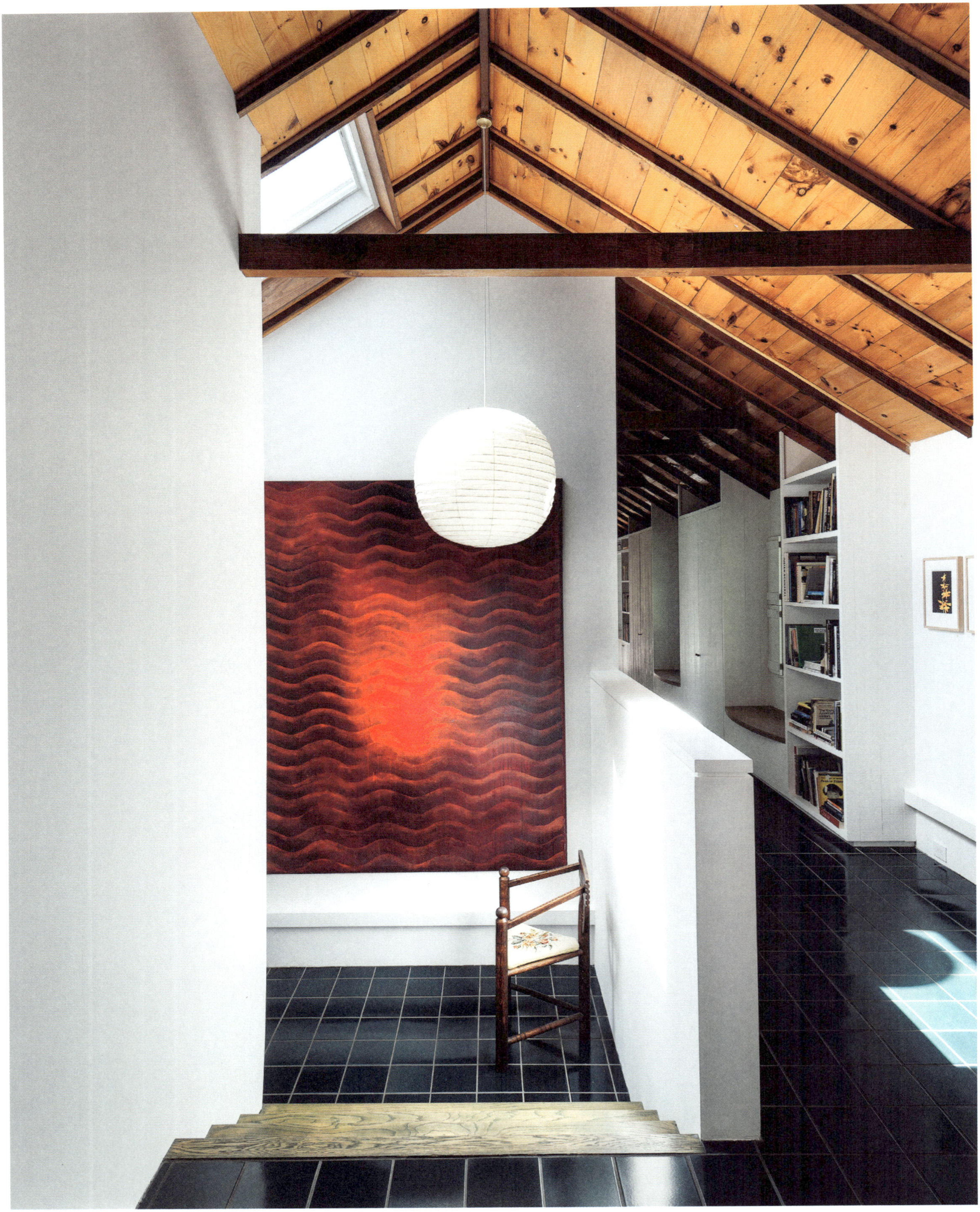

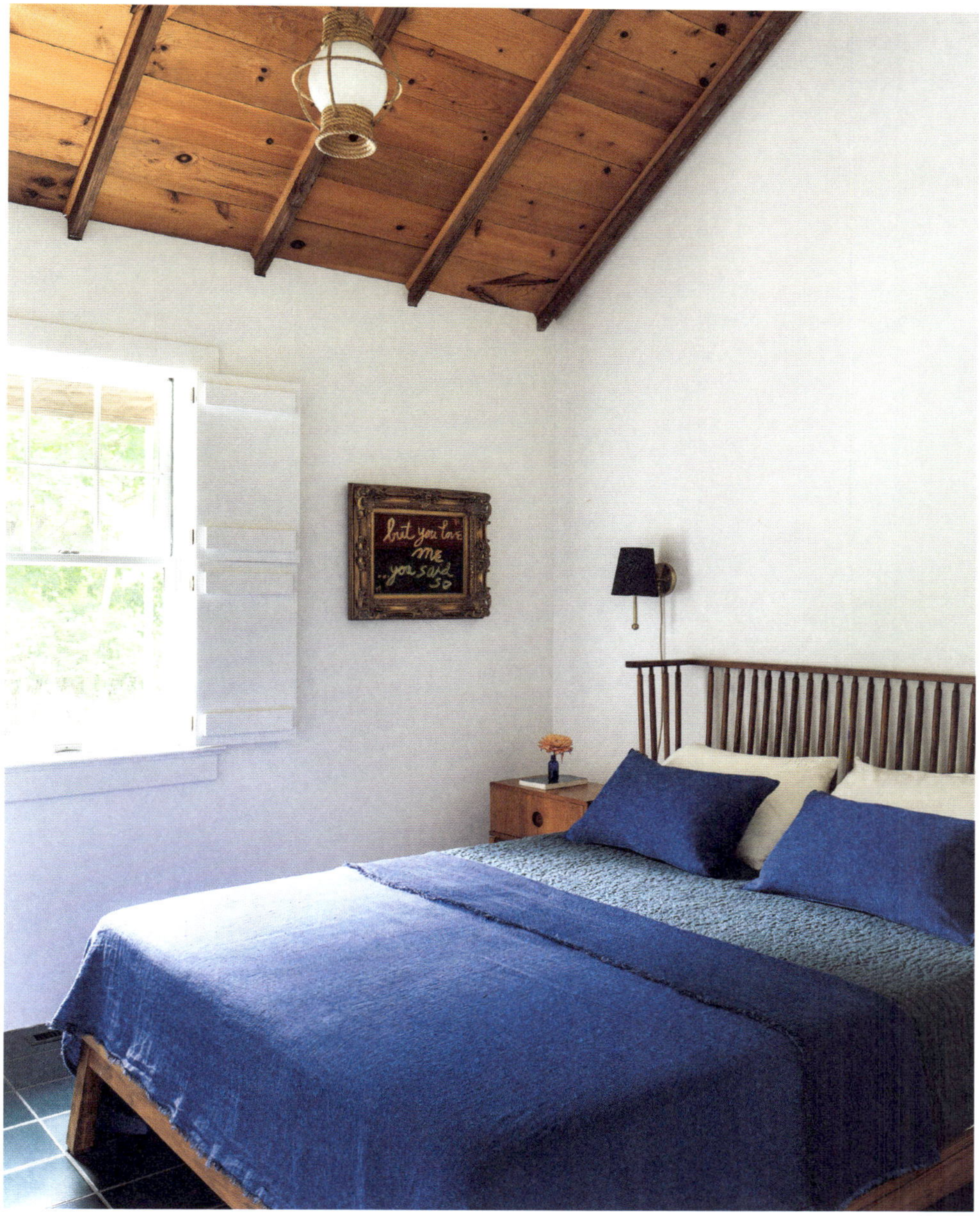

The pavilion was built in the 1940s by entrepreneur and New York grocery scion Giorgio DeLuca of Dean & DeLuca fame but was later purchased and remodelled by the interior designer and LGBT activist Melvin Dwork, who, when he sold it to Gavin, made him promise not to interfere with the simplicity of the layout. The 1,700-square-foot cottage had a single bedroom and not much else, but its sea-green tile floors and 15-foot-high cathedral ceilings made it stand out from the 19th-century clapboard houses and pre-war estates that populate the island.

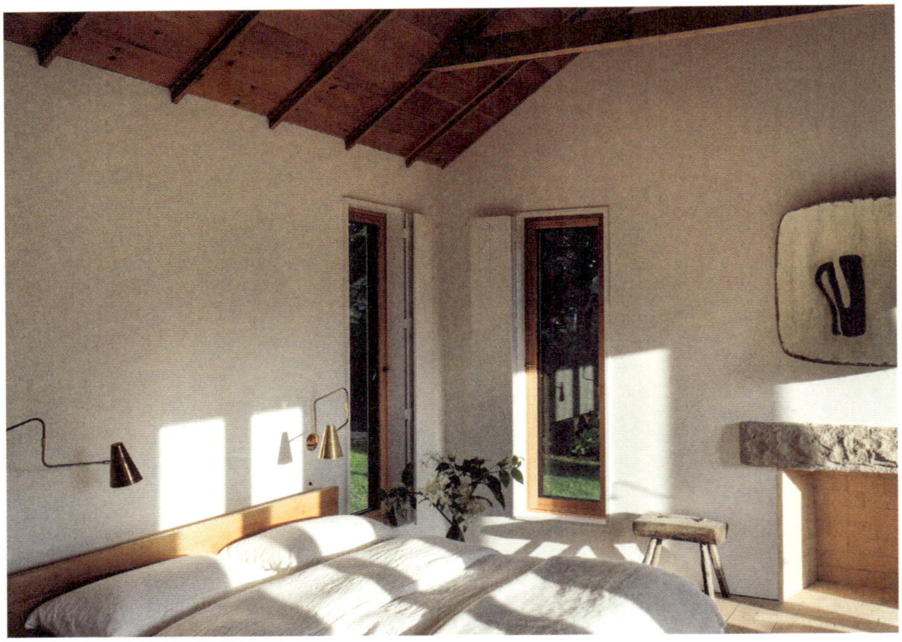

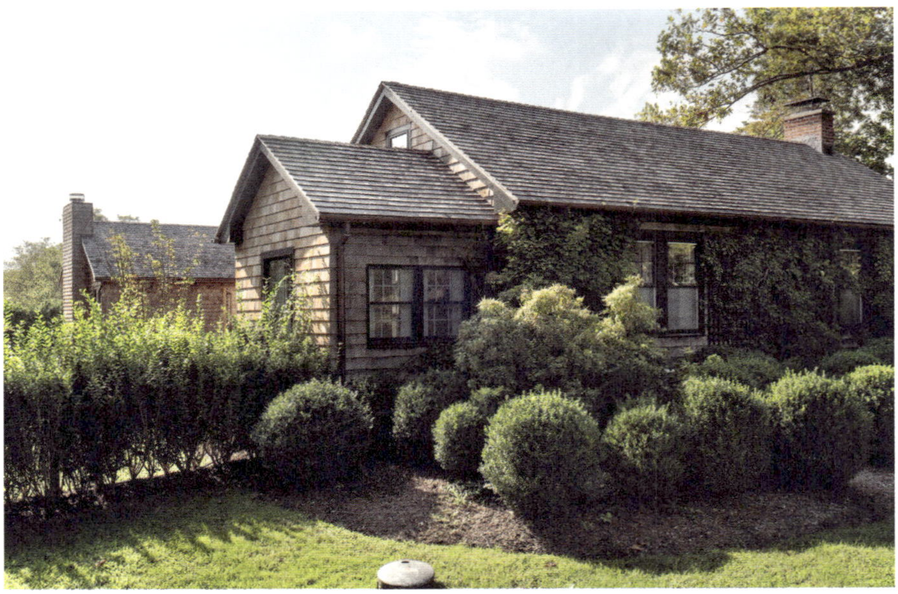

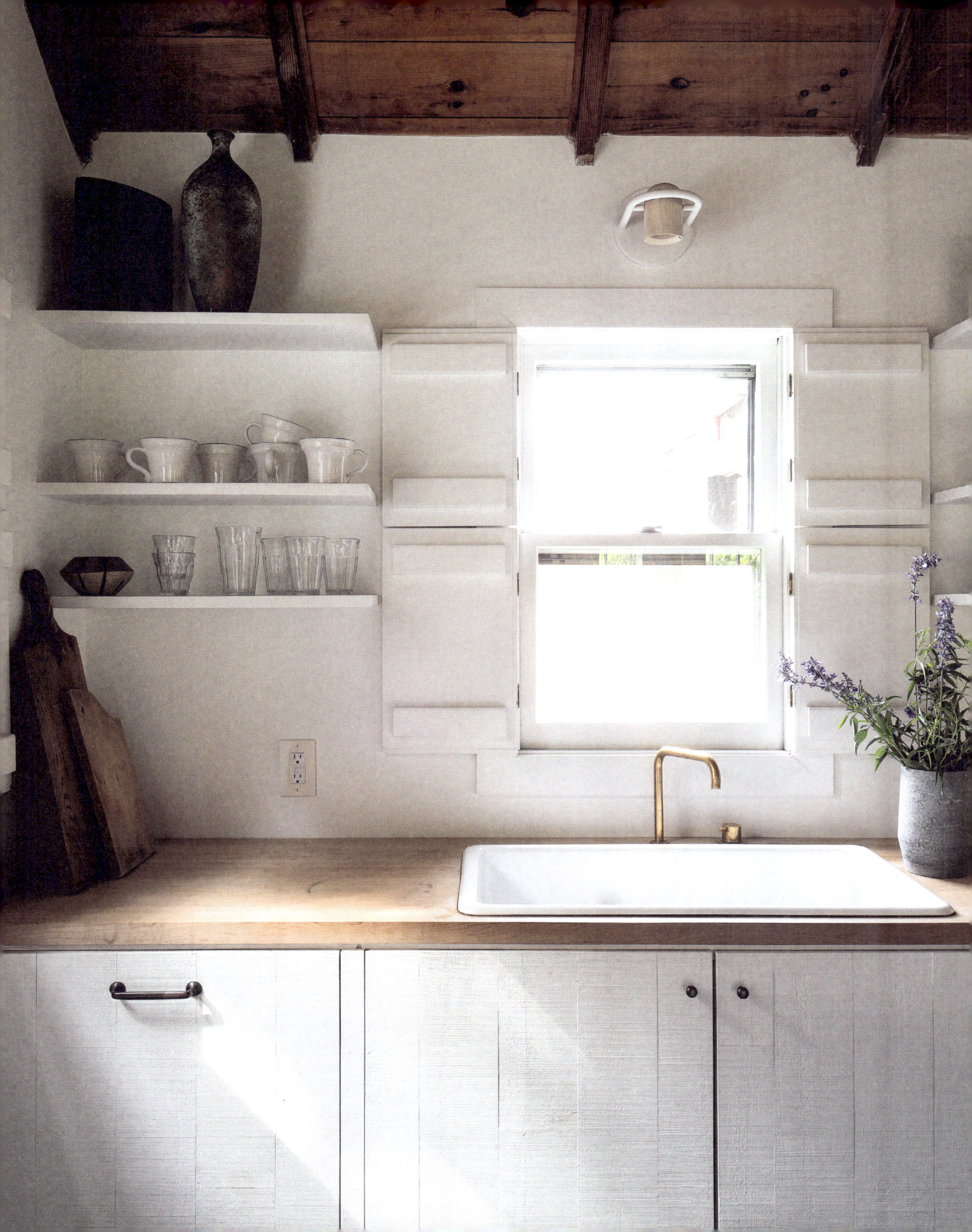

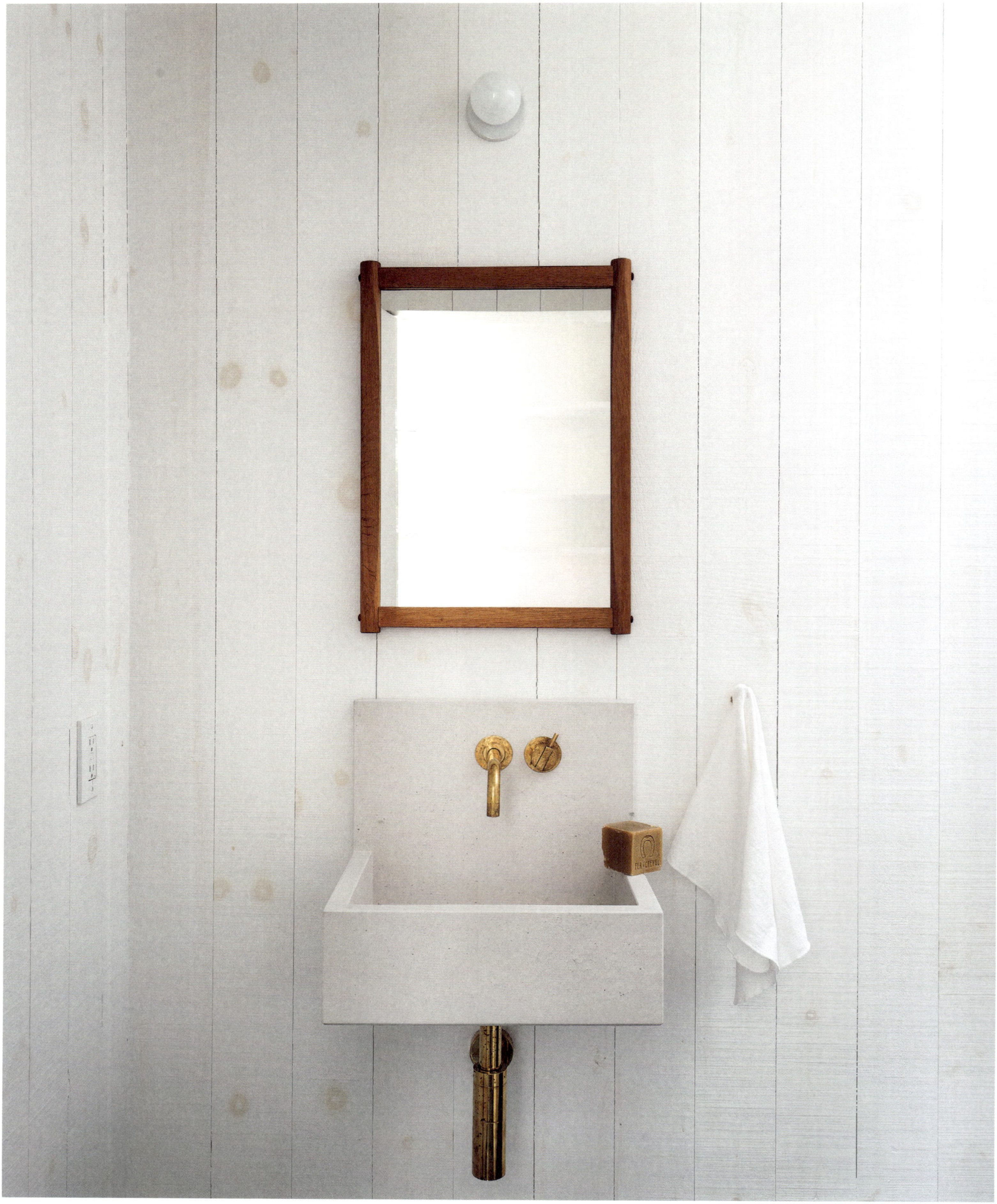

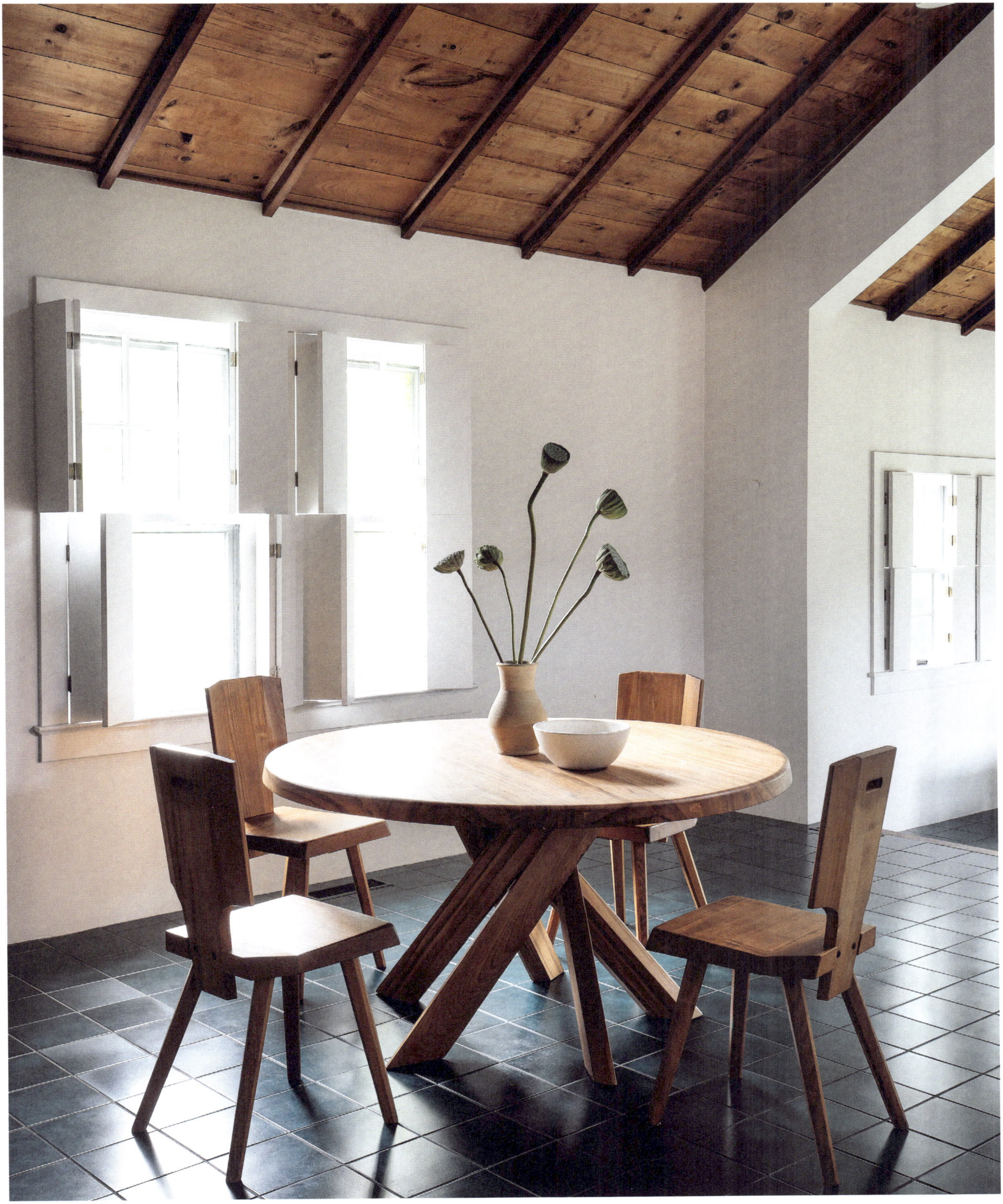

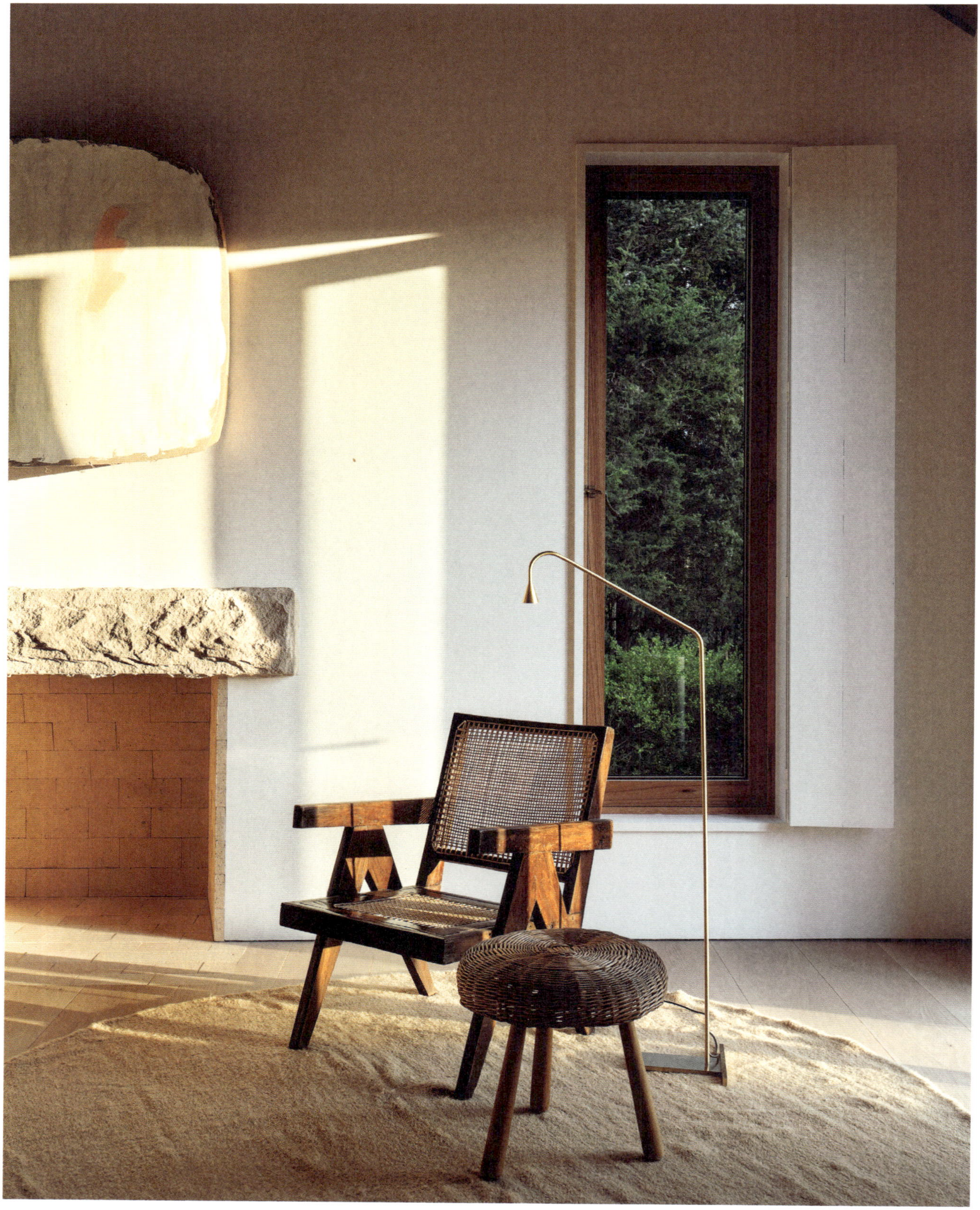

At first, Gavin was content to keep the space as-is, but a marriage and a baby later he knew some extra room would be required. He asked Brooklyn-based design firm Workstead to come up with a plan that would sympathetically modernise the home and add much needed square footage without breaking any promises to Dwork. What they came to him with was a second structure, built in the same style as the original, that could house an all-new primary bedroom and bathroom suite for Gavin and his wife, Katrin Thormann.

Workstead designed a breezeway in glass to connect the two structures, taking care not to make the new addition feel jarring or out of place. The design features of the new room – a pine-panelled gabled ceiling, painted white window shutters and a similarly minimal palette – thoughtfully echo the adjoining space.

In reorganising the original pavilion, they left the common areas as simple and uncluttered as they found them, choosing furniture, such as a Pierre Chapo dining table and a custom daybed set into the living room alcove, and rethinking the kitchen, where they added rough-hewn pine cabinets, maple countertops and open shelving, in a way that would mesh well with the home's quietly unpretentious aura.

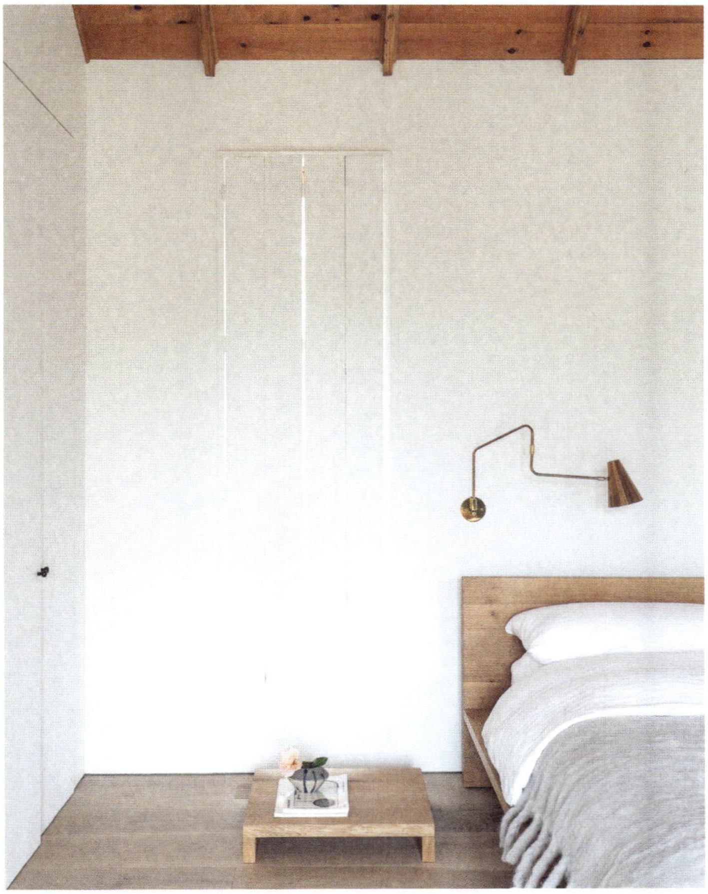

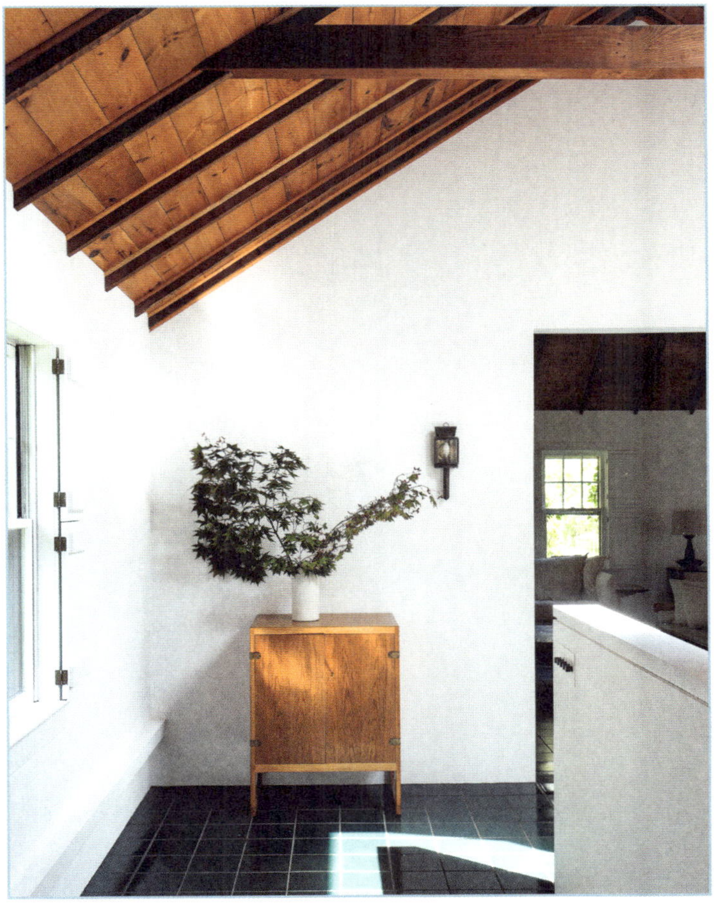

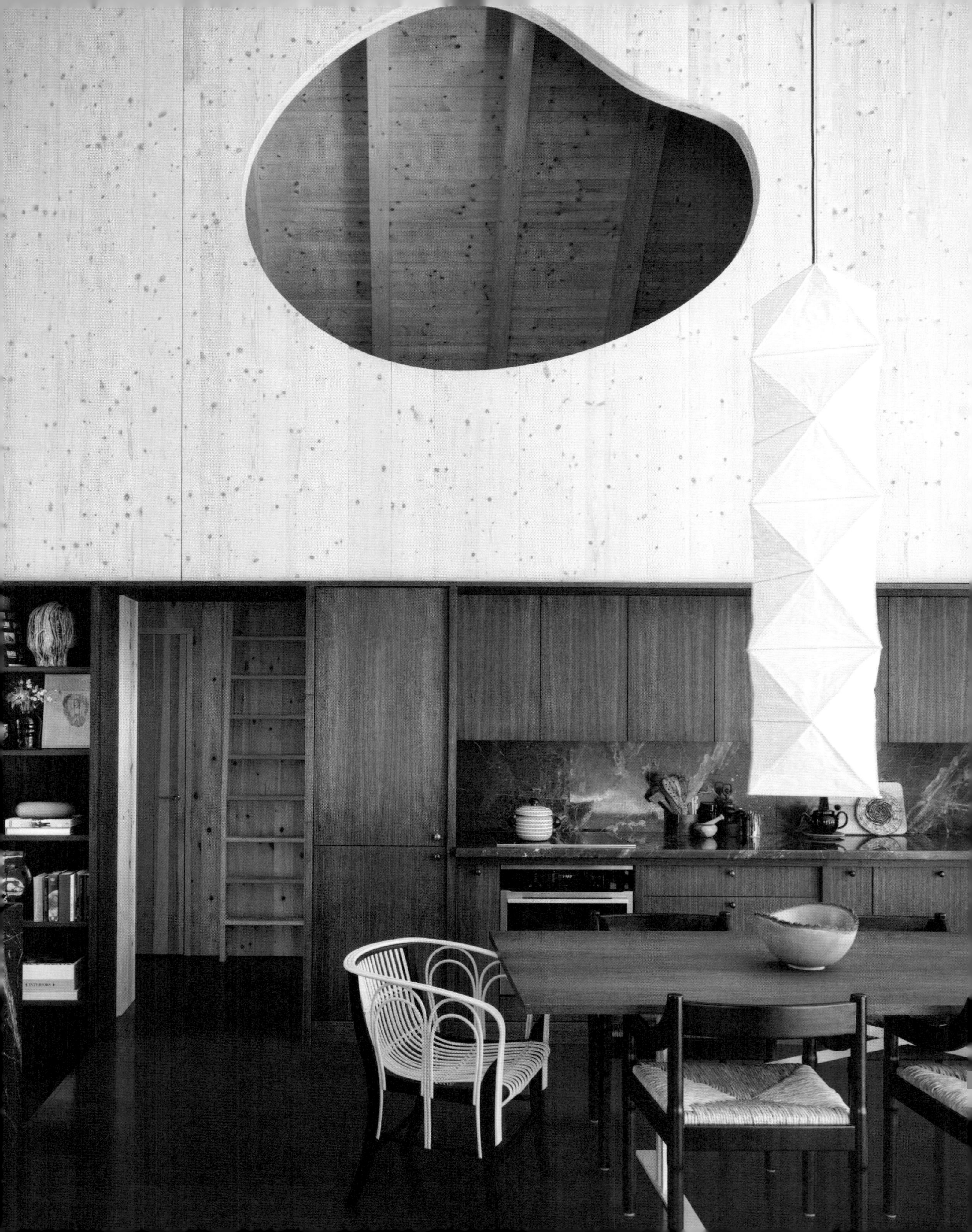

A Modernist-Inspired Nordic Cabin

BLIDÖ, STOCKHOLM ARCHIPELAGO (SW)

CHRISTIAN & RUXANDRA HALLEROED

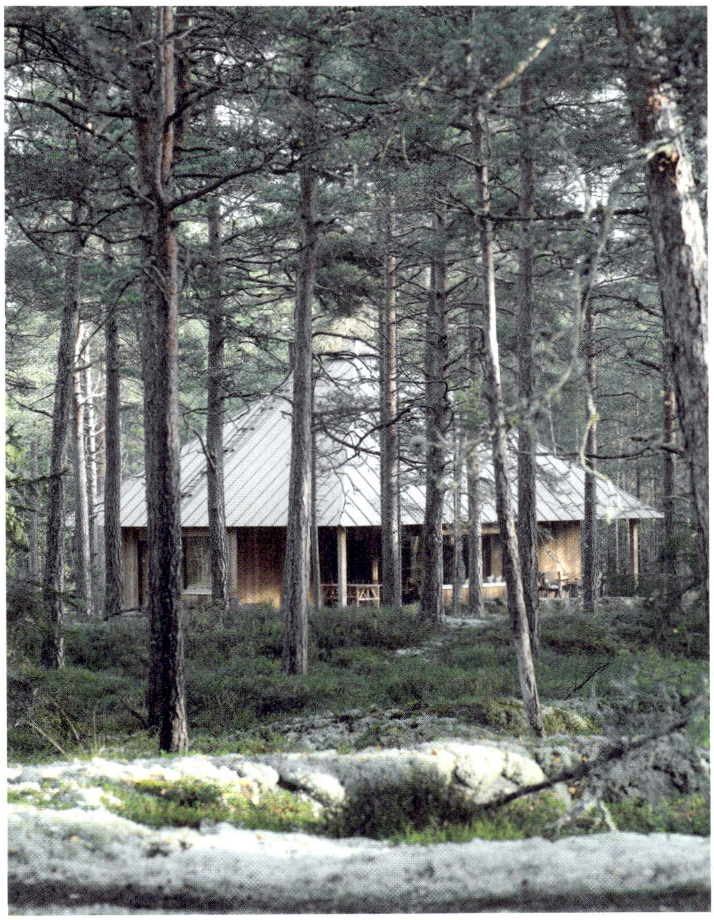

Several hours north-east of Stockholm, past the rugged outcroppings of land sprinkled throughout the Baltic Sea that makes up the Stockholm Archipelago, sits the island of Blidö, among the furthest and most remote of them all. There, hidden within the scraggly trees and the moss-carpeted forest floor, is the getaway home of Christian and Ruxandra Halleroed.

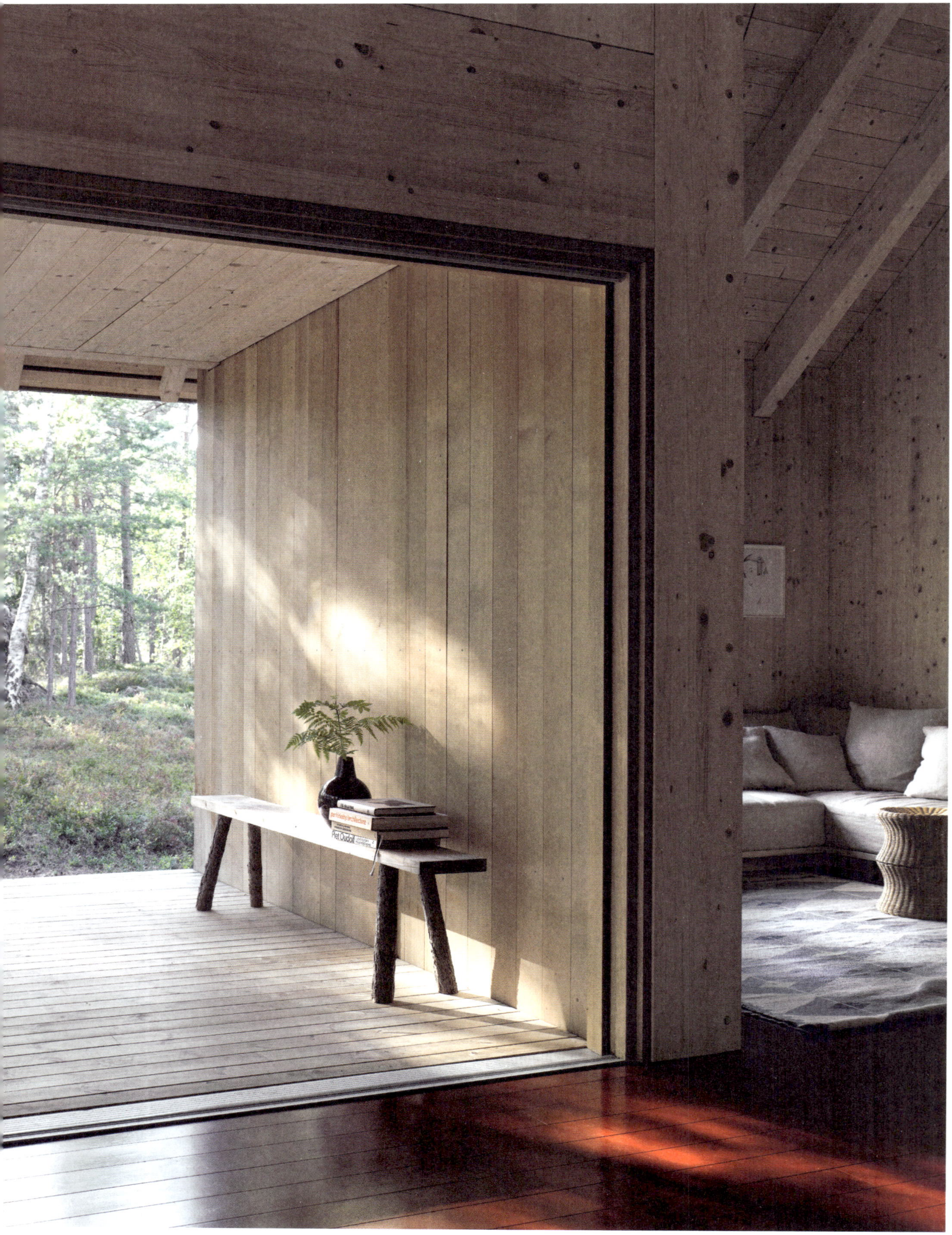

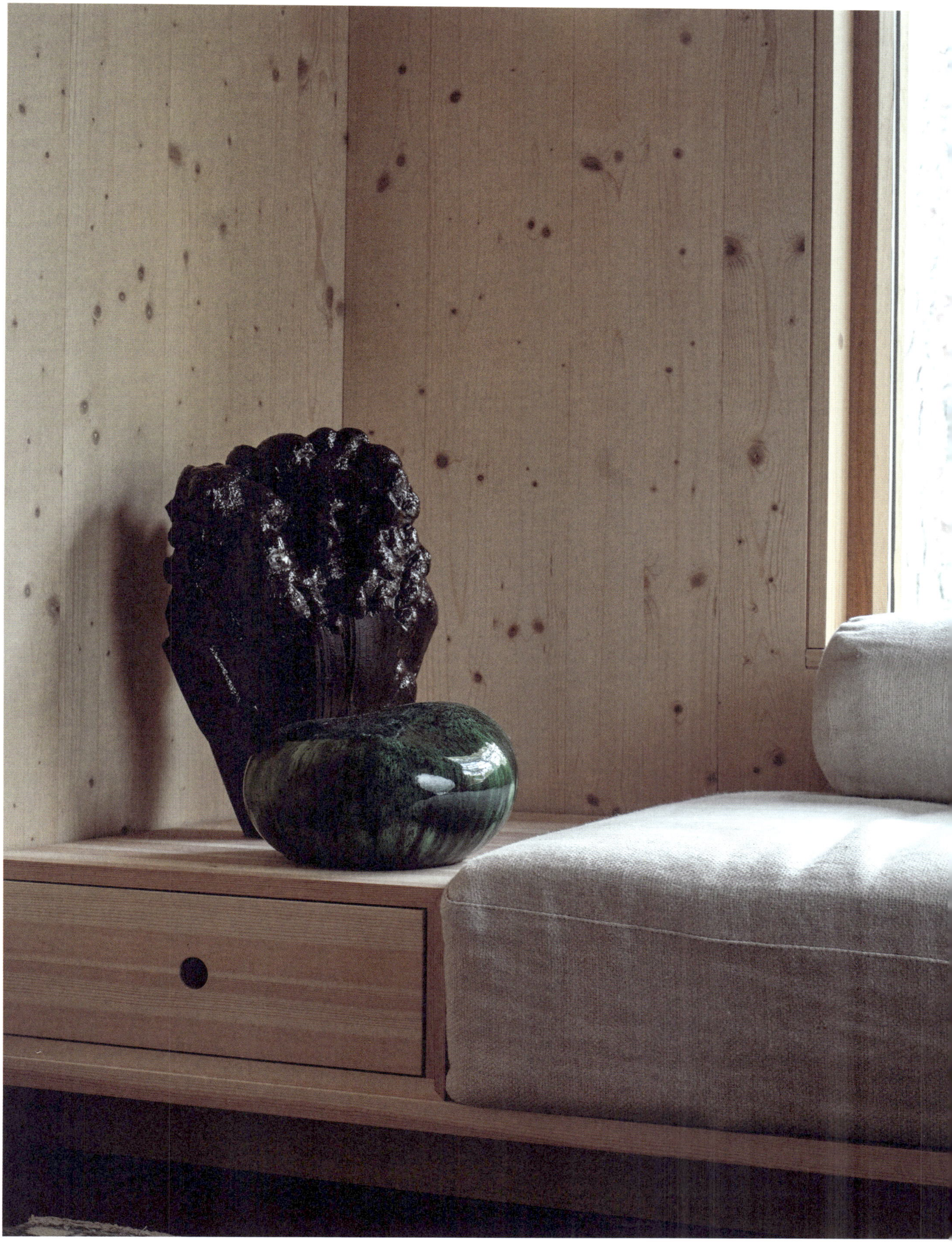

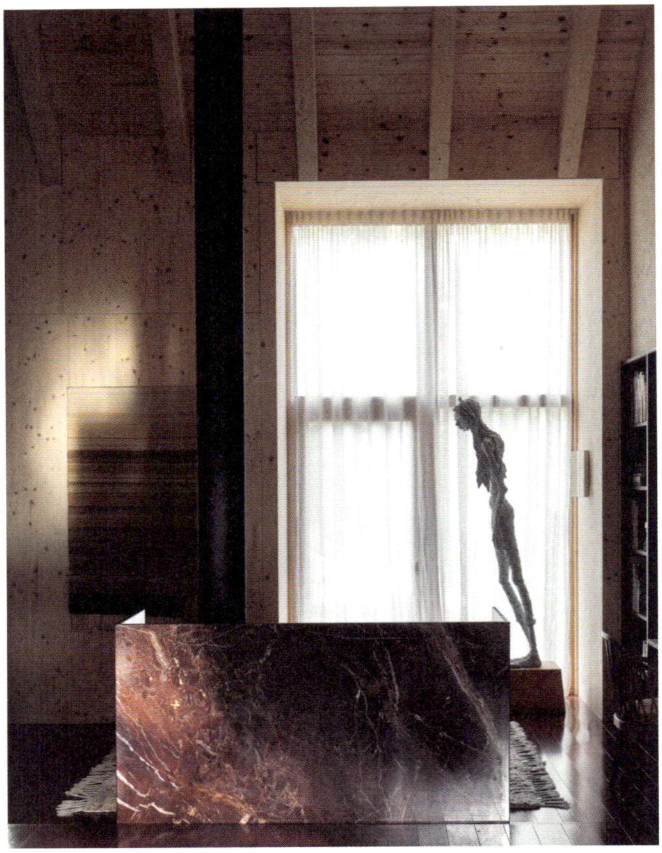

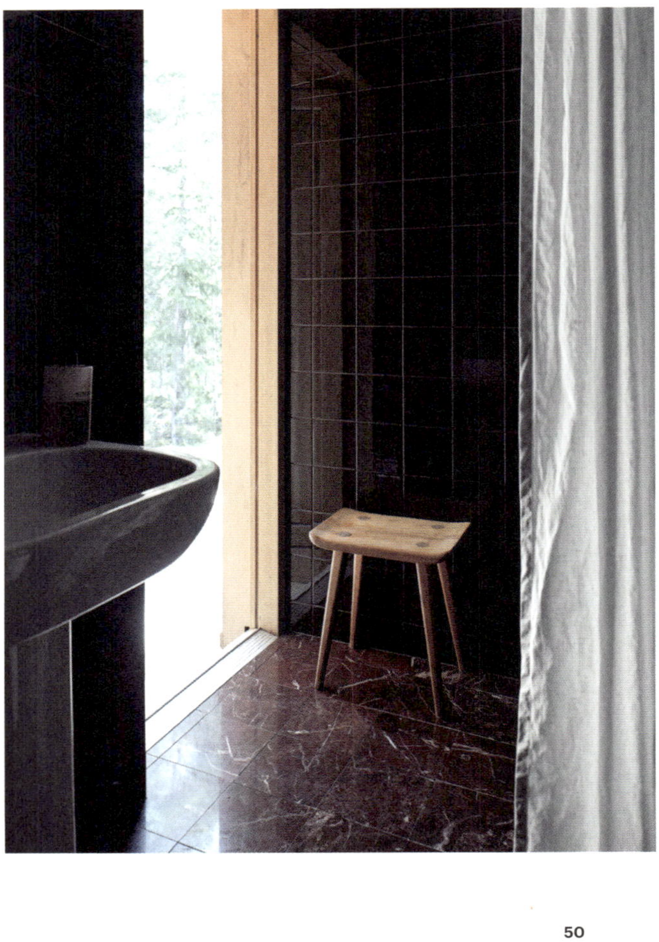

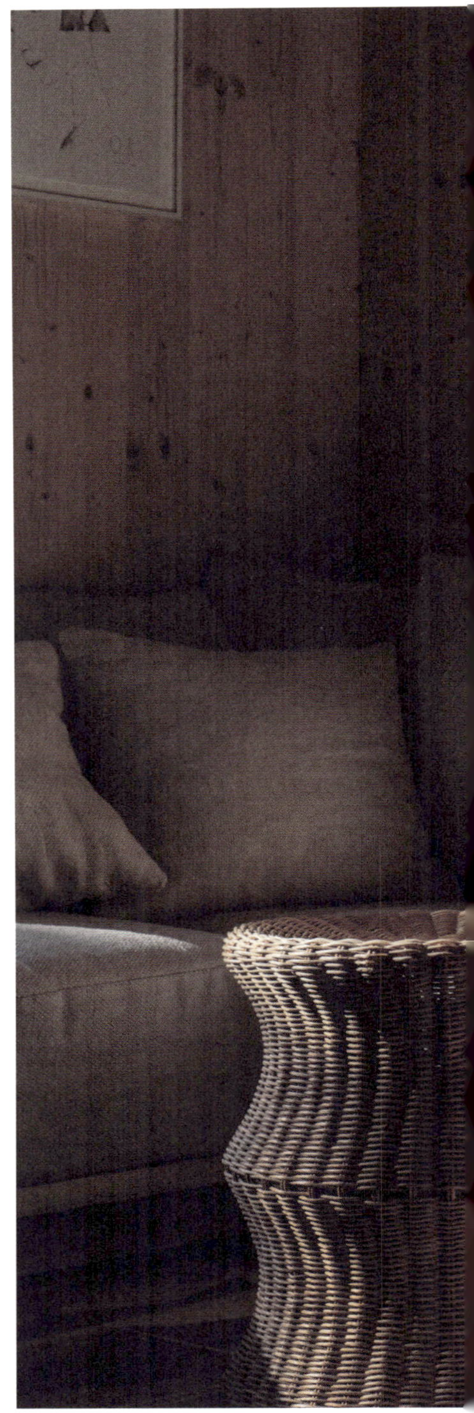

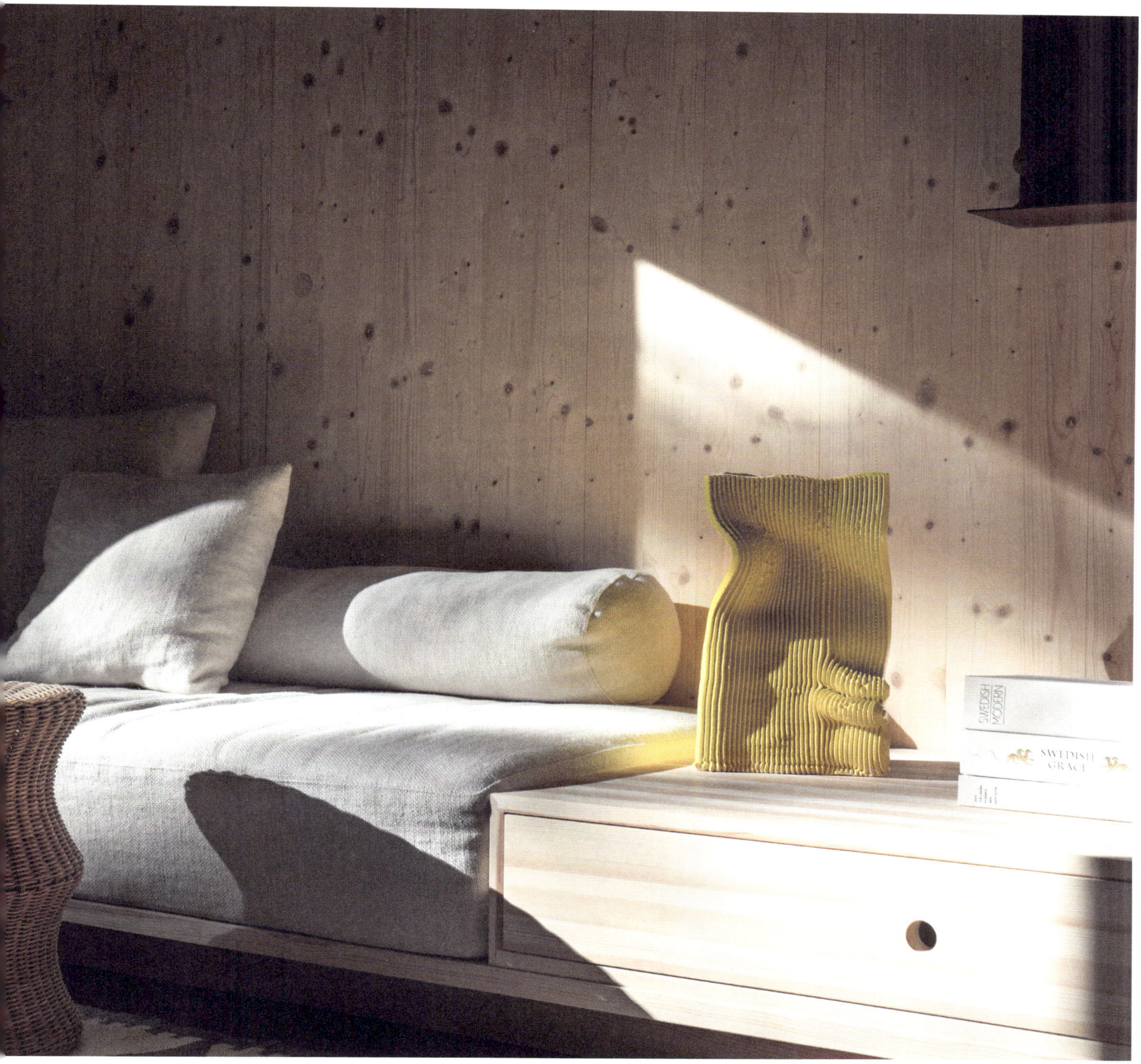

Both designers themselves, Christian and Ruxandra are best known for their commercial interiors of seemingly surgical precision, characterised by gleaming steel and sharp lines. But at their Nordic island escape, they chose instead a more organic approach. Soft, pale woods and natural materials such as blond cedar, unfinished spruce and red jasper marble define the palette of the two-floor, 1,100-square-foot home. Organised over two levels, the main floor comprises the living and dining room, reading nook and two bedrooms, while the upper level hosts an open-plan loft, which looks out over the kitchen through an amoeba-shaped porthole that Ruxandra sketched freehand during the construction process.

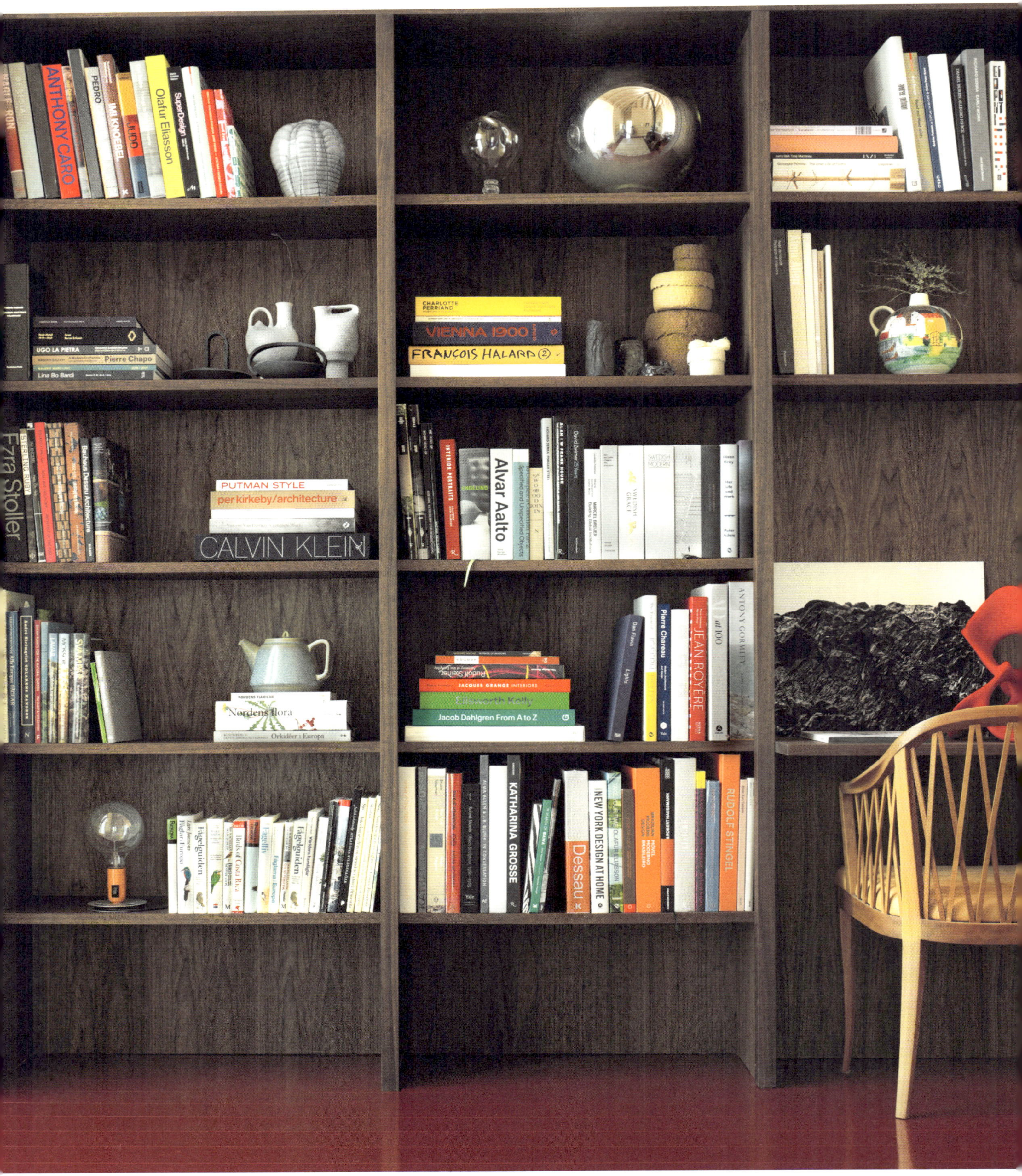
ANTHONY CARO
PEDRO
IMI KNOEBEL
JUDD
Olafur Eliasson
SuperDesign
UGO LA PIETRA
Pierre Chapo
Lina Bo Bardi
CHARLOTTE PERRIAND
VIENNA 1900
FRANÇOIS HALARD
Ezra Stoller
STERLING RUBY
Bauhaus Dessau Architecture
PUTMAN STYLE
per kirkeby/architecture
CALVIN KLEIN
INTERIOR PORTRAITS
Alvar Aalto
Specified and Unspecified Objects
ALAN I W FRANK HOUSE
SWEDISH MODERN
Nordens flora
Orkidéer i Europa
Rudolf Steiner
JACQUES GRANGE INTERIORS
Ellsworth Kelly
Jacob Dahlgren From A to Z
Pierre Chareau
JEAN ROYÈRE
ANTONY GORMLEY
Fågelguiden
Birds of Costa Rica
KATHARINA GROSSE
Dessau
NEW YORK DESIGN AT HOME
OLAFUR ELIASSON
RUDOLF STINGEL

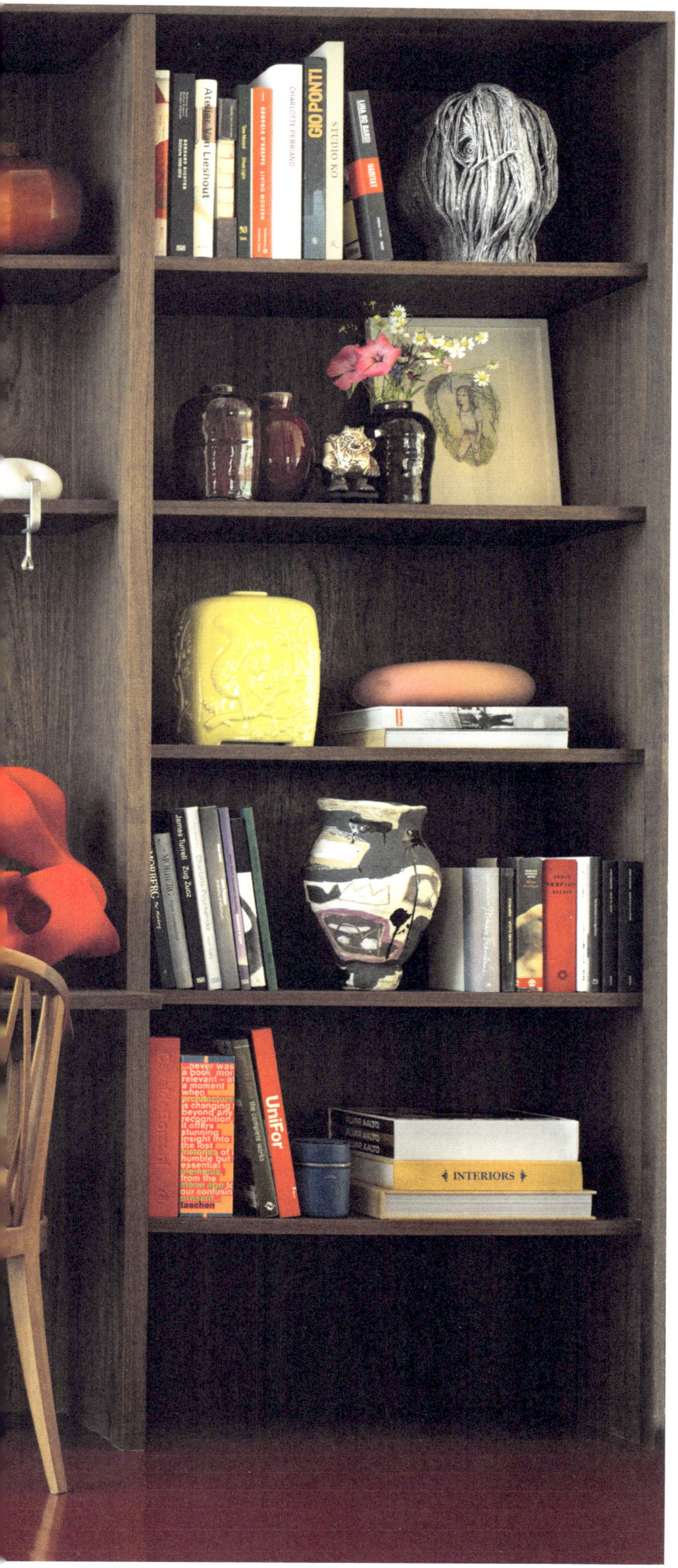

The pair folded a phalanx of modernist references into the home's architectural inspiration. The asymmetrical floor plan was informed by 1940s-era country houses by Josef Frank, while the steeply pitched standing seam aluminium hip roof pays homage to the woodland chapels designed by fellow Swede Gunnar Asplund in the 1920s. Both keen design collectors, the Halleroeds furnished the space with a treasure trove of covetable objects and furniture – among them, chairs by 20th-century masters Italian Luigi Caccia Dominioni and Swede Carl Malmsten, handcrafted blankets from Svensk Hemslöjd, vintage Rörstrand porcelain, Moroccan rugs and a Göran Malmvall armchair from the 1950s.

But the references are not solely high-brow; nostalgia played an essential role in guiding the design, too. The deep reds that define the cabin's interior palette were chosen as a nod to the natural paint falu red, derived from copper waste and used on the exterior of traditional Swedish clapboard houses. The home's austere profile is influenced by the simple pine shacks that populate the wilds of northern Sweden, similar to those in which Christian and his parents would pass the winters of his childhood.

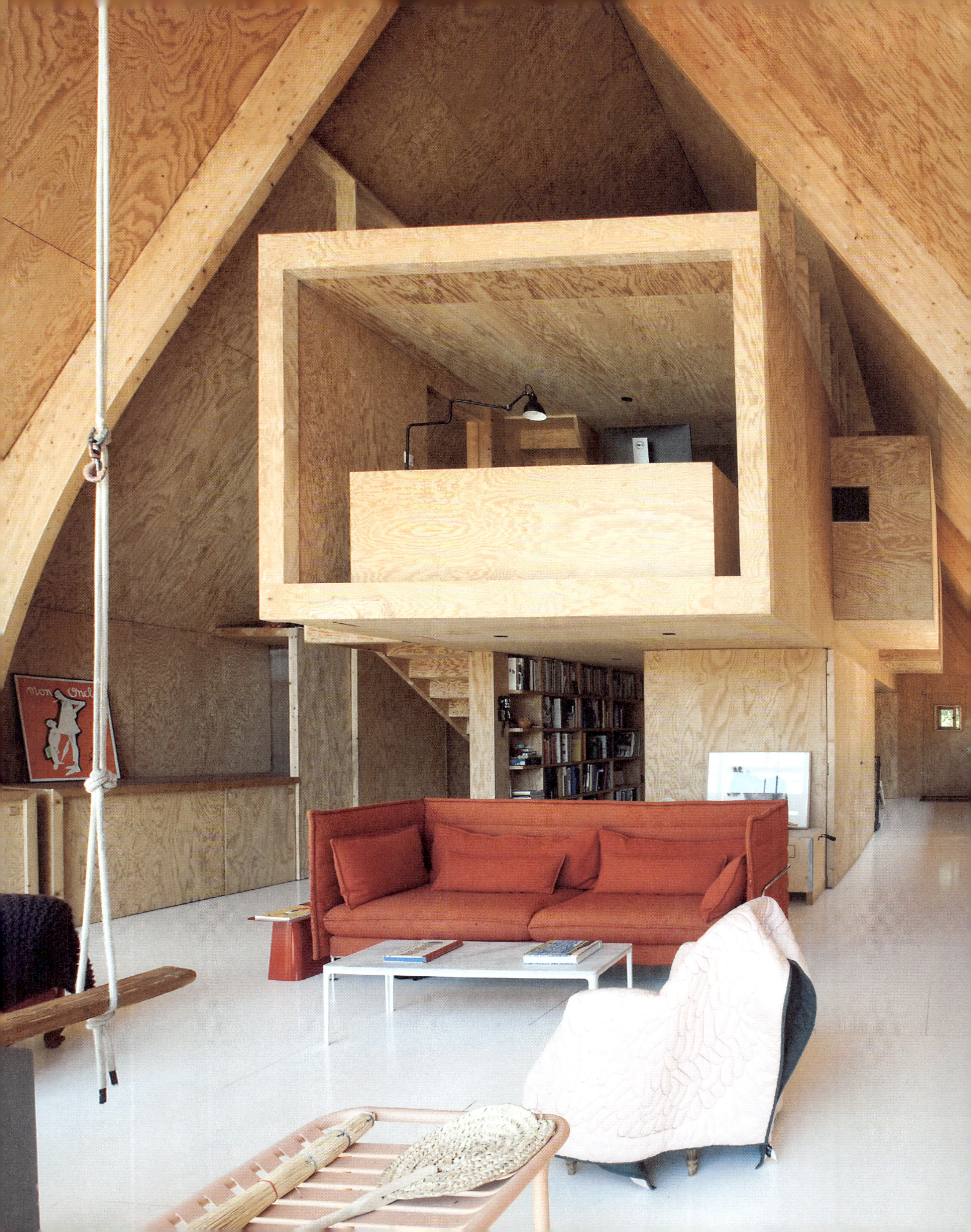

A Sustainable Countryside Sanctuary for a Designer

AUVILLIERS, NORMANDY (FR) **IONNA VAUTRIN**

Parisian industrial designer and illustrator Ionna Vautrin found her perfect countryside getaway in a windswept wooded knoll close to Auvilliers, Normandy, about two hours north-west of Paris. 'I live and work alone with my cat in this wonderful house,' says Vautrin, who purchased the cottage in 2017 and has since moved there full time. 'I had lived in Paris for almost 20 years and I felt the need to reconnect with nature.'

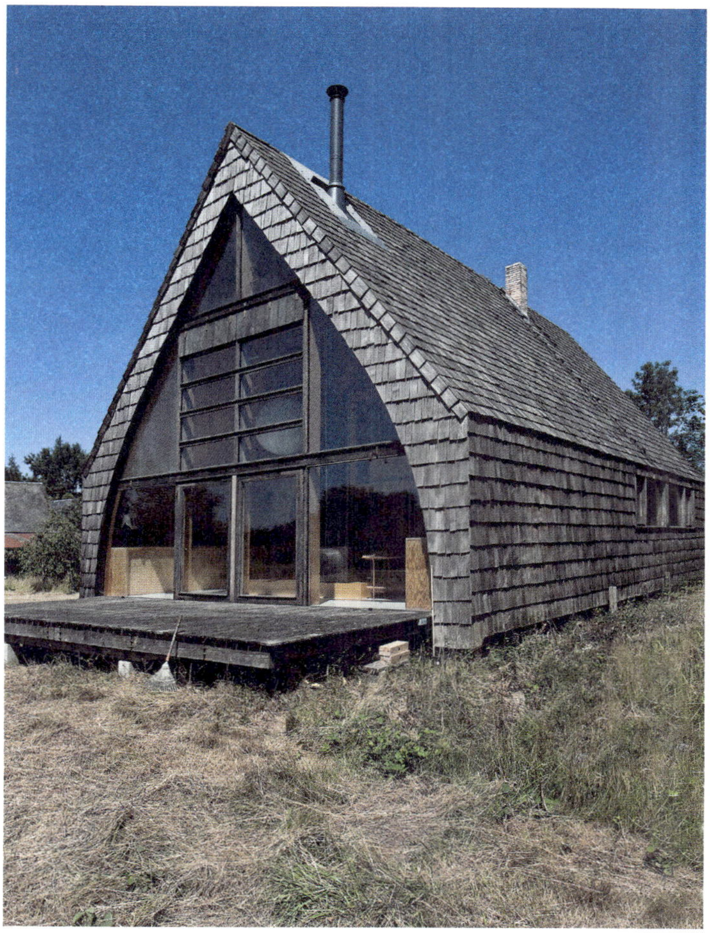

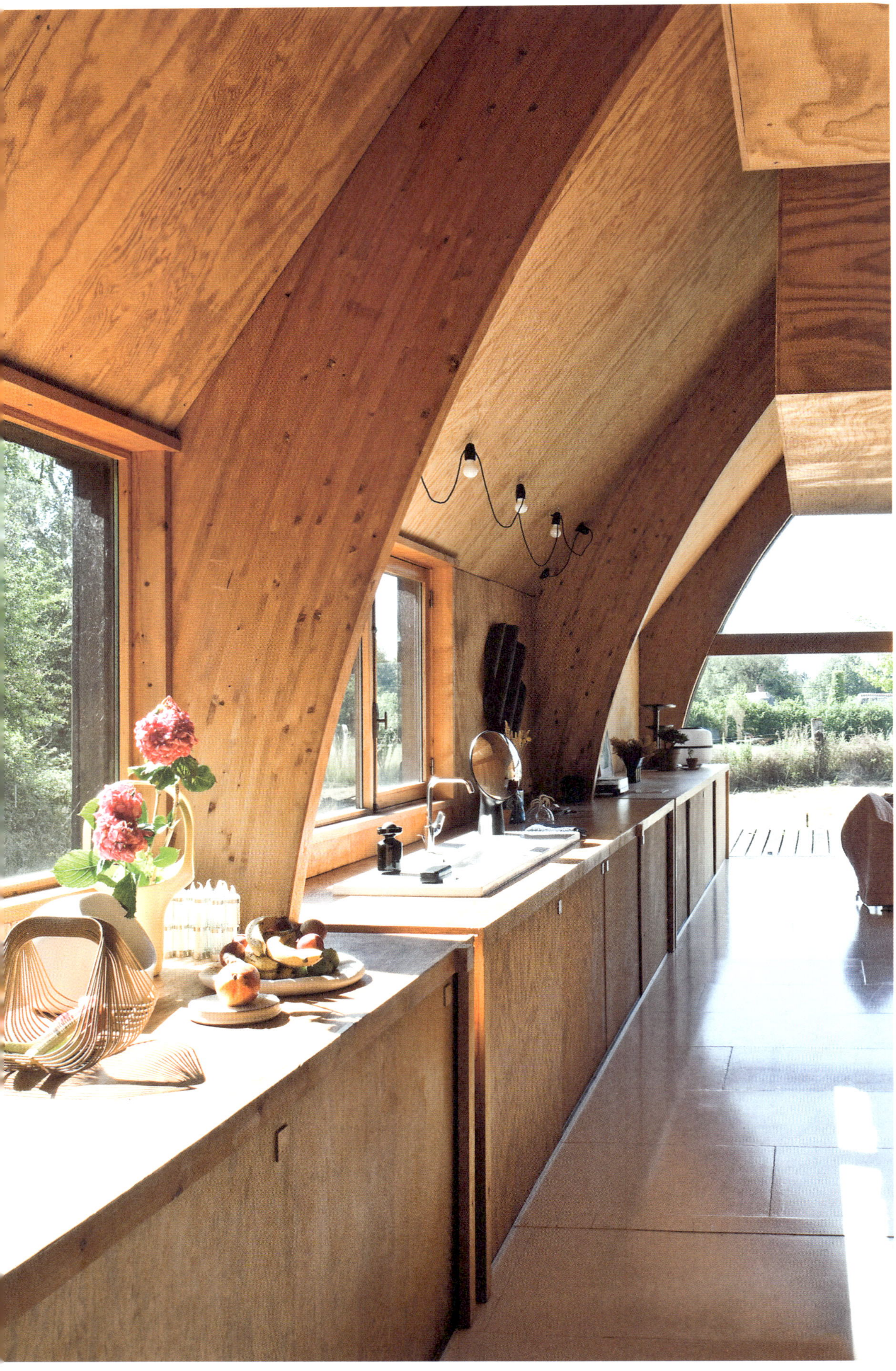

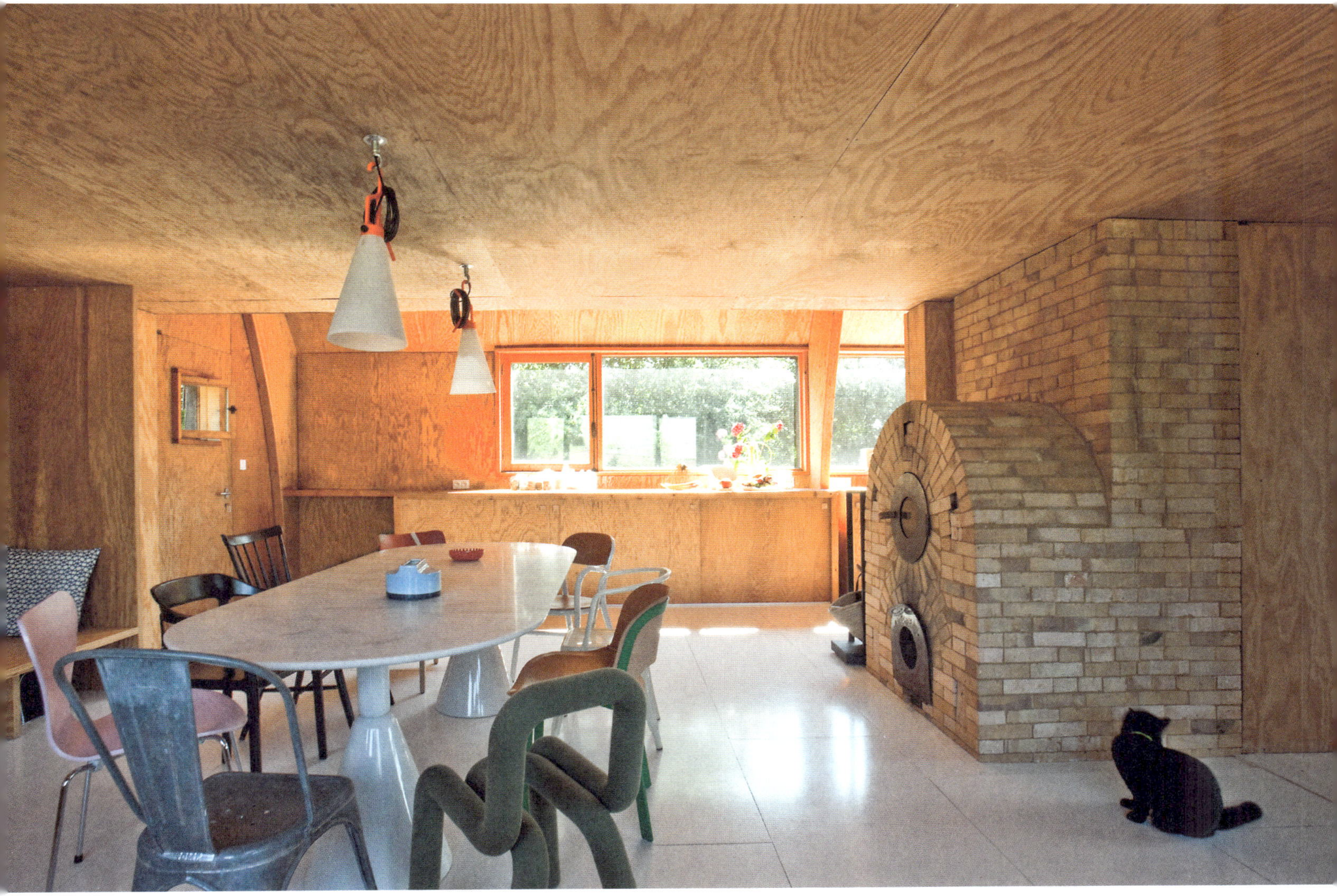

Weathered timber shingles were used to clad the steeply pitched A-frame roof, designed to vaguely resembles a simple country chapel. 'Its outer skin is made entirely of red cedar tile,' explains Vautrin, 'while its interior is made from flamed pine plywood.' This unfinished pine plywood, coupled with the plain white floors that make up the interior, pull the focus towards the bright furniture and unconventional forms that define the home. 'A large open space on the ground floor accommodates a kitchen, dining room, bathroom, living room and a library,' Vautrin explains. 'The first floor offers a dormitory with three alcove beds and an office, and the top floor houses a large plateau, the only closed space.' The structure's main architectural gesture, the second-floor loft, hovers above the double-height living room like an incoming spaceship.

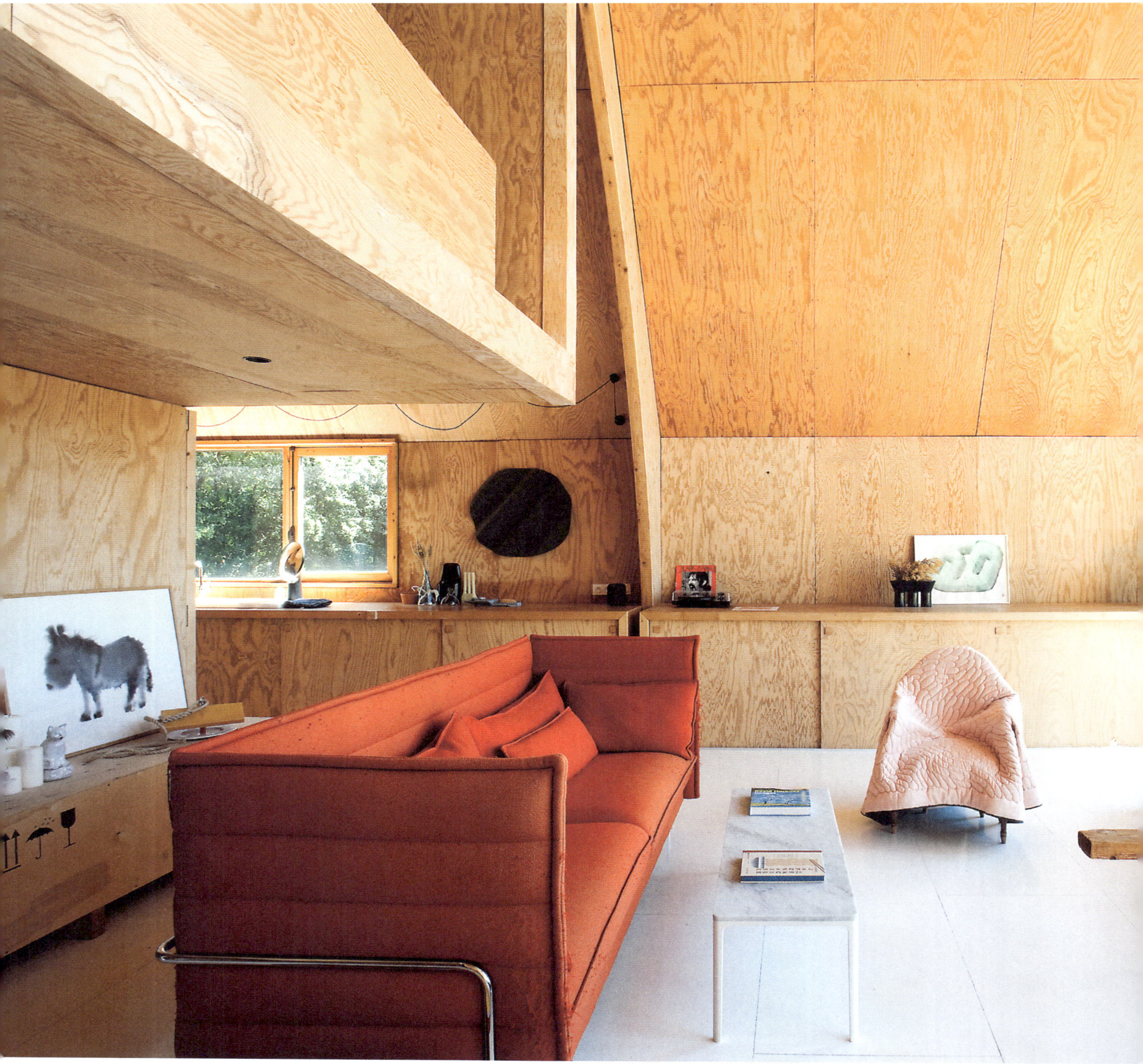

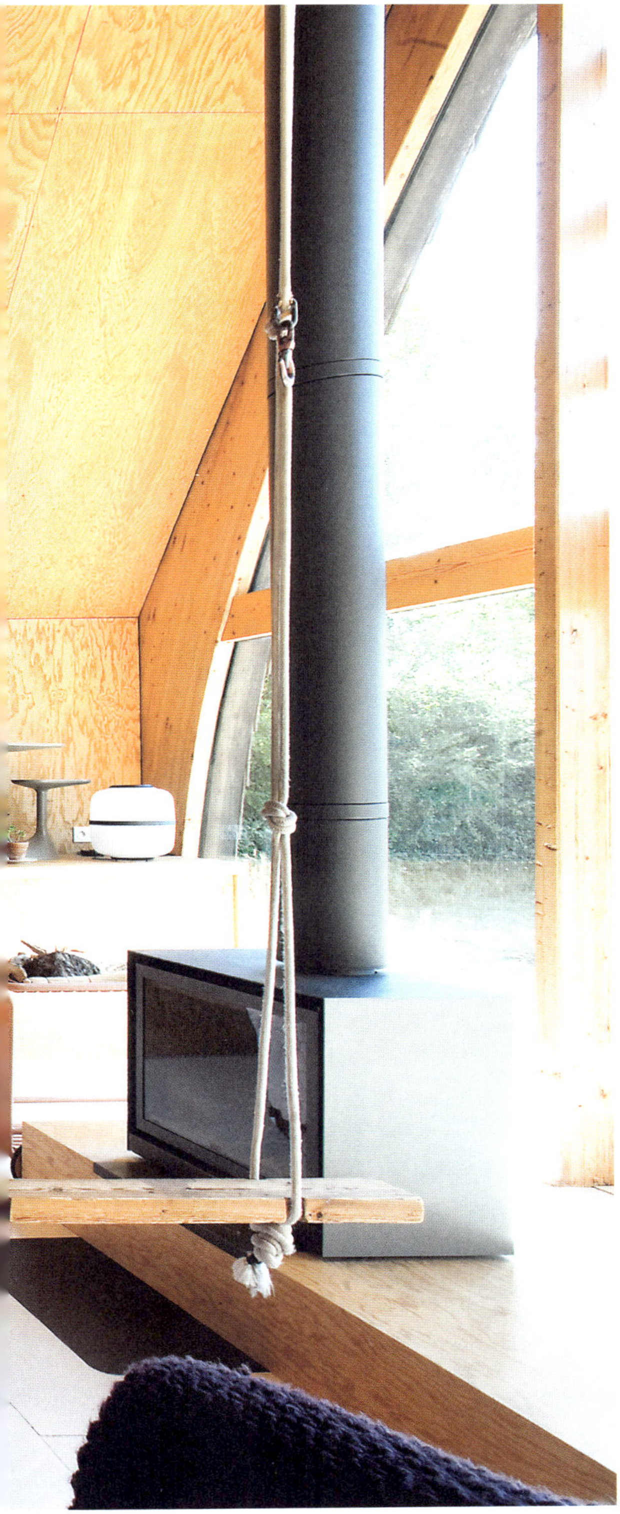

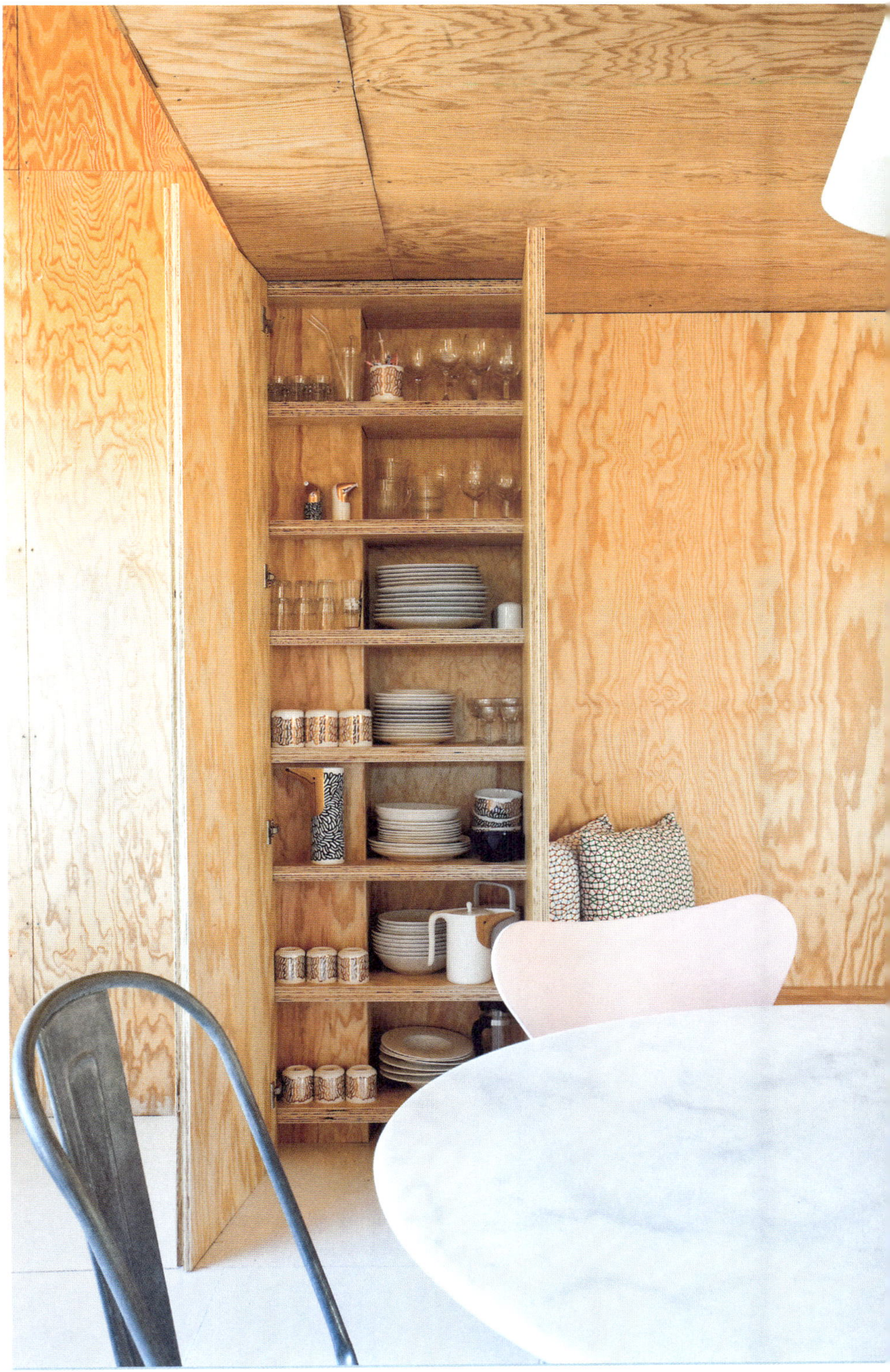

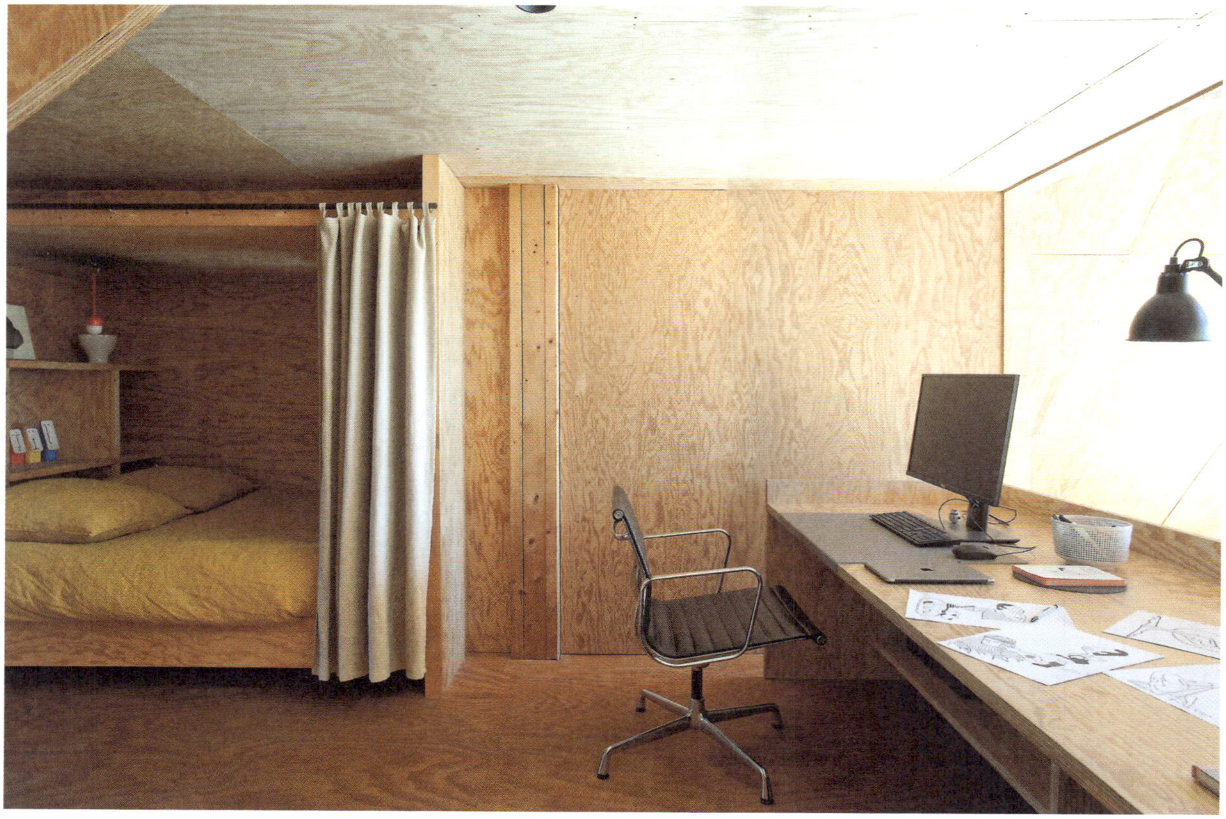

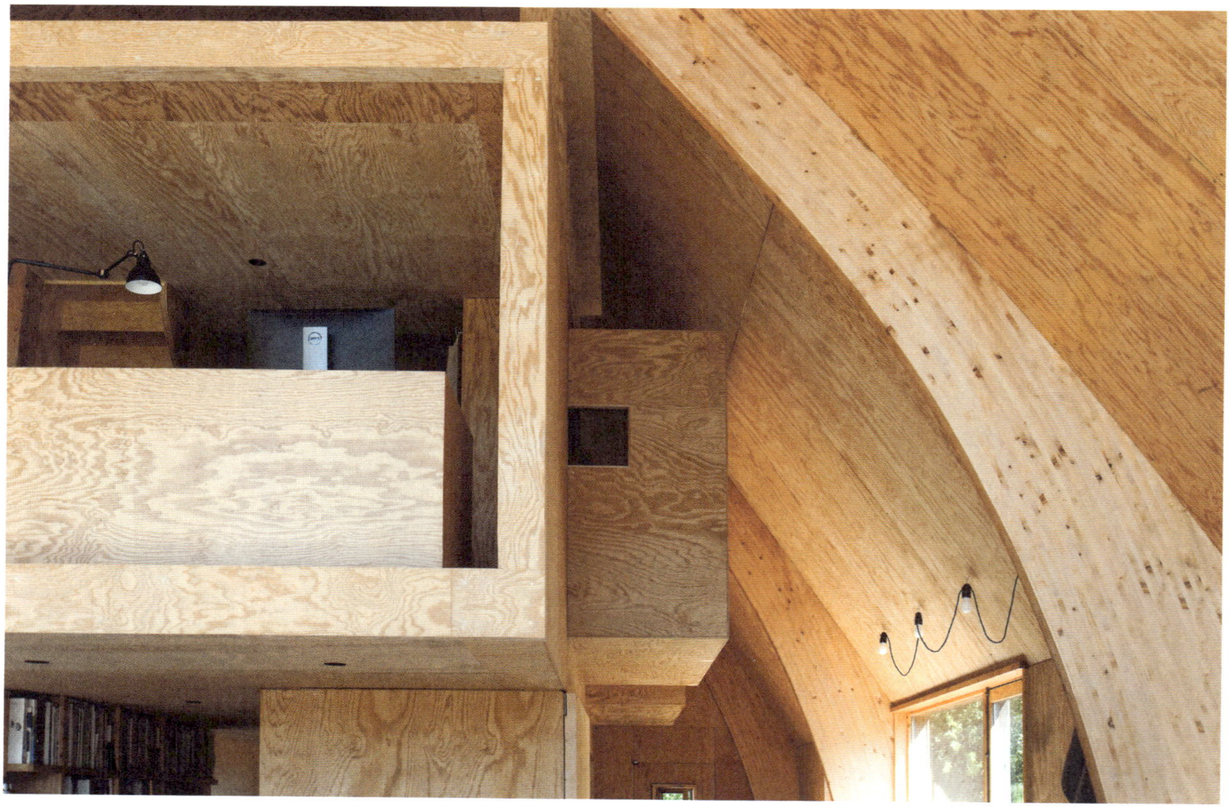

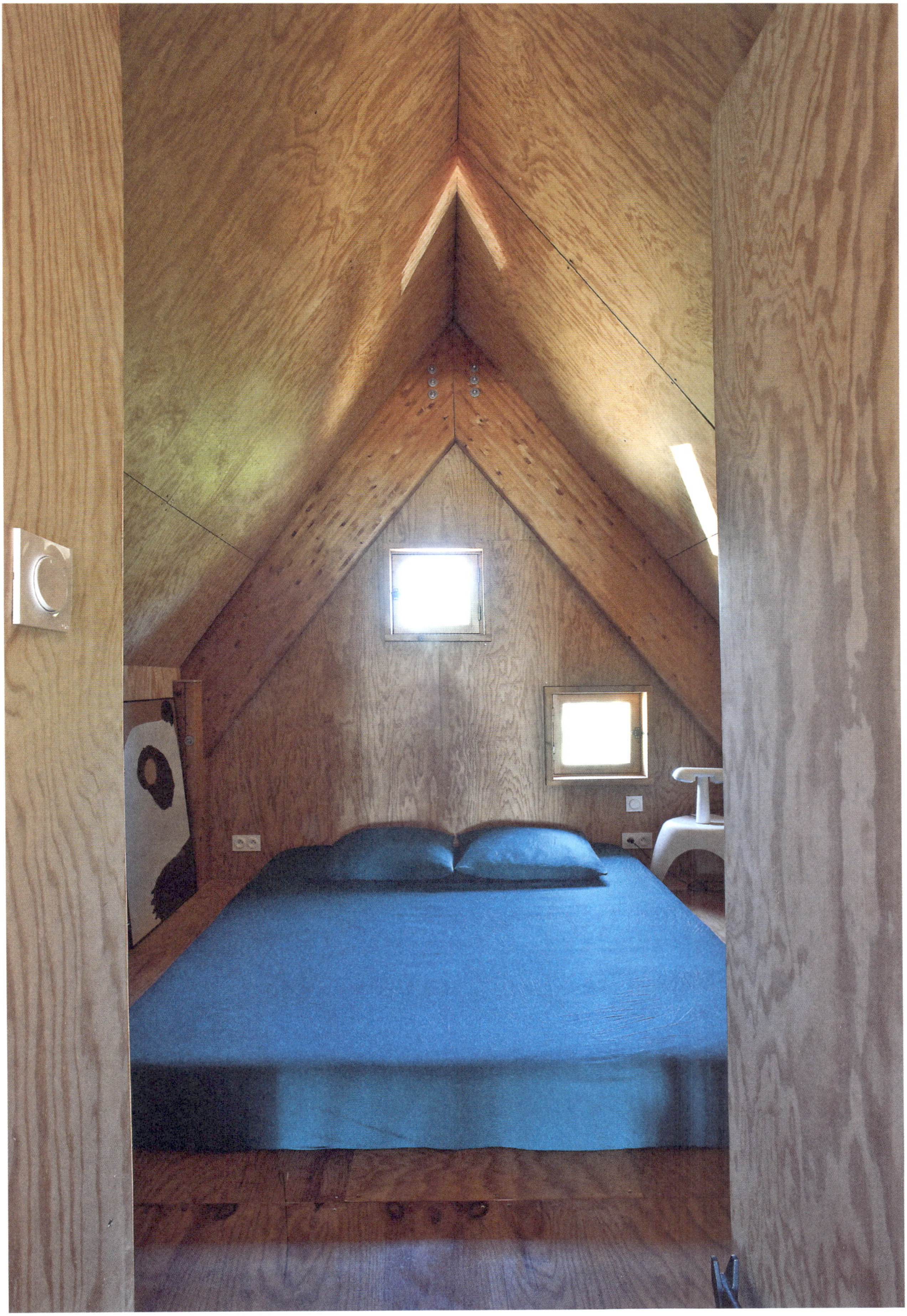

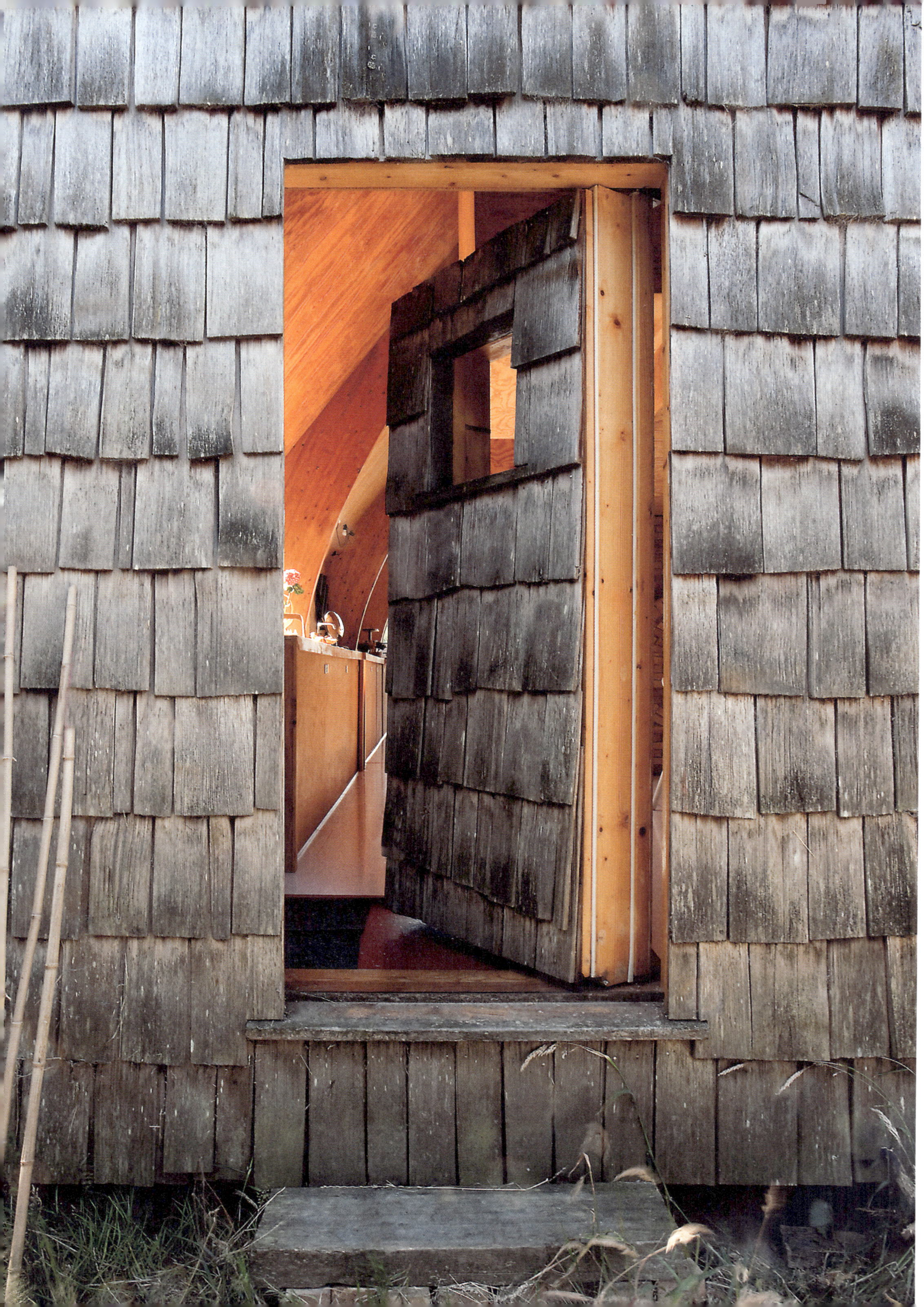

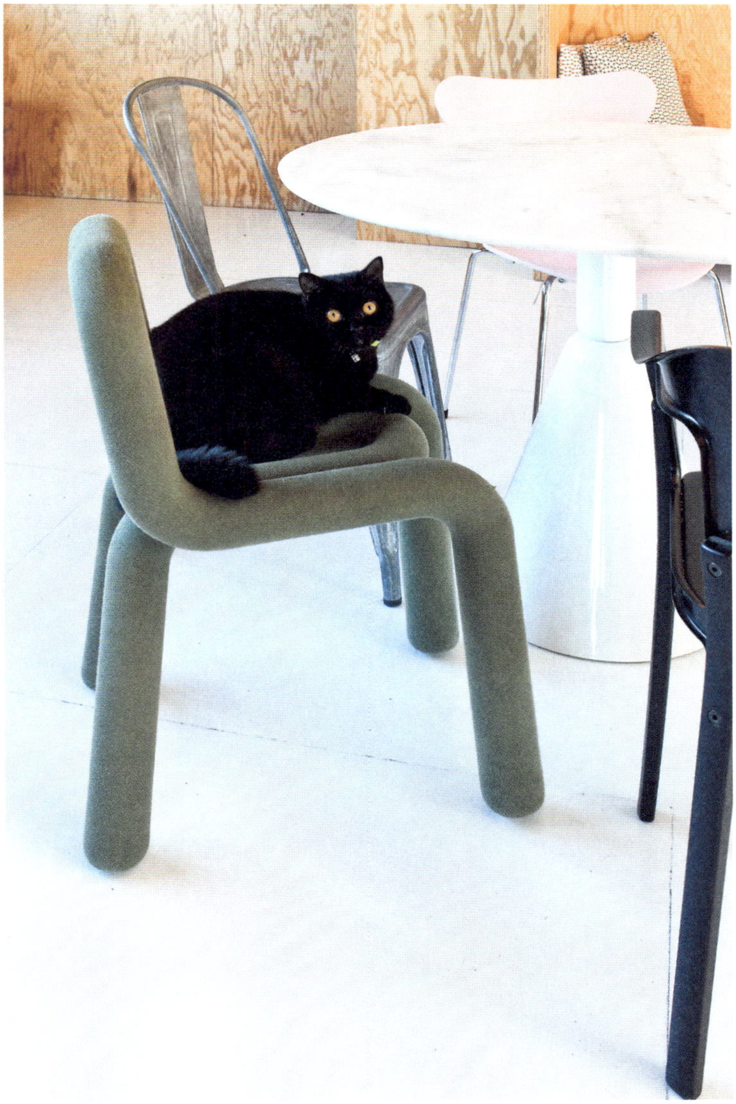

In the main living area below, which frames views of the countryside through a double-height window, a cherry red sofa by the Bouroullec brothers, with whom Vautrin cut her teeth as a young designer, and a squiggly green Big Game bench by Moustache are arranged next to a rope swing that hangs from the vaulted ceiling – all pieces that speak to Vautrin's playful artistic attitude.

'I am an industrial designer and this house made me think a lot about the meaning and impact of my profession,' she says, referencing the sustainable ethos of the original architect, Jean-Baptiste Barache, who constructed the majority of the structure himself over the span of 18 months, using only passive solar energy and a wood stove for heat. Initially, the house did not have electricity but Vautrin has since connected it to the grid. 'Its objective was to design a passive house that he could build himself,' she adds. 'He saw this cabin as an experience of living without connection to contemporary life.'

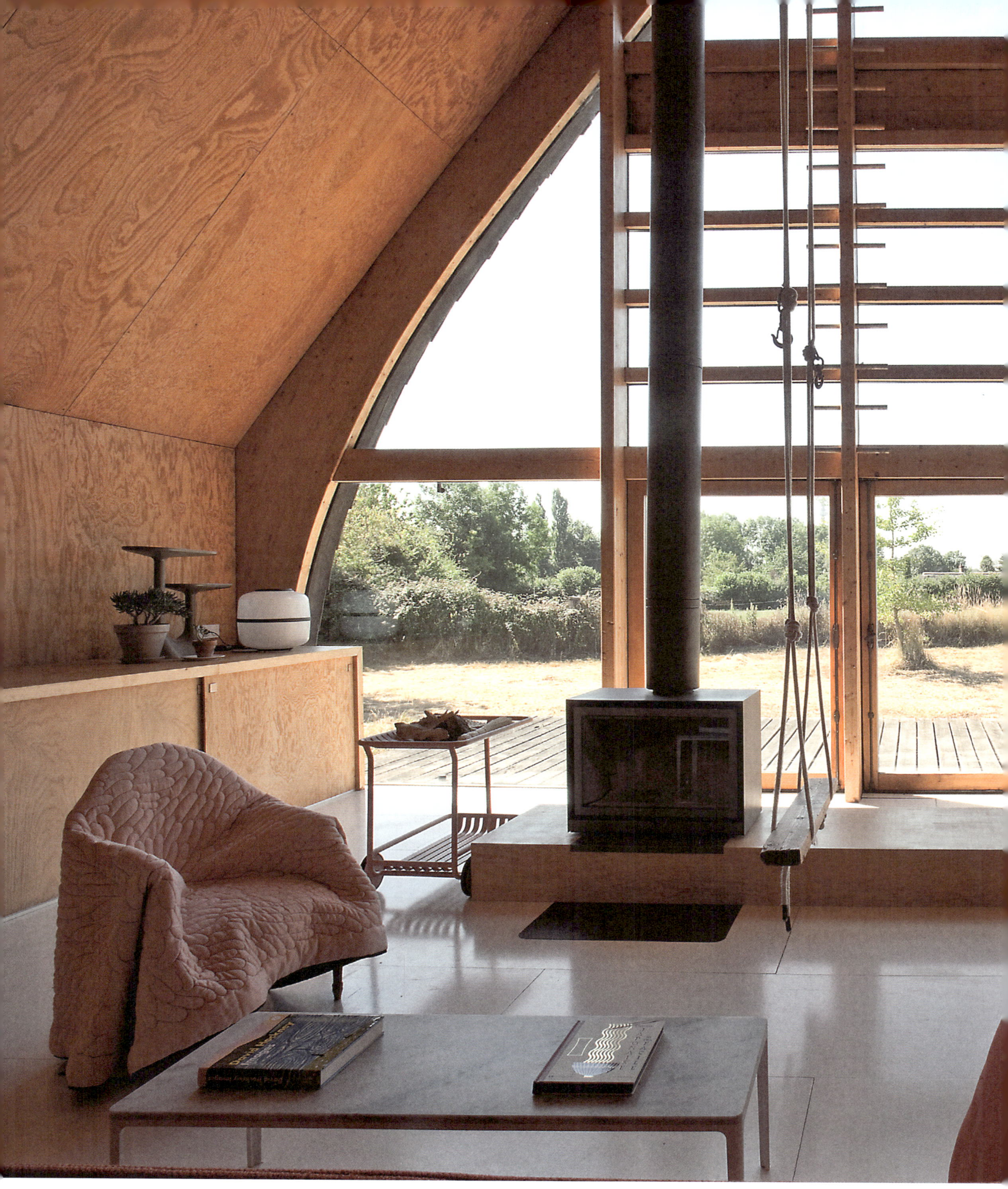

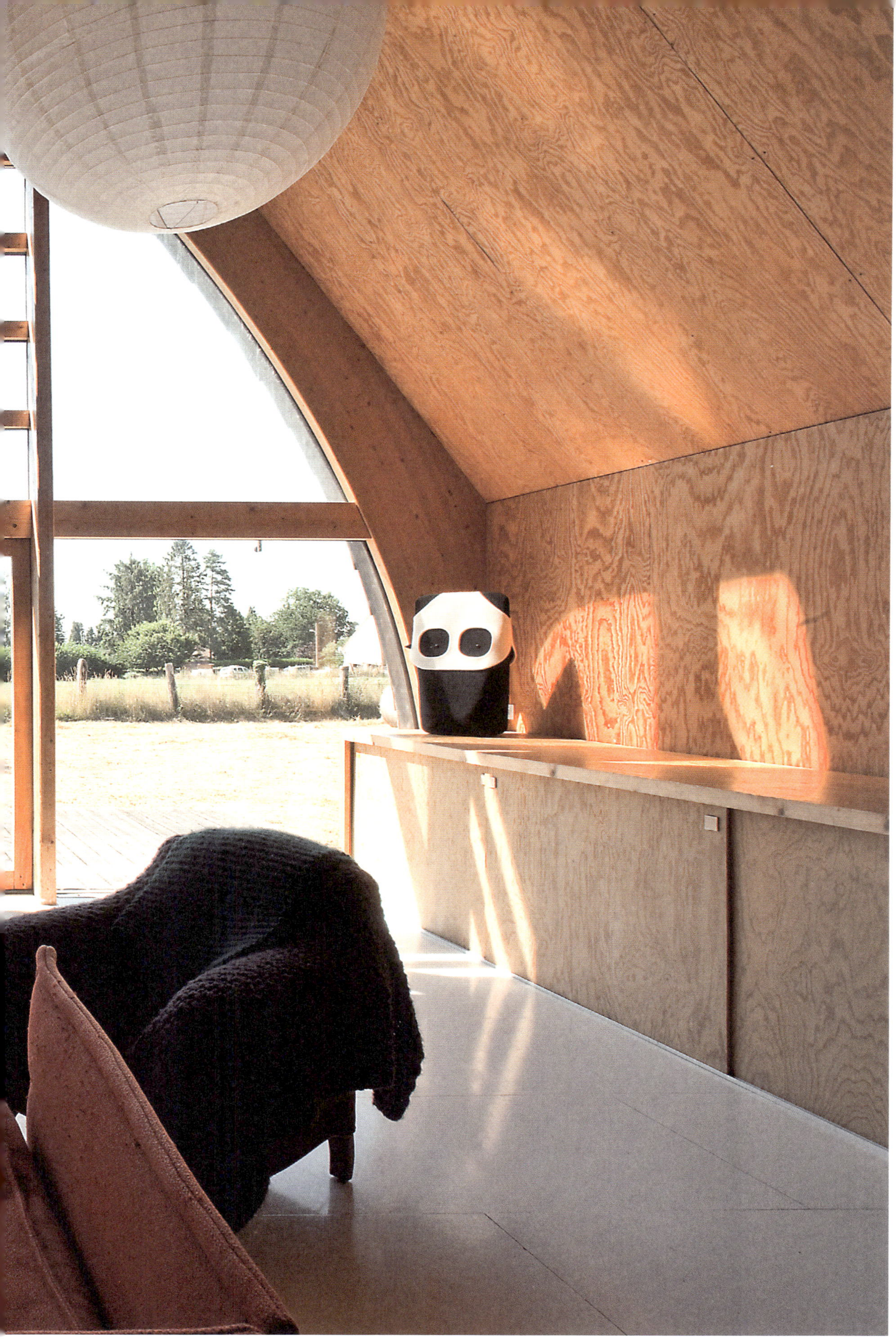

A Modernist Icon's Second Life as an Artistic Family's Retreat

FIRE ISLAND, NEW YORK (US) **JAMES & HARA PERKINS**

Fire Island, a narrow strip of land to the south of New York's Long Island, is known as a historic haven for the LGBT community and a lively beach resort just a short trip away from the city. But what is less known about Fire Island is that it is a mecca for modernist architecture, mostly due to the influence of one man: the architect Horace Gifford. From the 1960s to the 1980s, Gifford produced a trove of modest beach houses characterised by a profound connection with the landscape – sustainable thinking well before its time.

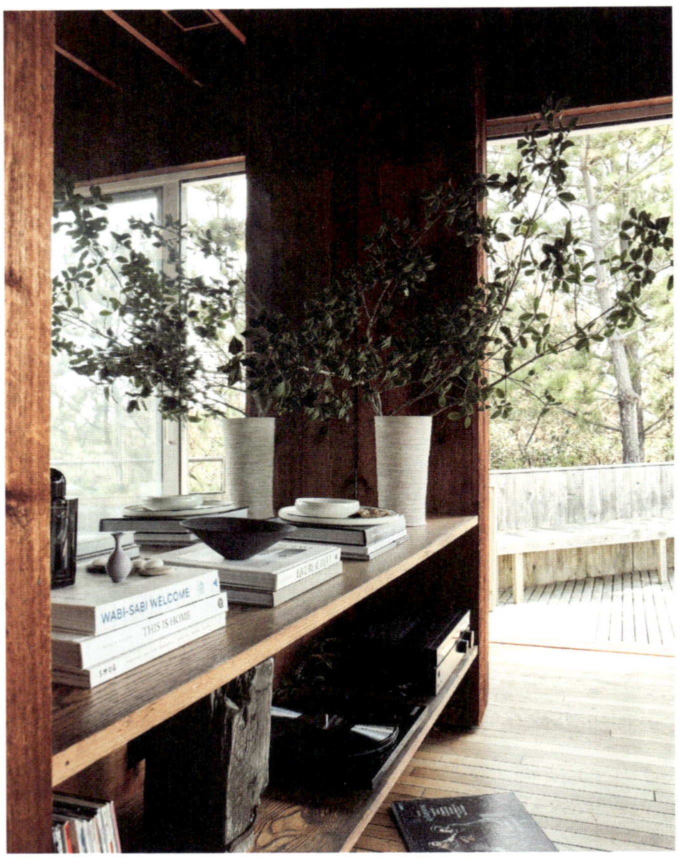

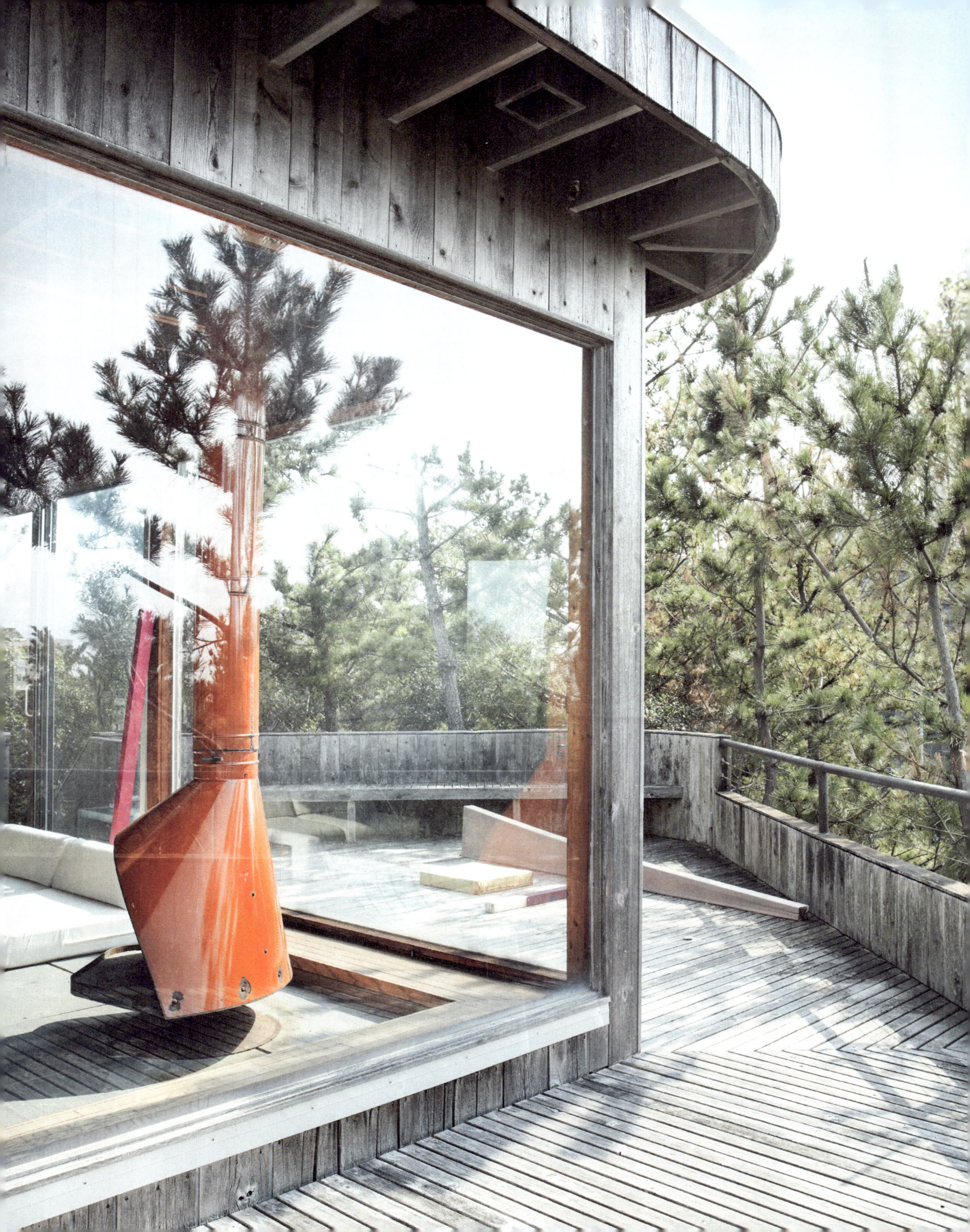

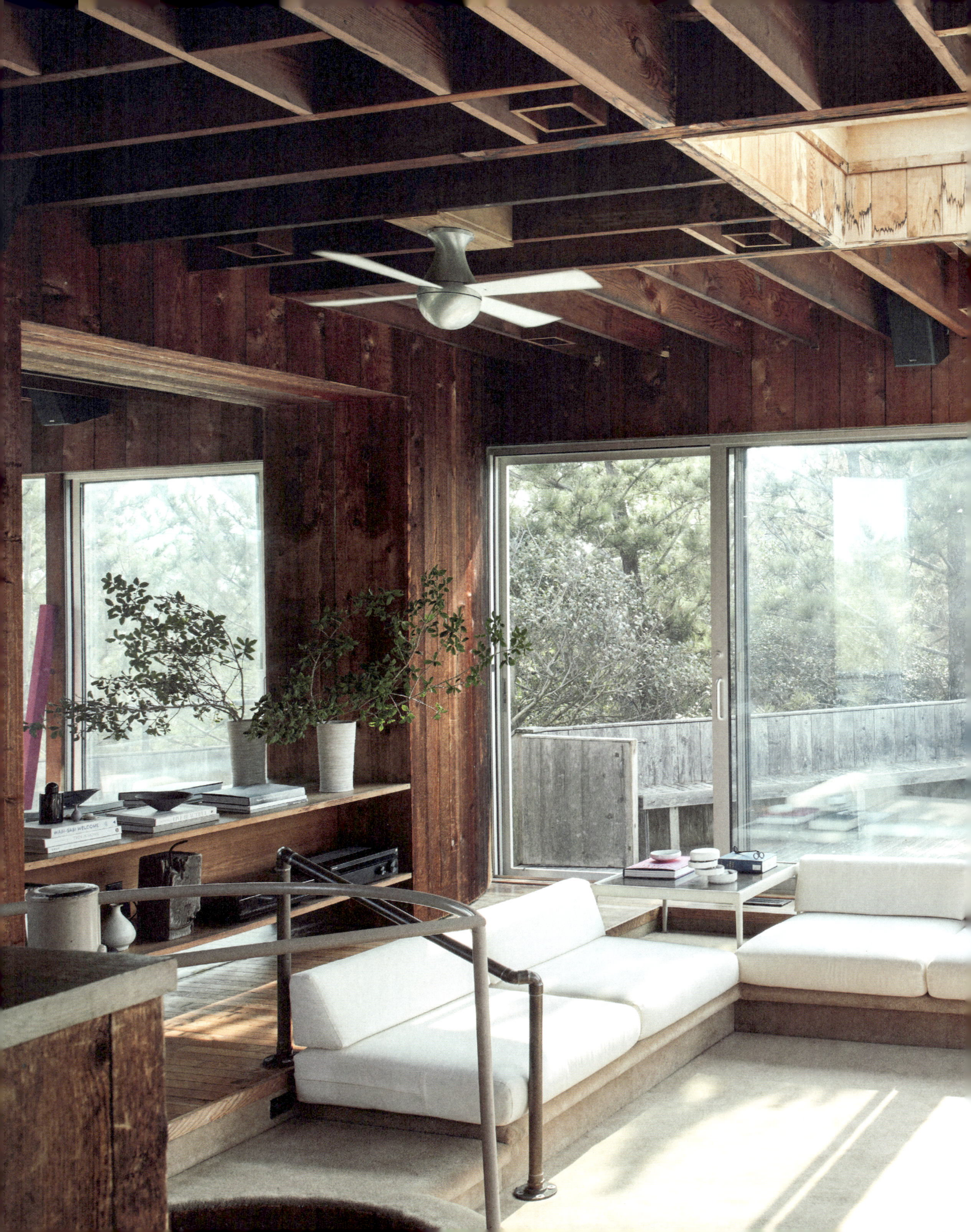
WABI-SABI WELCOME
THIS IS HOME

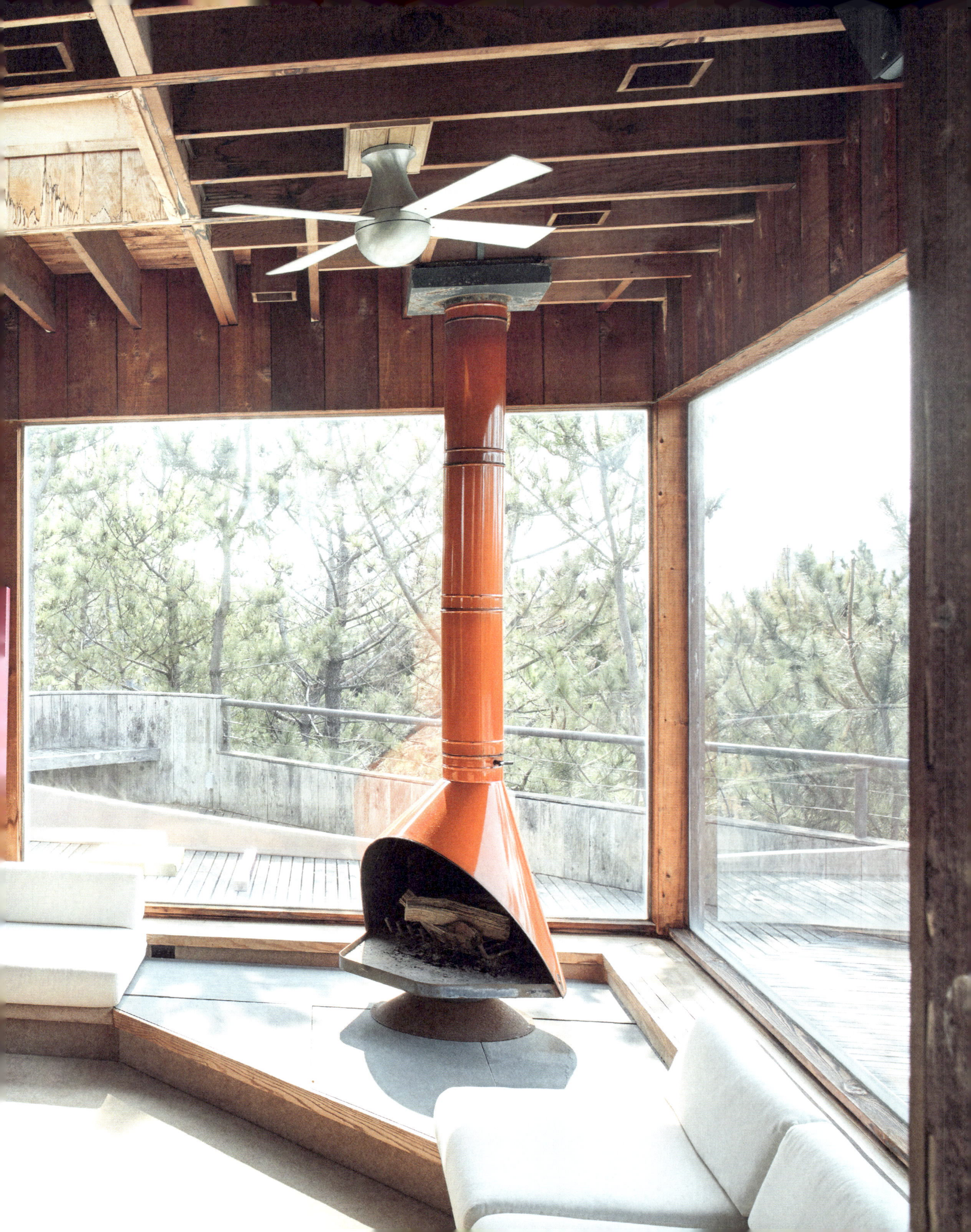

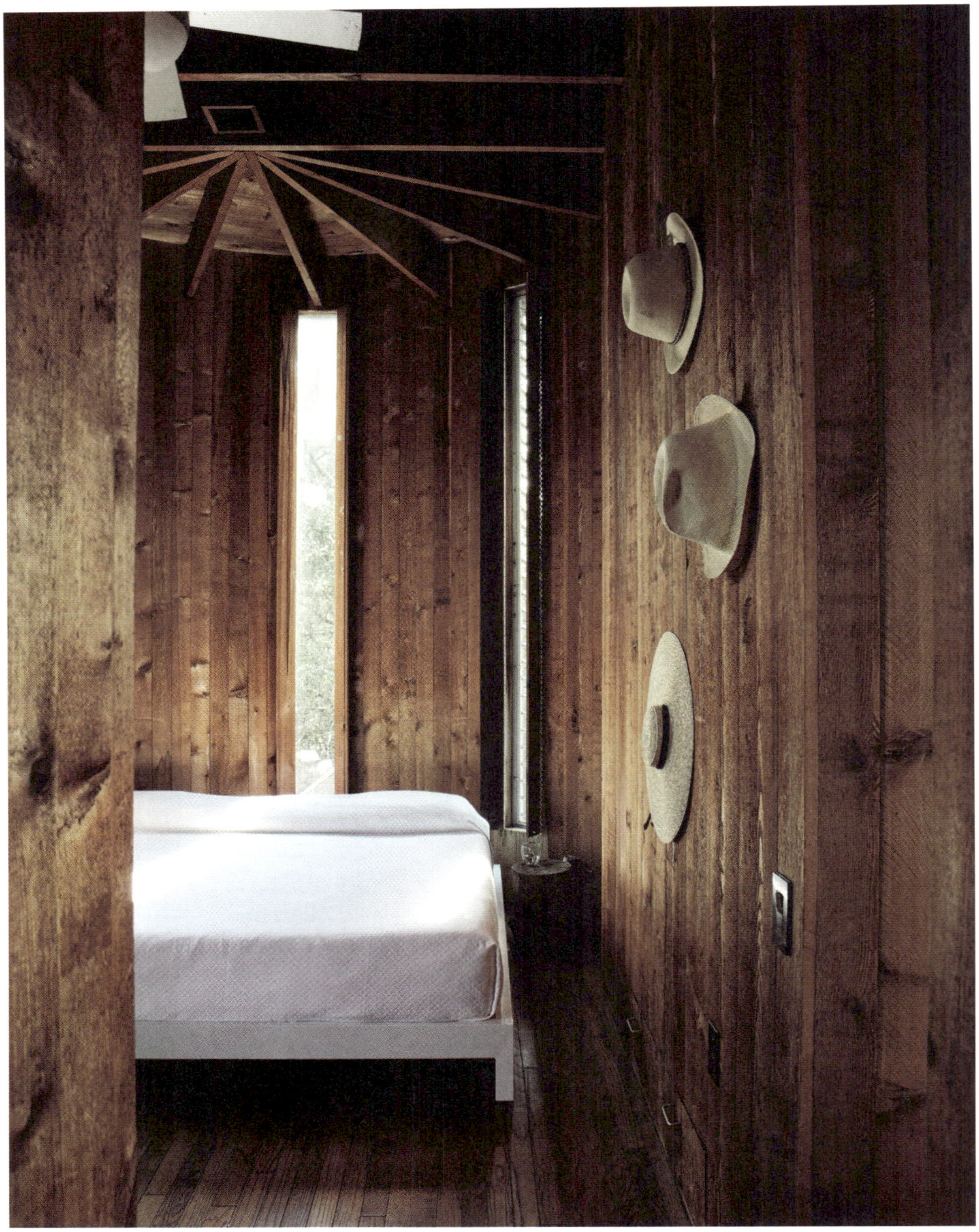

James and Hara Perkins purchased their Fire Island refuge after falling in love with the work of Gifford. When they took possession of the property in early 2020, just before the first pandemic lockdowns, it had been in the same family since it was first built in the 1960s. They spent the early months of quarantine renovating the space themselves, stripping back the layers of time to restore it to its original glory.

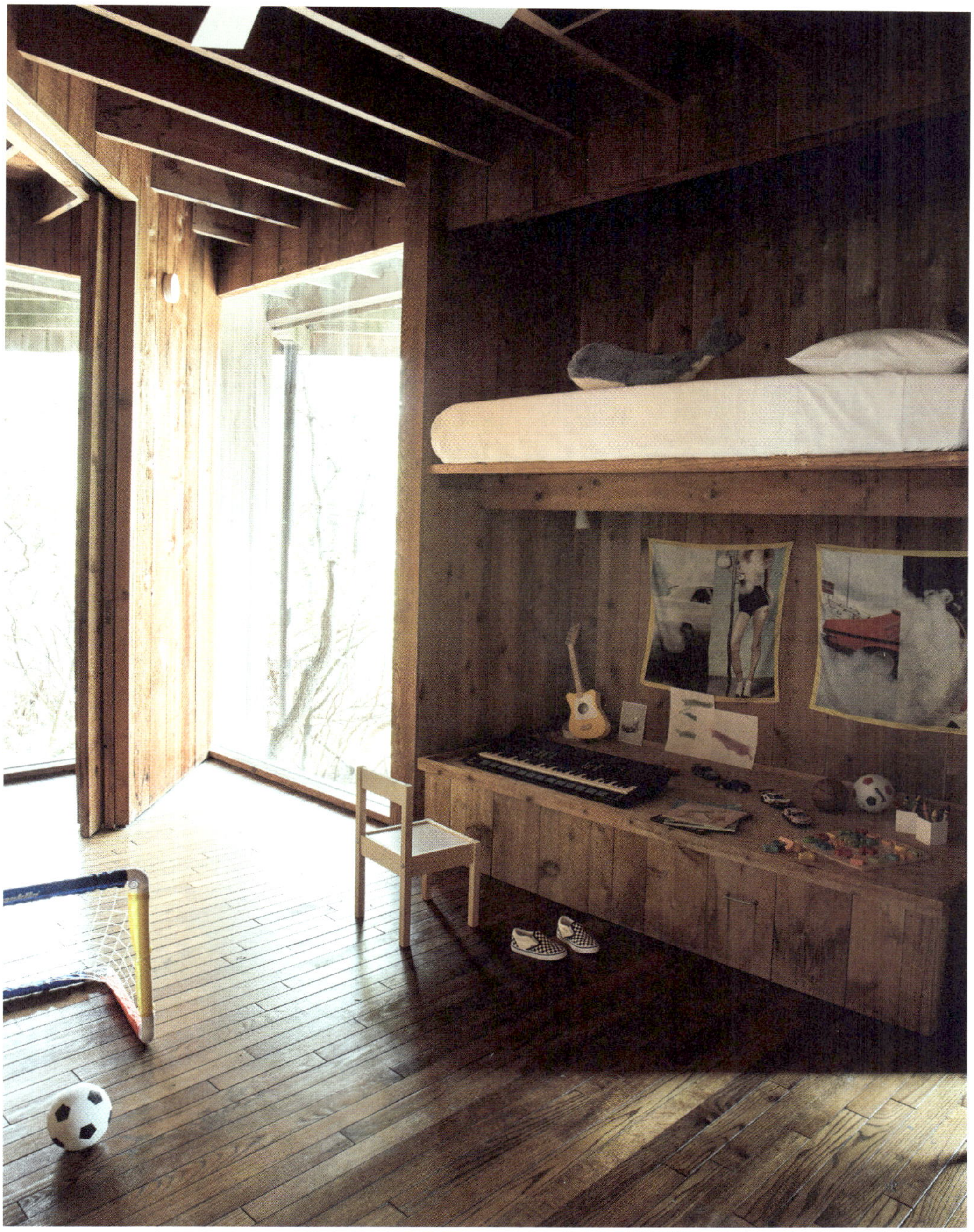

Considered one of the prime examples of Fire Island modernism, a term used to describe the Gifford-designed homes that populate the island, the Perkins' house boasts a number of striking features – including a sunken living room with built-in sofas and floating fireplace; floor-to-ceiling windows that look out onto the ocean and a wraparound deck; curved walls and clever multifunctional bedrooms that can be divided or opened up at will – all lined with natural cedar planks constructed by legendary local carpenter Joe Chasis.

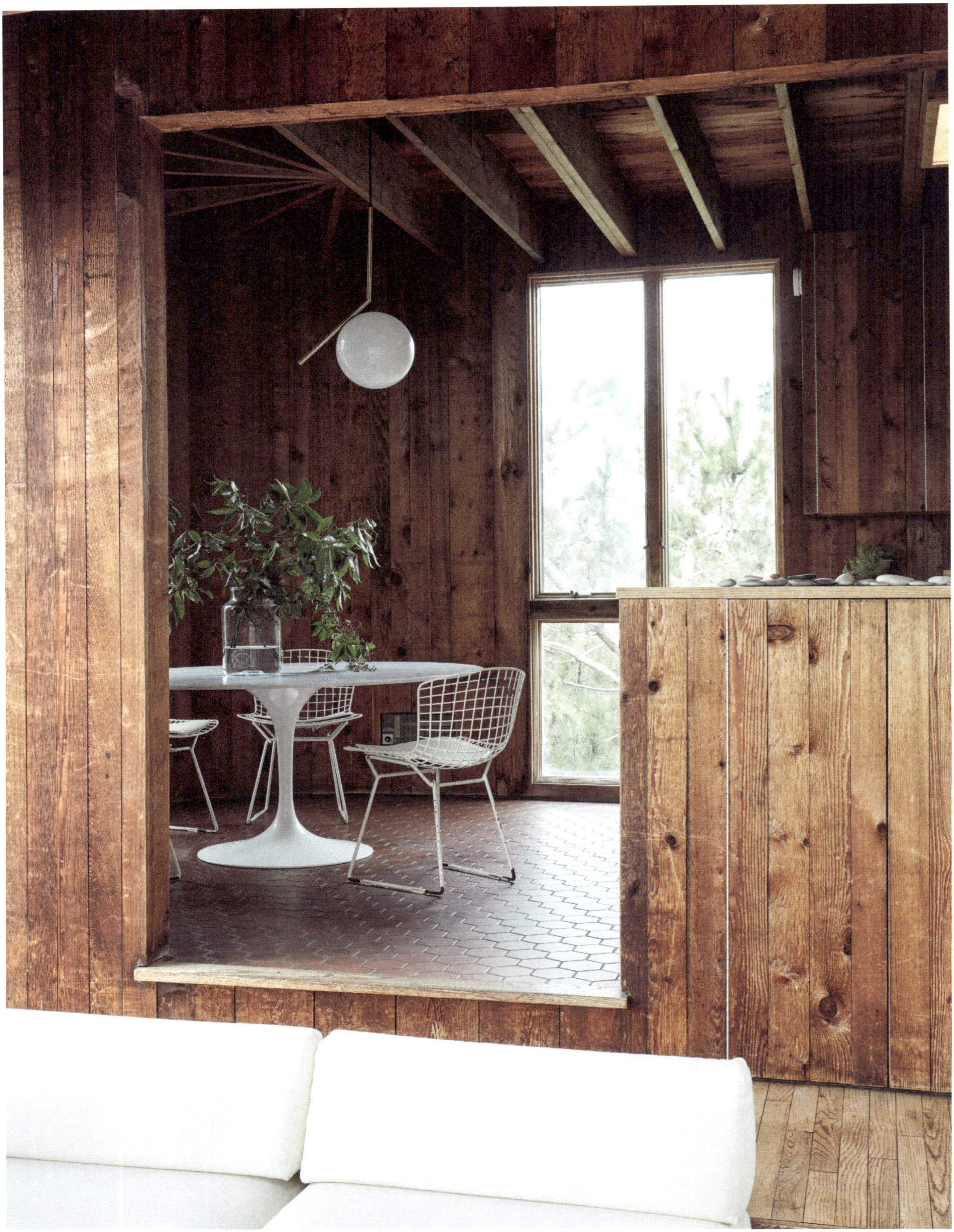

The pair kept the furnishings as close to the original design as possible, only adding pieces that felt true to Gifford's plan. 'One of the things you notice studying Gifford's work is his use of specific pieces of Knoll furniture to the point where architectural elements are designed to hold certain pieces,' James says of the interior decoration. 'For instance, the circular dining has an Eero Saarinen Tulip table which we placed in the kitchen with the steel-mesh Harry Bertoia chairs that were already in the house.' According to James, every corner and sight line of the home was carefully thought out by Gifford. 'He smartly put a huge mirror behind the stairs in what he called on the blueprints "the audio shelf", where we now keep records and books,' he says of the layout. 'So if you choose a couch with your back to the ocean, it appears as though you are still looking at nature.'

The ground floor hosts their son Judd's bedroom and James' sculpture studio, where he creates colour-forward sculptural installations that often dialogue with Fire Island's landscape. 'We whitewashed the space to see colour better as opposed to the rough-cut cedar,' he explains. 'We then cut a huge window in the door to bring more nature into that room that was initially an afterthought. Now, it has a similar energy to the rest of the house.'

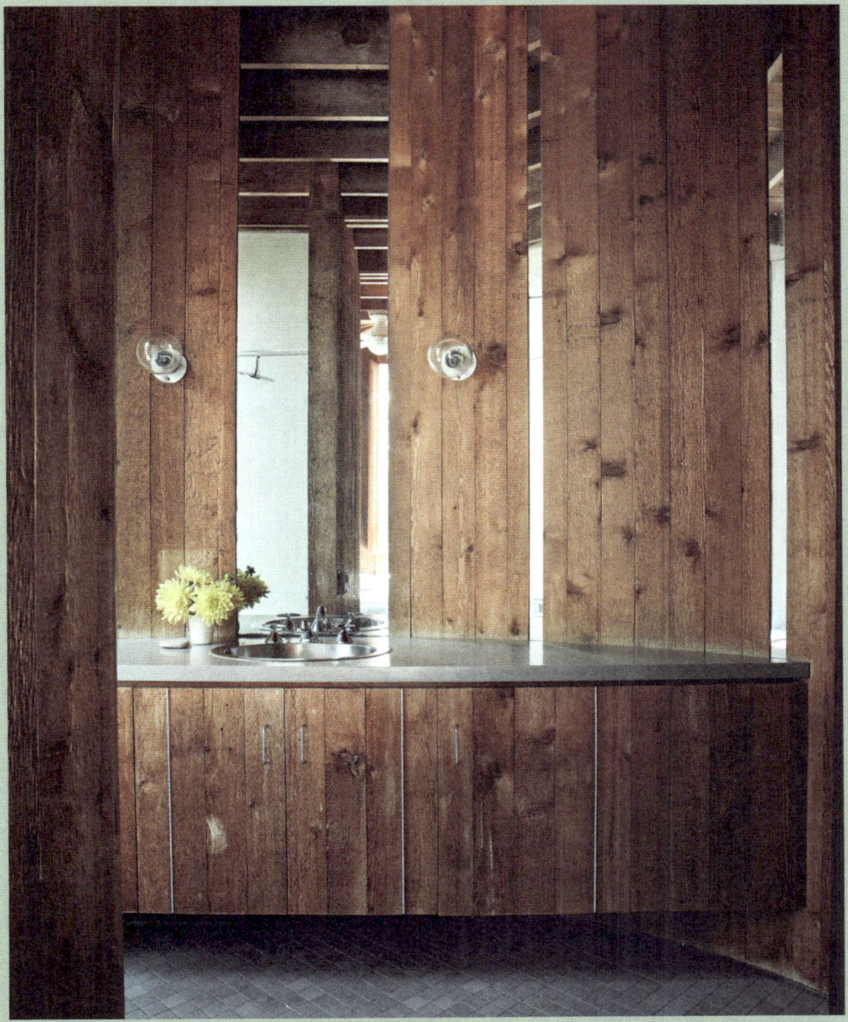

Interview

James Perkins, a sculptor and multimedia artist, and Hara Perkins, a partner at a law firm, met as students at Yale University. They both lived in the same residence, the Eero Saarinen–designed Ezra Stiles College, which they attribute to igniting their mutual love for modernist architecture. Along with their young son, Judd, they split their time between Manhattan and their mid-century escape on Fire Island.

James & Hara Perkins

Tell me a little bit about the home. Why did you choose Fire Island?

JP: My wife's family have had a house on Fire Island on the bay for about 40 years. She grew up walking past this house her entire life on her way to the beach. I had been out once or twice before as a visitor, but when I started going with Hara it was an entirely different experience as a resident. The island means so much to both of us. After we got married, we spent the first five years at our family's property, which Hara's parents acquired when she and her brother were very young children. Now, they are both married with kids and we were looking for more space. There is a book by Christopher Rawlins on Fire Island architect Horace Gifford, and our favourite picture in the book was this centrefold of what is now our living room. I actually didn't know that it was the house down the street – Hara probably did – and I remember walking into the house the first time and being blown away, almost like meeting your idol or something. It didn't disappoint, and as the house is lived in it gets better.

Why were you drawn specifically to the work of the modernist architect Horace Gifford?

JP: Horace Gifford's work is entirely singular. He has this way of working that is both organic and elegant. His specific use of the curved space is comforting and feels natural. No room is a square. Hara and I actually met at Yale and both were in the residential college Ezra Stiles which was designed by architect

Eero Saarinen. Stiles is interesting because it juxtaposes all the beautiful classic Gothic architecture that you find in the Ivy League, but with Stiles, none of the interior walls makes right angles, many of rooms are furnished with built-in desks and bookshelves, and the college was once heated by a system that warmed the stone floors. It is my opinion that Stiles makes you highly aware of architecture and the possibility for different ideals. I soon was no longer sad about missing out on living in Gothic buildings and realised I was having the opportunity to live in a groundbreaking piece of architecture. Some things that are really lovely about this particular Horace Gifford house are the built-in couches, pocket doors, and the rooms designed in a way that suggest the activity and mood. In fact, my son's room reminds me of my room in Stiles College with its angles and built-ins.

You mostly renovated the entire house yourselves. What was that process like? What were the challenges?

JP: Yes, we did. We were kind of forced into this during the pandemic. We moved out to the house earlier in the season than usual in anticipation of lockdown. We just went to work really not overthinking it. Hara grew up doing many projects on her family's home down the street on the bay. I would later start helping her father and brother with projects, so it actually felt natural to start working on the house and to make it ours. I think of the house as a vintage Porsche or a watch that has this beautiful patina you don't want to touch, so doing these projects alone we had to be very careful not to damage any of the beautifully handmade rooms.

What was the building like when you found it?

JP: The structure had served one family for 50 years. After that time there is a lot of life built - that's how I looked at it. Kids had gone through different phases of their life, the parents had gone through different phases of their life and that was reflected in the property. The bones were incredible but the property needed some TLC, which the owners also realised, and living away from the property didn't allow them to do so. At least to our eye, you could just see this stunning property that needed attention and love inside and out.

What is your favourite place in the house?

JP: My favourite place is right off the deck looking at the ocean, where I like to sit with a drink and cigar. Judd's is probably the sunken den which is the perfect playpen. Hara's is the ocean view from the kitchen when we are all cooking together.

You've said previously that your son, Judd, had a say in the home's restoration. What was it like designing with a young child?

JP: Judd has strong opinions and a great eye. His suggestions of what colour to choose or where to place something are always really good. It reminds you to look and feel and trust yourself. We also remind ourselves that every object that enters the home should be a thing of beauty. It's OK to have toys out in every room if the train set is handsome, the stuffed animals share a soothing palette. You don't need to be crazy about making everything match, as long as there is some baseline standard of beauty. It's a good practice for all of us. And it then becomes more natural for our son to participate in not only design but maintenance and caring for those things, too.

What do you love about this area of Fire Island?

JP: Fire Island is such a magical place because, an hour from the noise and energy of New York City, you have this carless, barefoot, 30-something mile-long sandy-beached barrier island. That means, no matter where you are, you are literally steps from the Atlantic Ocean or a hop from a dip in the Great South Bay at sunset. Our house is one back from the ocean, on the second dune, in what feels like a very protected nook. We are lucky to be bordered by empty lots, with the native mix of bayberry, juniper, beach plum, cedars and choke cherries. It is natural and quiet, and yet somehow we have world-class tennis pros a block over, our only store is a family-owned market that has the best bread, cheeses, farmers market produce... And our neighbours create a sense of community that almost feels like a lost art these days.

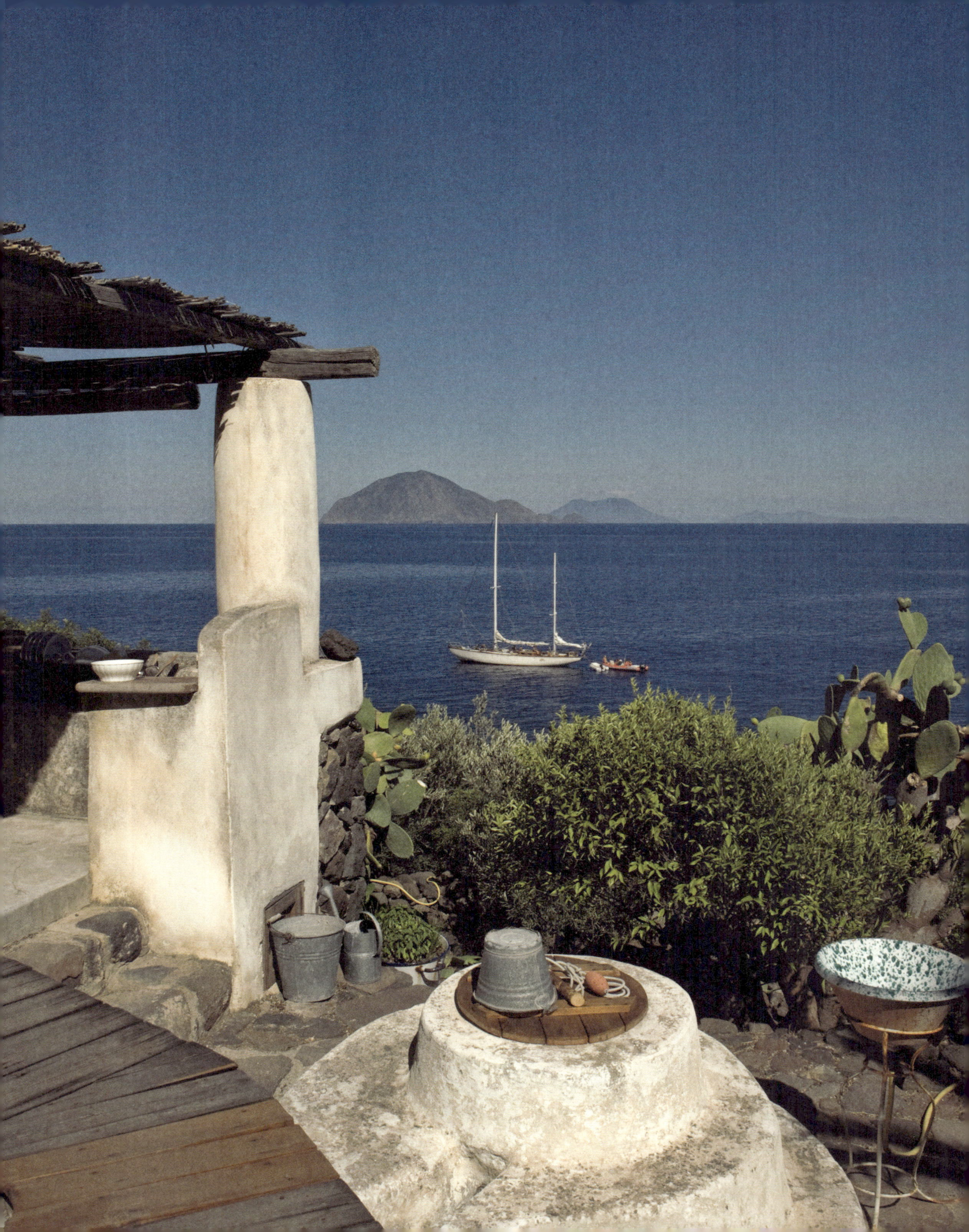

CHAPTER 02

Coastal Hideouts

Beach shacks and surf huts these hideouts are certainly not. Coastal living takes on an entirely new meaning in the hands of these homeowners and designers. Whether they are interpreting the spartan geometry of traditional island architecture or channelling the monumental forms of modernist masters, each dwelling is deeply influenced by its own sense of place.

A Five-Star Getaway in an Isolated Beachside Town

TRANCOSO, BAHIA (BR) **WILBERT DAS**

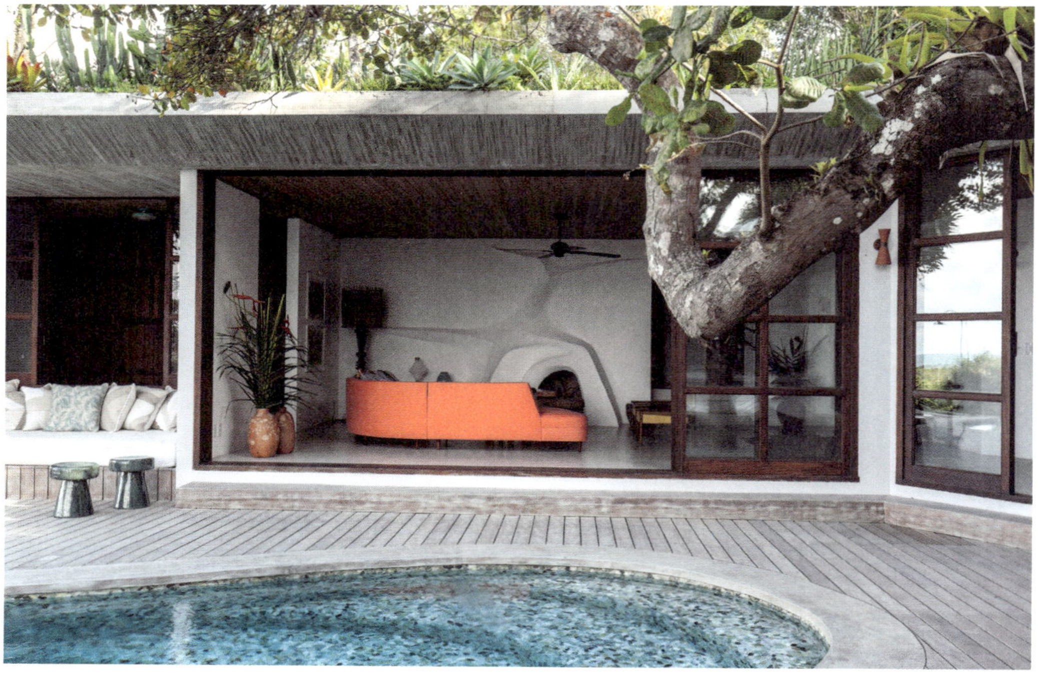

Few places are further off the grid than the Brazilian seaside town of Trancoso. Settled in the 1500s by Jesuit missionaries, this small fishing village in the state of Bahia has been left in relative isolation over the centuries, allowing it to develop its own unique culture and a knack for self-reliance. It is exactly this vibe – not to mention the lush surrounding jungle and white-sand shores – that first attracted fashion designer-turned-hotelier Wilbert Das to Trancoso.

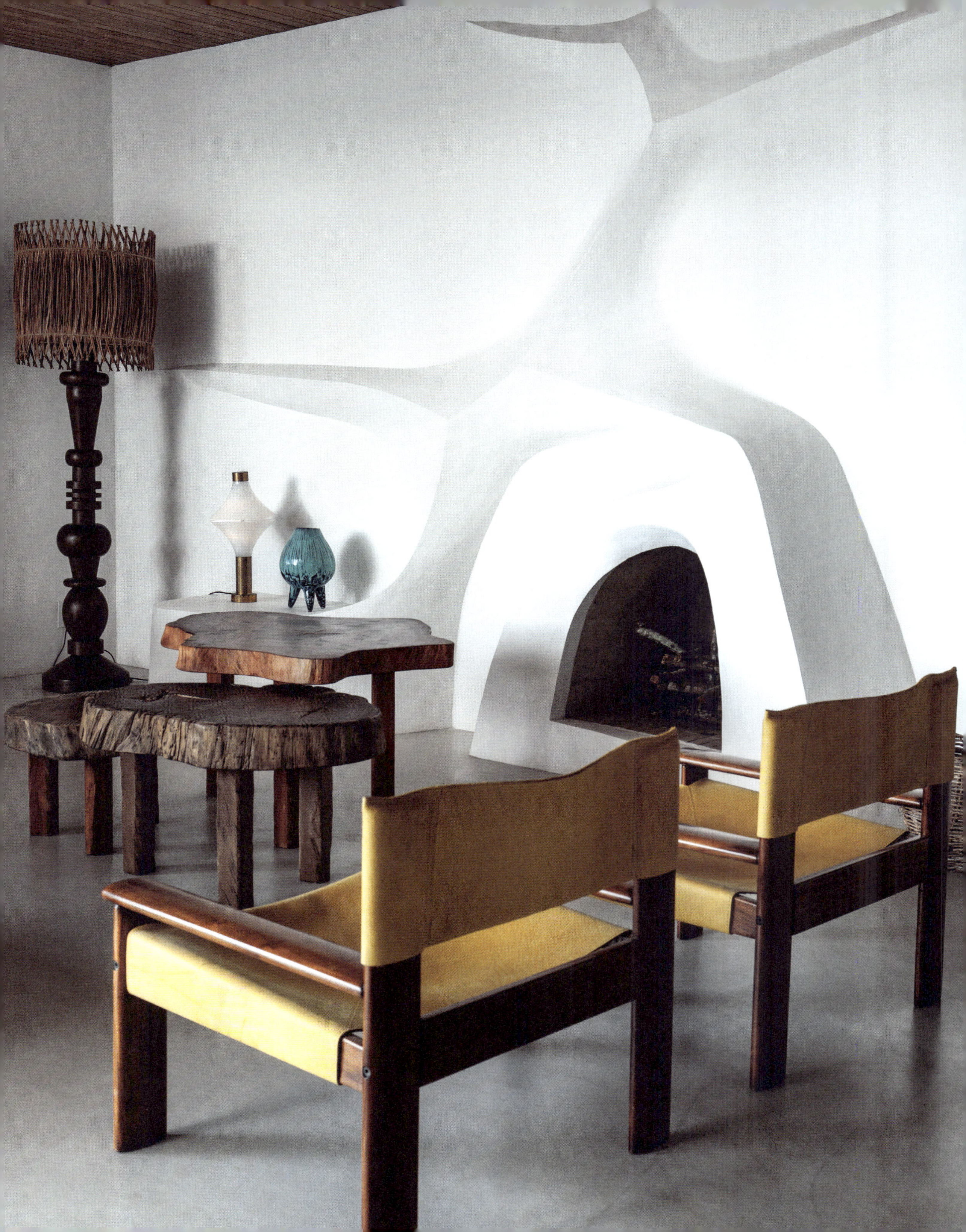

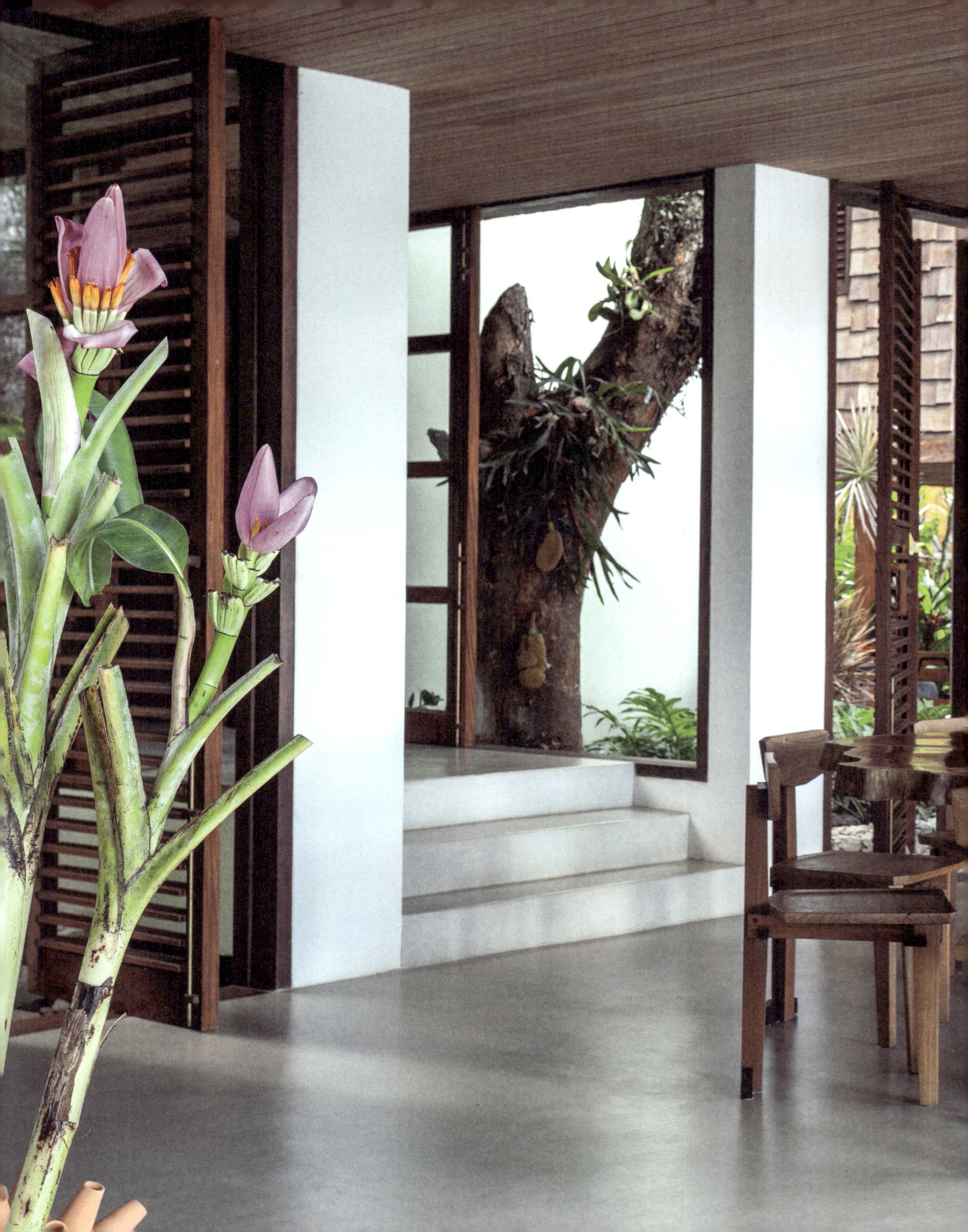

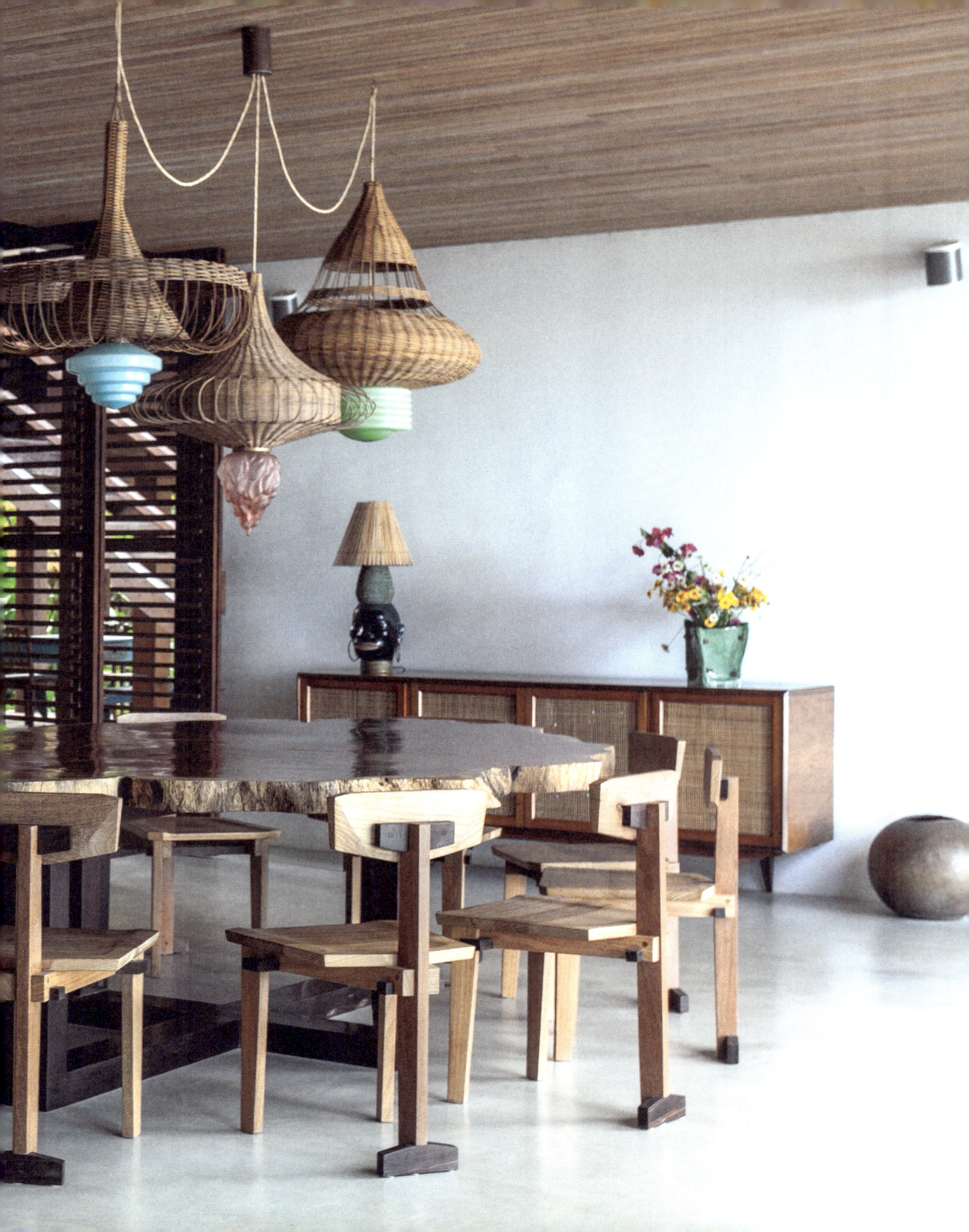

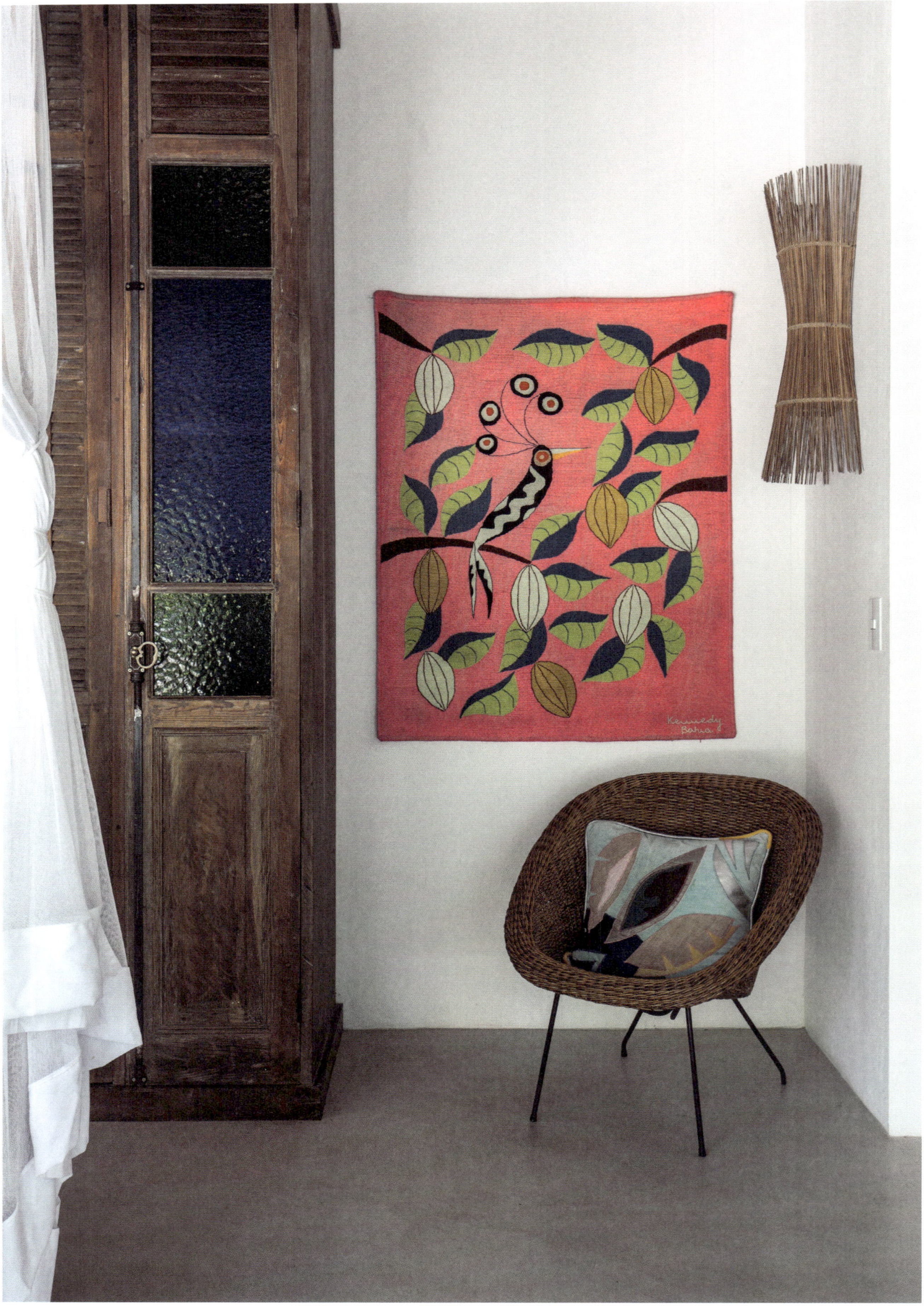
Kennedy
Bahia

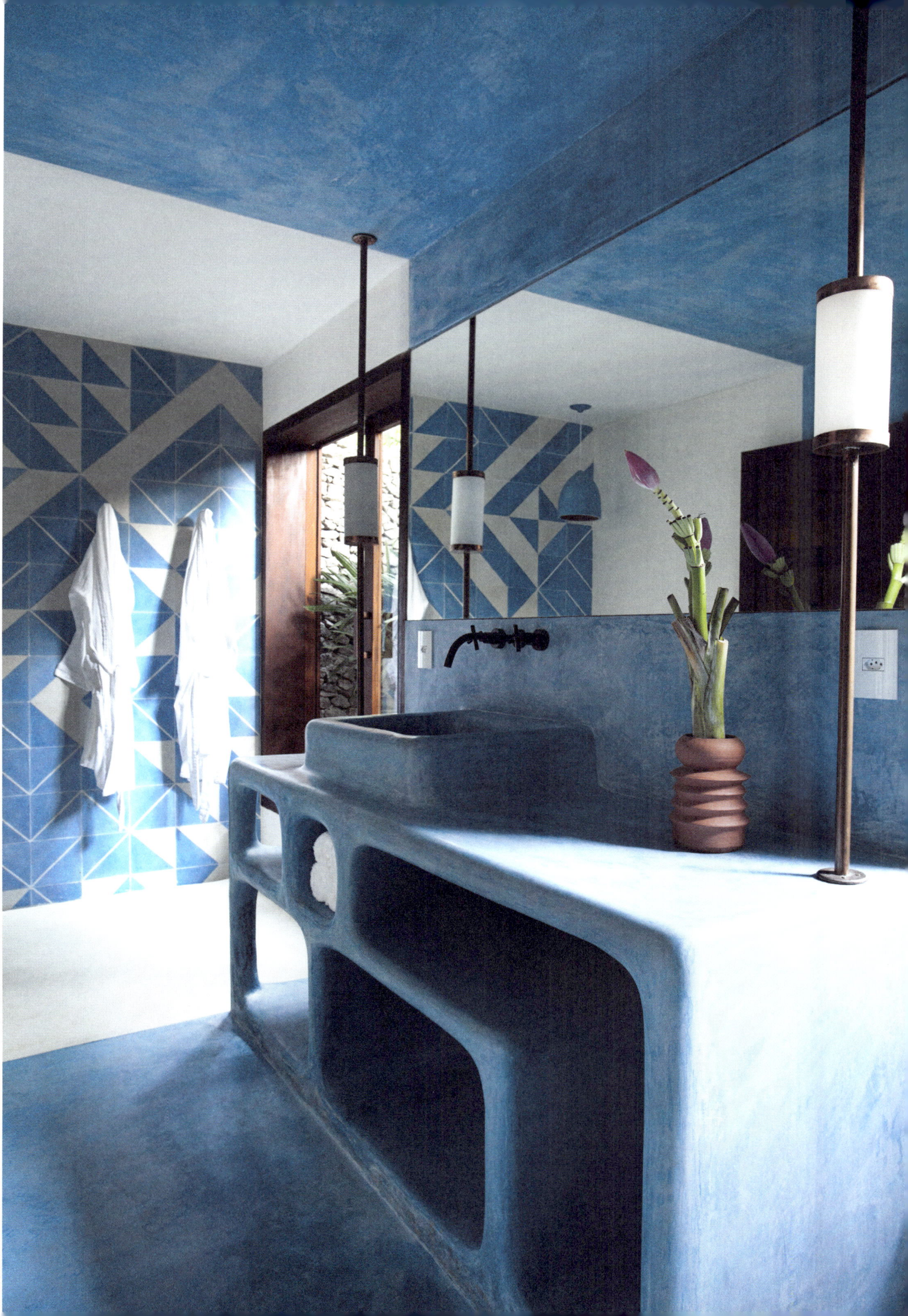

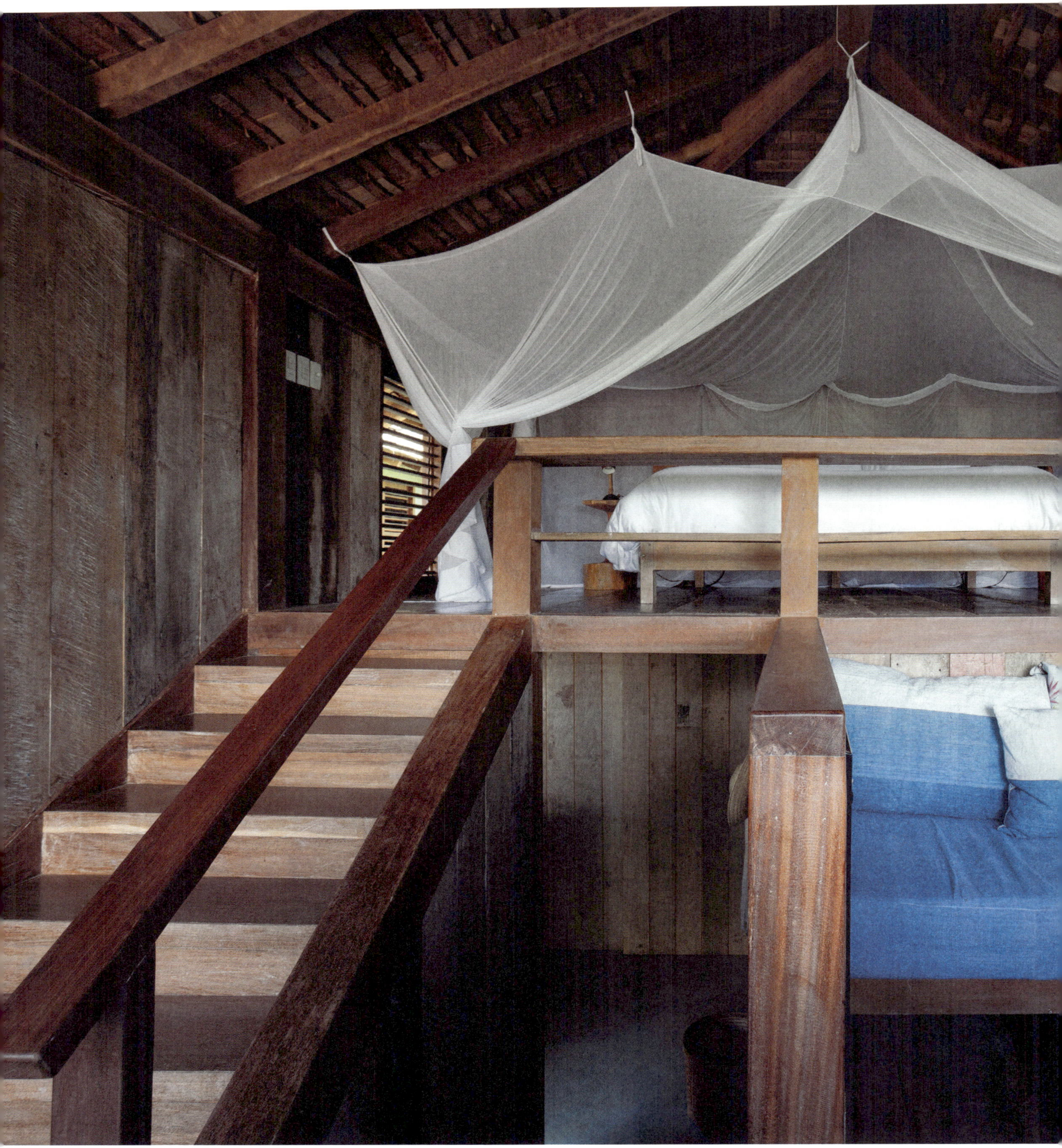

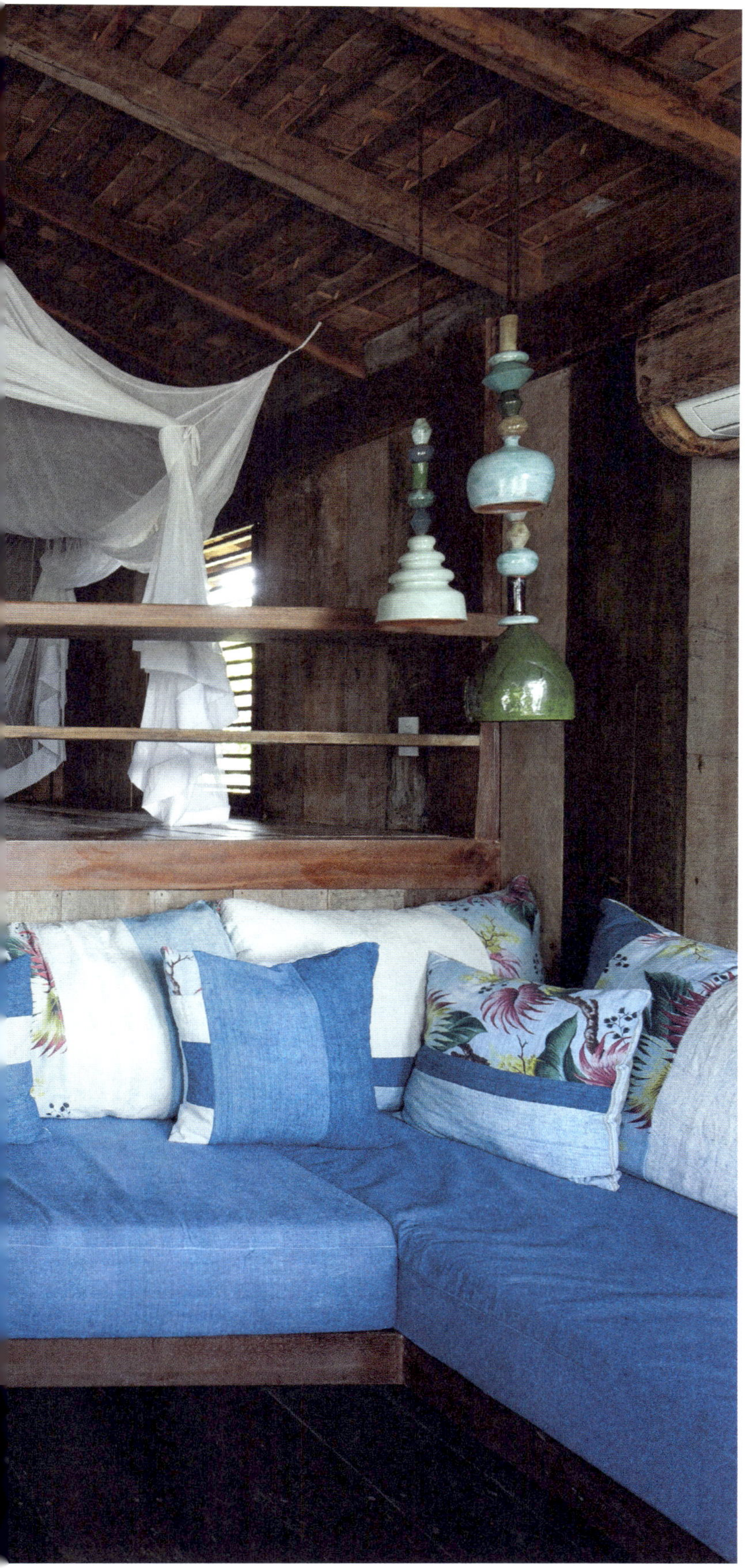

Das built this sprawling 12,000-square-foot home for a private client, a family of like-minded holidaymakers looking to unplug from modern life. When designing the home, Das followed the natural rhythm of the forest, organising its six pavilions around the property's existing foliage, taking advantage of the natural shade of the cinnamon, jackfruit and mango trees that pepper the grounds. Indeed, the home's name, Casa Cajueiro, stems from the towering cashew tree that sits at the centre of it all.

In designing the interiors, Das looked to the pantheon of Brazilian modernists for inspiration, a cohort of architects and designers who flocked to urban centres such as São Paolo and Rio de Janeiro in the first half of the 20th century, mixing the clean lines of the International Style with the abundant natural materials and bountiful local artisanship found only in Brazil. For example, the organically formed concrete and stucco fireplace that dominates the main sitting area, whose shape was inspired by the work of French designer Valentine Schlegel, was chosen to contrast with the natural pequi and jackfruit wooden coffee tables that were hand-painted by a local artist. For the sleeping pavilions, Das channelled the simple wooden frames and pitched, parajú wood roofs of fisherman's cottages that dot the Trancoso coast. While the public spaces and bedrooms are defined by organic materials and a minimal palette, Das opted for a geometric pattern of blue and white cement tiles for one of the en-suite bathrooms.

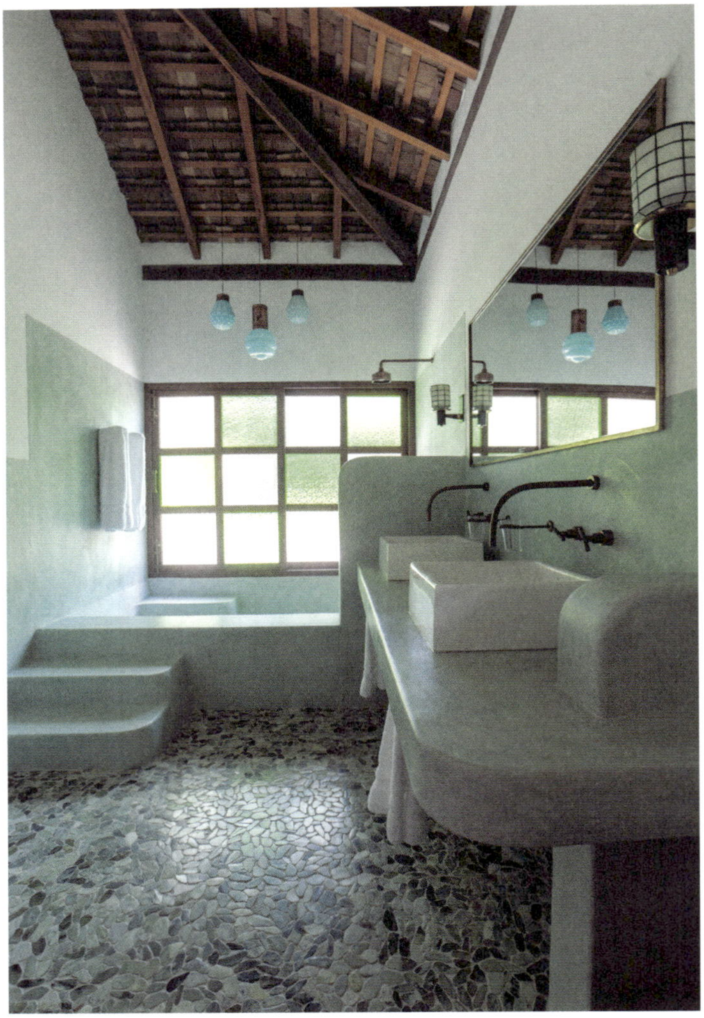

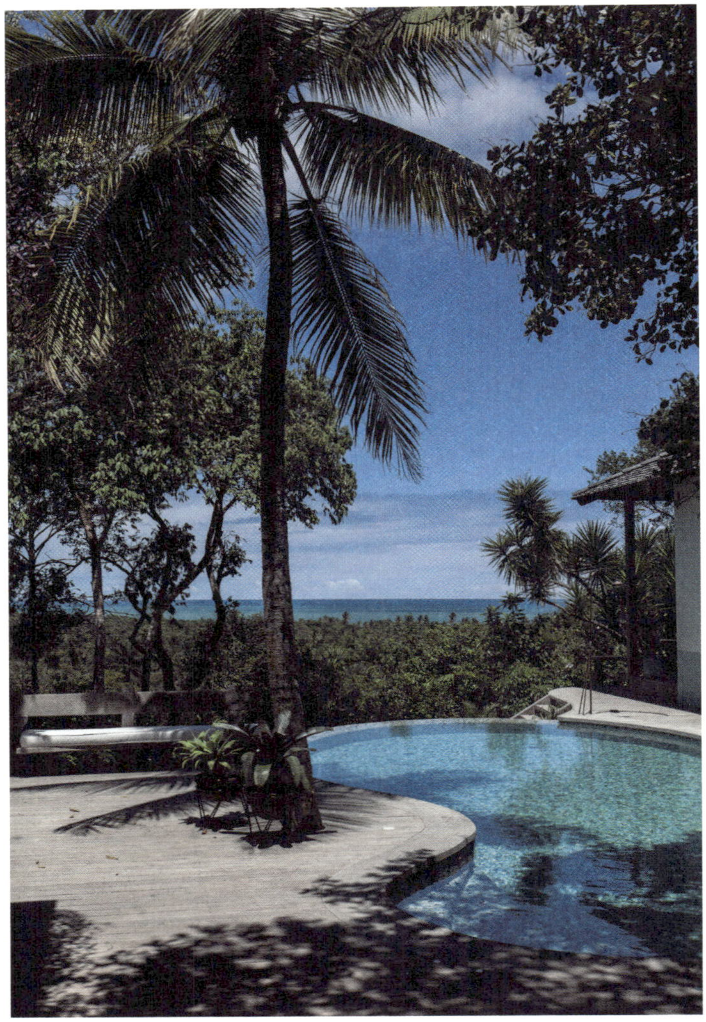

Das decorated the home with pieces from his collection, UXUA D.A.S, which was crafted by local artisans, as well as antiques sourced from the surrounding area. The dining table, designed and constructed by a Trancoso craftsman, was built from slabs of jackfruit wood, while its accompanying chairs were made from Brazilian cumaru, freijo and brauna woods and inspired by the Brazilian architect Lina Bo Bardi.

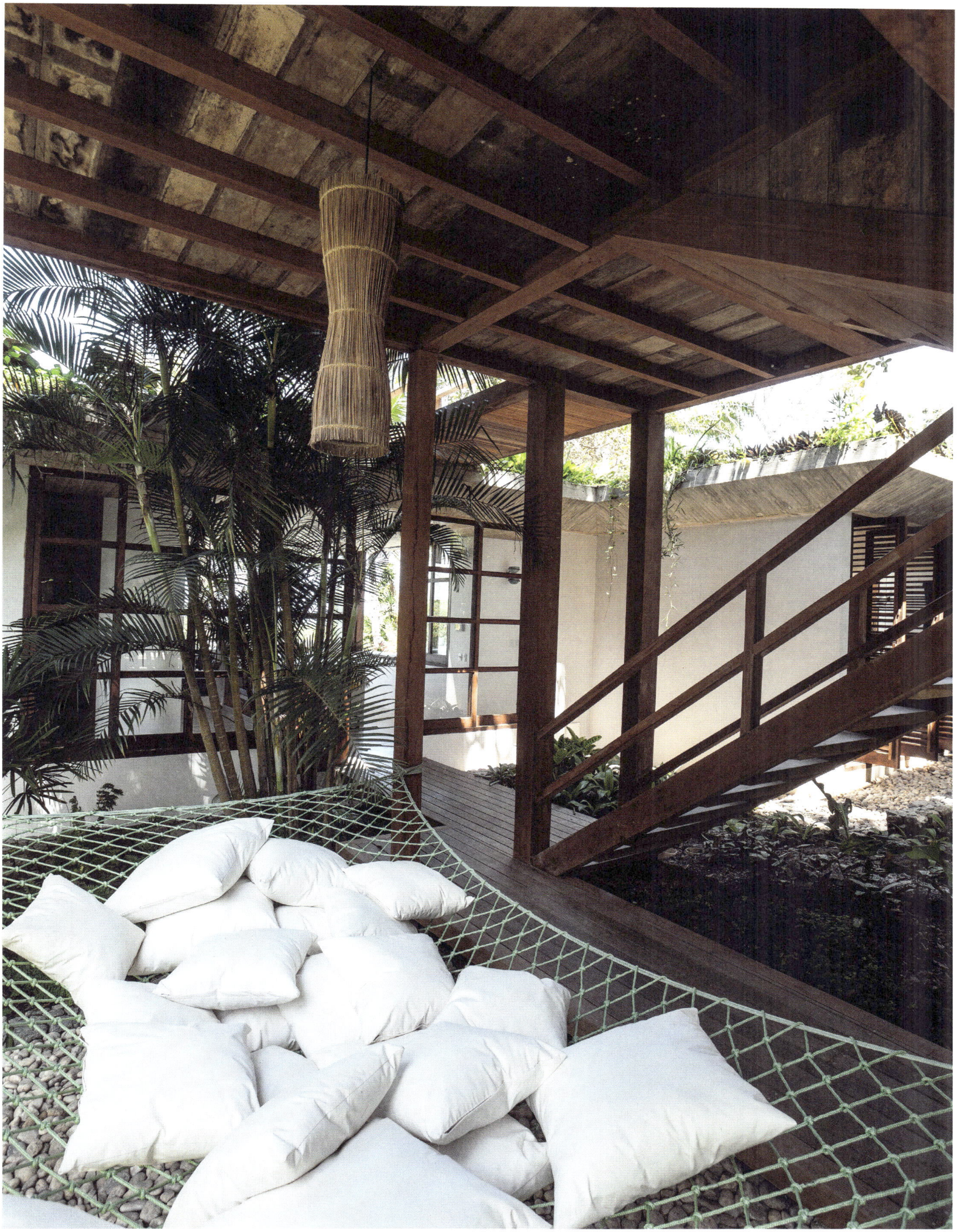

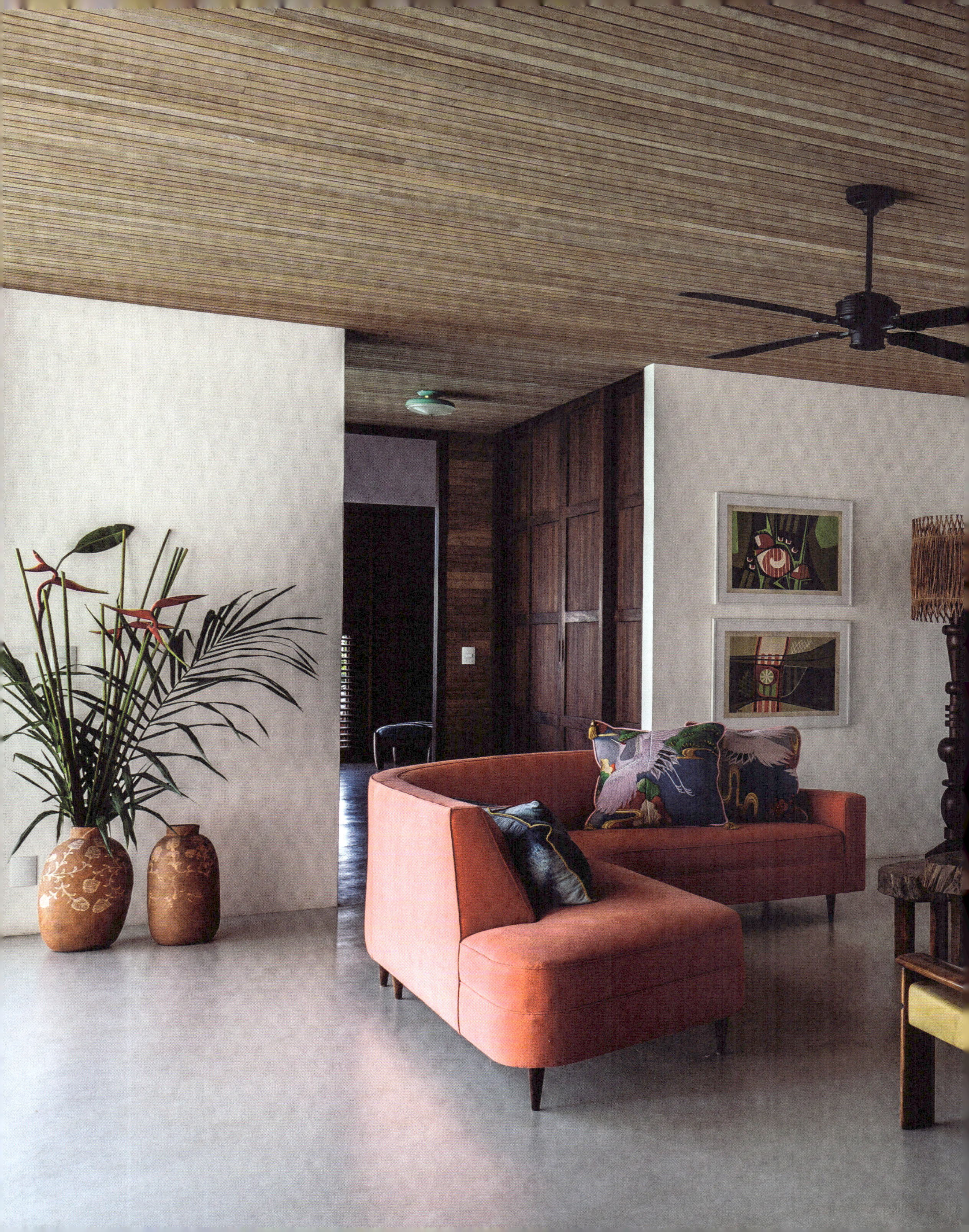

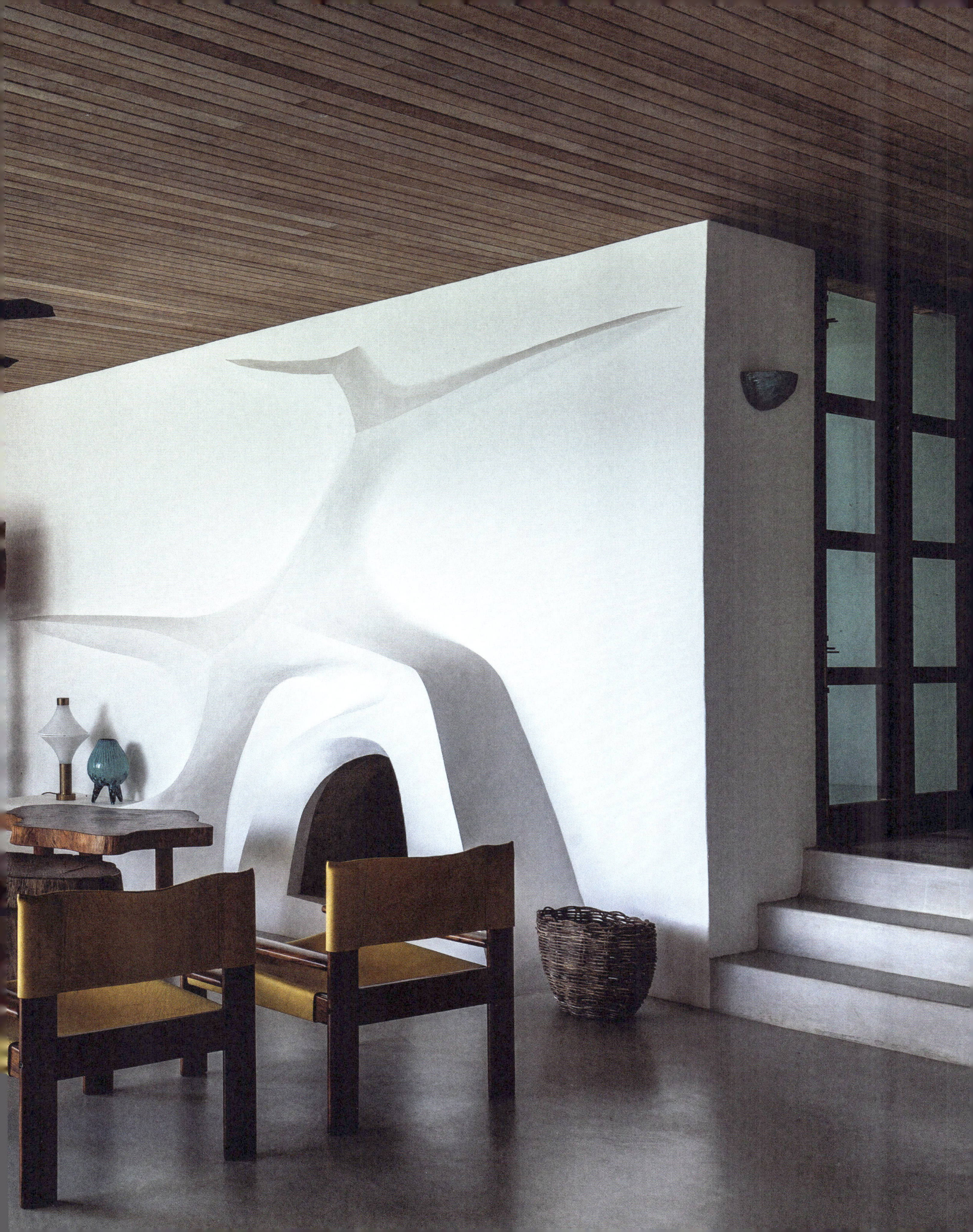

A Spartan Island Home with Volcanic Views

ALICUDI, AEOLIAN ISLANDS (IT) **ANONYMOUS**

The group of seven rocky outcroppings – Lipari, Vulcano, Salina, Stromboli, Filicudi, Panarea and Alicudi – that make up the Aeolian Islands, dotted in the Tyrrhenian Sea off Sicily's northern coast, are as steeped in legend and myth as you can get. Named for Aeolus, the Greek god of the winds, these remote but fertile isles appear in the *Odyssey*, where King Aeolus provides the fair winds that the hero Odysseus needs to return to his homeland of Ithaca. Known for their black sand beaches and the occasional eruptions of lava that burst from the still-active Stromboli and Vulcano islands (from the latter of which the geological feature gets its name), they remain some of Italy's wildest and most enchanting islands. Alicudi, the westernmost island of the group, now hosts a small community of year-round residents.

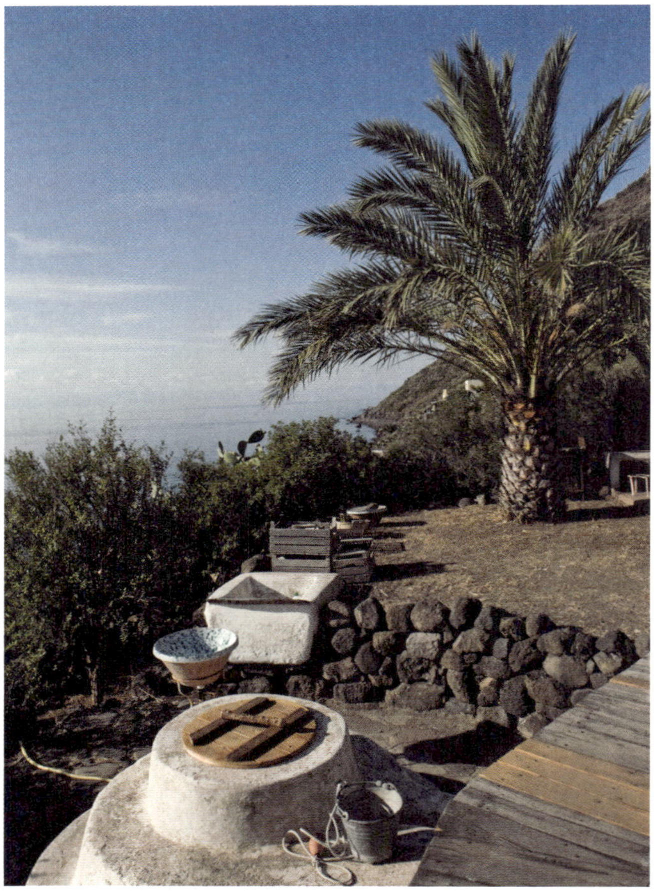

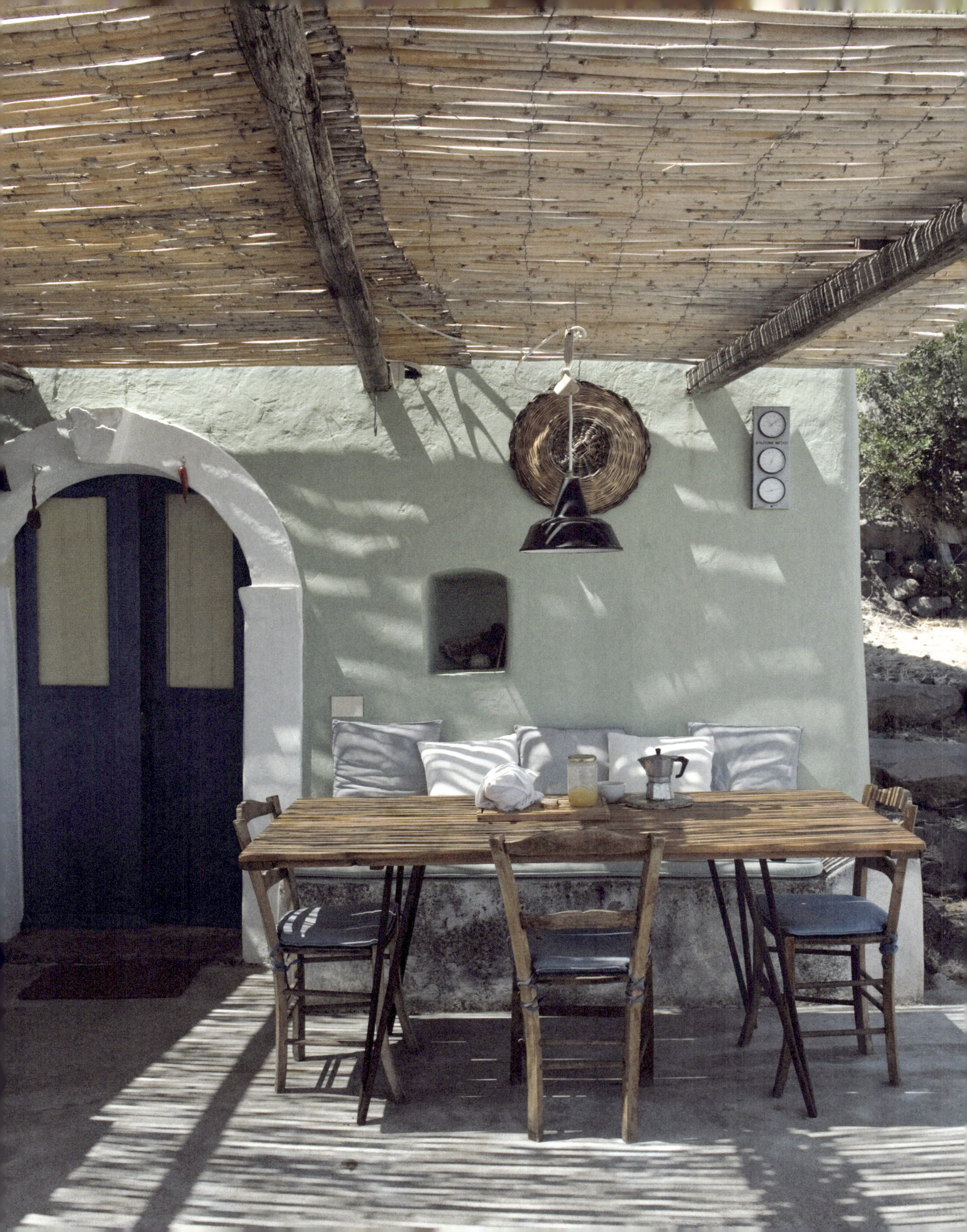

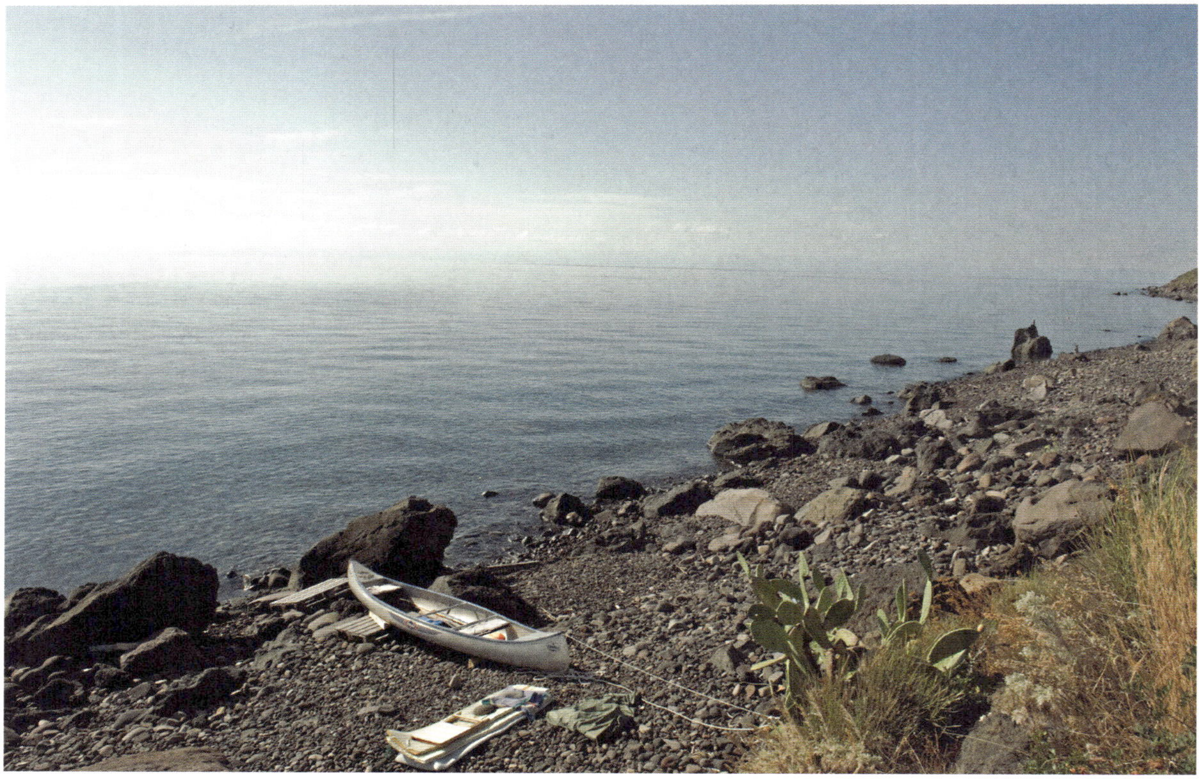

There are no cars or conventional roads on Alicudi, so in order to reach this spartan stone retreat from the island's main port, one must either arrive on a small boat, or hike over an hour down a narrow trail etched into the hillside. Because of the islands' difficult, remote terrain, traditional Aeolian homes are defined by a simplicity of form and an economy of materials. Whittled down to the essentials due to the struggle involved in transporting material to secluded and somewhat treacherous locations, dwellings are generally made up of lime plaster and fragments of volcanic stone, known as lapilli, found on site.

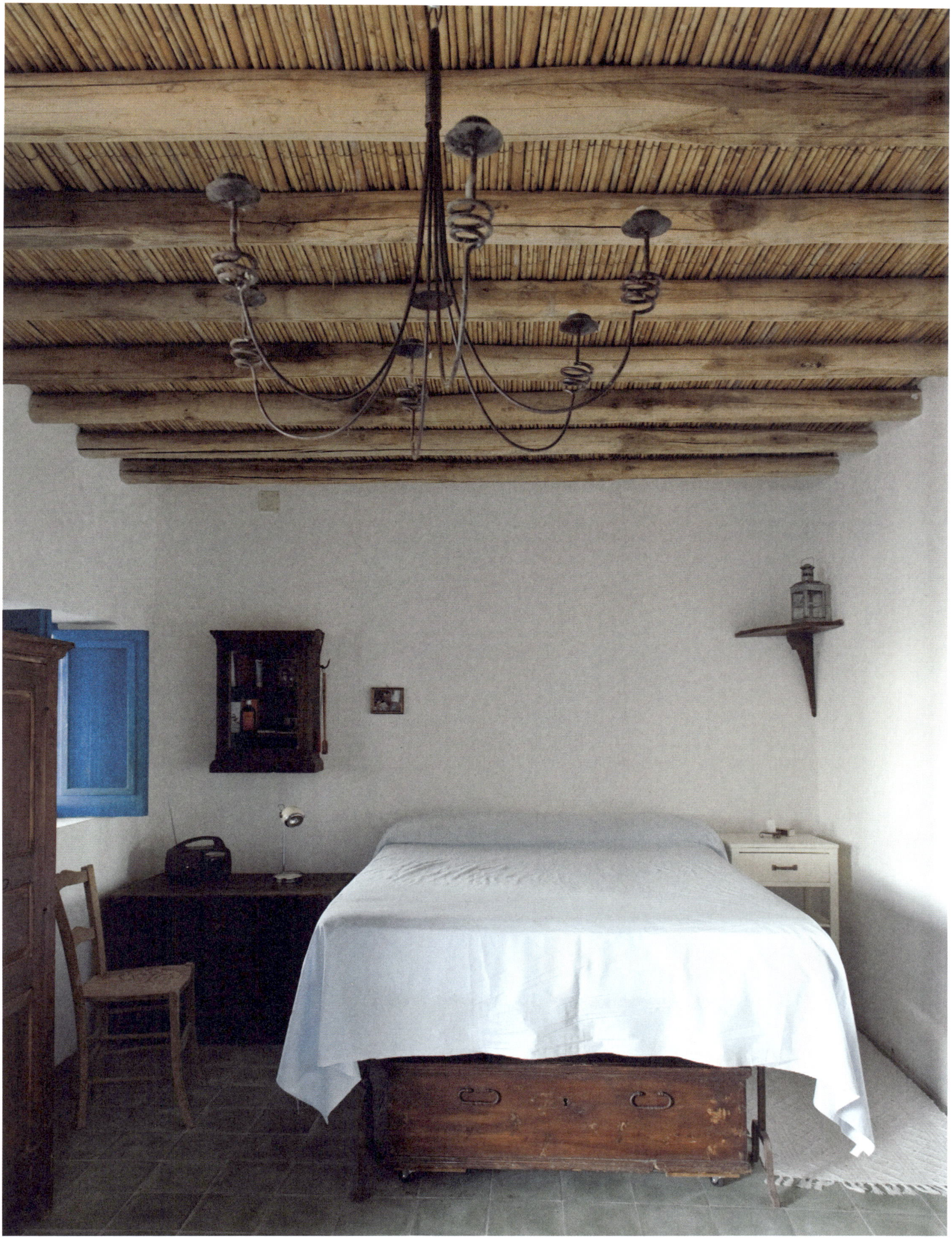

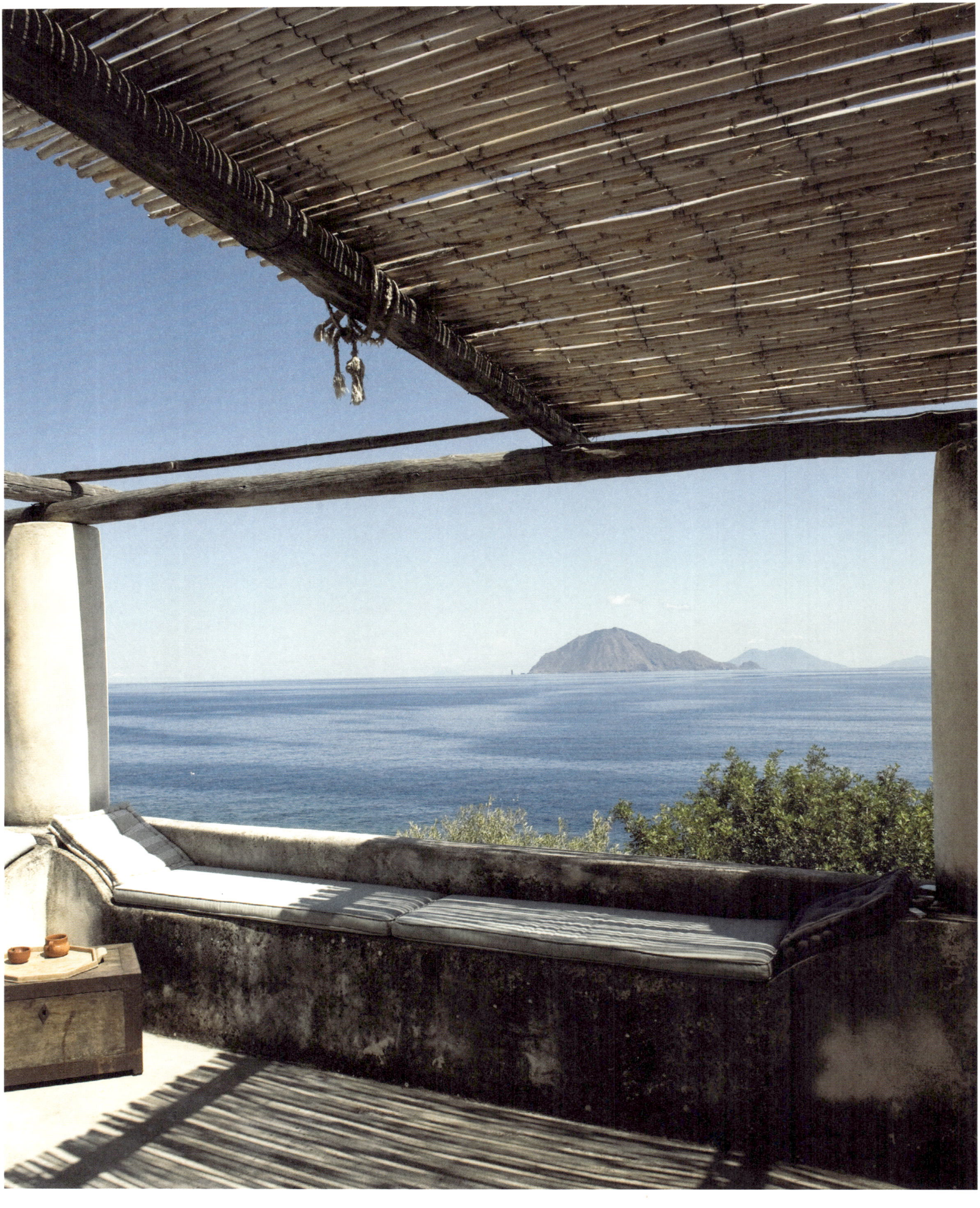

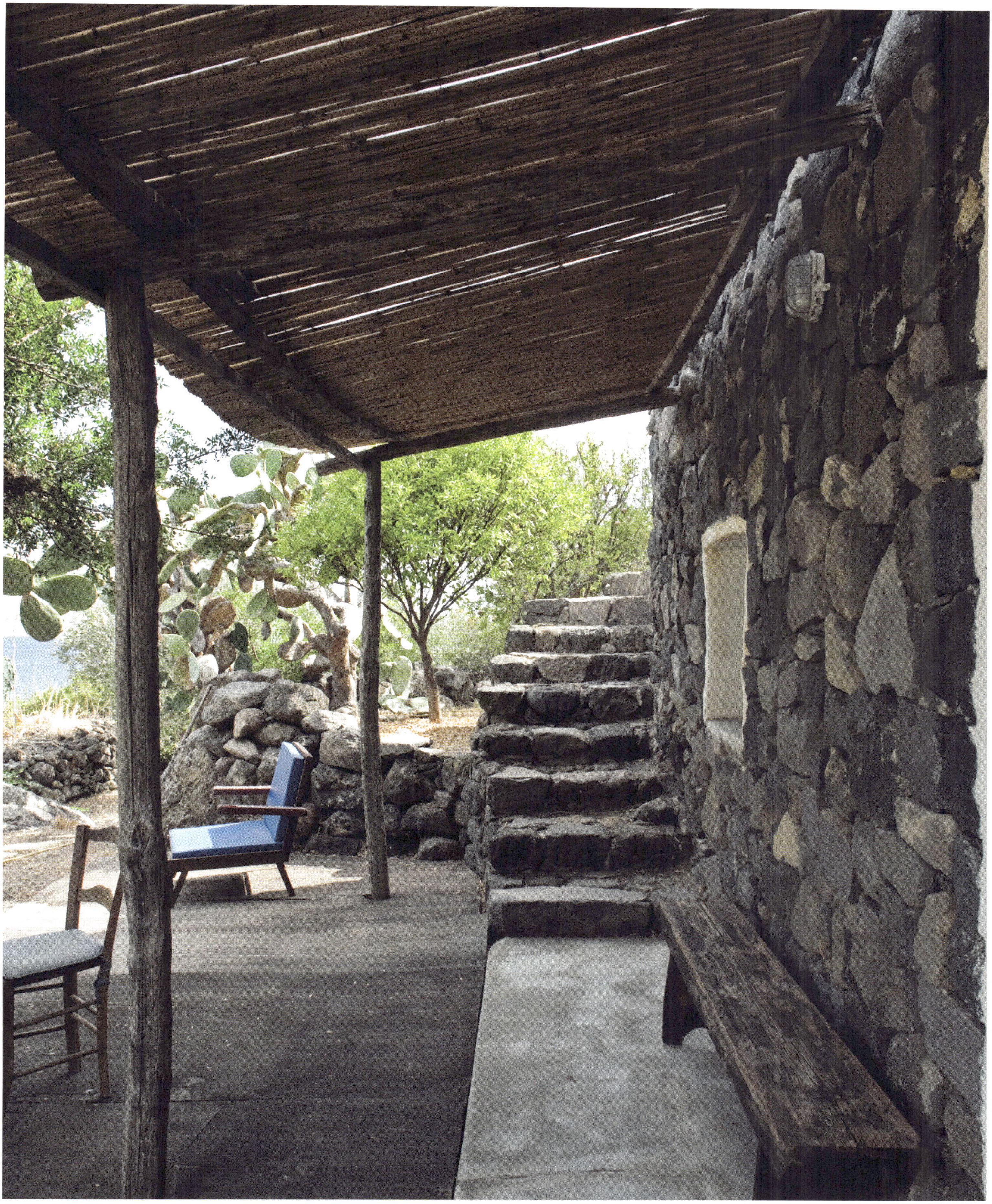

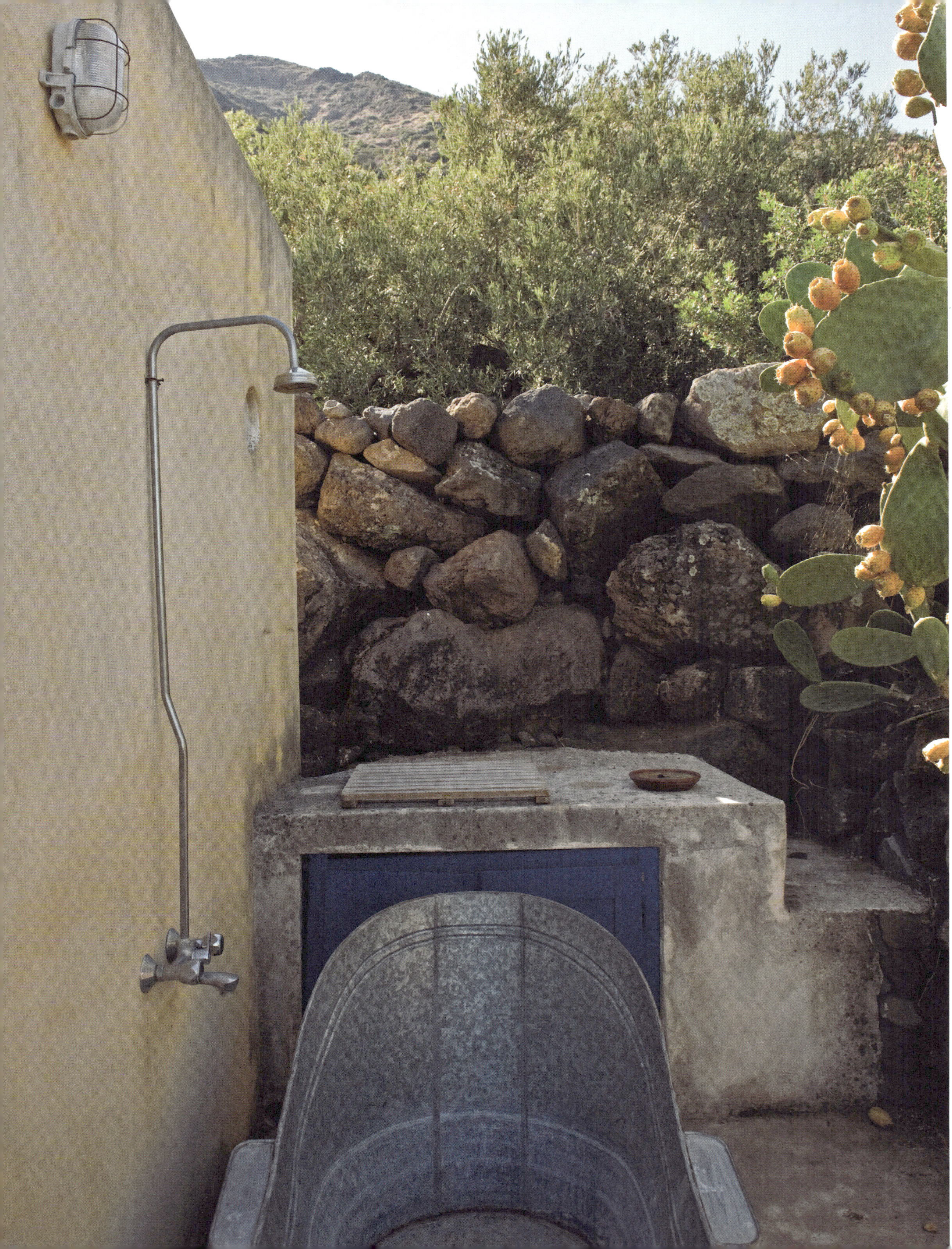

Shaded by a canopy made of reeds harvested on the shore, a large terrace, called a *bagghiu* in the local dialect, surrounds the simple square volume, composed of only a kitchen and sleeping area. Outdoor spaces such as this are an essential element of Aeolian architecture and the site of most gatherings and meals, where families break bread while looking out onto the inky sea and mighty volcanoes in the distance.

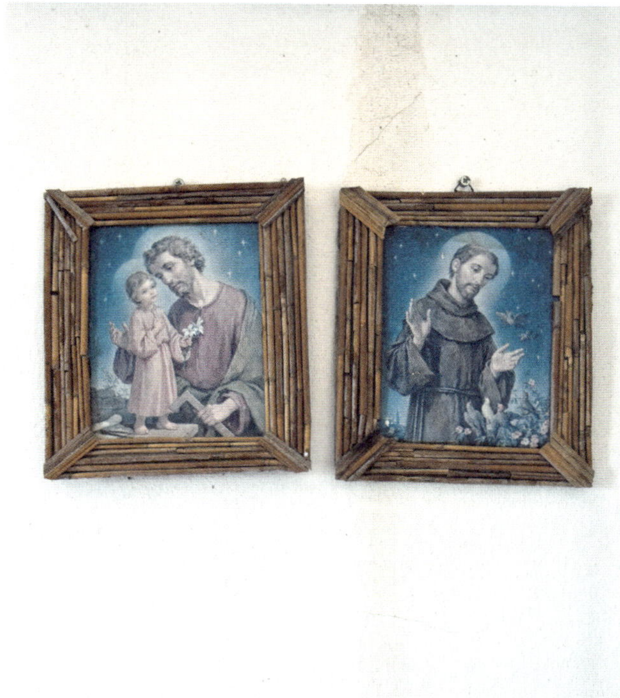

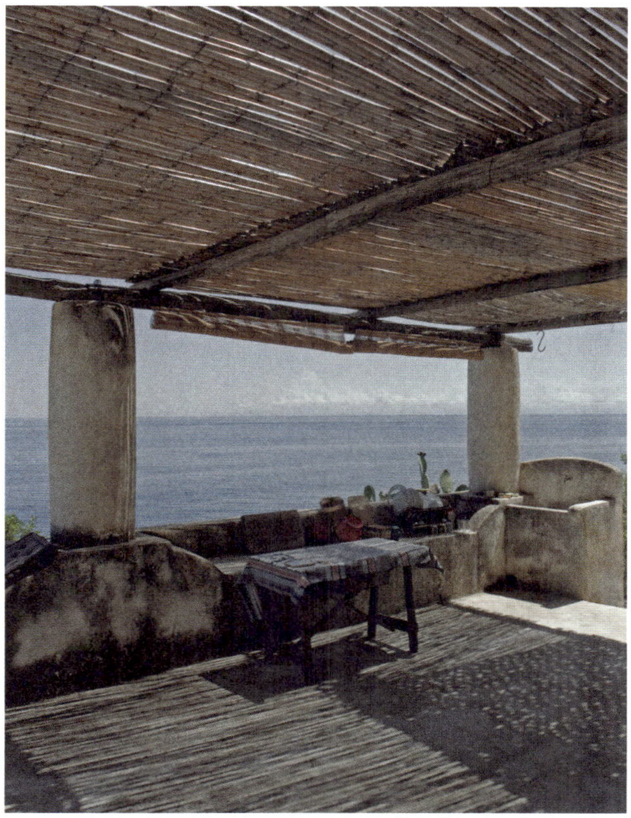

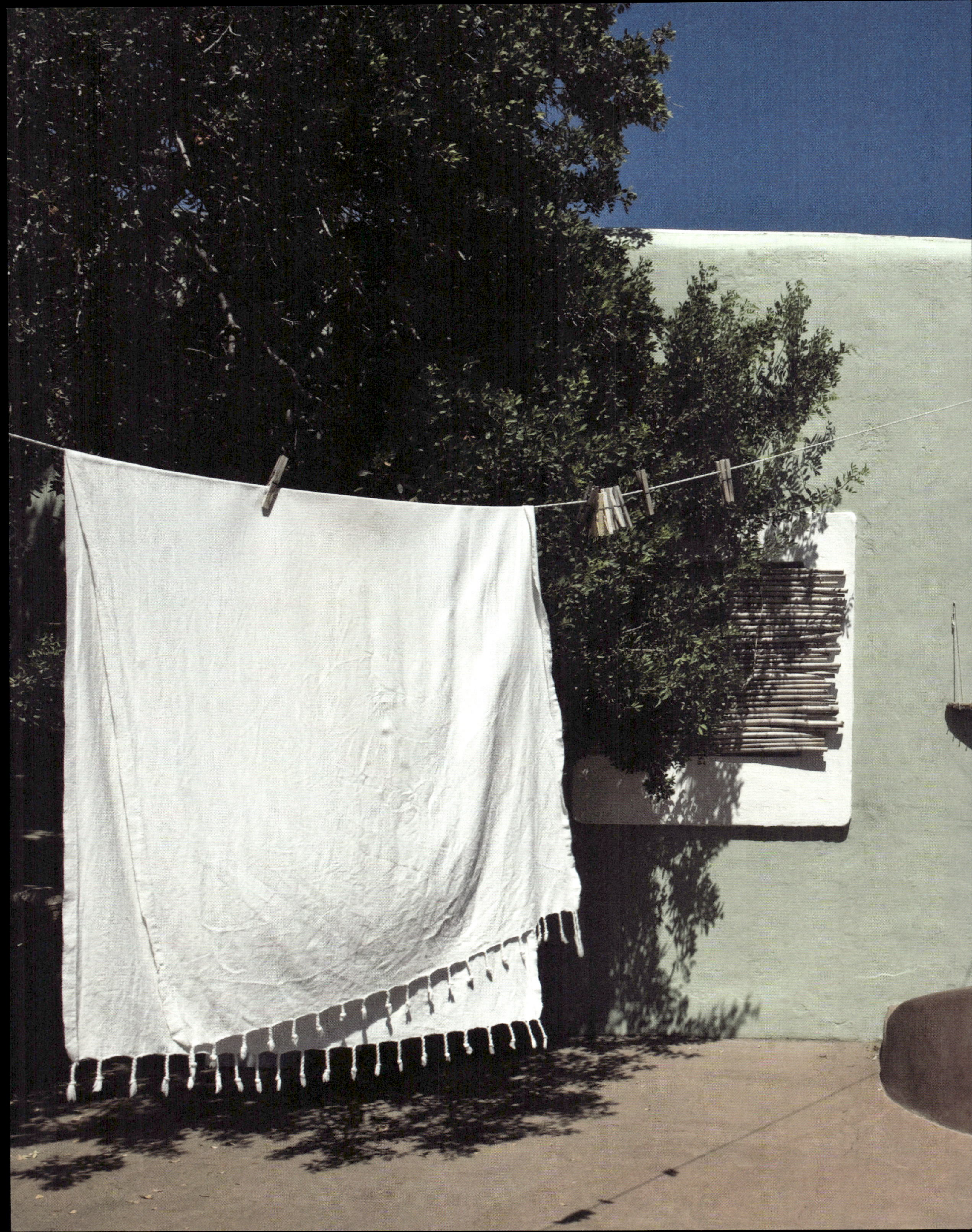

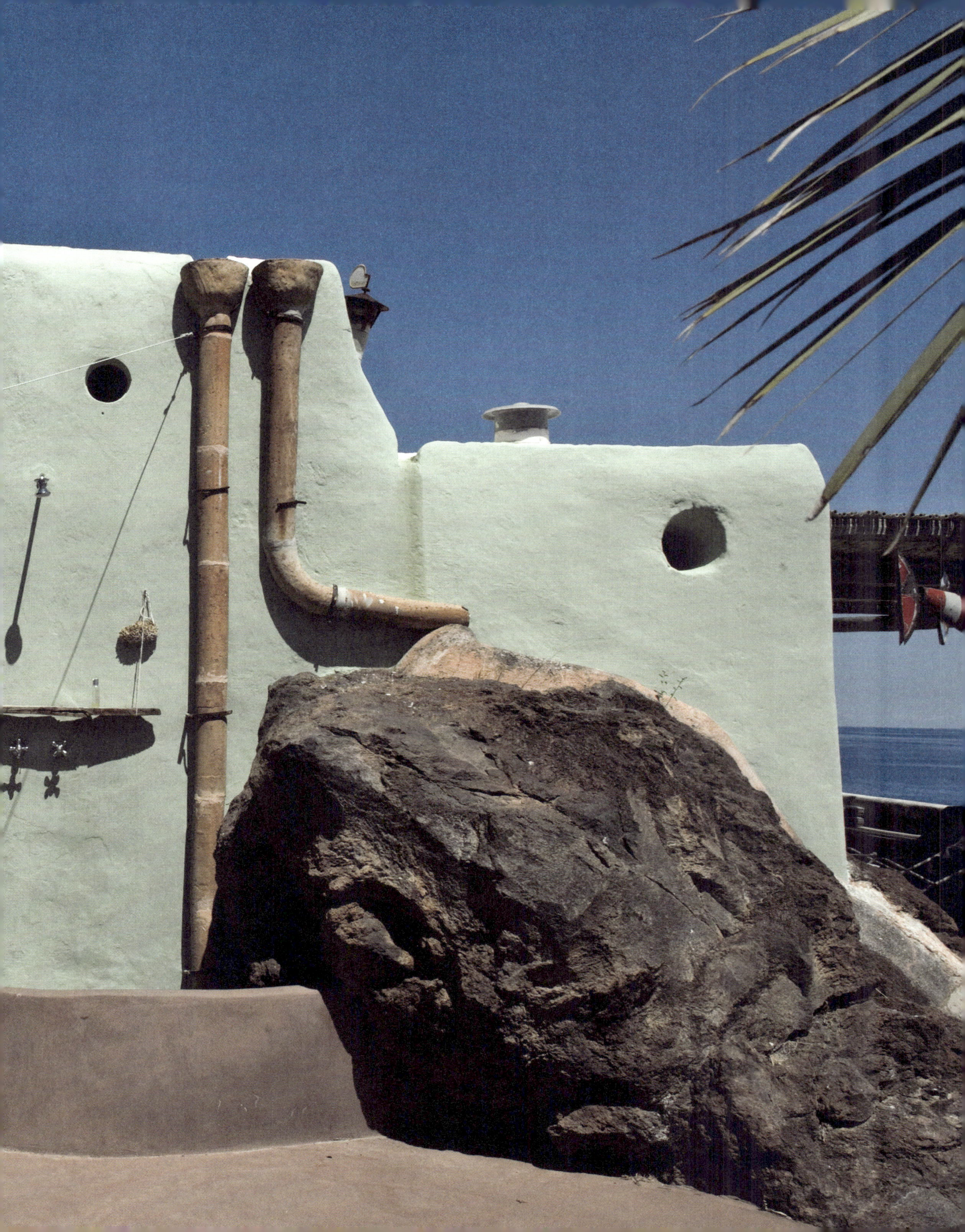

A Balearic Bachelorette Pad

IBIZA, BALEARIC ISLANDS (SP) **HAUVETTE & MADANI**

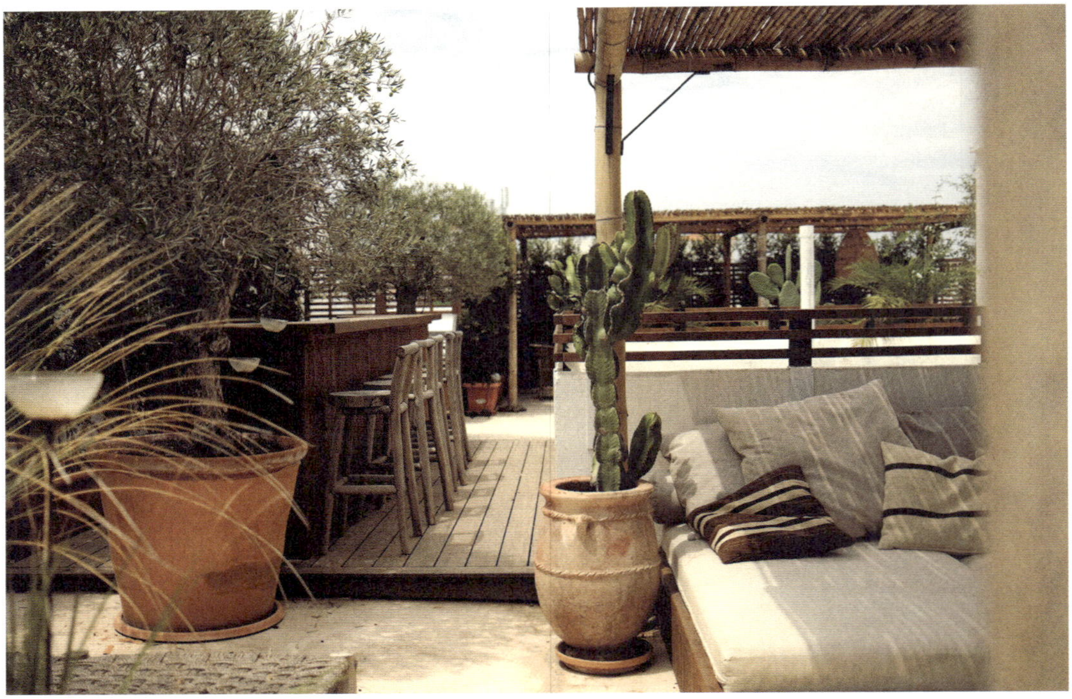

The island of Ibiza, a rugged, sand-ringed promontory in the Balearic Islands just off Spain's Mediterranean coast, is probably best known as a nightlife hotspot teeming with youthful revellers dancing and drinking at thumping clubs until the early hours of the morning. But what is less known are Ibiza's rural charms. Away from the bustling, tourist-filled towns are tranquil villages and ancient farmsteads that have nestled in this idyllic land for centuries – long before the package holidays and techno DJs arrived.

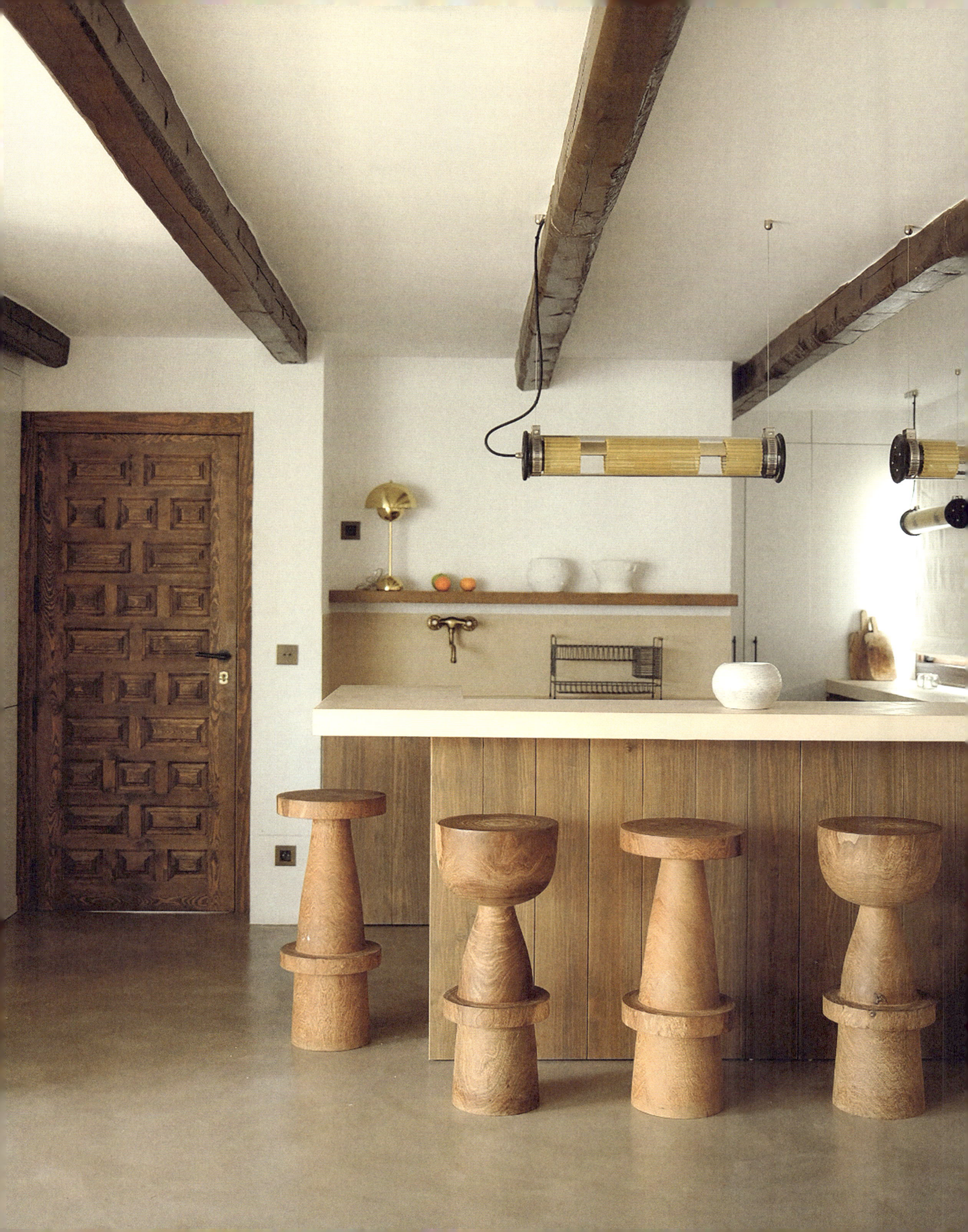

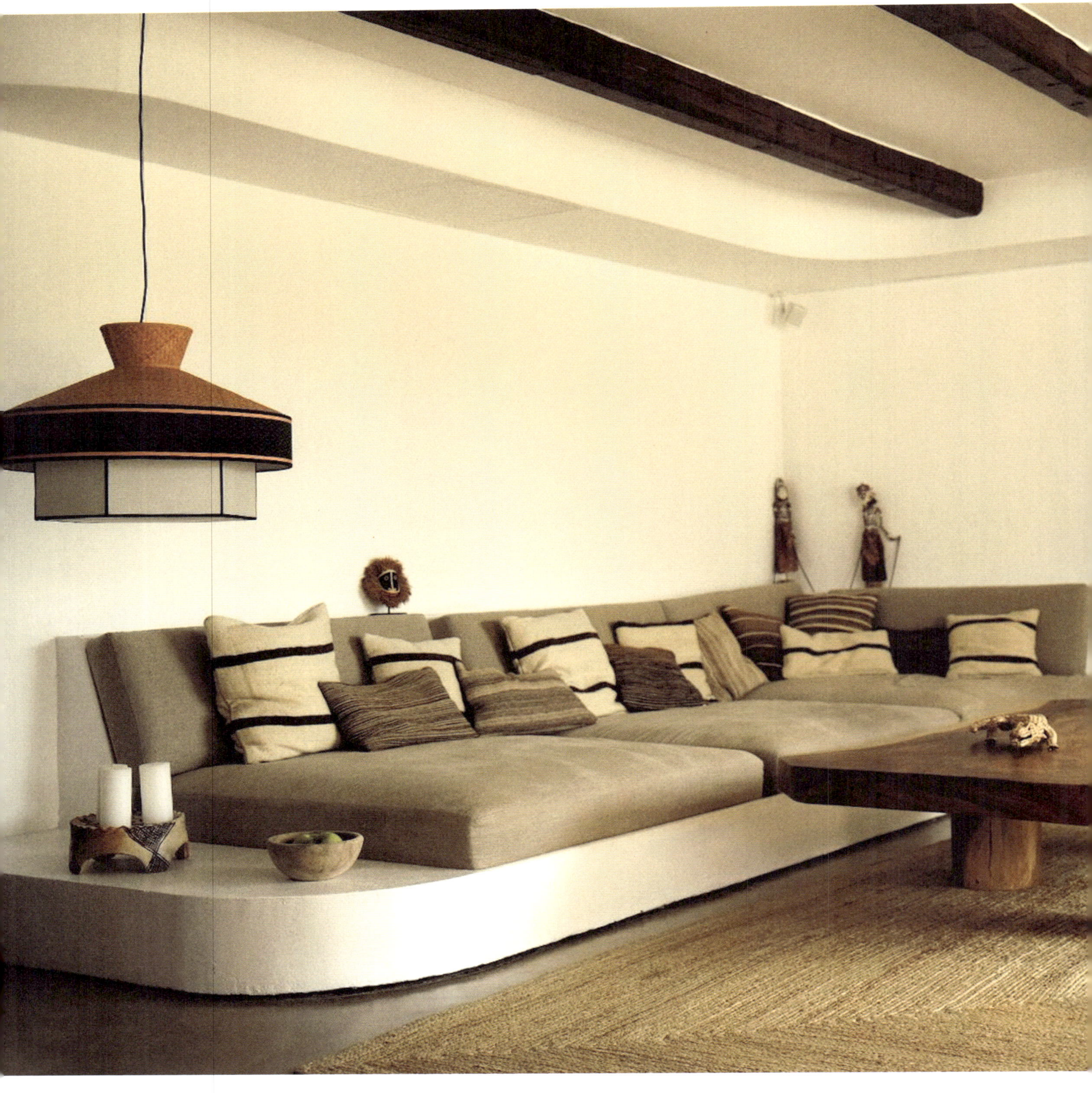

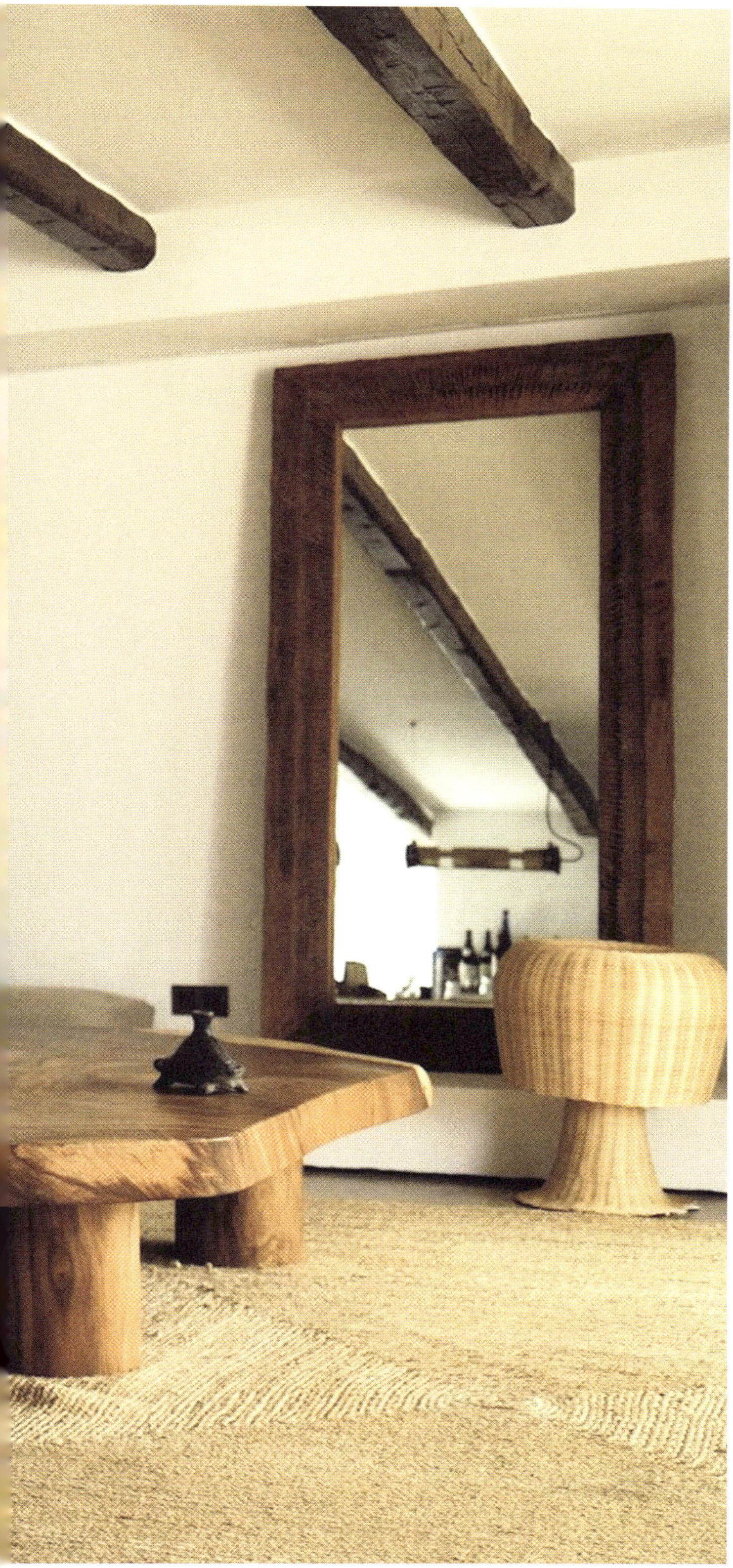

The island's built history was the inspiration for Parisian design duo Hauvette & Madani – formed of Samantha Hauvette and Lucas Madani – when coming up with the interior concept for this penthouse apartment in Ibiza for a client who wanted her very own pied-à-terre on the island, both for entertaining and escape. 'We decided to design it in the style of a local finca,' says Hauvette, referring to the traditional whitewashed rural dwellings found across the island, spartan shacks made of whatever materials could be found nearby – usually dry stone, sand and clay, and juniper for the long-weathered timber ceiling beams. 'But we changed everything about it,' she continues. 'The bones, the structure, everything. If you looked at the building from the outside you would never guess what was inside.'

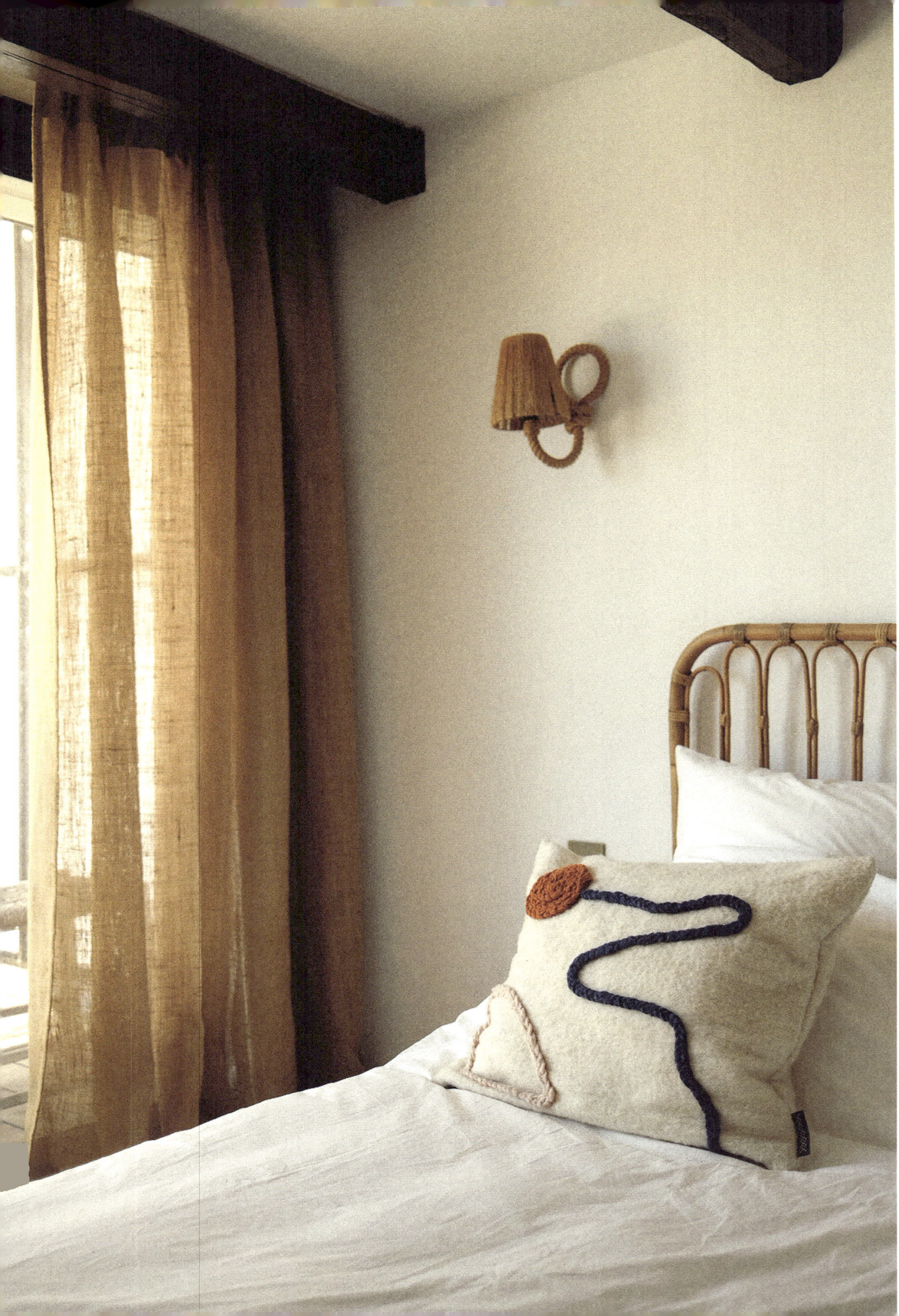

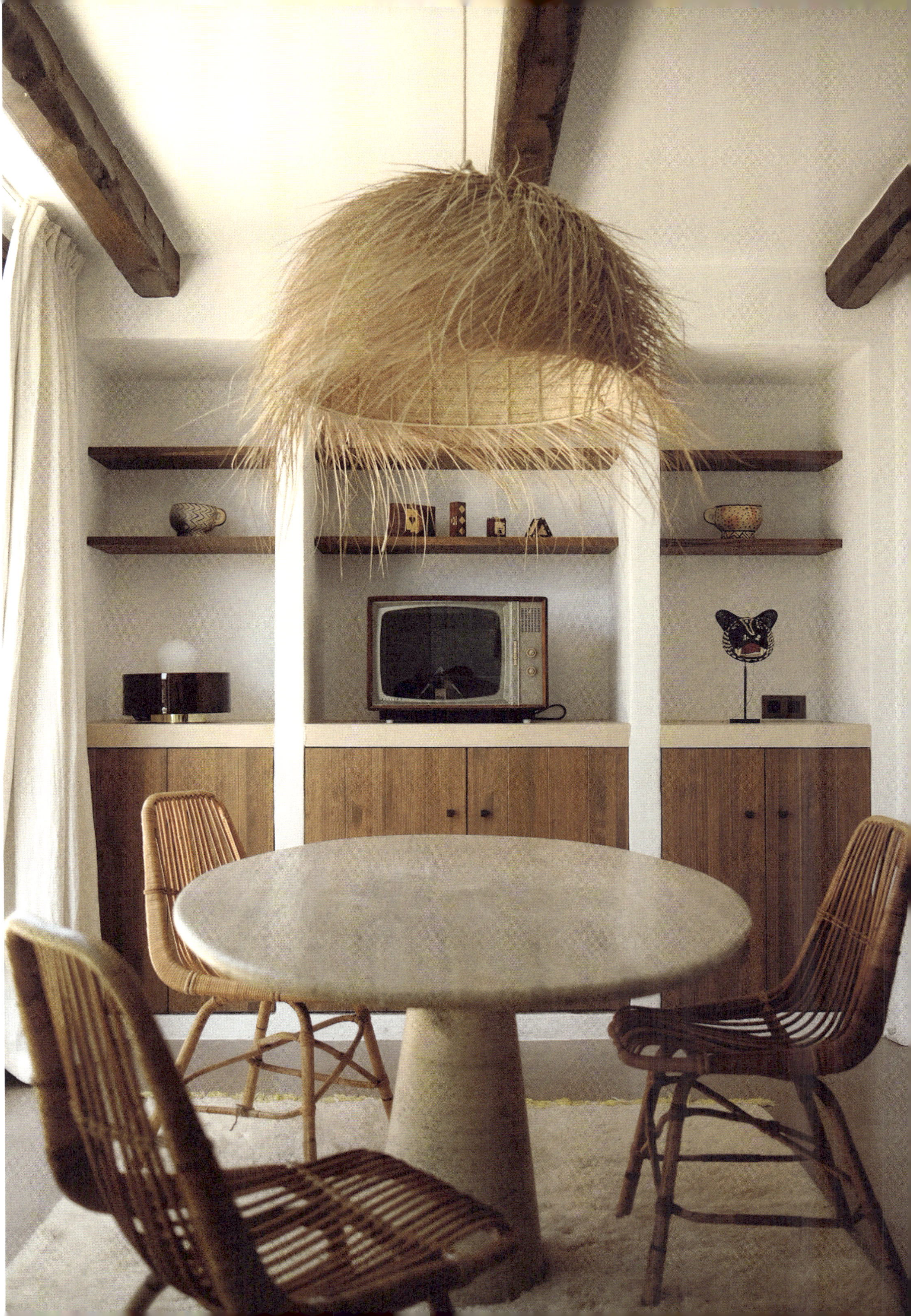

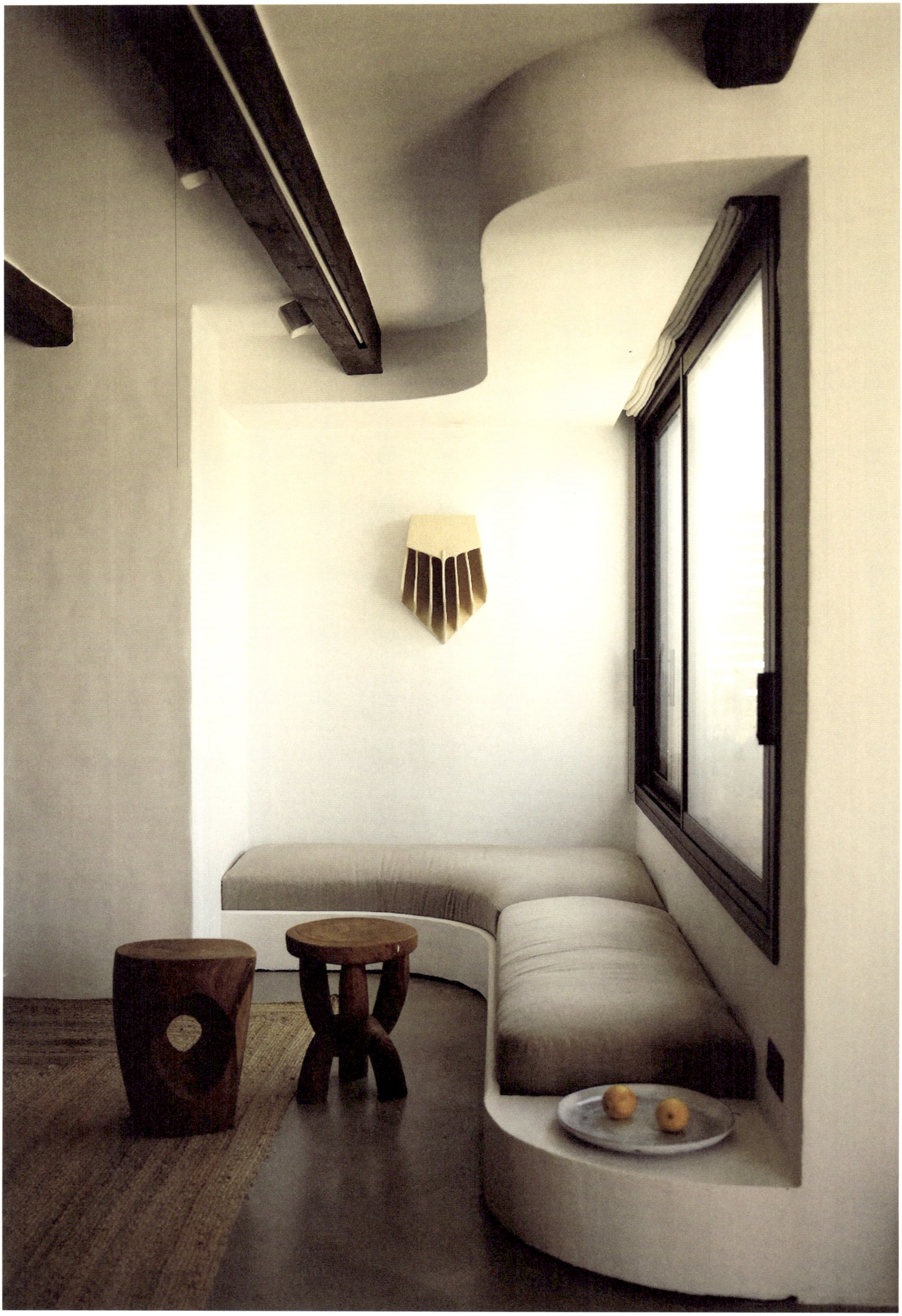

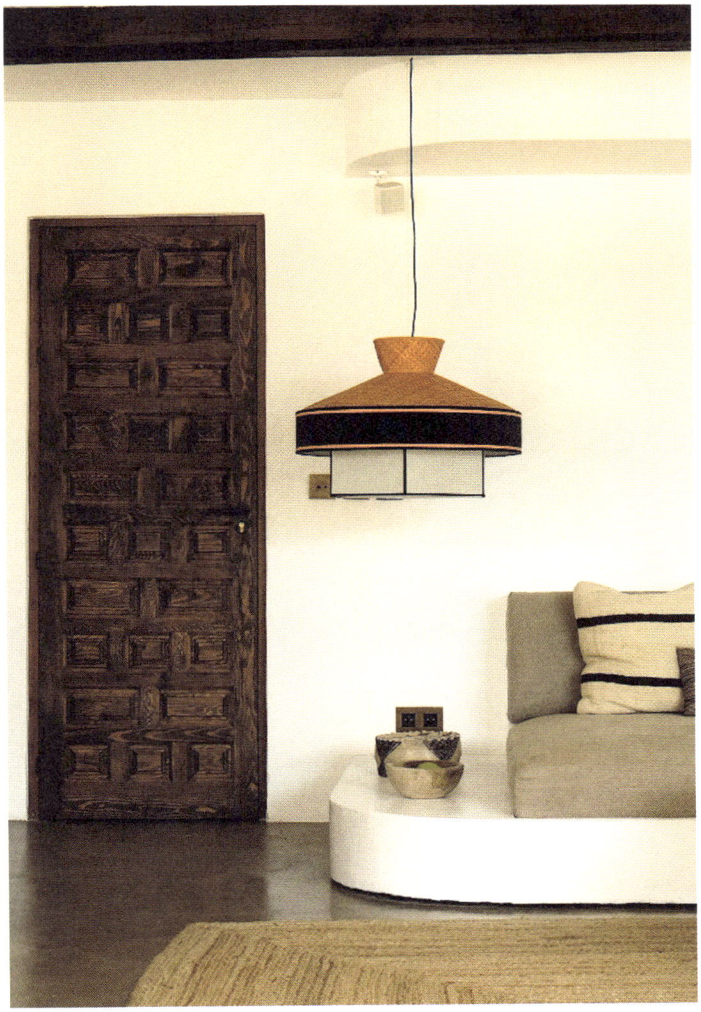

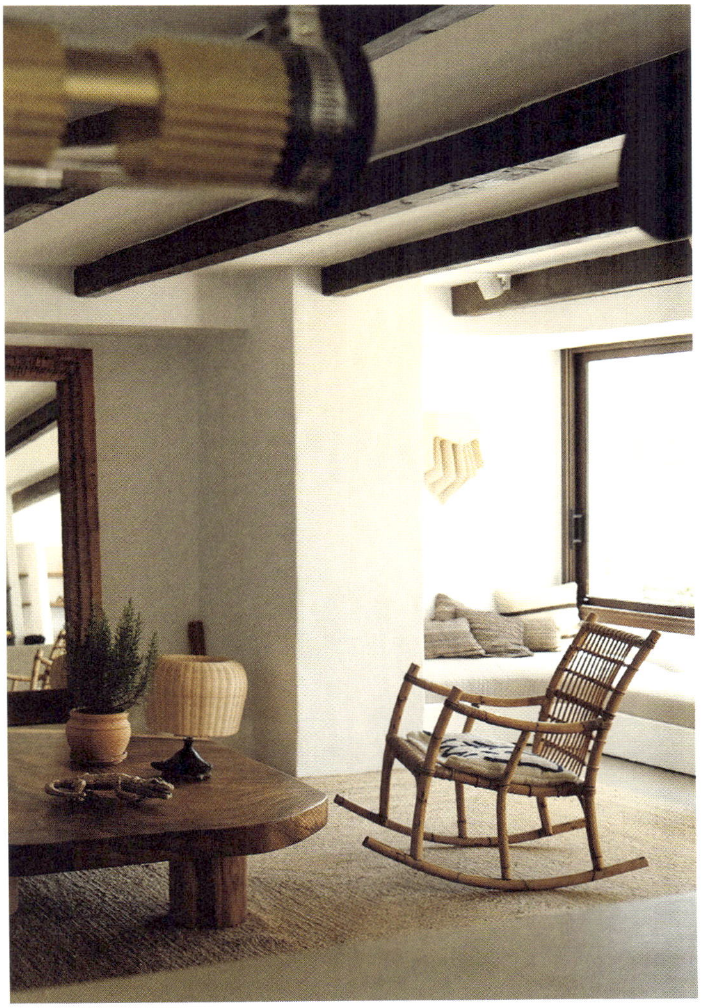

The pair kept within a palette of warm whites and organic wood tones, wrapping the living room with deep, comfortable sofas carved in the style of traditional plasterwork. A wooden bar space was installed opposite, which is clad in a paler shade of wood and ringed with monolithic stools that were hewn in Senegal and imported to Spain. They kept the furnishing to a minimum, opting for natural materials – including a bent bamboo bed frame, wild-grass pendant light, travertine stone dining table and asymmetrical coffee tables made from Indonesian teak. 'We then added woodwork to the doors,' says Hauvette of the final details, 'to make them look like the typical Ibizan doorways that you can see all across the island's historic villages.'

Tropical Brutalism in Bali

CANGGU, BALI (ID) **DANIEL & HILDA MITCHELL**

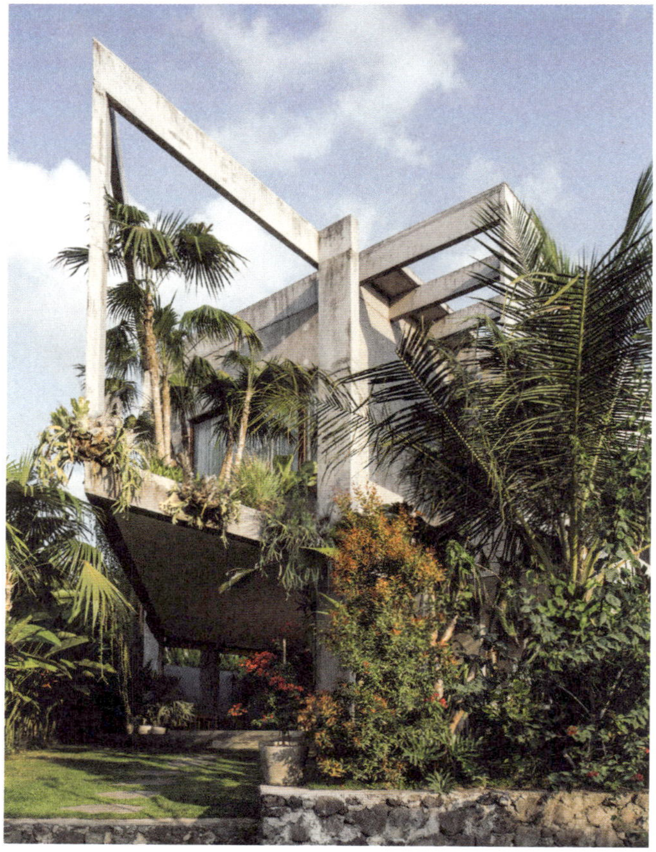

The beachside village of Canggu occupies an idyllic slice of land on Bali's Indian Ocean–facing western side. Characterised by a think inland jungle and vibrant shoreline resorts, this tropical paradise is where designers Dan and Hilda Mitchell happily absconded to after more than a decade of living in London. 'After years of visiting the island, we always thought about moving to Bali to live a more sustainable lifestyle,' says Daniel. The final straw was the birth of their first son. In 2014 they packed their bags, determined to raise their brood outside of the chaos of the city and closer to Hilda's family, who hails from Jakarta.

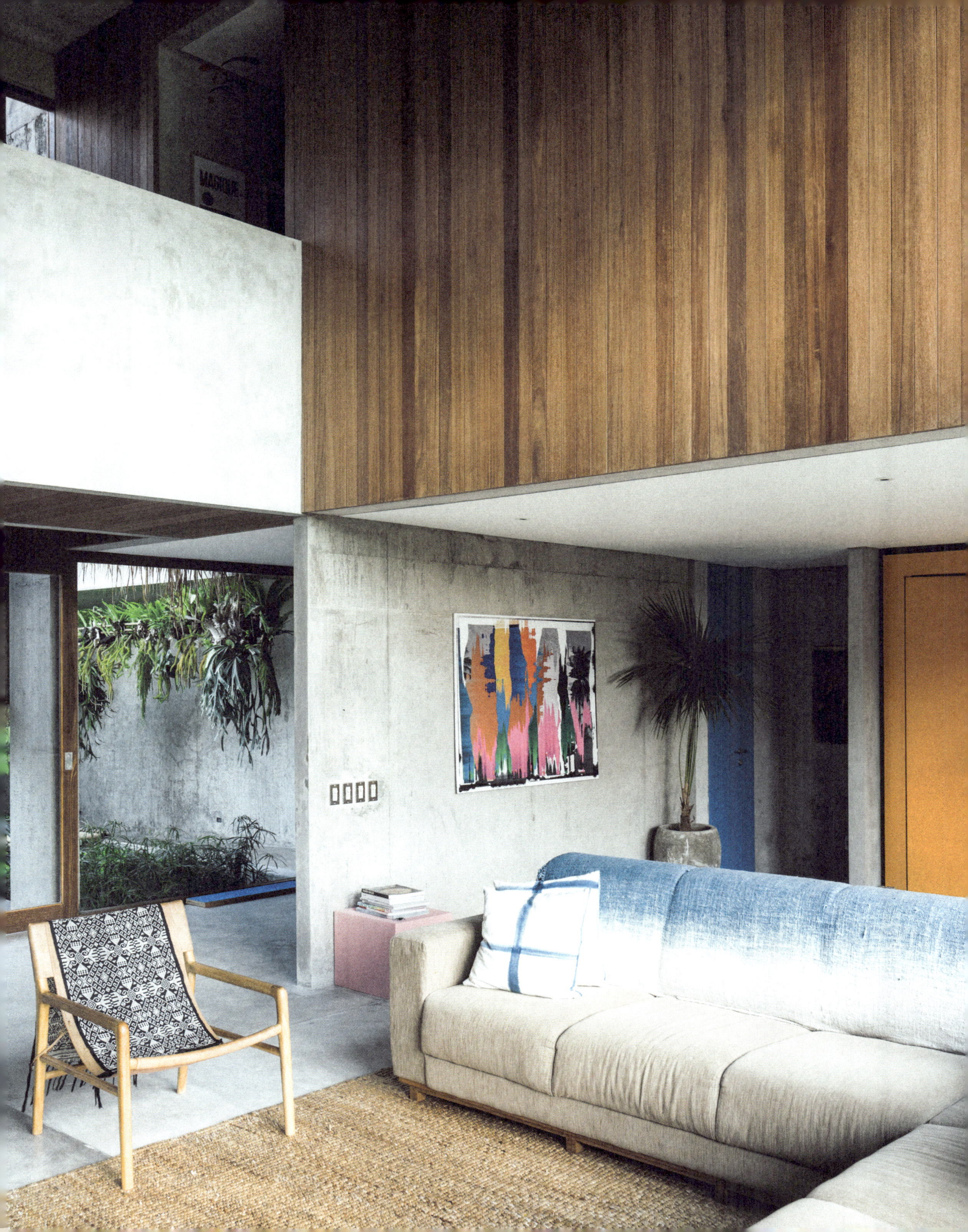

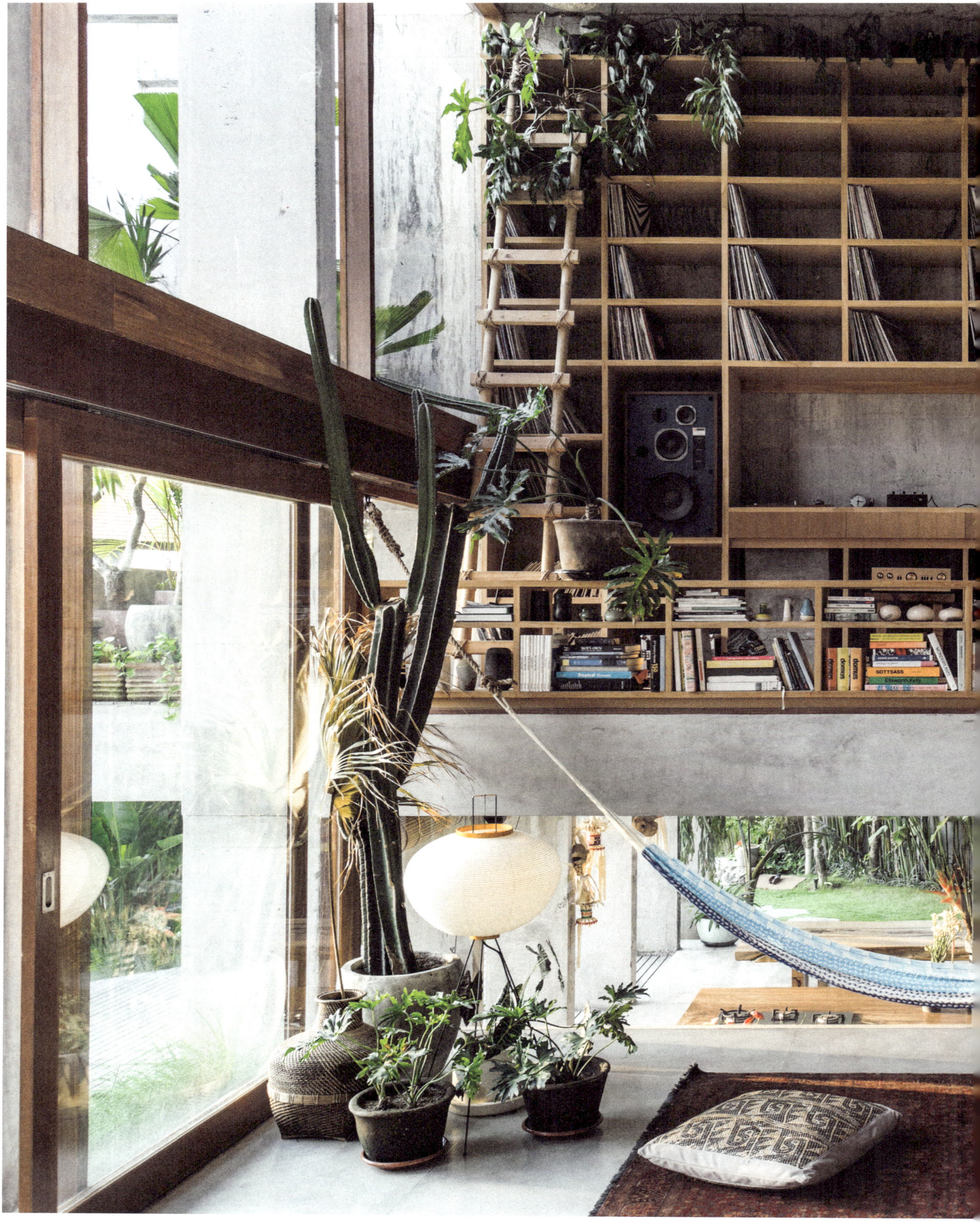
BOY'S OWN
Tropical Houses
domus
domus
domus
SOTTSASS
Ellsworth Kelly

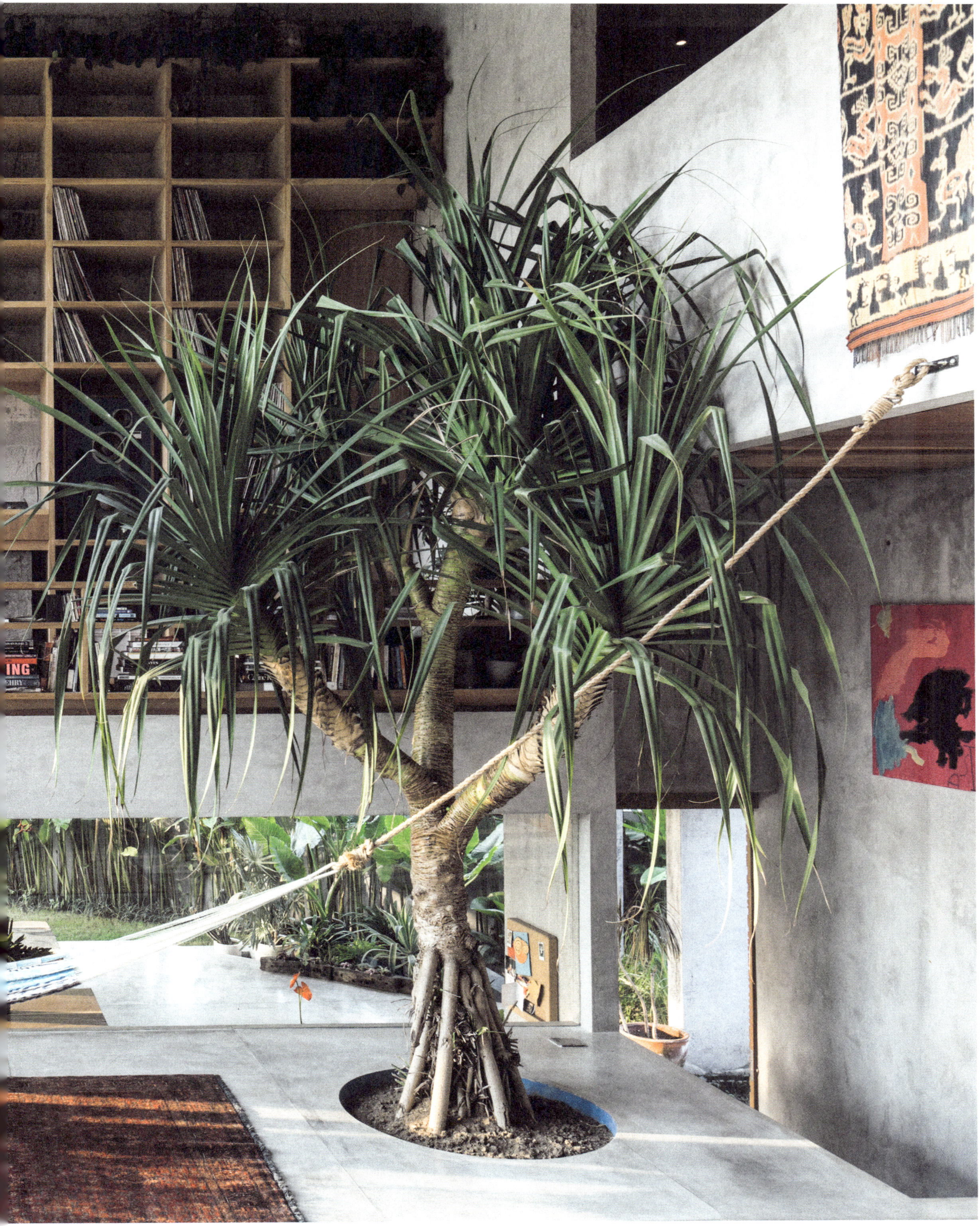

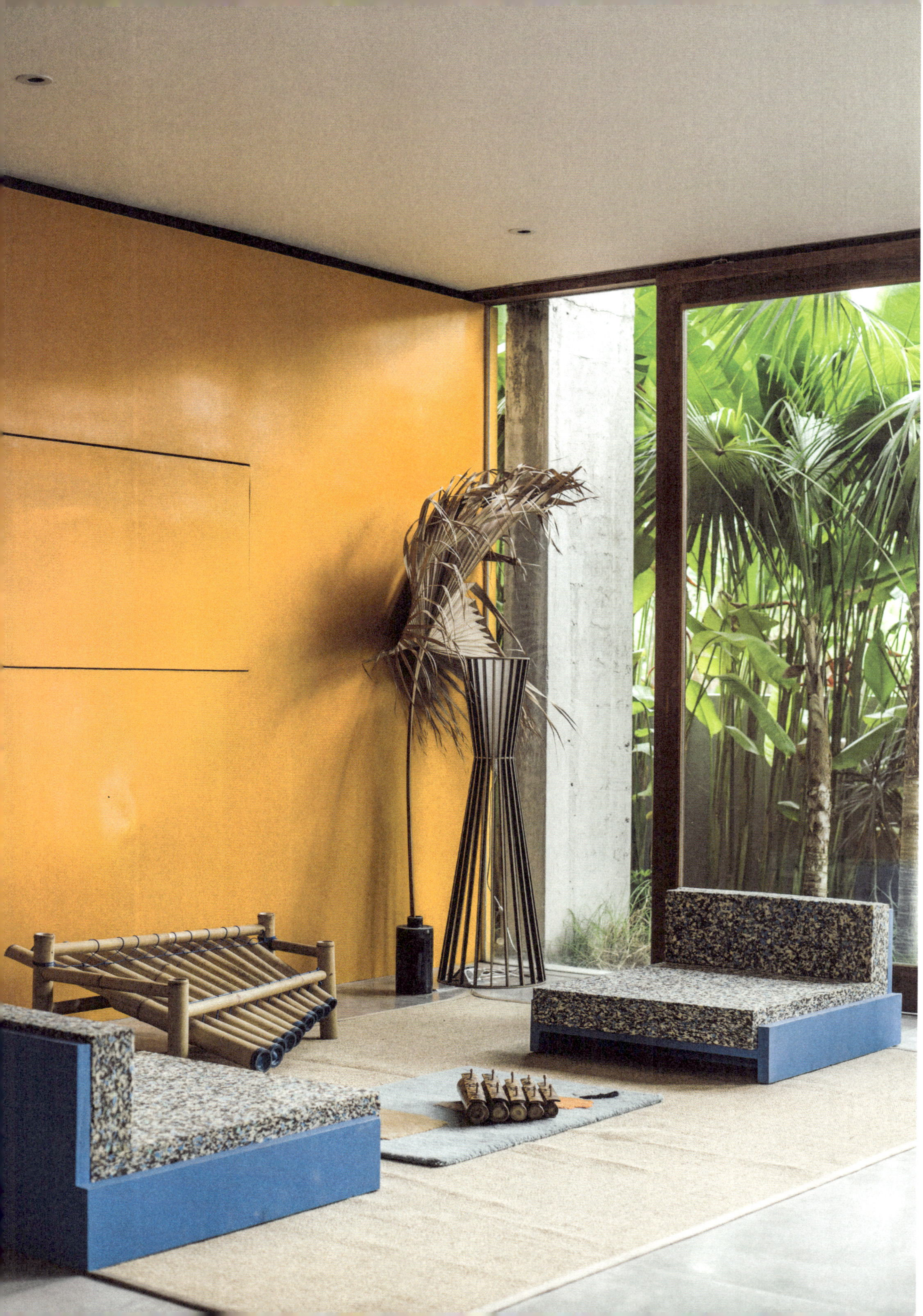

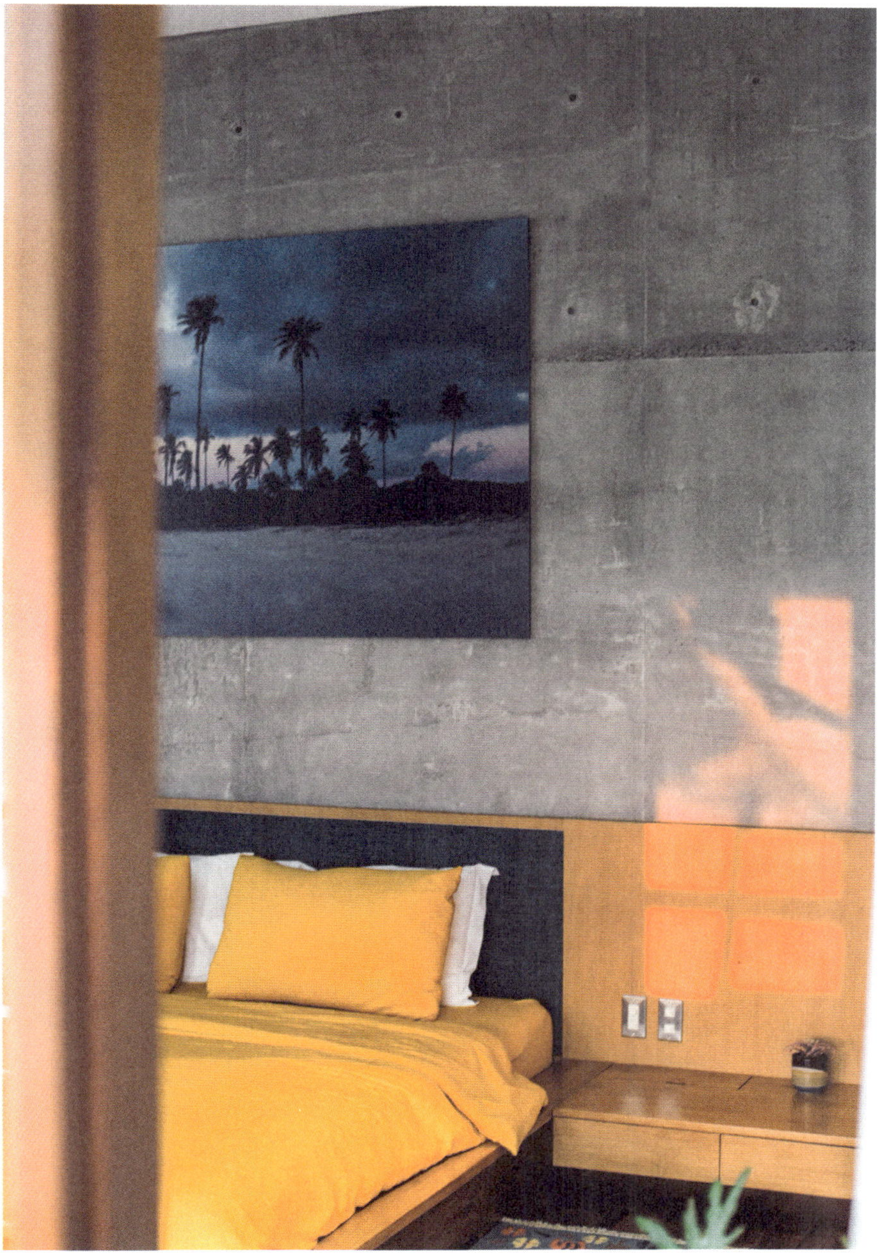

In designing the home, the couple wanted a space that 'felt comfortable and was very open and very airy, ' says Daniel. They organised the concrete structure, a Brutalist-inspired villa that brilliantly contrasts with the surrounding jungle, over a series of half levels connected by steps. 'Because of the split levels, the different rooms feel together and separate at the same time,' he says of the layout, which allows uninterrupted sight lines between the adjacent rooms. From the living room, you can simultaneously peer into the kitchen below and the second floor above, connecting the disparate spaces visually while maintaining a sense of independence.

According to Daniel and Hilda, the heart of the home is the living room. 'Everything we love is on display there,' Daniel says of the double-height space, where a six-metre-tall shelving system was built into the wall and stacked with books, beloved objects and audio equipment for the couple's extensive collection of vinyl records.

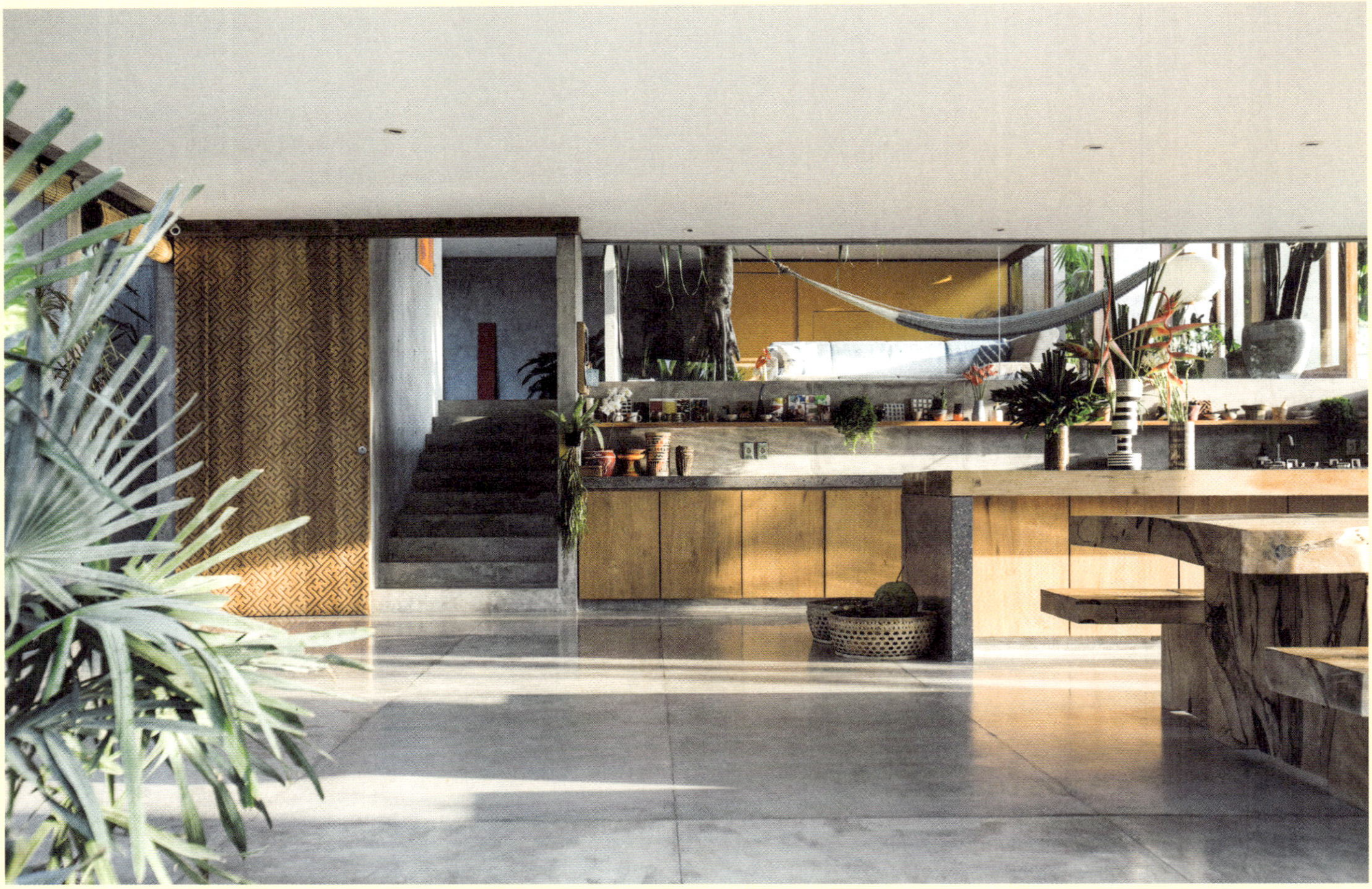

The couple called on local craftspeople to create much of the furnishing found throughout the space. The long dining table and accompanying benches were hewn from a tree that had fallen naturally in the jungle, while just opposite a wooden sliding door was hand-carved in a pattern depicting the Balinese peace sign by island artisans. They acknowledge that the concrete that makes up the home's structure differs from local architectural styles, but they added an awning made of local ylang-ylang grass, a typical vernacular element in Bali, to aid in shielding the home from the hot midday sun.

Elsewhere in the home, furniture is a mix of pieces repurposed from previous houses or passed on from family: the hammock, strung between two trees planted in situ in the living room, was bought second-hand on the island; the rug below was shipped from London when they relocated, and the sofa was repurposed from Hilda's mother's house. The artwork hung in the living room, Daniel proudly states, is another family heirloom: colourful, finger-painted canvases by the couple's two young sons.

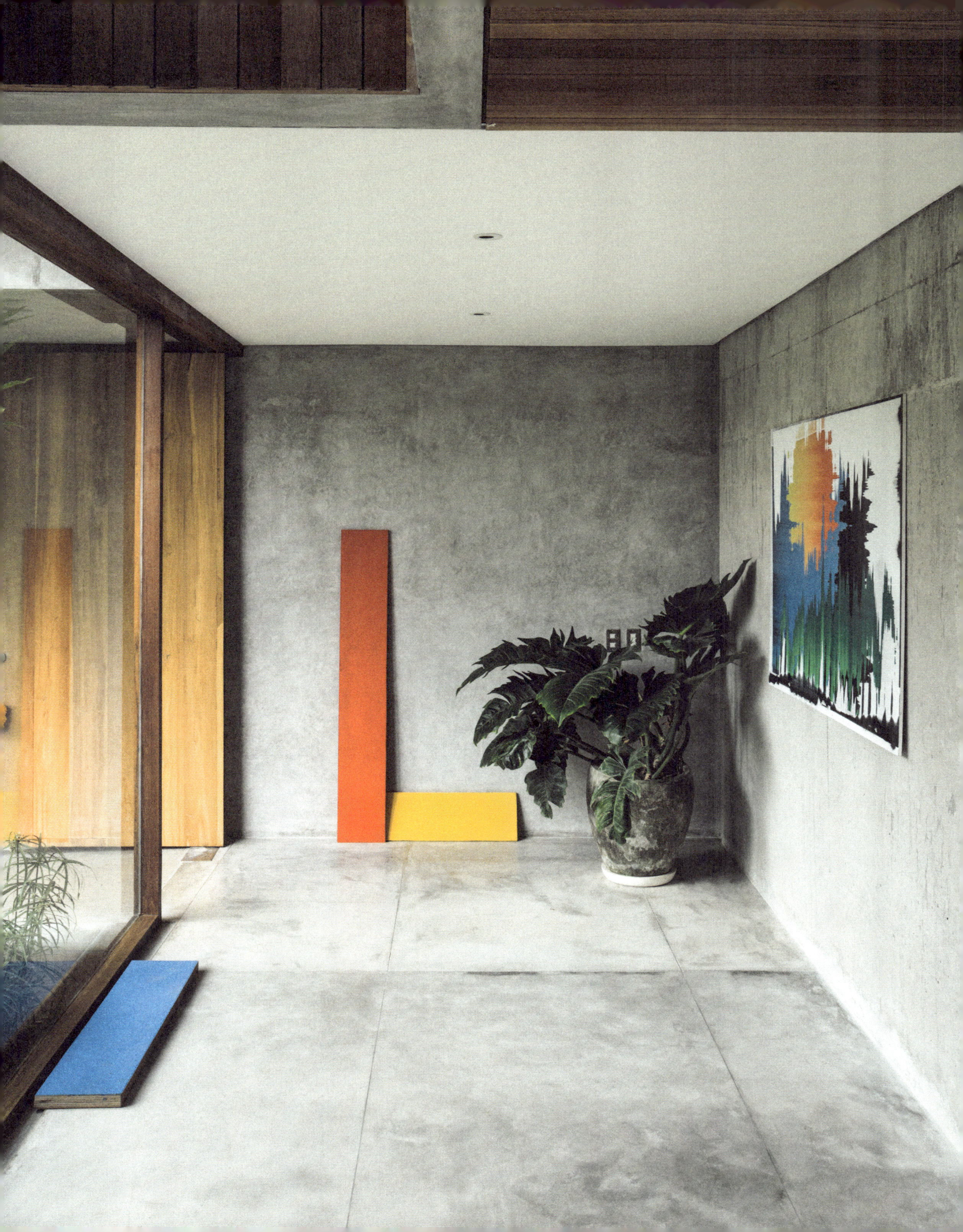

Interview

Daniel Mitchell, the creative director behind Bali's Potato Head Resorts, and Hilda Mitchell, a fashion designer and owner of children's clothing label Zephyr Blues, together run the design firm Space Available, a research-based studio that creates furniture and objects from recycled plastic waste. Daniel, who is from England, and Hilda, from Indonesia, met in London where Daniel was running his former cult clothing store, LNCC. They now live in their concrete dream house in the beachside village of Canggu with their two sons.

Daniel & Hilda Mitchell

What was the initial concept behind the house?

DM: The goal was to create a comfortable family home and a creative space where we wanted to spend the rest of our lives, with a structure that would remain there for hundreds of years. We also wanted to create something that adapted to the local environment, even though the material choices aren't necessarily natural – we played into that contrast. We wanted to clash with the landscape using something quite foreign in terms of material choices. It was important to us to bring a lot of nature inside, so we included a lot of plant life within the layout of the house.

One of the design references behind the house was American modernist architect Ray Kappe's home in Los Angeles, which was built in 1967. How did you integrate his ideas into this home?

DM: That's where the split-level concept comes in. The house is actually on multiple levels, but not necessarily on different floors. From the entranceway and living room, you can see several spaces at once. You can see into Hilda's workspace, up into the kitchen and dining room, but still, all the spaces are separated. And the inspiration for that was the Kappe House, the modernist residence by Raymond Knappe in Pacific Palisades, Los Angeles. I always found that to be a very comfortable way of living, because each room was separate but you didn't have the conformity of walls.

There are a host of sustainable features built into the design of the house. Can you share some details about those aspects?

DM: There are several energy-saving aspects such as solar panelling and rainwater harvesting, which we use for the showers and things like that. But in terms of how the house was designed, we didn't want to have air conditioning, even though Bali is a tropical climate, so we created a sort of overhang that shades the living room window. We knew we wanted to have a lot of glass, and obviously, glass isn't the best in a hot climate because of direct sunlight, so the overhang protects the house and keeps it cool by creating shade. It allows the house to breathe when all of the sliding doors are open. Because there are no walls between the spaces, the air circulates and we can feel a constant breeze throughout the day without using any electricity. We used concrete, even though it's not the most sustainable of materials, because of its cooling properties. I wouldn't call it a completely sustainable house. We're not off the grid, but we try to reduce our footprint as much as we can.

Your design studio Space Available works with waste materials and recycled plastic. Was that incorporated into the furnishings of the home?

DM: Yes, the Space Available furniture is made from 100% recycled plastic waste, which is saved from landfills and rivers here in Bali. Before we started producing the furniture with Space Available, though, we experimented with using recycled material for pieces in the house. For example, the low-sitting blue chairs were made in collaboration with a local artisan from discarded foam and plywood, which we now use as meditation chairs.

Within the house, some elements point to a love of music: traditional Balinese instruments in the meditation area and a large-scale sound system in the living room. Was that something you consciously incorporated into the home?

DM: Music has always been a big part of our lives. When I first founded LNCC it was one of the first listening spaces in London, which has now become a big trend globally. I was first introduced to this concept when I started visiting Japan in 2006 and discovered these listening spaces for audiophiles. They would have these old studio monitors and stacks of records and people would just sit and listen to music through high-fidelity audio systems and have a nice drink. So when we were creating the house we wanted to have a turntable room that was really the centrepiece of the house. So when you first walk in, you first see the big tree, then behind it, there is the huge built-in shelving system where all of the music equipment is. It's very much the centrepiece of the house.

Many elements in the house were inspired by local craft traditions. What was that design process like?

DM: The wooden door in the kitchen is hand-carved by local craftsmen. The symbol is the Balinese peace sign, which is also the Hindu peace sign. You see it at every temple on the island. Balinese houses will often have it carved above the doorway, so we took that and turned it into a repetitive pattern for the door. It was important to us to have that element of Balinese craft within the house, to honour the local culture.

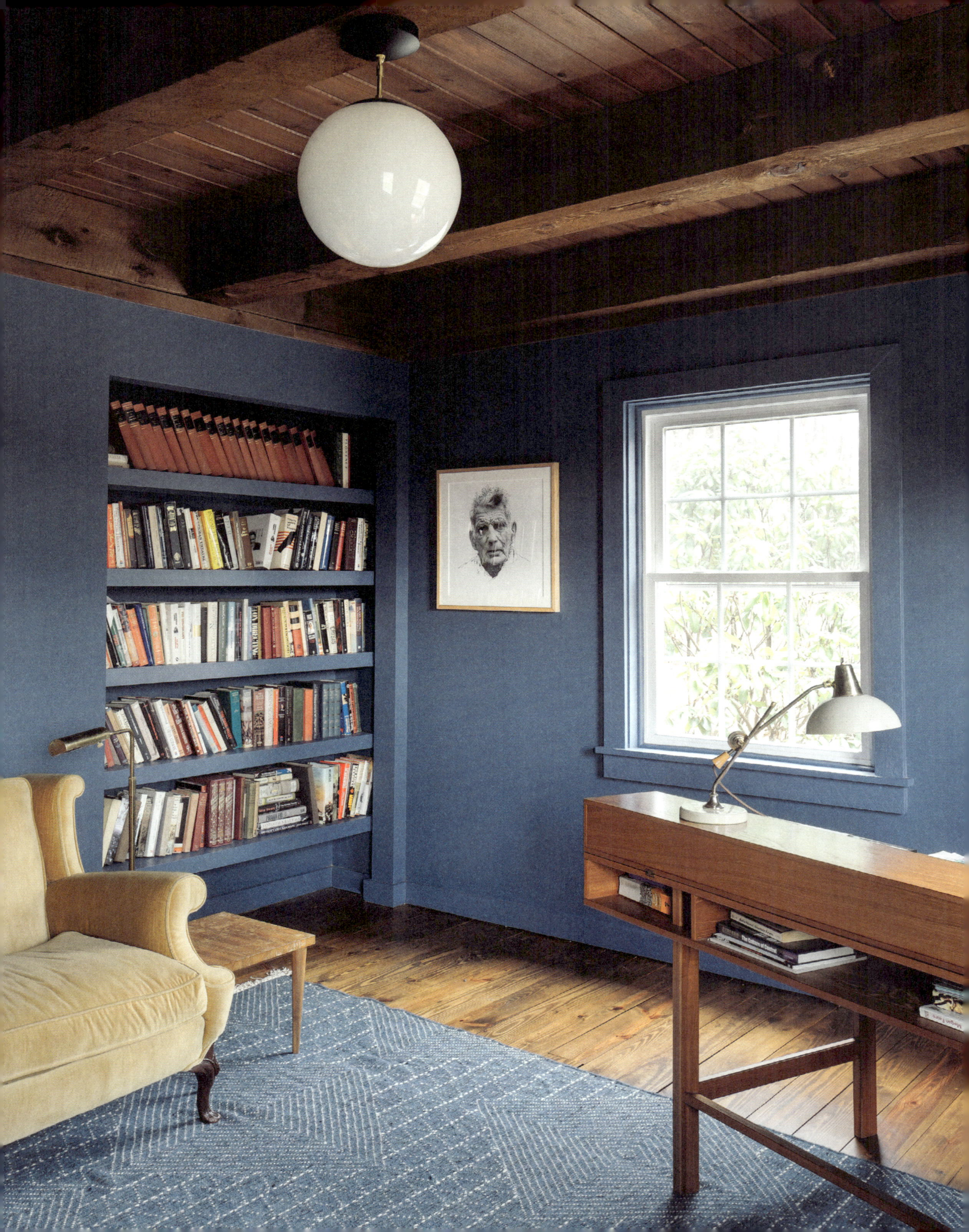

CHAPTER 03

Reimagined Farmhouses

The pastoral charms of a farmhouse are hard to beat. Surrounded by fertile land and endless space, these countryside retreats are the definition of bucolic. But, more than an exercise in charming aesthetics, these converted spaces are a lesson in how to thoughtfully restore historic homes — homes that nonetheless look optimistically towards the future.

A Sustainable Home on a British Farm

CAMBRIDGESHIRE, ENGLAND (UK) **PRACTICE ARCHITECTURE**

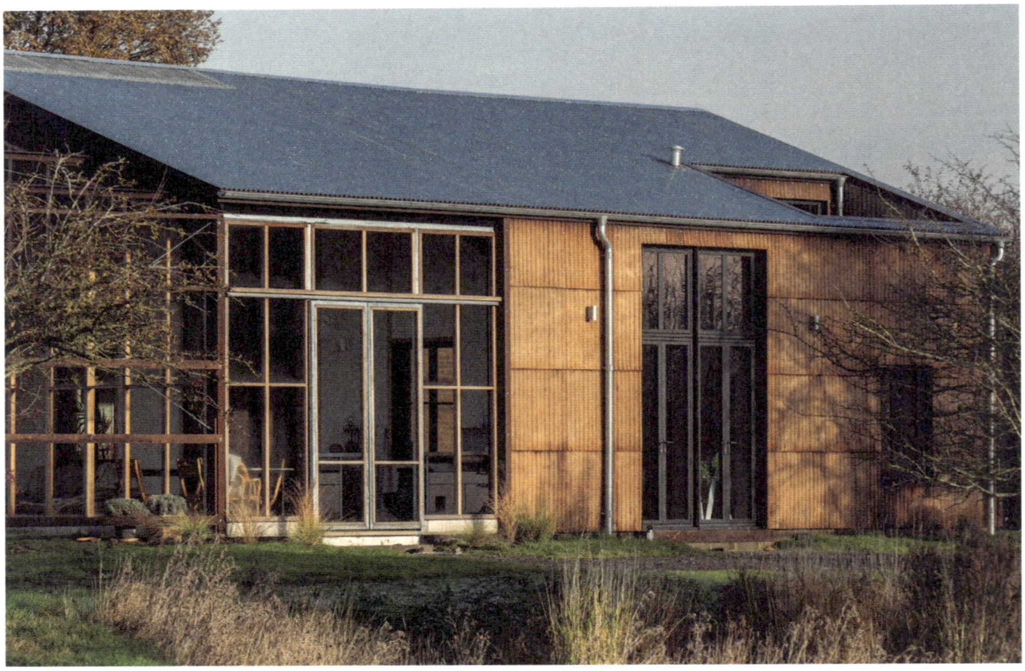

Hemp is a thoroughly misunderstood plant. Known primarily for its associations with cannabis, it is in fact a surprisingly resilient and eco-friendly building material. When dried and mixed with lime, a white powdery substance derived from limestone, the resulting solution becomes hempcrete, a fast-growing sustainable material prized for its fire-retardant properties, strength and ability to capture excess carbon. Over the past few decades, architects and designers have slowly been catching on to hempcrete's potential as a non-polluting alternative to standard building materials.

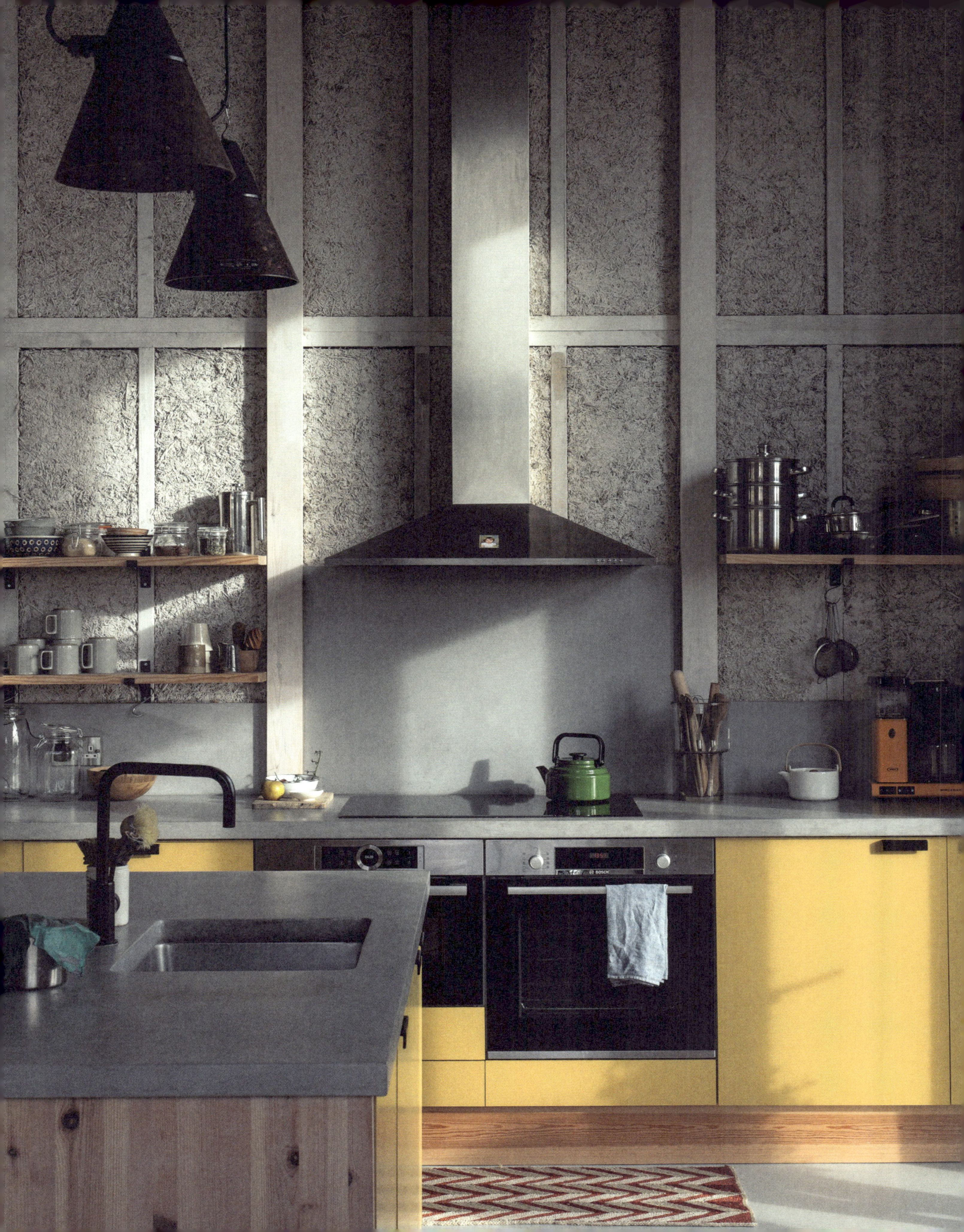

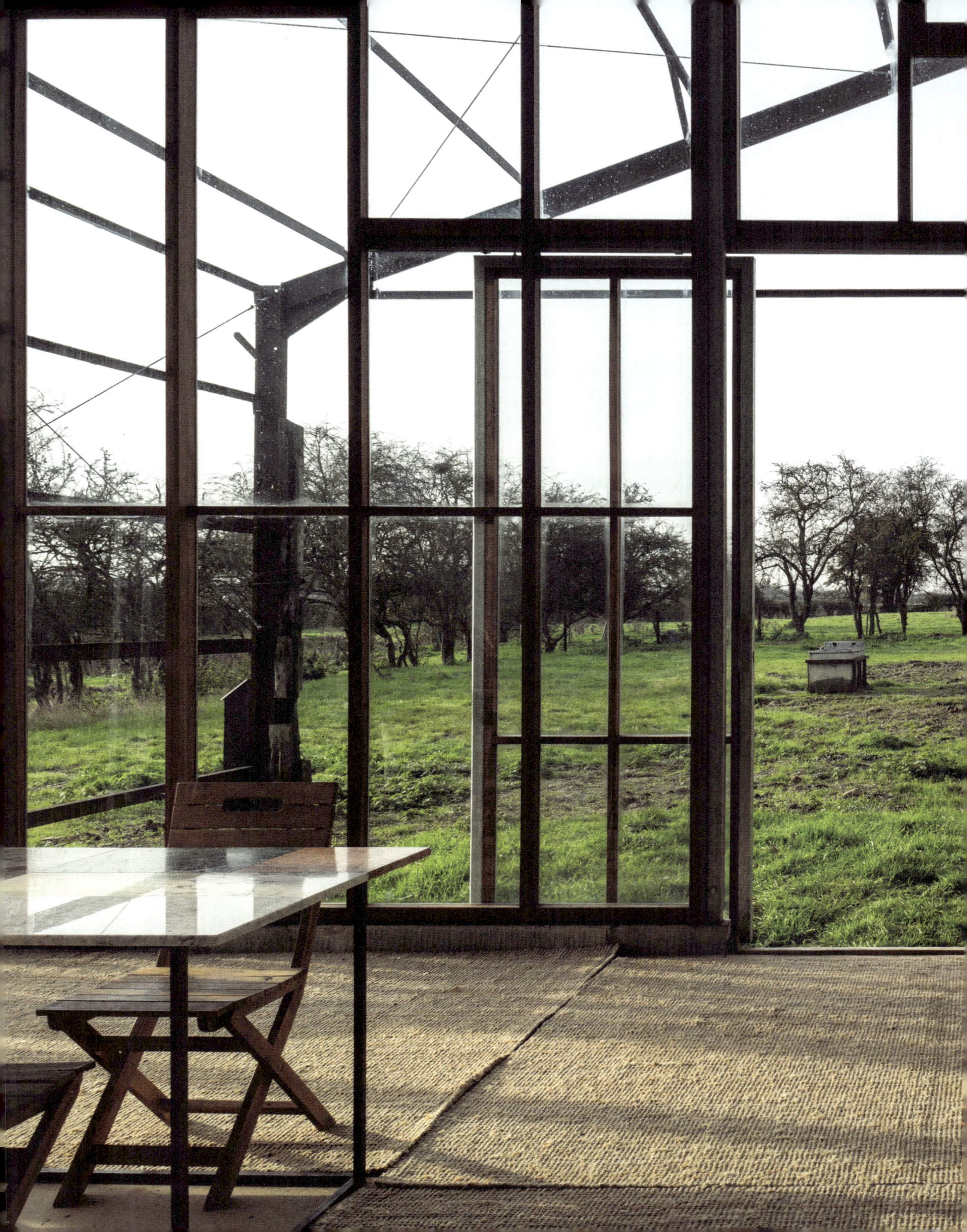

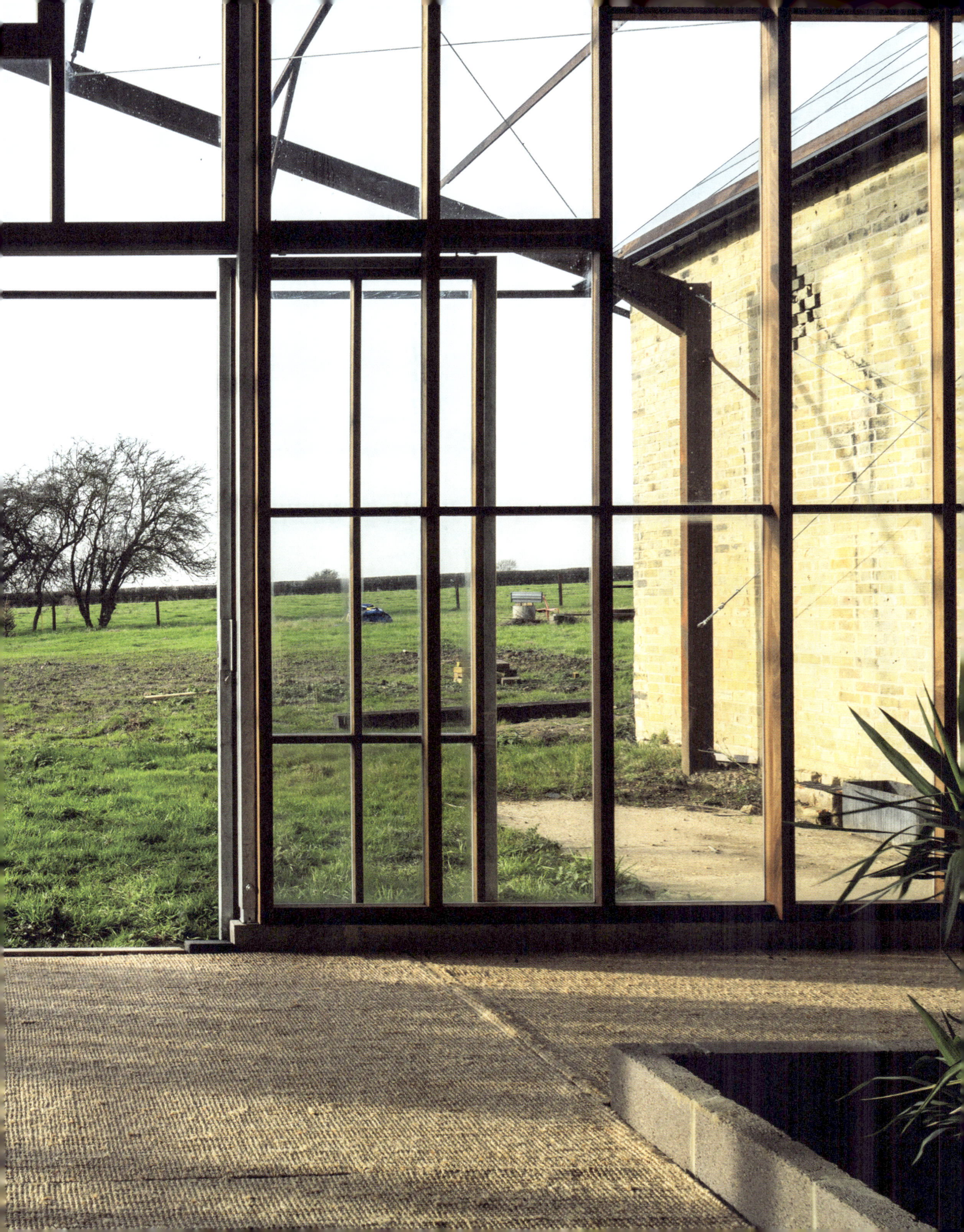

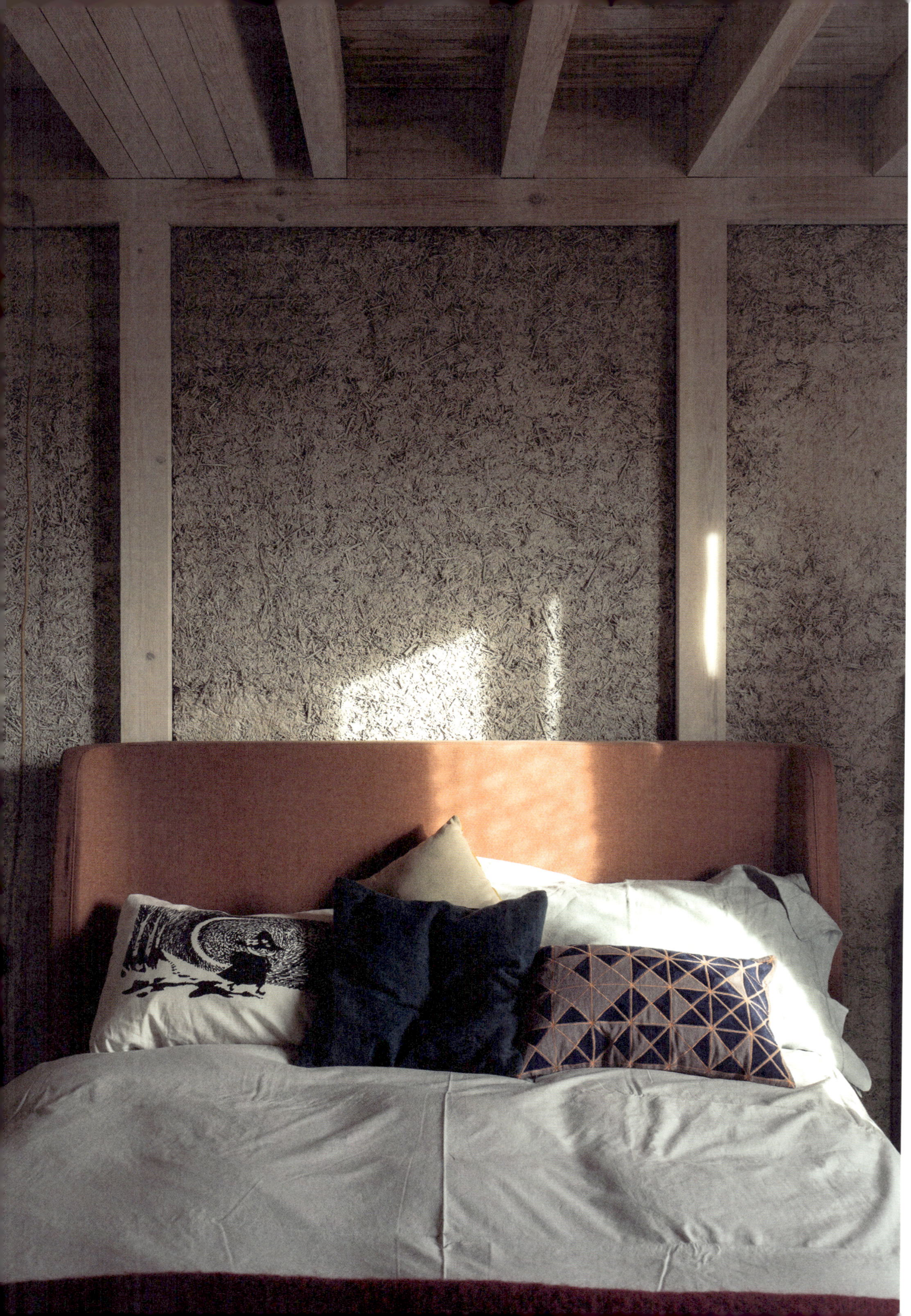

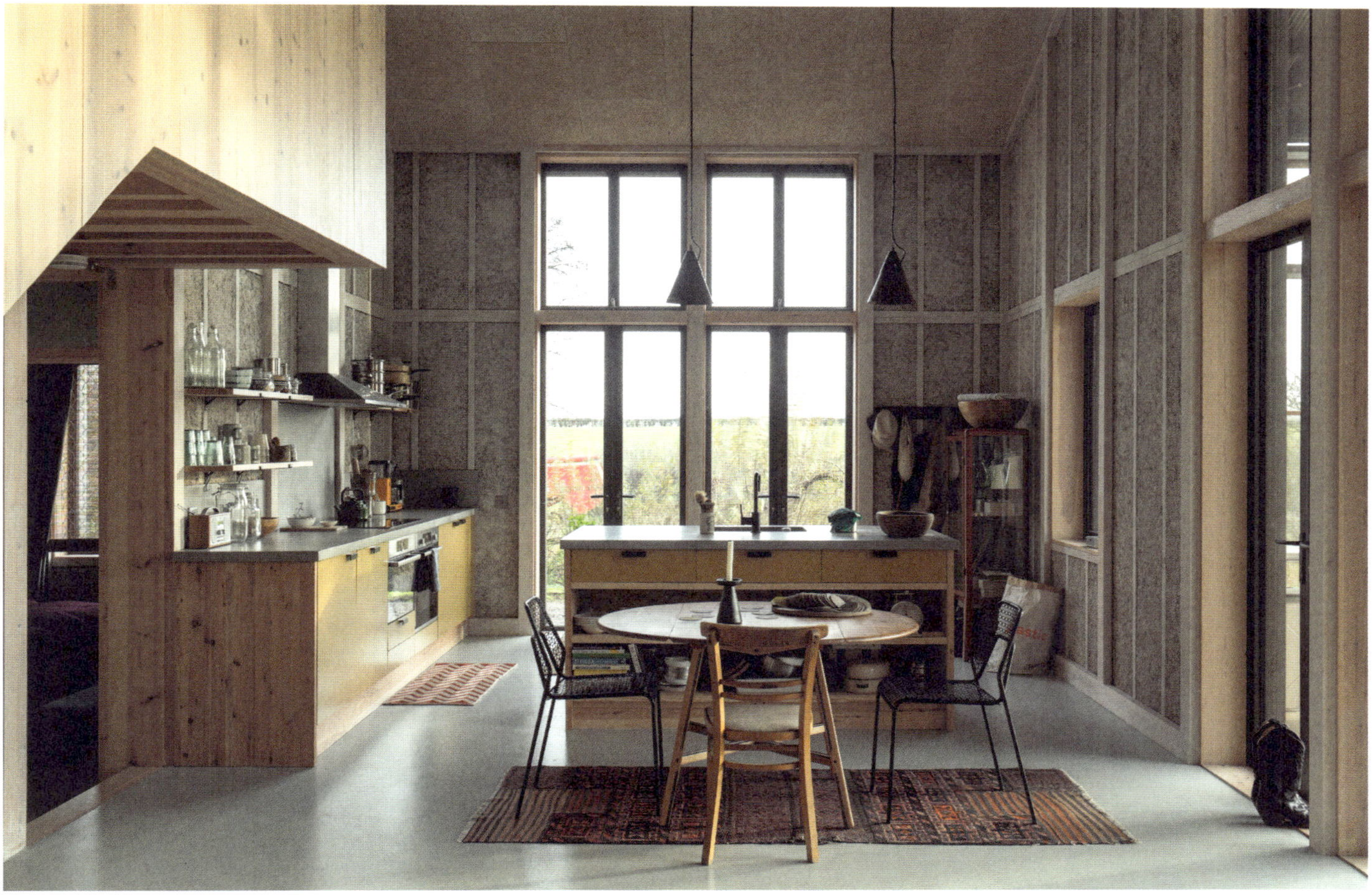

Margent Farm, the brainchild of film director Steve Barron, is a 50-acre hemp farm in a hilly pocket of the Cambridgeshire fenlands that is committed to developing sustainable bio-based plastics. For the on-site residence, Barron commissioned London design firm Practice Architecture to develop a home that would highlight the low-carbon building potential of hempcrete. The result, named Flat House, is a 1,000-square-foot, two-storey farmhouse formed of a timber frame and a system of structural insulated panels made from the experimental material.

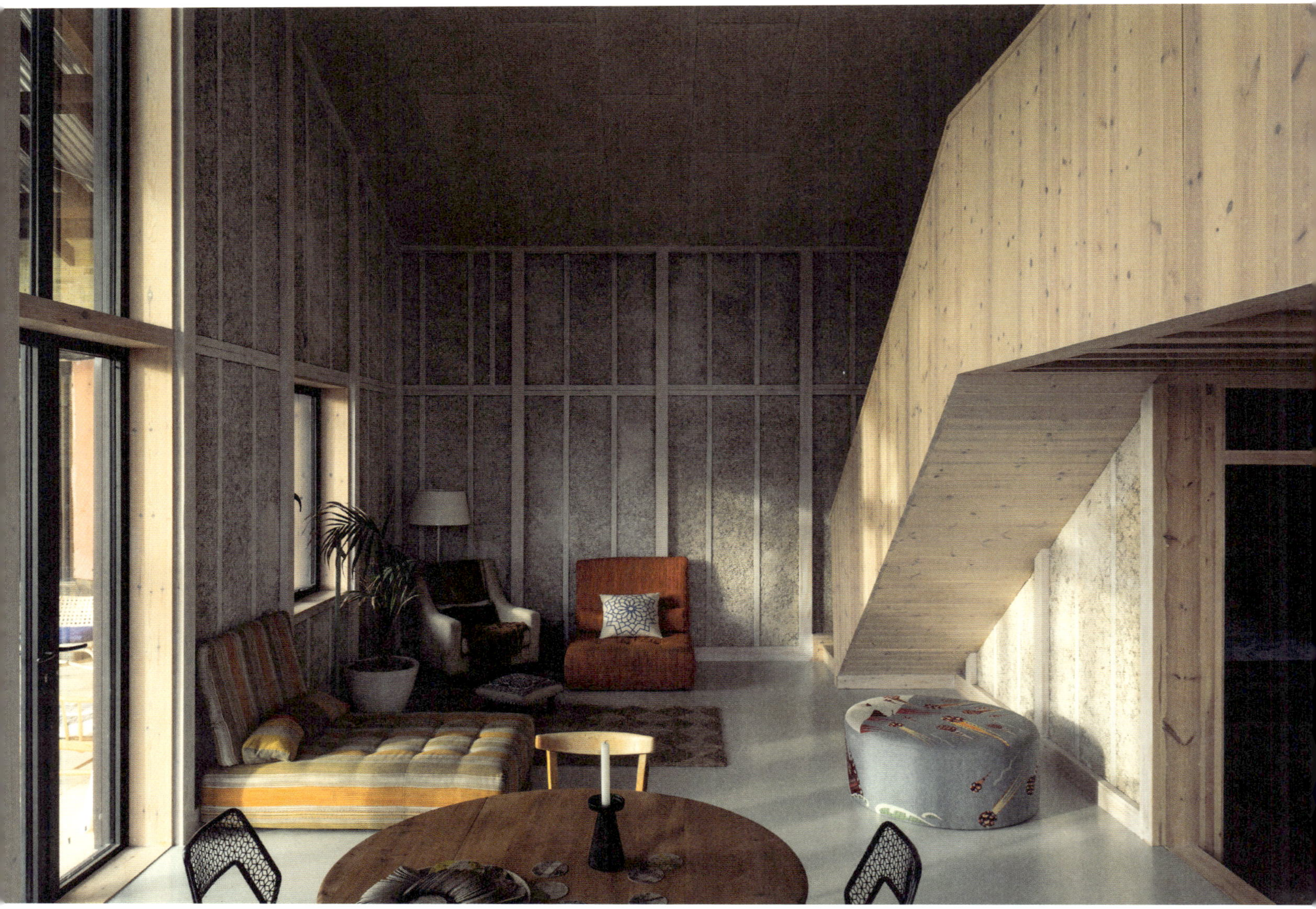

The home occupies the site of a former working barn and largely conforms to a conventional layout: the two-floor gabled roof structure features a double-height kitchen and living room, ground-floor bedrooms, a second-floor office and a glassed-in sunroom overlooking the marshy fields beyond. The architects visually foregrounded the use of the hempcrete material by leaving the brown-grey insulated panels unfinished, creating a rough, organic effect on the interior walls. For the exterior, they developed a system of hemp-fibre tiles, which together with the insulating panels naturally regulate the moisture and humidity within the house. Flat House acts both as an idyllic countryside dwelling and an experimental inquiry into the potential of sustainable building materials.

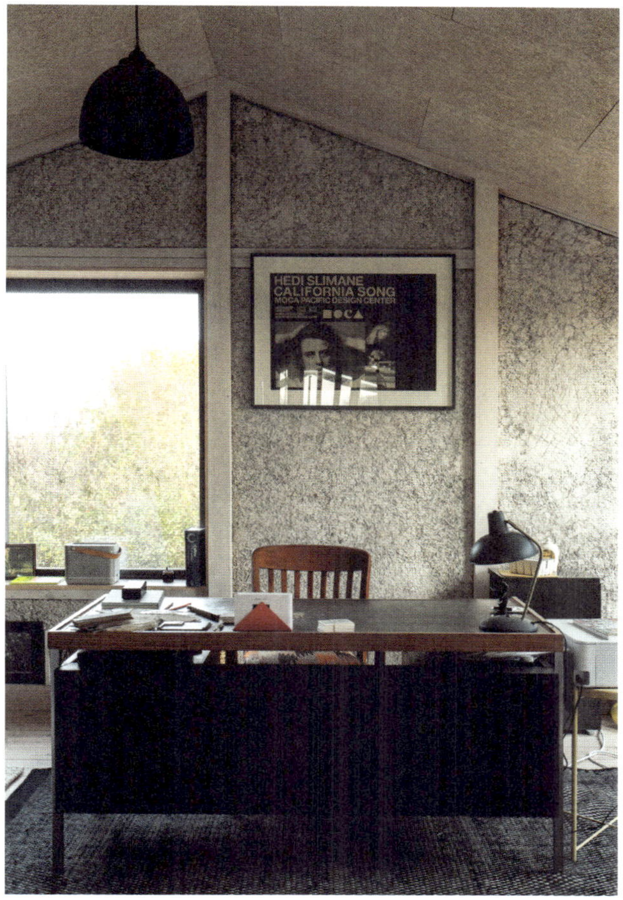

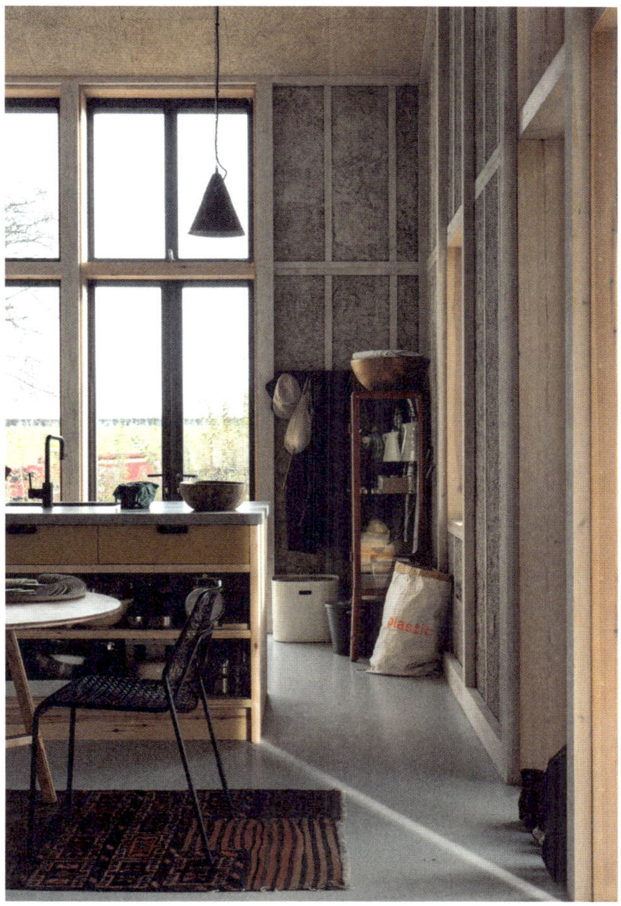

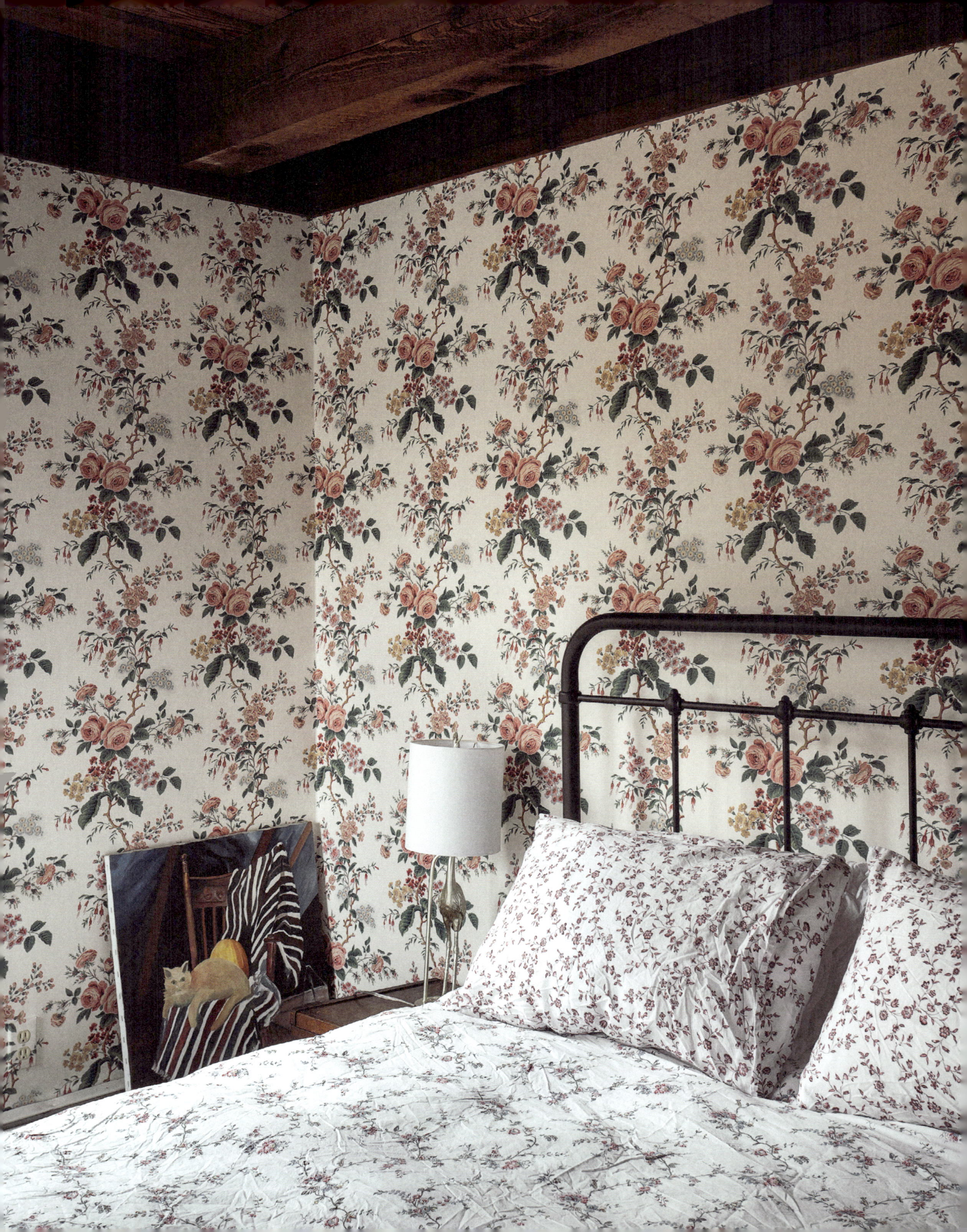

A Classic Post & Beam in Upstate New York

HUDSON, NEW YORK (US) **GENERAL ASSEMBLY**

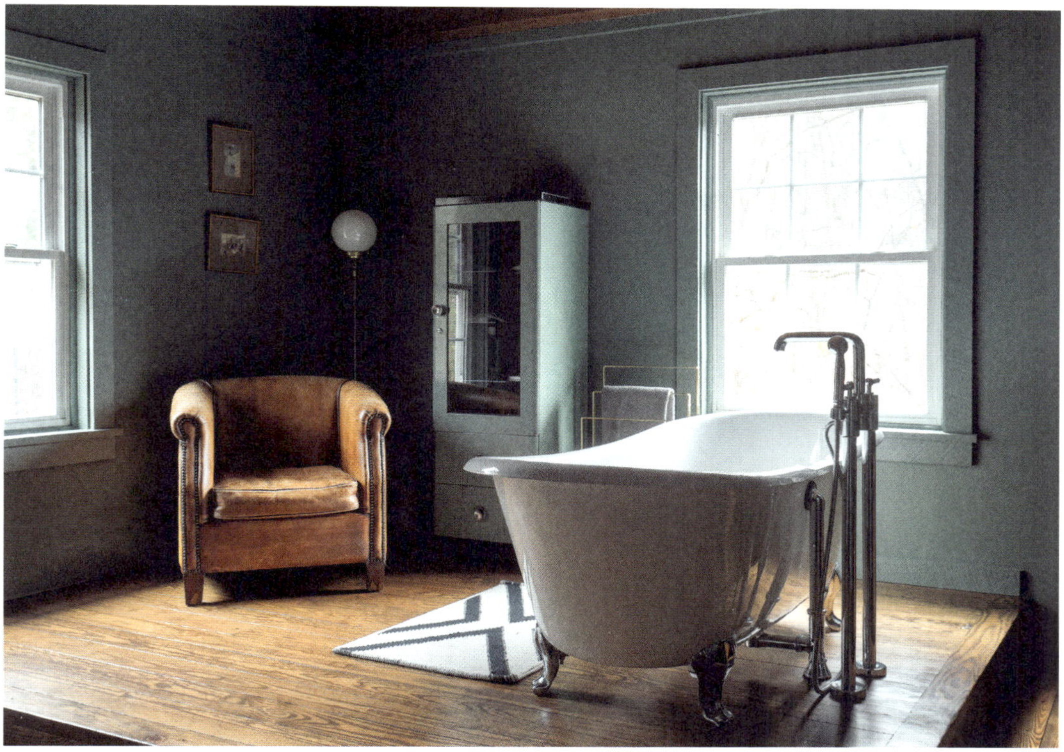

The town of Hudson, New York, just a few hours' drive north from New York City, has long been a refuge for erstwhile city dwellers looking for a simpler life – even if it's just for the weekend. Once a primarily agricultural community in the fertile Hudson Valley, which runs along the eponymous river and is known for its fruit orchards and organic farms, the town has become a buzzing cultural centre, which is why a bi-coastal family that works in the film industry chose this vibrant village as the site of their country getaway.

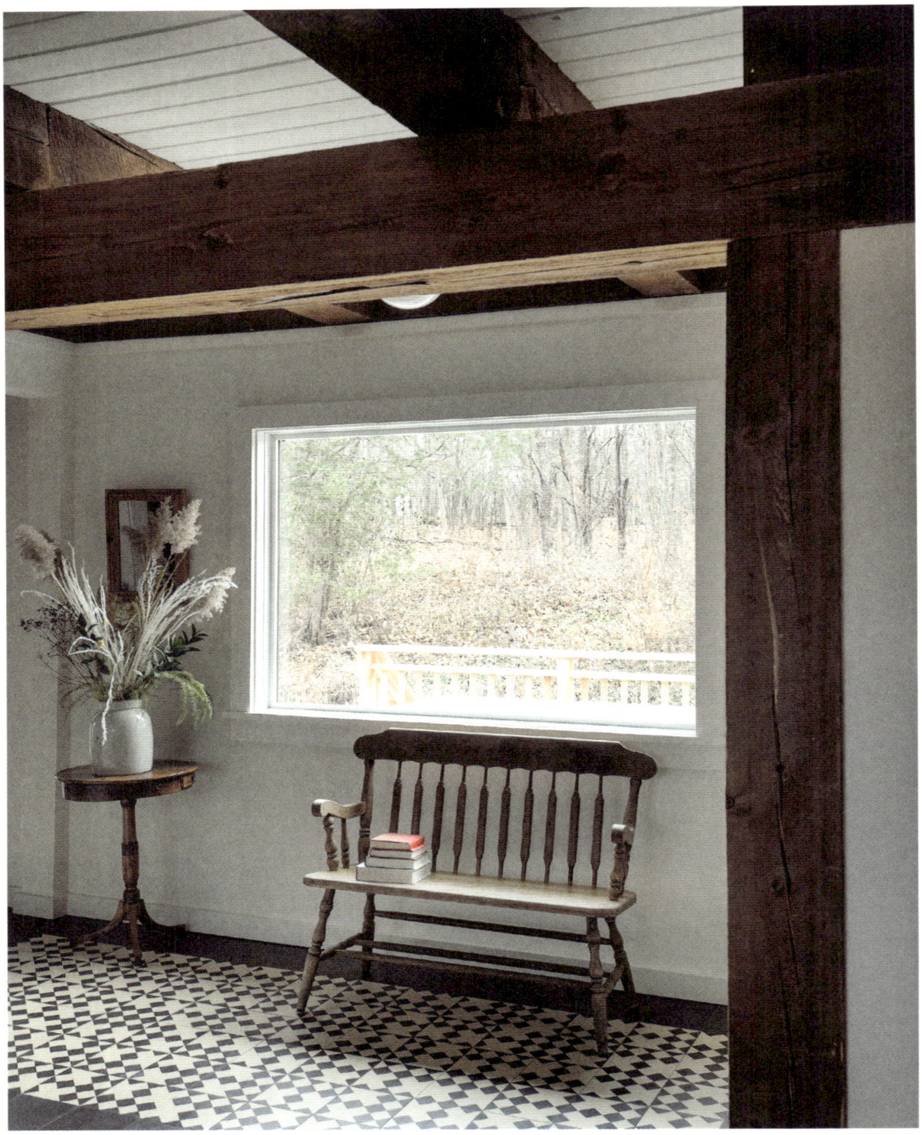

Originally built in 1977, this rustic former farmhouse was given a new life by Brooklyn-based firm General Assembly. Previously a rabbit warren of small, separate rooms, it was transformed by the firm's architects Sarah Zames and Colin Stief, who let the light in by pulling down non-essential walls and creating a single, communal space that centres around a whitewashed brick fireplace. The designers left the home's original dark-hued timber framing in place but chose to keep the vibe fresh and light by painting the walls and ceiling a subtle shade of cream and choosing furniture with natural wood tones. The couple turned a small corner of the main floor into a music room, a lively meeting place for friends and family where they keep an all-white grand piano – a family heirloom passed down from the previous generation.

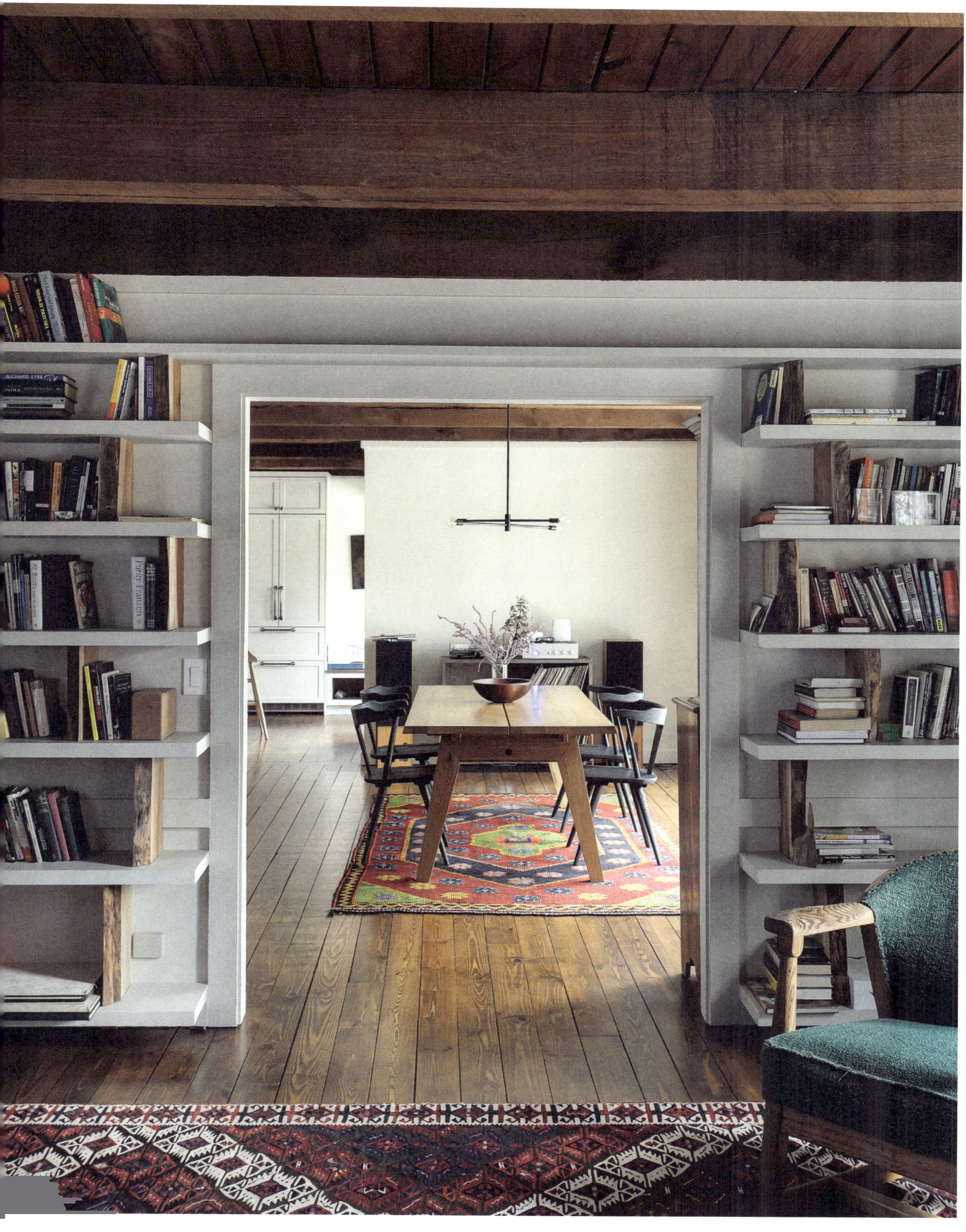
RICHARD EYRE
Ali Smith
Purity Franzen

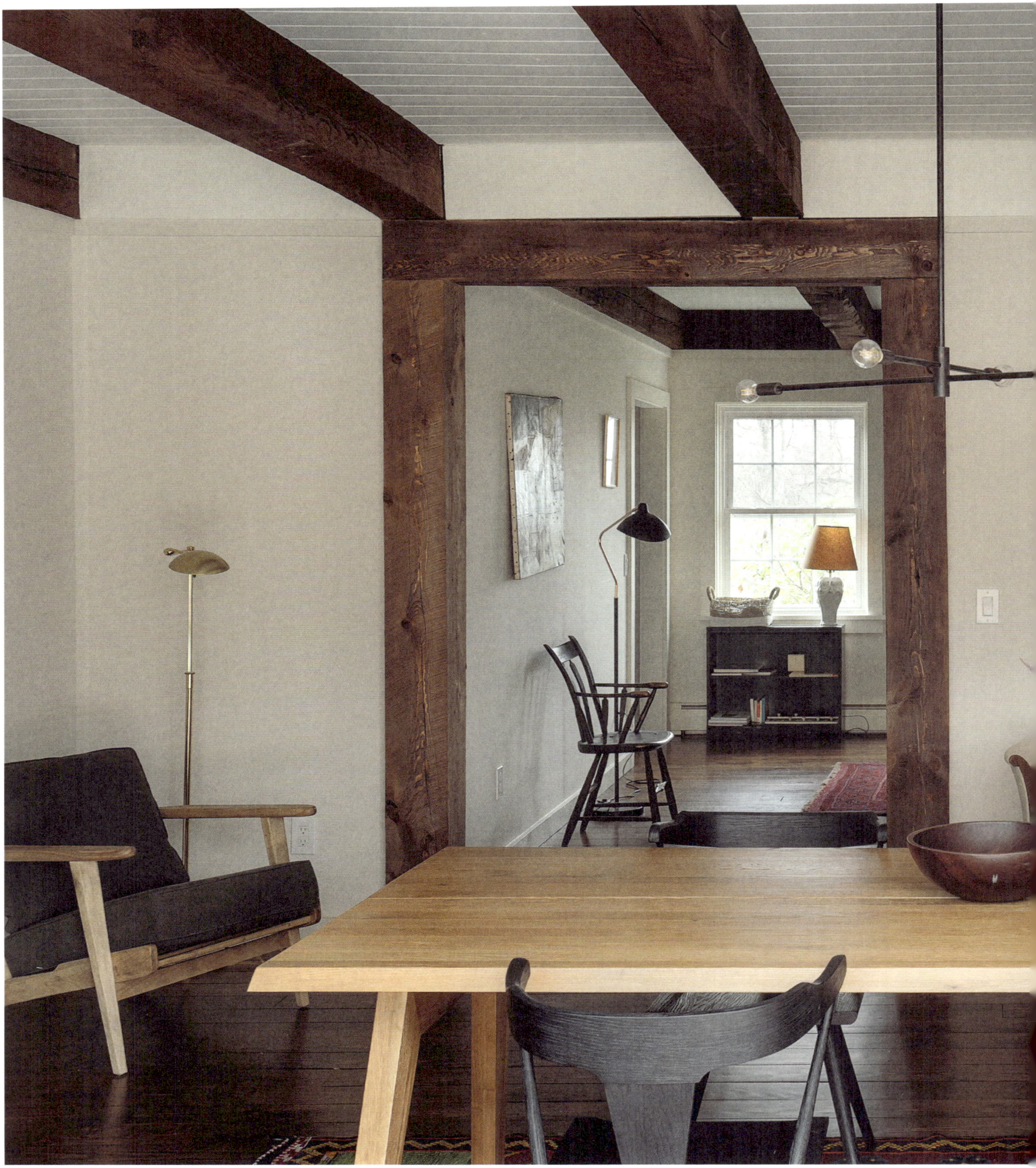

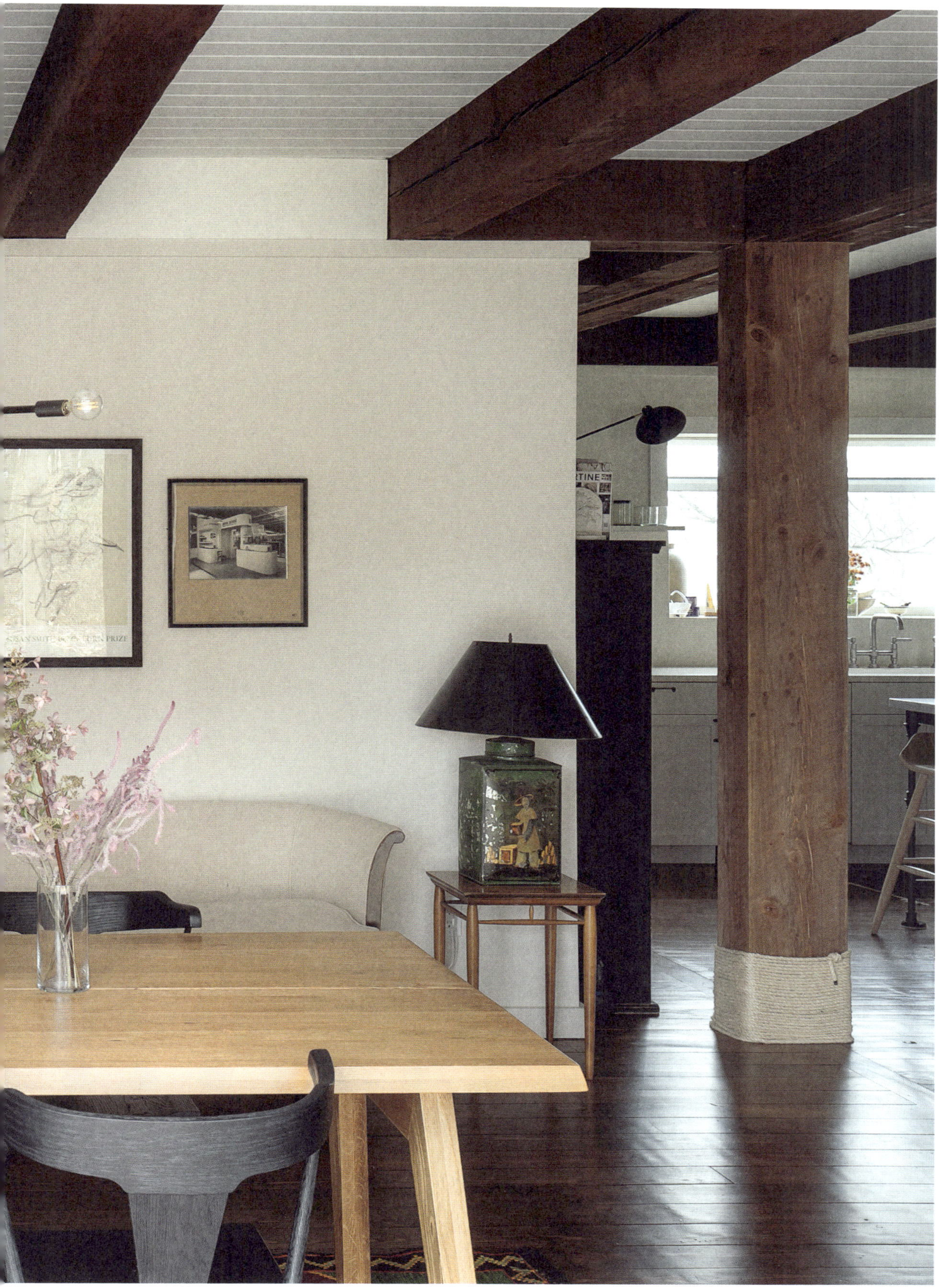

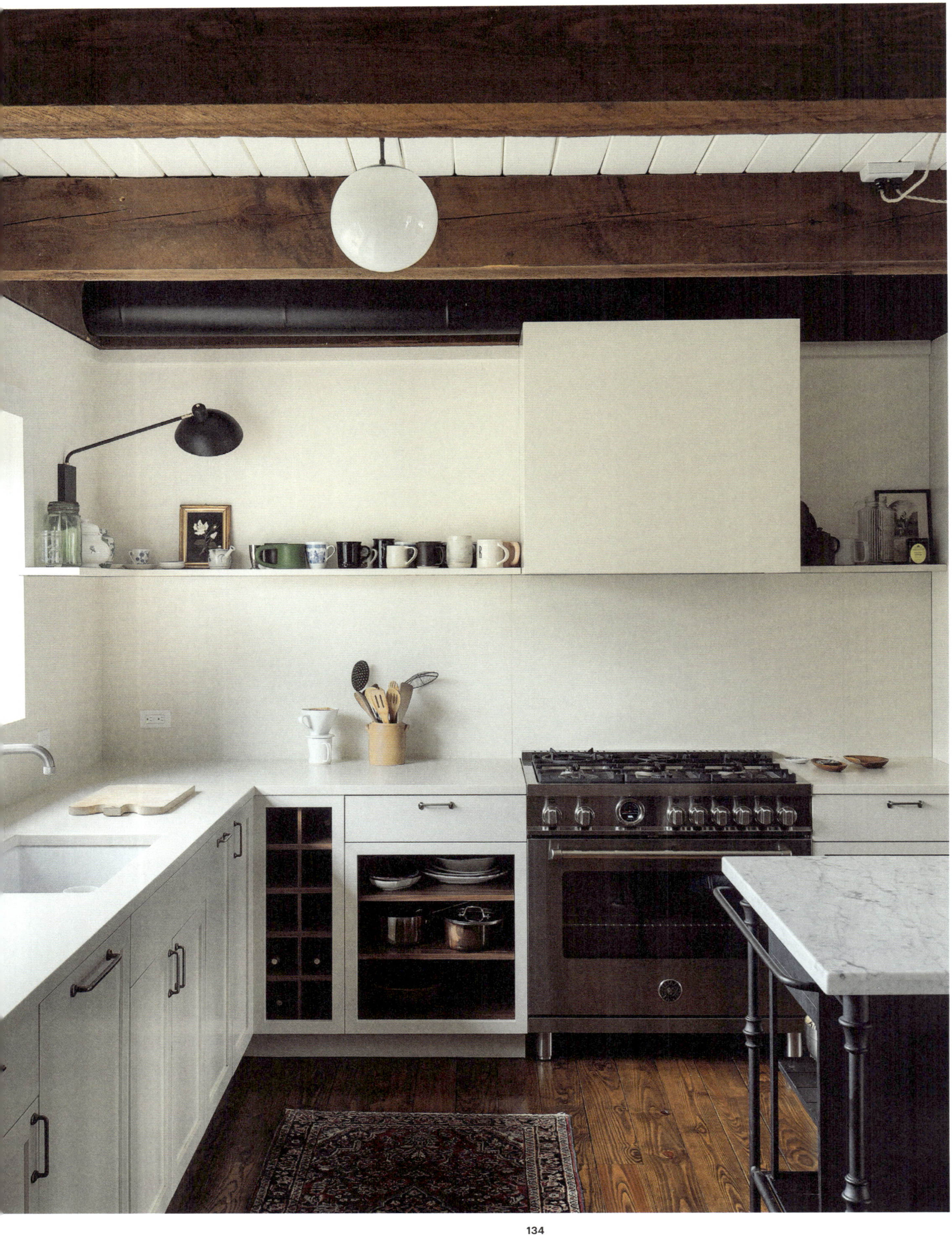

In the smaller, more private rooms – the office, main bedroom and guest room – they opted for a bolder palette and more eclectic furnishings, while also managing to leave part of the home's heritage intact. A pink-toned floral wallpaper, a remnant of the home's previous 1970s-era design, dominates the guest bedroom with its playfully chintzy motif. Another small bedroom was converted to a spacious bathroom with a free-standing claw-footed tub and painted a soothing shade of sage green – the ideal vantage point for soaking in the forest beyond.

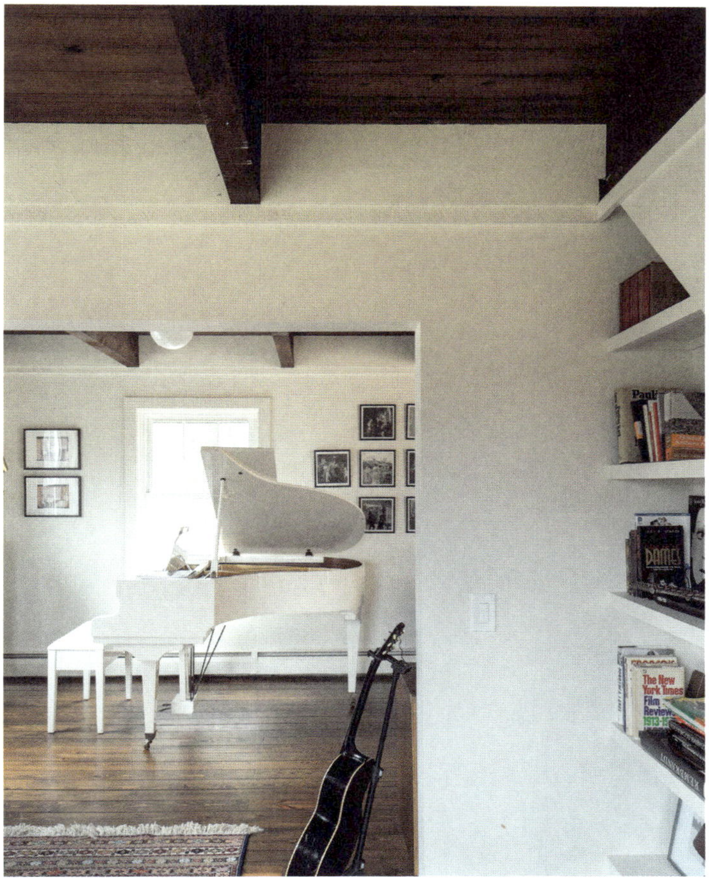

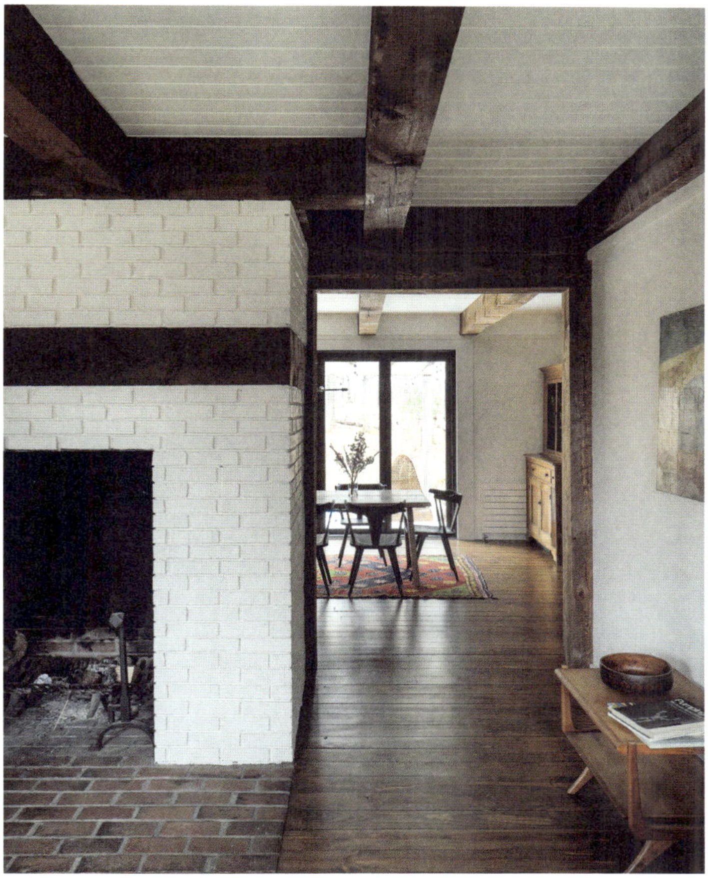

A Multigenerational Retreat in the French Countryside

VAUCLUSE, PROVENCE (FR) **TIMOTHEE MERCIER OF STUDIO XM**

The craggy hills and dense oak forests that make up the region of Vaucluse in south-eastern France are rich in history. Known as the Province of the Popes, the capital city of Avignon was the home of the papacy during the 14th century, and the Gothic architecture of the surrounding villages reflects this storied legacy. But, for architect Timothee Mercier of Studio XM, this pastoral refuge, roughly an hour and a half from the Côte d'Azure's turquoise waters, has long been the pilgrimage place of his family each holiday season. So, when his parents decided to renovate a broken-down farmhouse on their property, they kept the commission in the family. 'It was very special for me to be working somewhere I had spent most of my summers as a child,' Mercier says of the project.

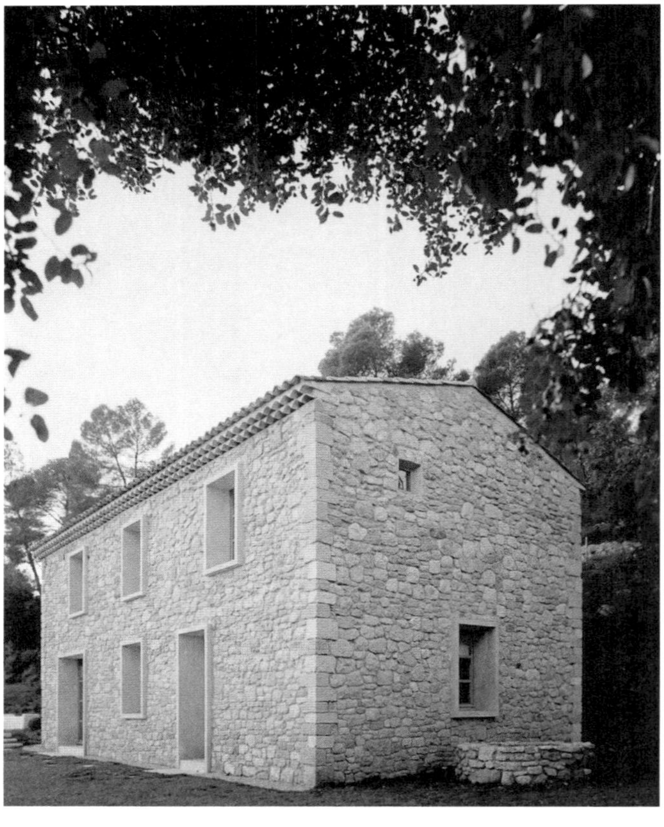

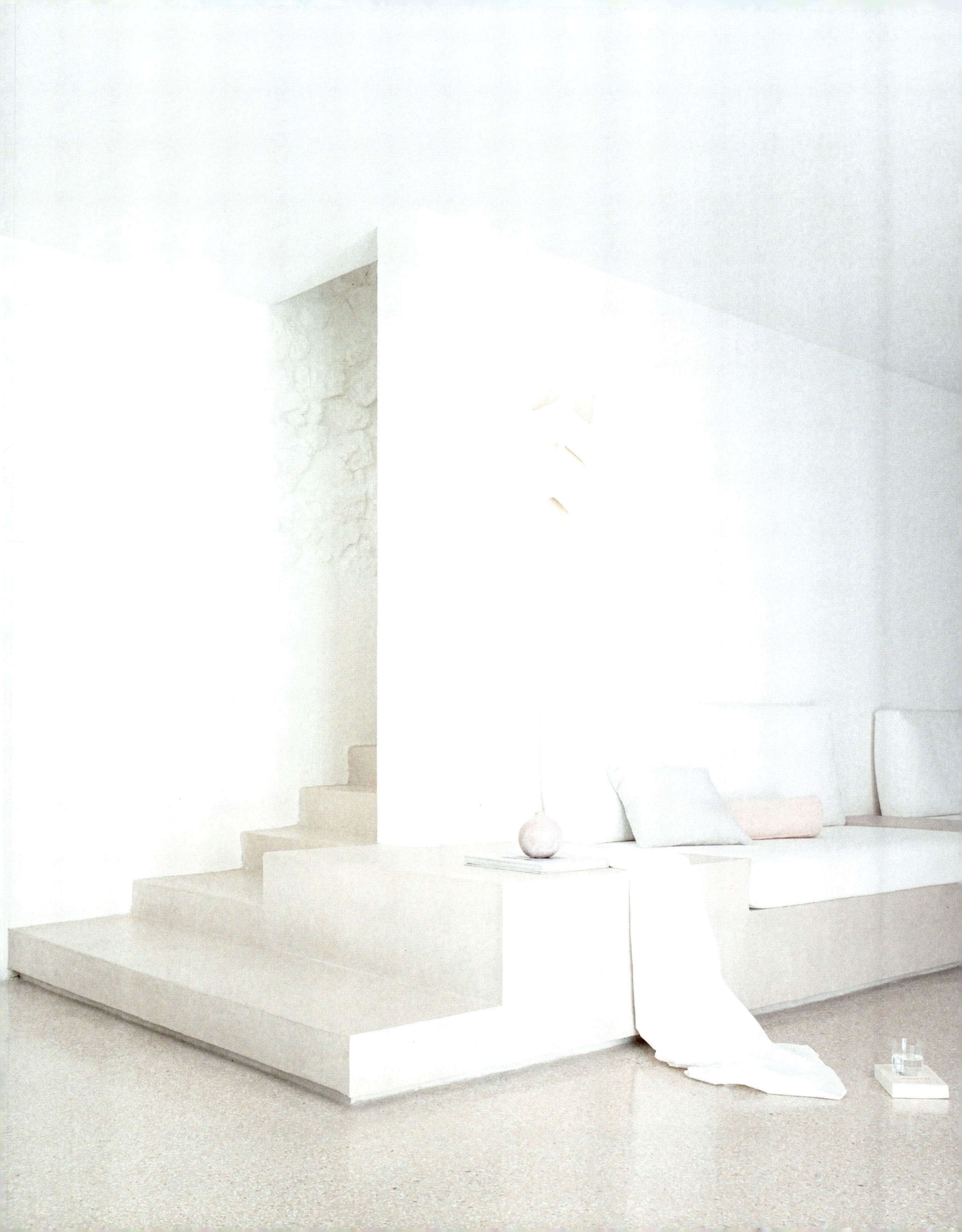

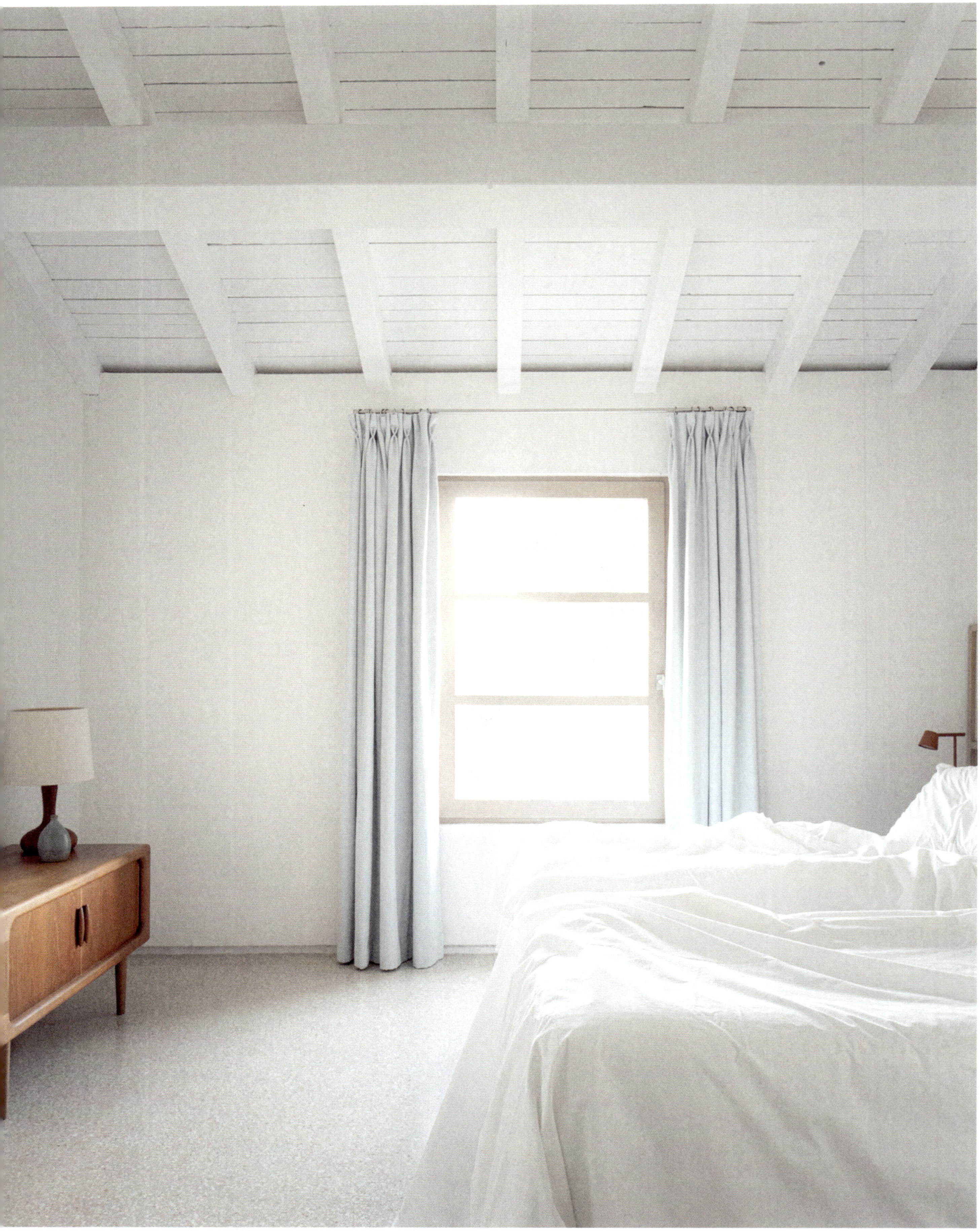

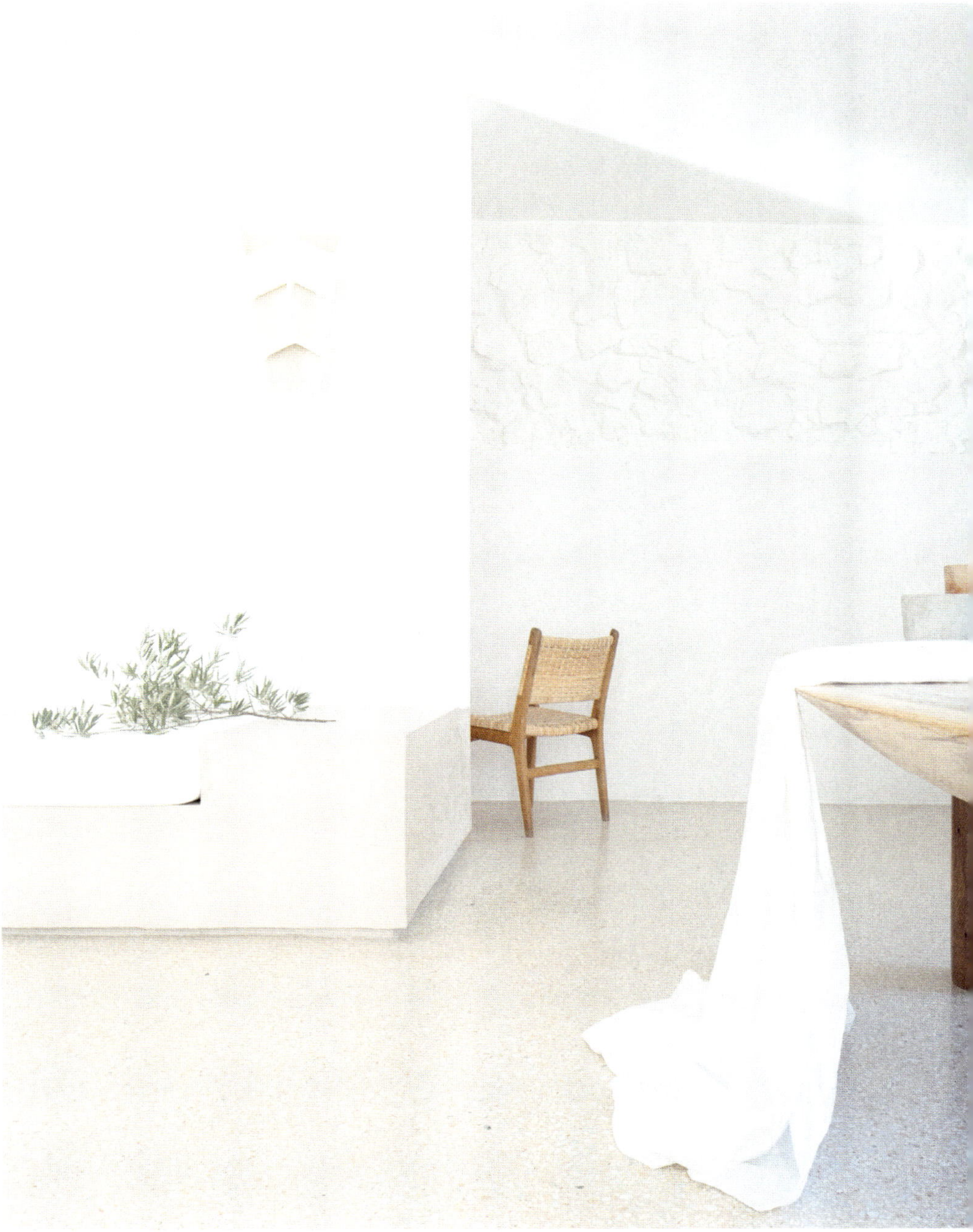

‘The site itself is very intimate,’ he continues. ‘The house sits at the base of a small, tree-covered hill in the middle of the countryside. When summer comes around it gets progressively nestled in the forest, without ever losing views of the vineyard below.’

While the exterior of the house was faithfully restored to its former rough stone glory, he kept the interior concept minimal in order to create a feeling of total zen. He finished the walls with *chaux*, a local lime plaster that imbues the surface with an organic, handmade texture, while the windows casings, door frames and kitchen cabinetry were carved from local oak, contrasting the stark white with a uniform shade of blond wood.

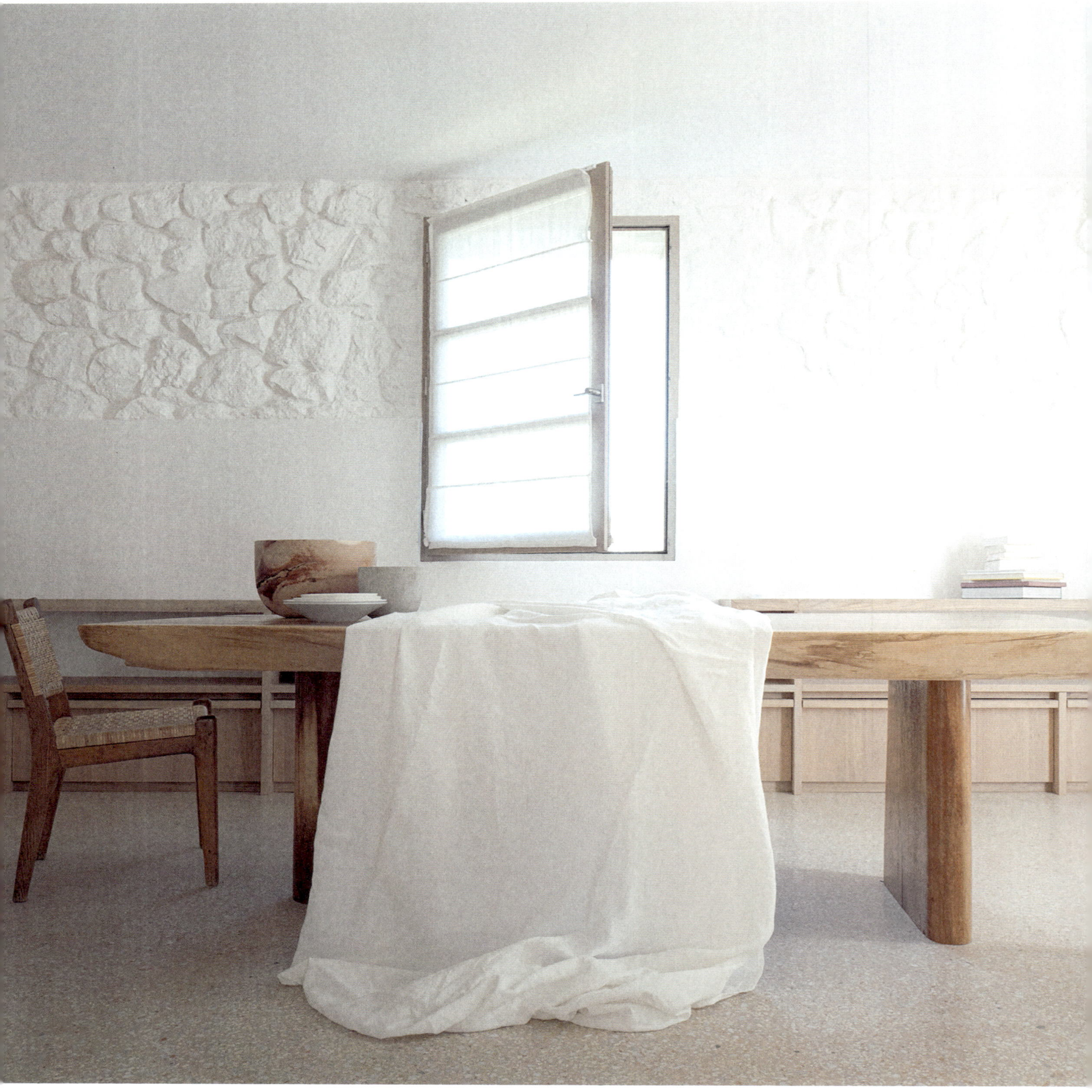

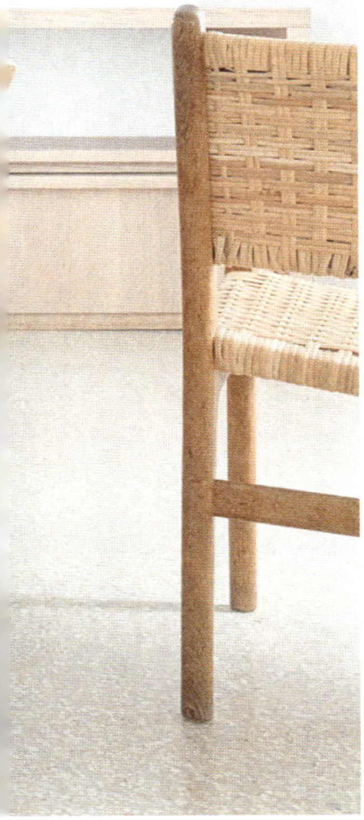

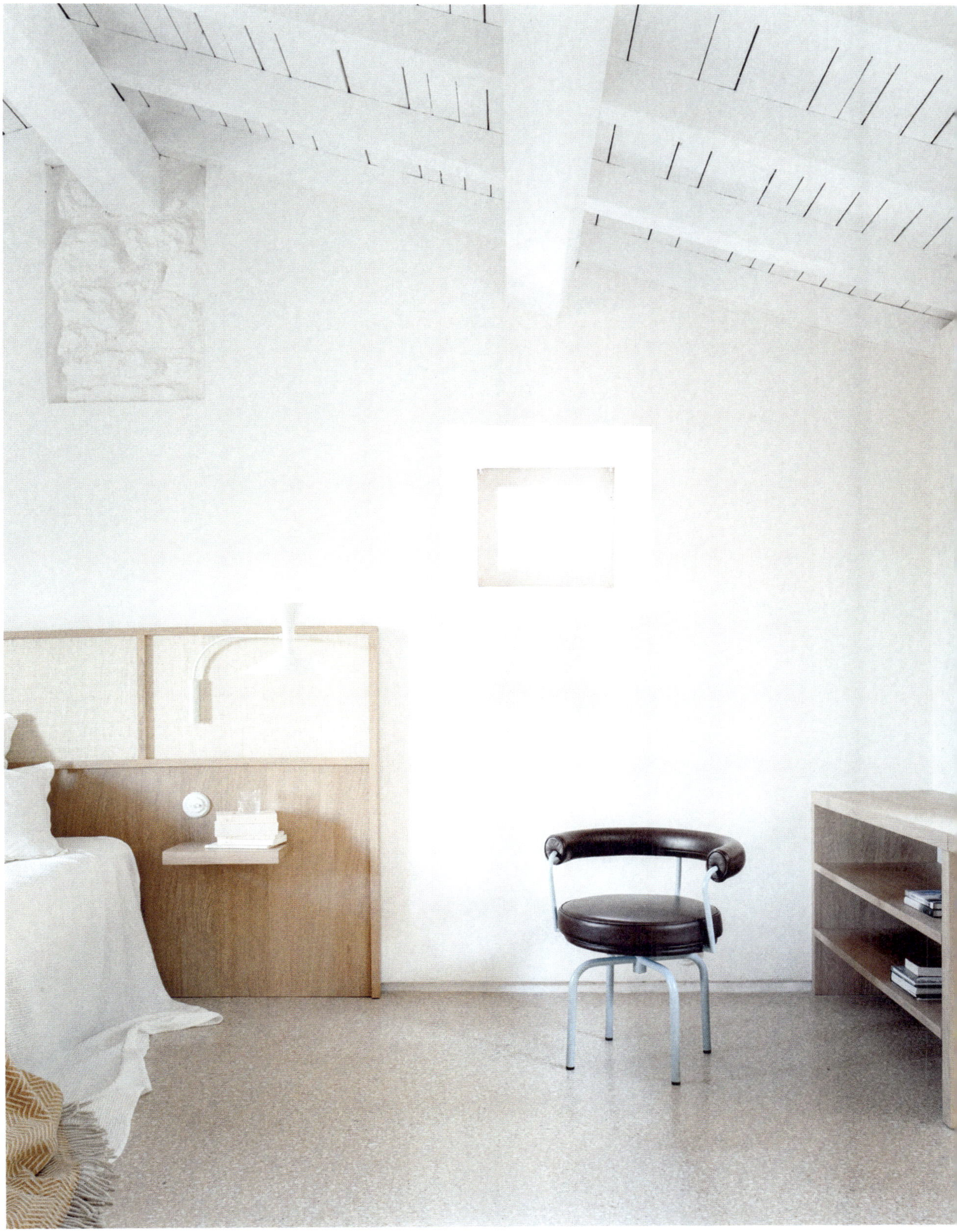

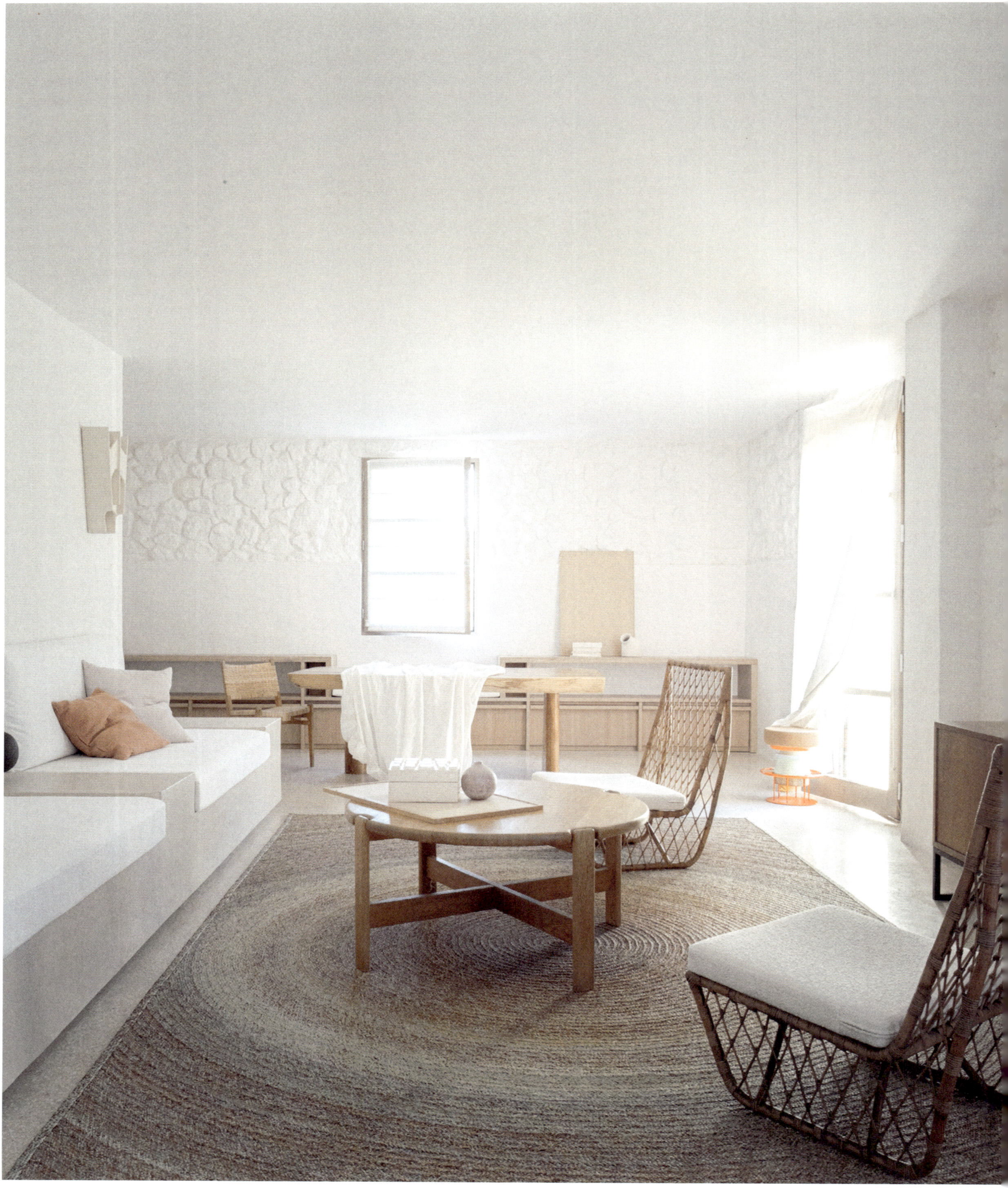

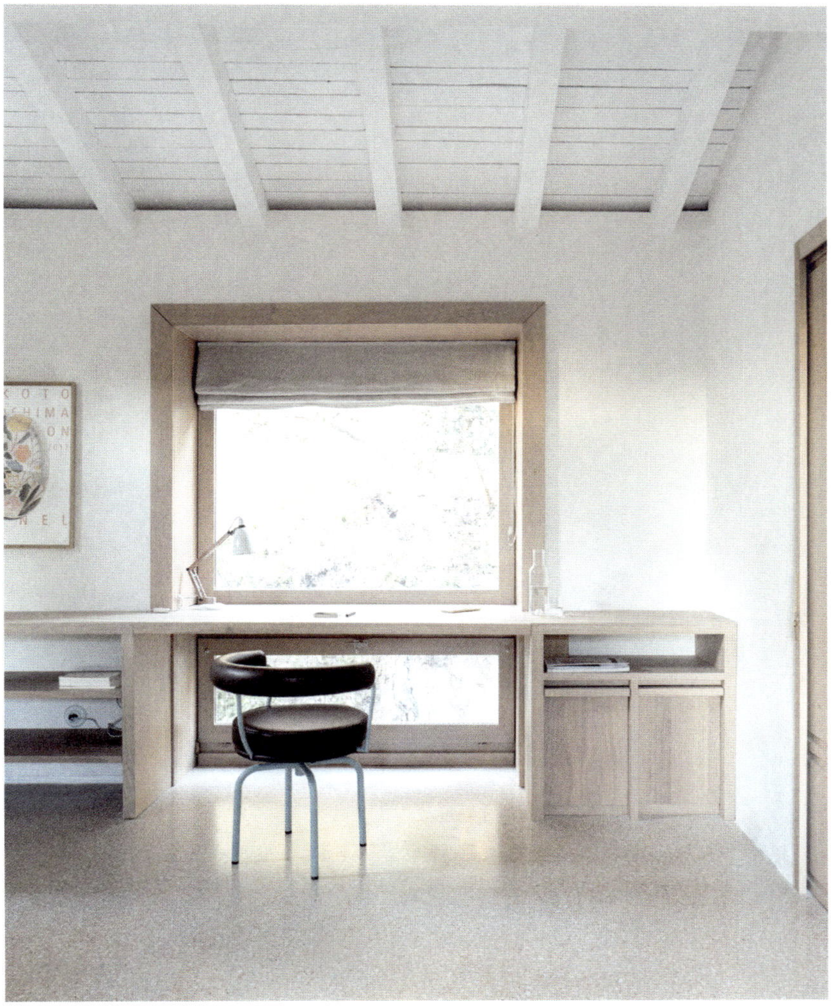

'I decided early on to infuse the house with the monastic qualities of its surroundings,' he explains of the design, made up of a succession of sparsely furnished rooms. He chose a mix of humble pieces like rattan chairs, simple wooden tables and vintage lamps – much of which was picked up at a flea market in nearby Marseille – alongside design icons by French mid-century masters such as Charlotte Perriand and Le Corbusier. 'It had to be a spectacle,' he adds, 'but a discreet one.'

A Whitewashed Holiday House among the Orange Groves

TAVIRA, ALGARVE (PT) **ATELIER RUA**

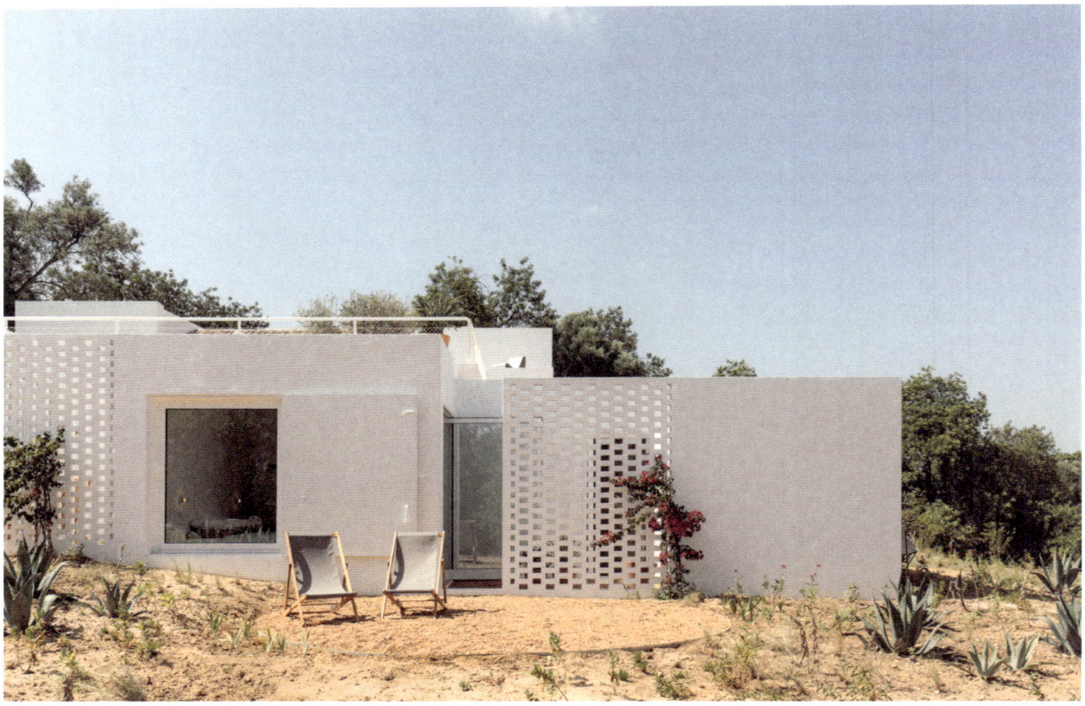

The Algarve region of Portugal often gets a bad rap. Known for package holidays and all-inclusive resorts, it is not often associated with sophisticated boltholes or secluded escapes. But just inland from the hustle and bustle are a network of quiet farming towns, their rural charms perfectly preserved in time. It is exactly this pastoral appeal that attracted Belgian hospitality entrepreneurs Ludovic Beun and Bert Jeuris of The Addresses to this part of the country – a 30-minute drive from the Spanish border and butting up against the picturesque Ria Formosa Natural Park. 'We wanted to honour the simplicity of the Portuguese countryside past by uplifting it with modern architecture that meets the standards of today's travelling nomads,' the pair say of their motivation to base their first venture, Casa Um, here.

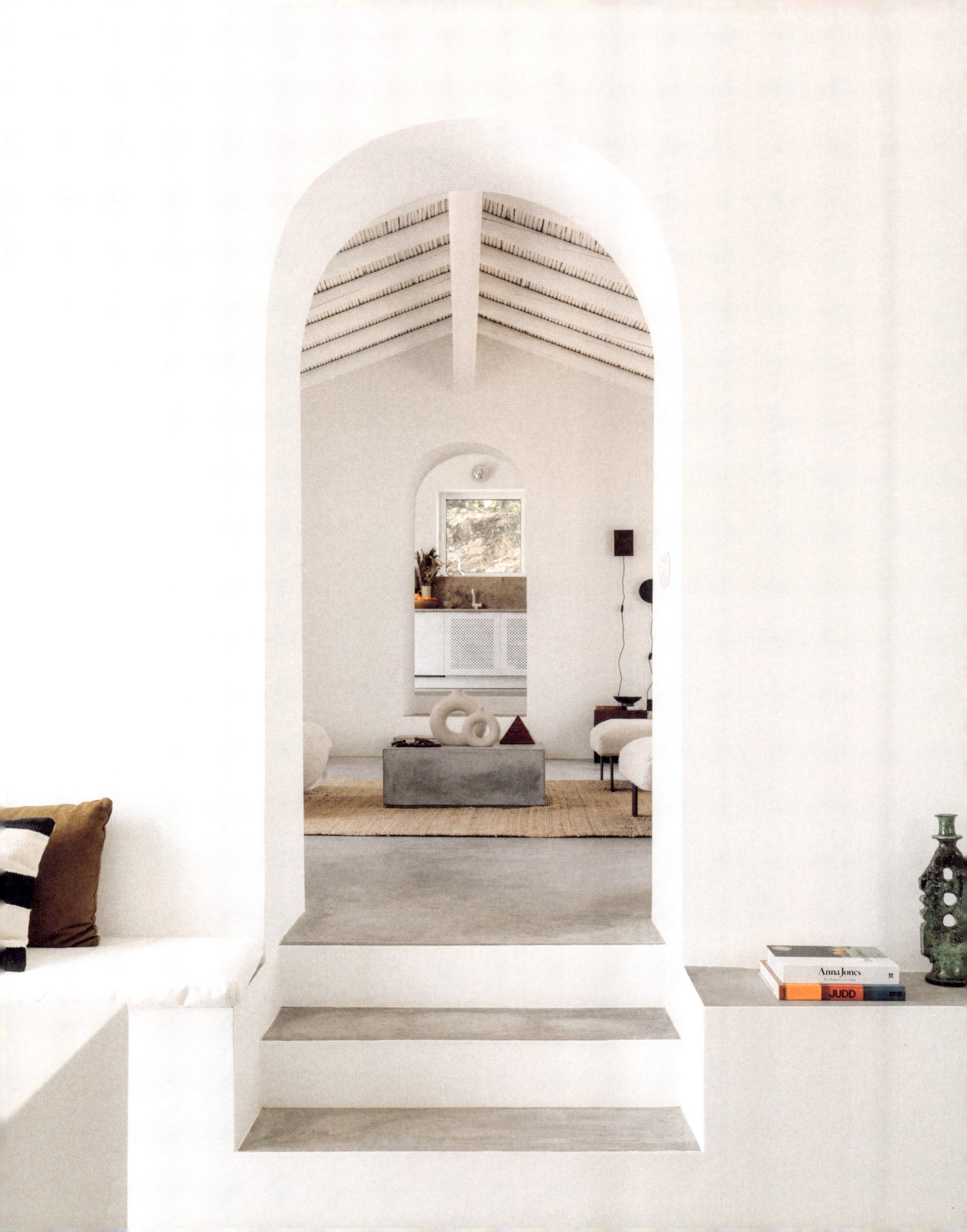
Anna Jones
JUDD

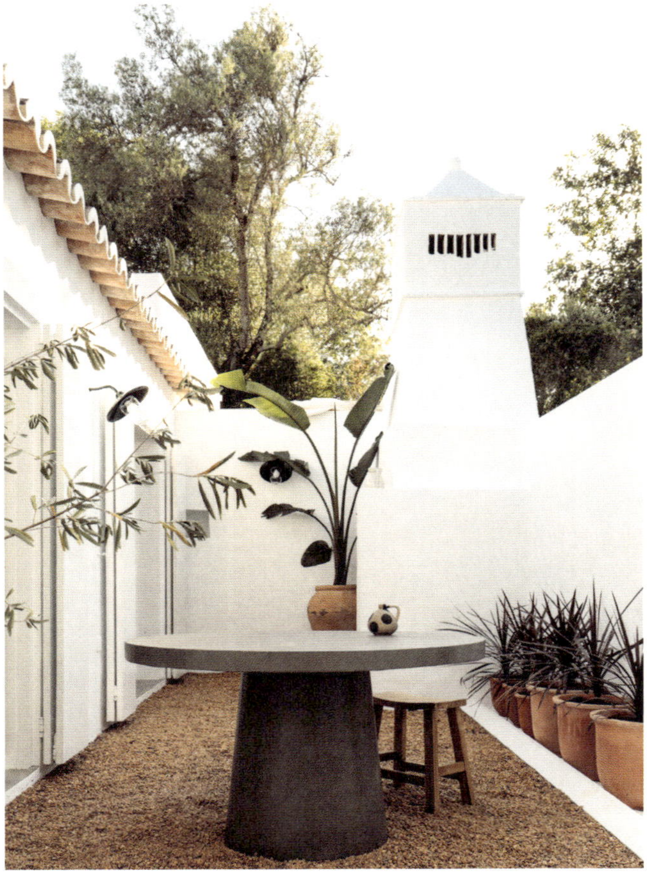

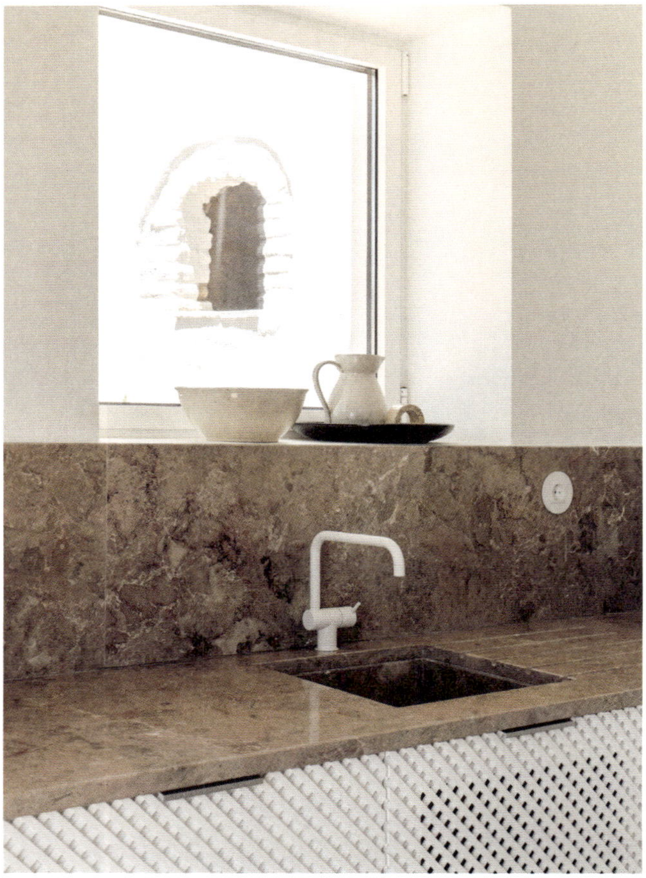

A renovated Portuguese quinta (a traditional farm surrounded by a vast agricultural property, usually planted with either citrus groves or vines) provides the structure for this minimal-minded holiday home, designed by the Lisbon-based Atelier Rua, which describes the home as 'a modernist take on Portuguese traditions'. Following a palette of whites, creams, greys and natural materials like marble and wood, the designers stripped back the layers of this old stone building to create a truly inviting retreat.

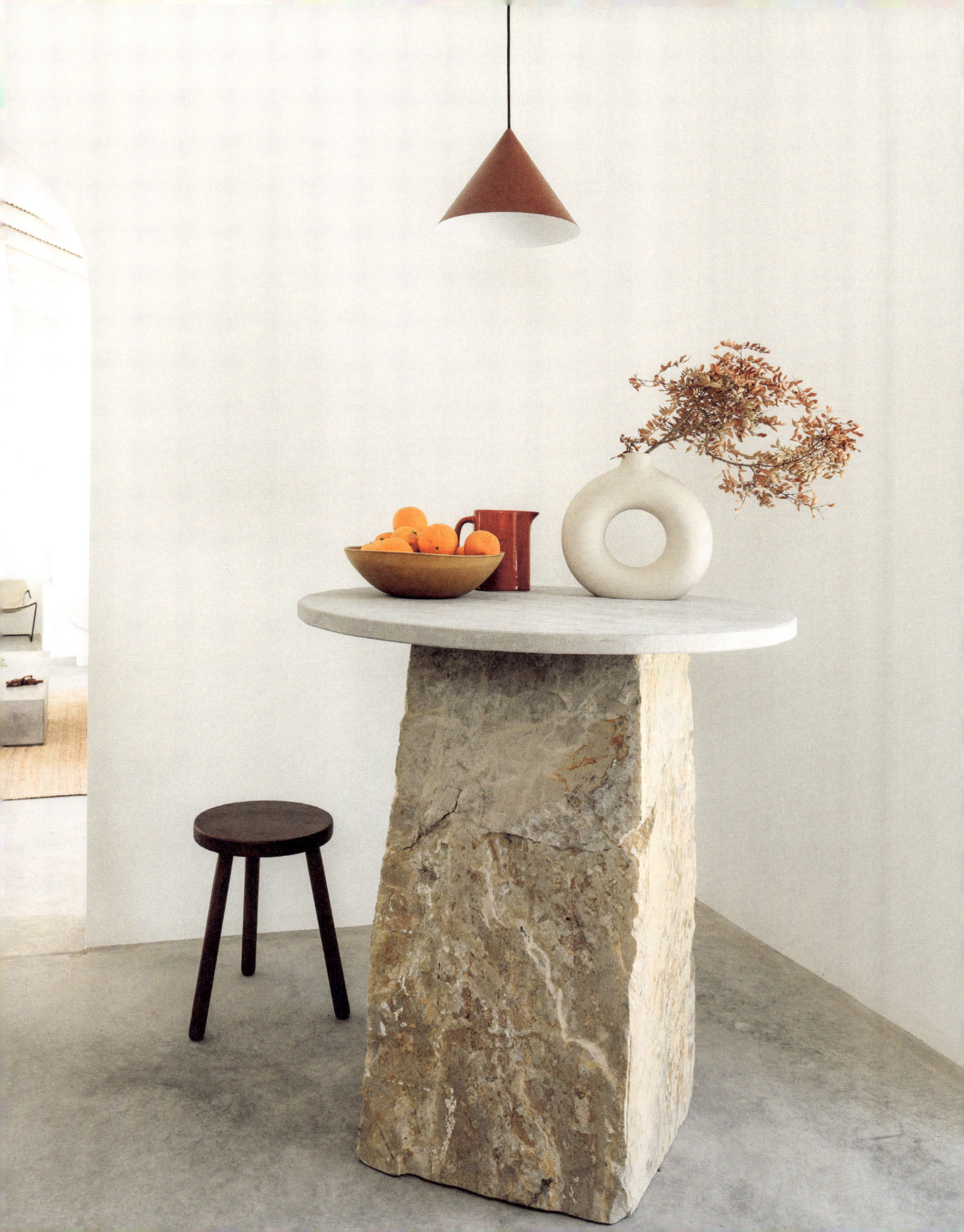

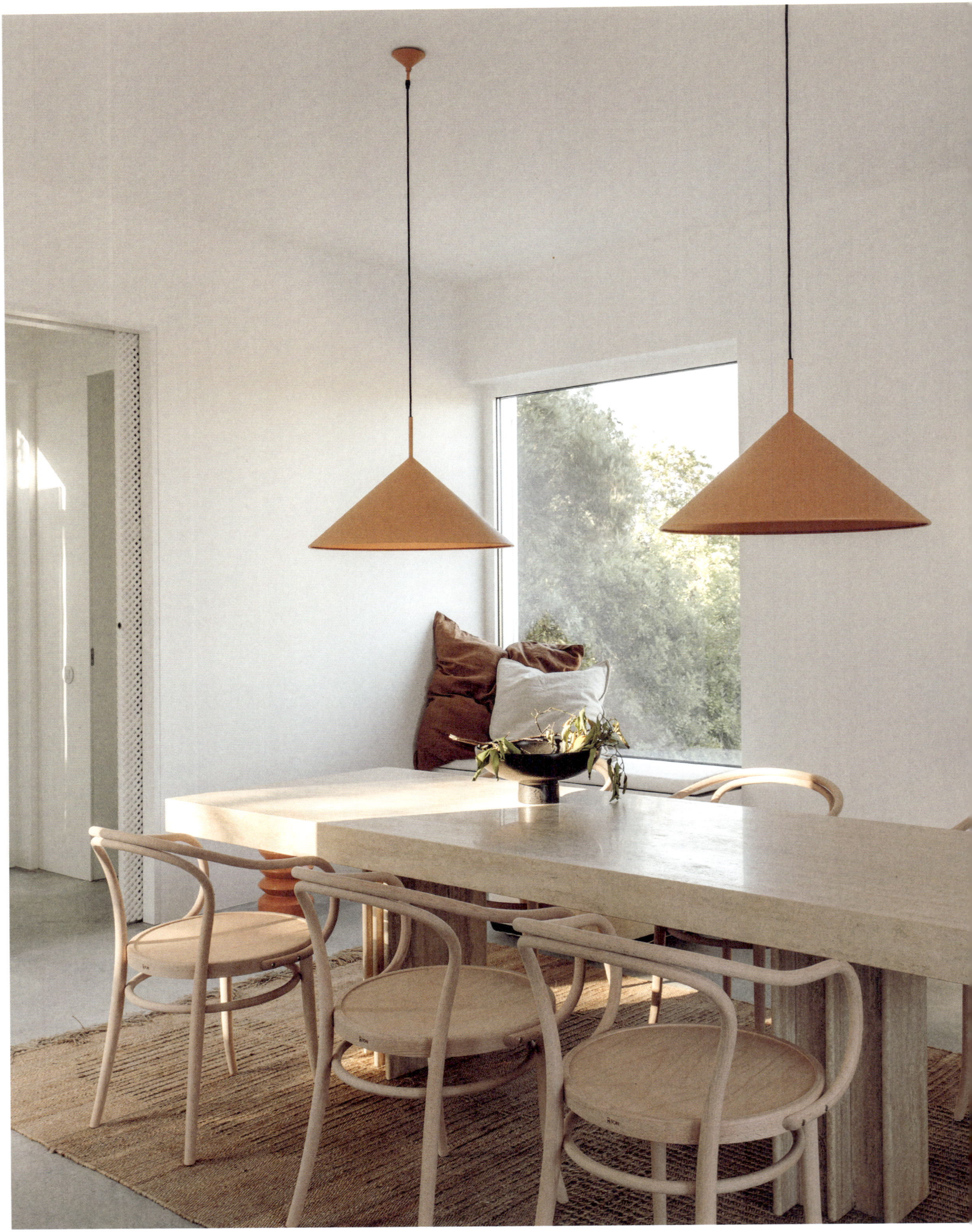

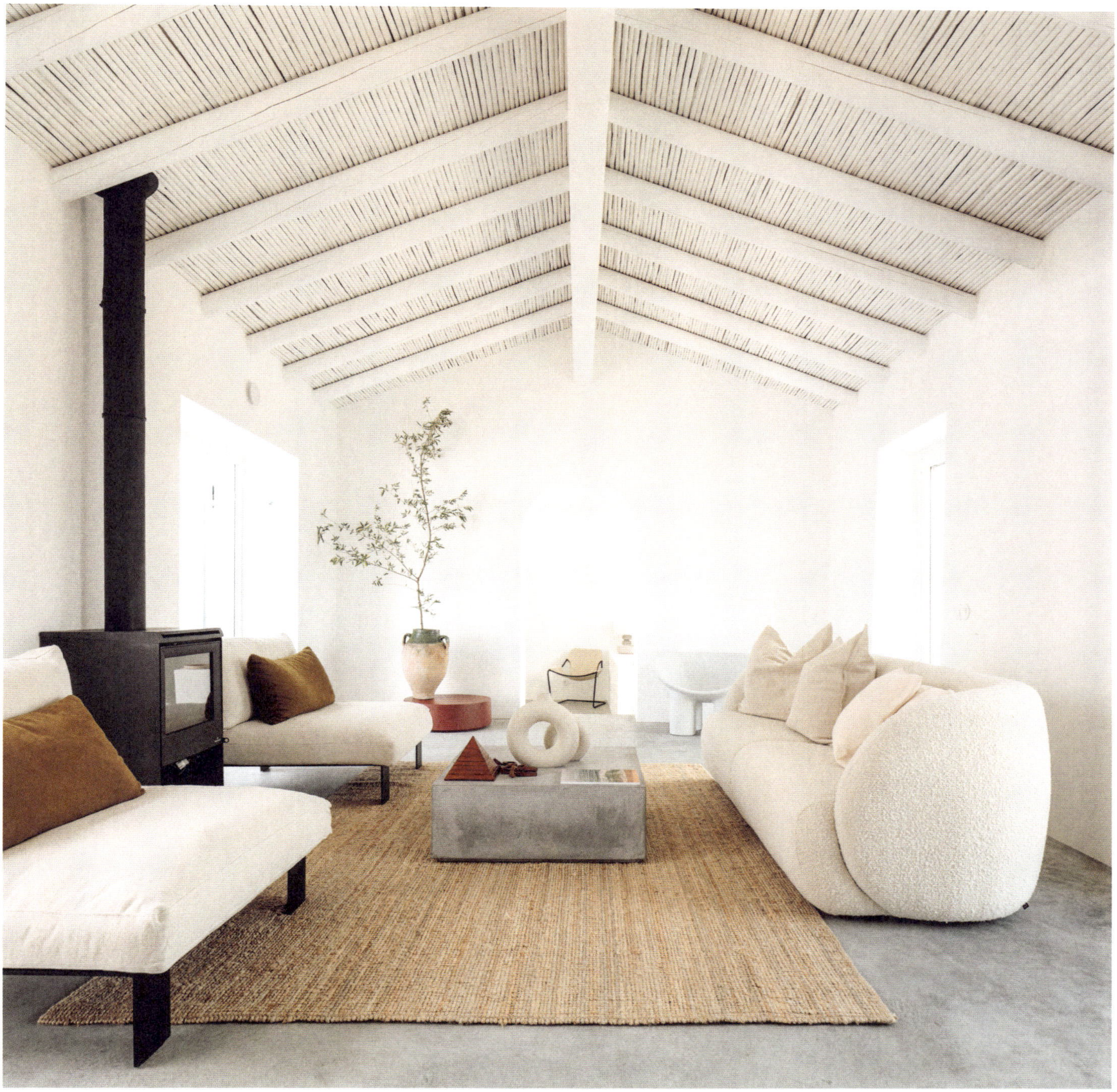

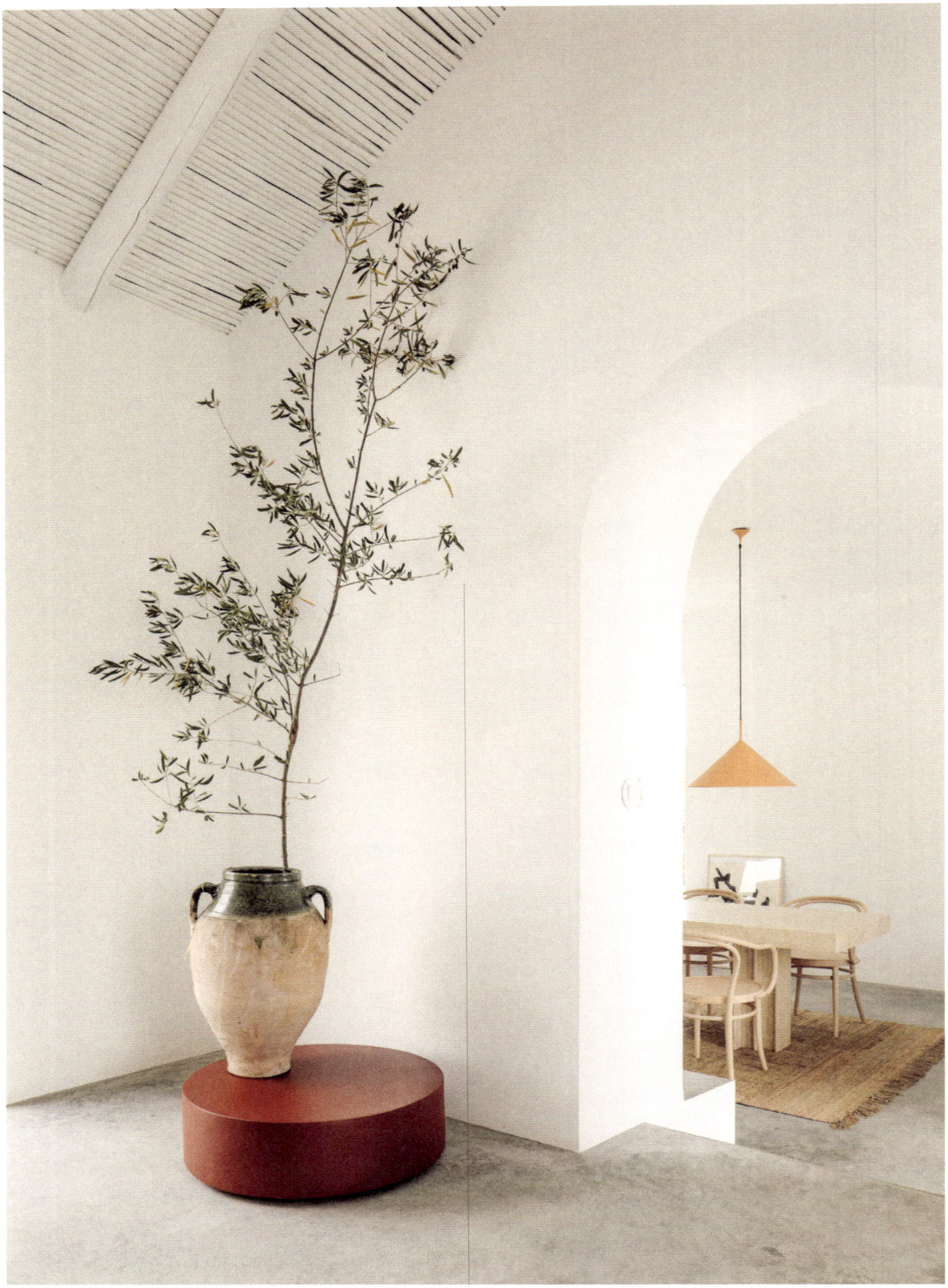

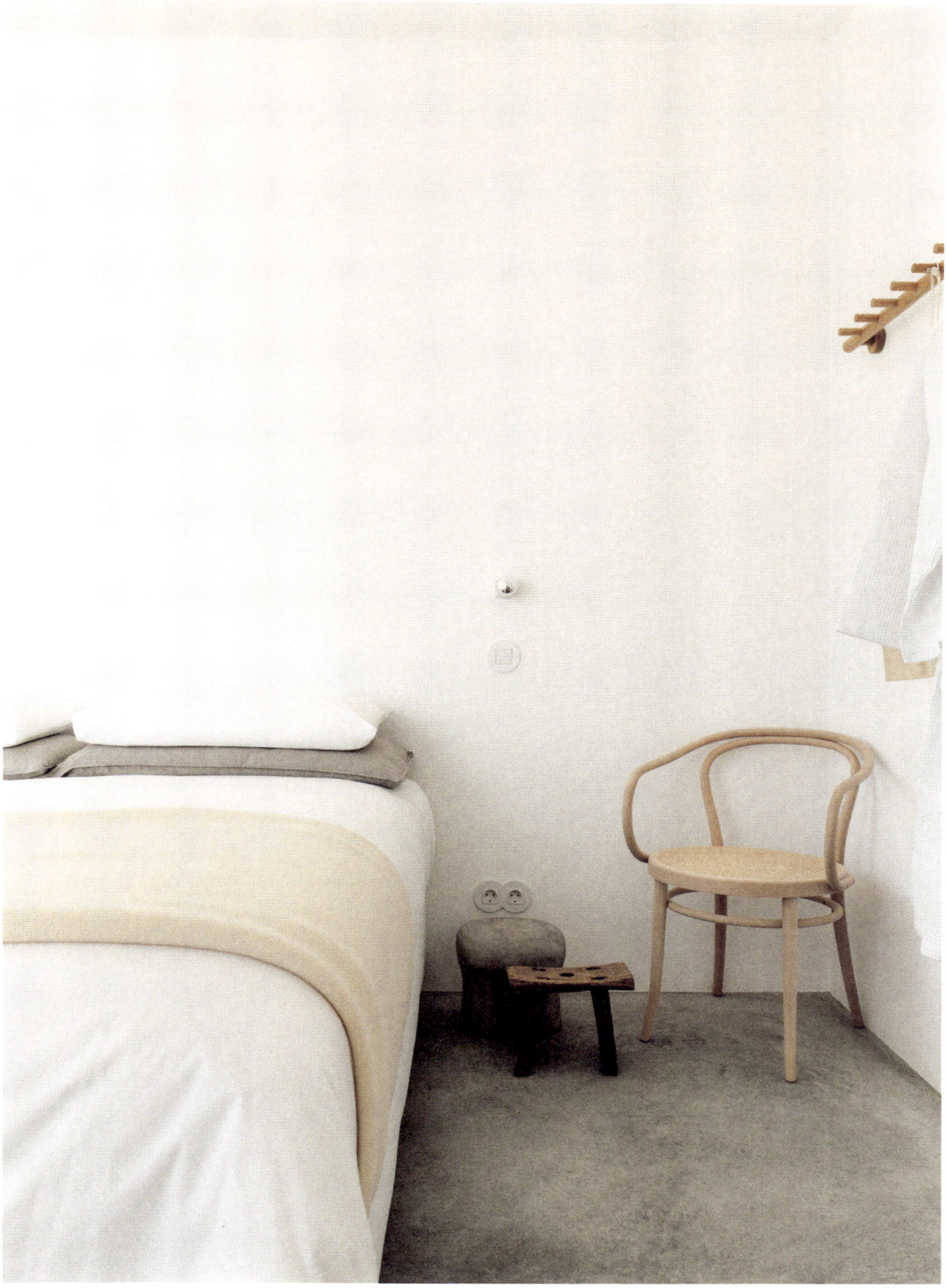

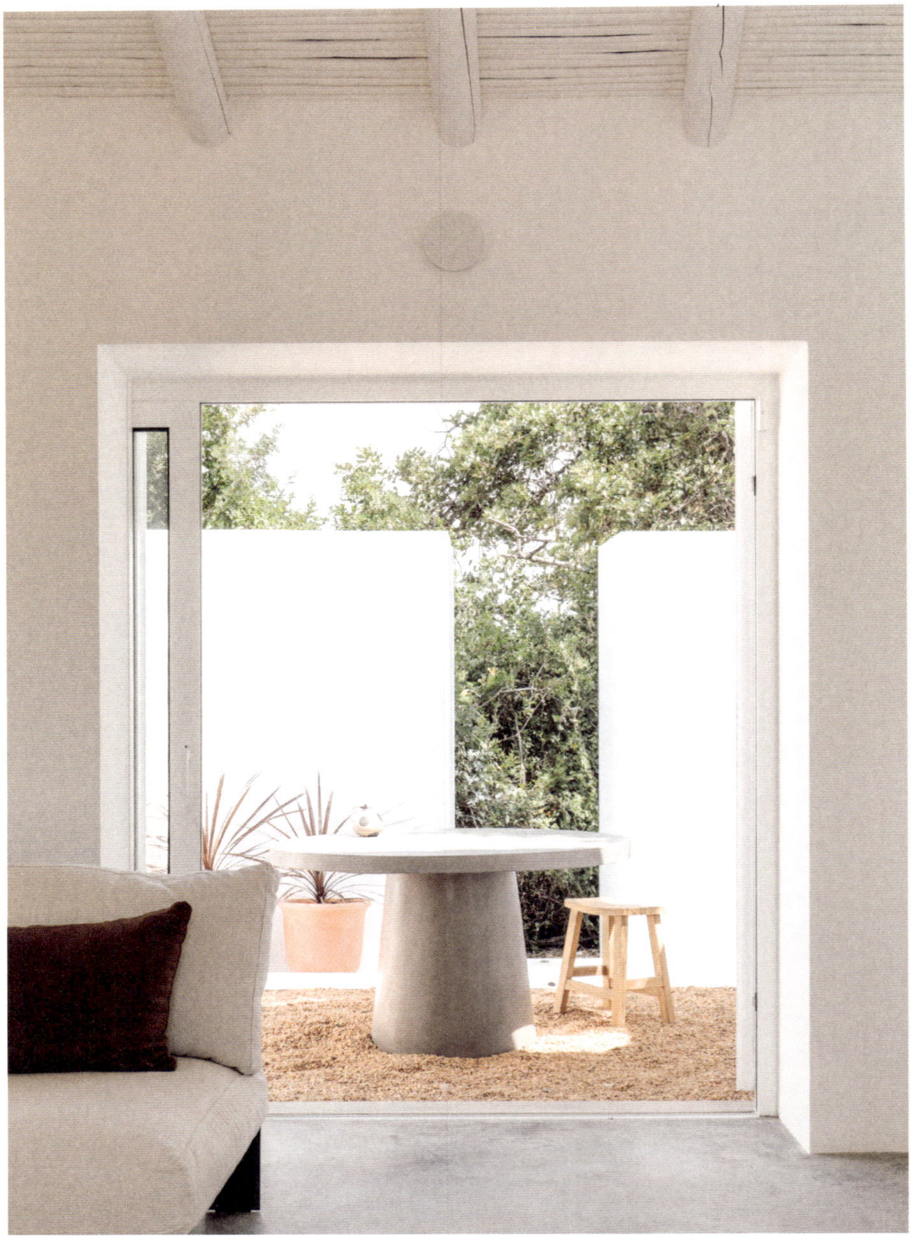

The property's main farmhouse was converted into the living room, a spartan but cosy lounge with overstuffed sofas and a cast-iron stove to warm the home in colder months. The architects left the original volume largely unaltered – including the gabled wooden roof, which was painted white – but cut generous openings in the walls to allow the sun to naturally filter in as well as provide access to the intimate terrace. On the opposite end of the property, the former stables were turned into a dining room, which looks onto the pool and, just beyond, rolling meadows bursting with fragrant citrus trees.

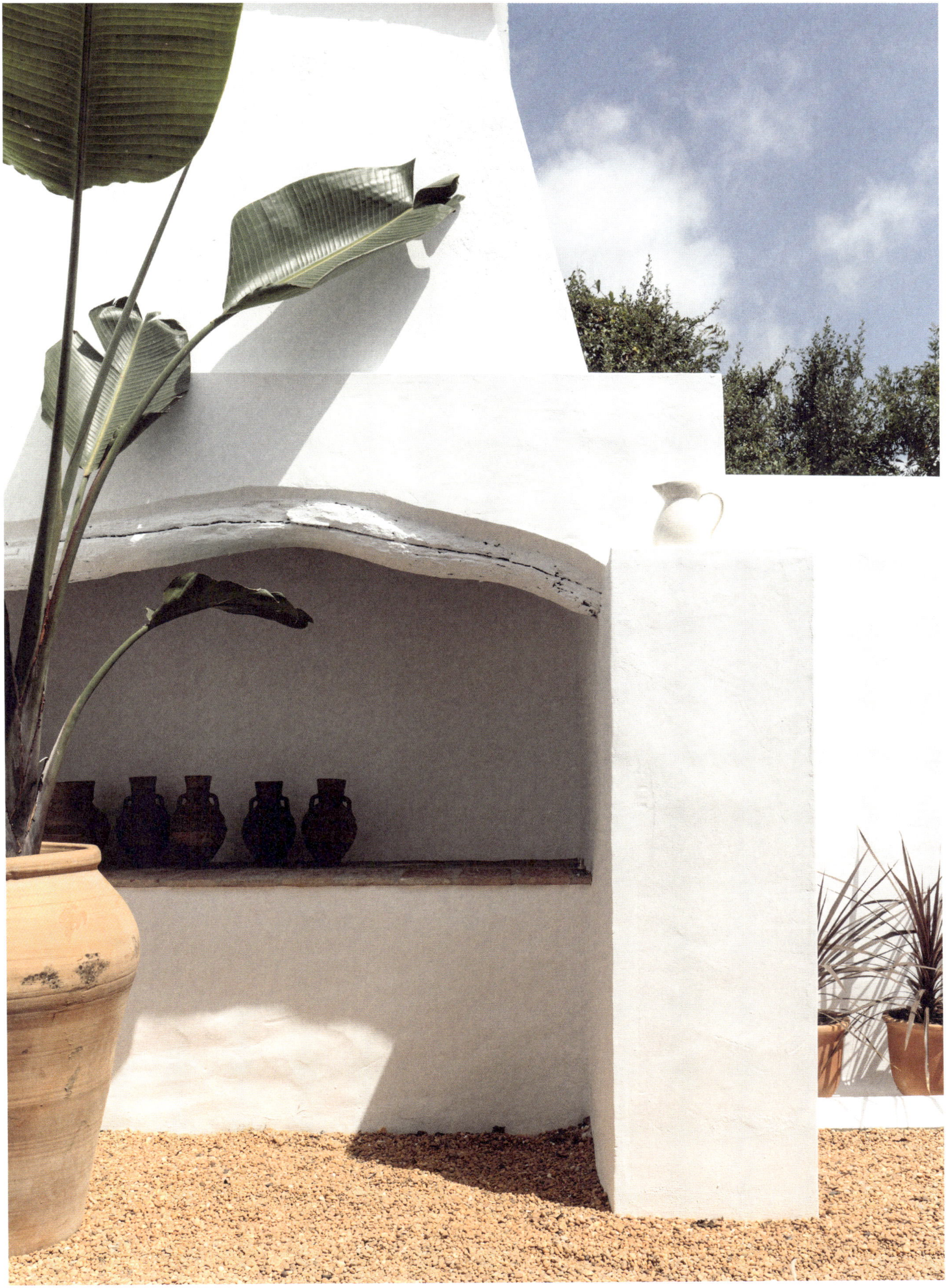

A Centuries-Old Stone Farmhouse in the Canadian Countryside

PRINCE EDWARD COUNTY, ONTARIO (CA)

JOHN BAKER & JULI DAOUST BAKER

The fertile farmlands that make up the south-eastern fringes of the Canadian province of Ontario are known for their abundant fruit orchards and miles of vineyards. A popular weekend getaway for city dwellers hailing from the nearby metropolis of Toronto, the region, which was settled by Scottish and Irish immigrant farmers in the 1700s, is still populated by quaint Victorian villages and rustic homesteads nestled into the hilly landscape. In 2018, the founders of design shop Mjölk, John Baker and Juli Daoust Baker, came into possession of their very own slice of Canadian history in the form of a run-down stone farmhouse from centuries past.

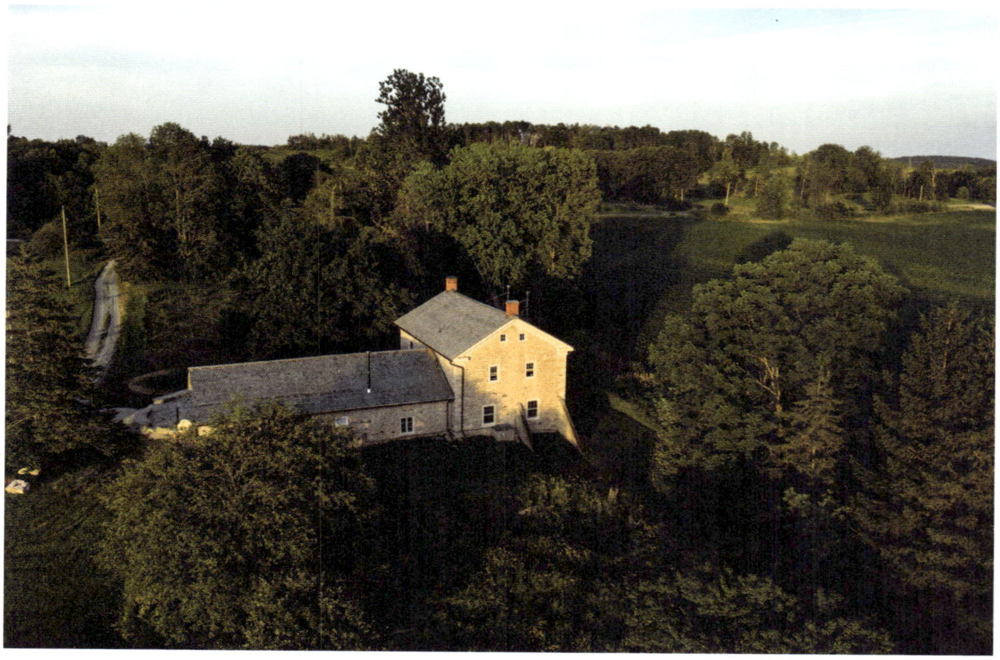

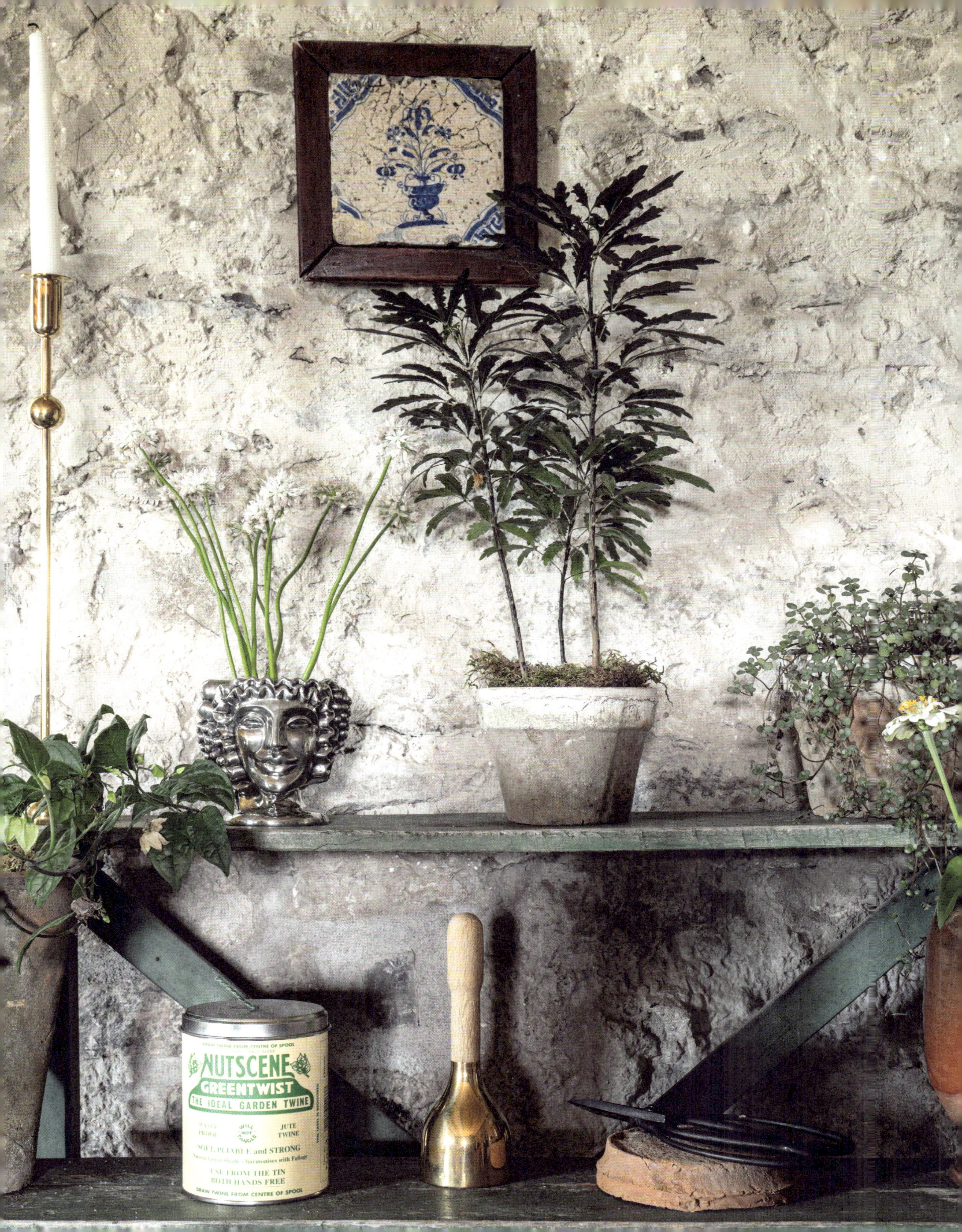
DRAW TWINE FROM CENTRE OF SPOOL
NUTSCENE
GREENTWIST
THE IDEAL GARDEN TWINE
WASTE PROOF
WILL NOT TANGLE
JUTE TWINE
SOFT, PLIABLE and STRONG
USE FROM THE TIN
BOTH HANDS FREE
DRAW TWINE FROM CENTRE OF SPOOL

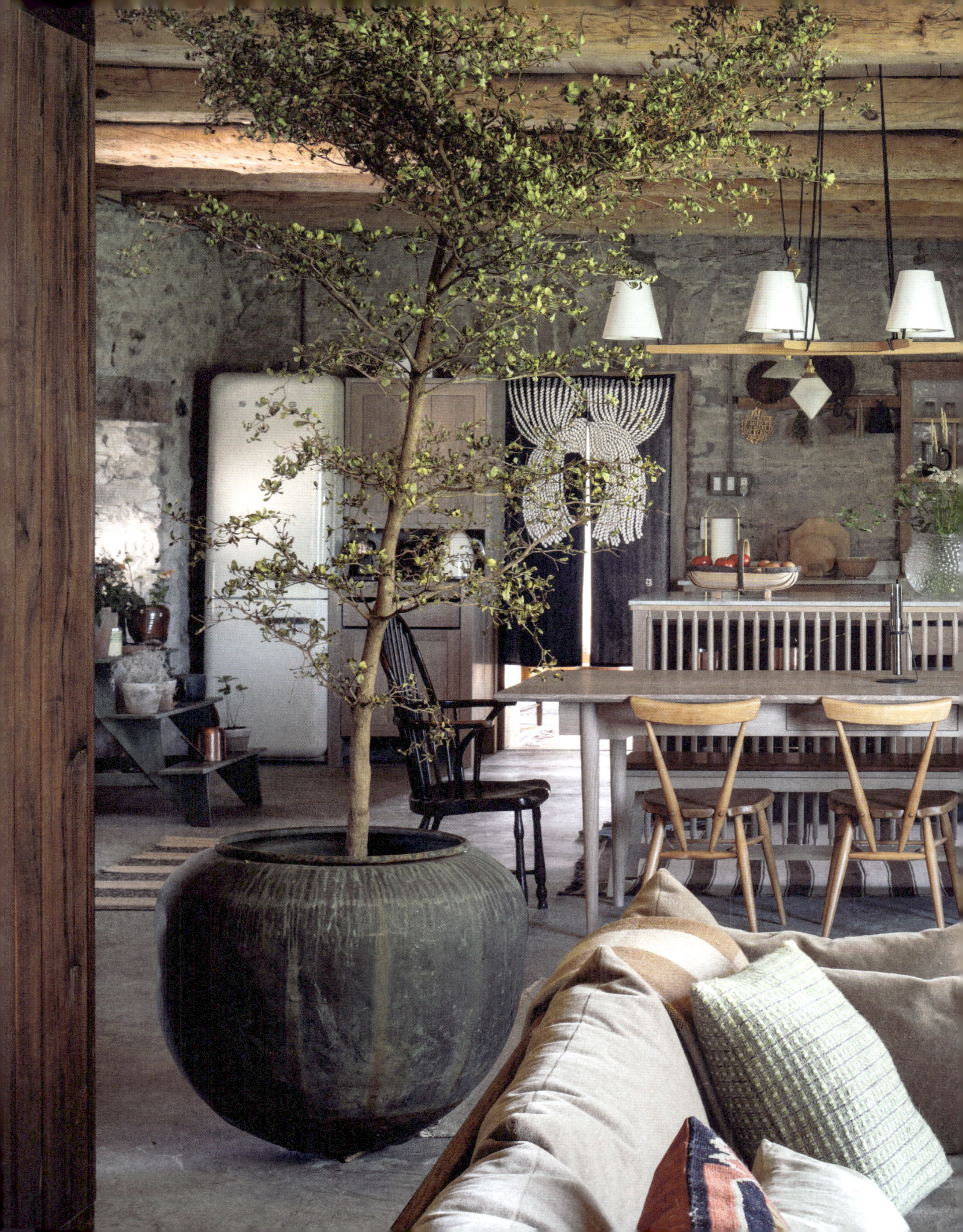

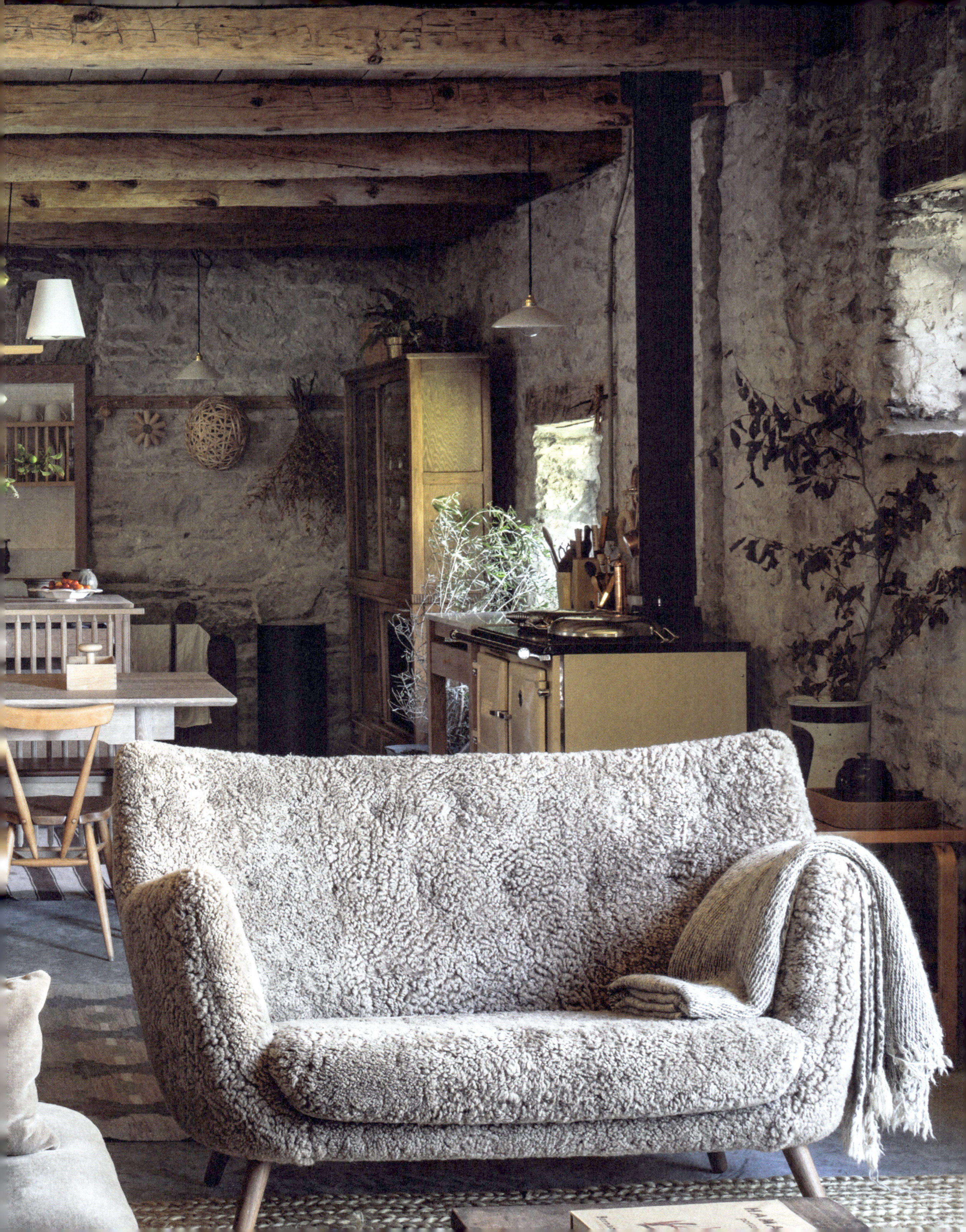

When they found the home, it had been abandoned for a decade and was desperately in need of some TLC. 'It's a metaphor that's overused, but it had really good bones,' John recalls of the structure's metre-thick stone walls that had stood strong for nearly two centuries. 'We knew we could put some love into it and make it something special.'

At the time, the house was nearly devoid of all modern conveniences. 'There was no electricity built-in, just a few extension cords running from a power box outside. Everything was very much original,' he says. But, rather than a total revamp, they decided to lean into the homesteading vibe, eschewing comforts like Wi-Fi and a conventional oven, choosing instead to cook with a wood-burning stove. 'It was a restoration instead of a renovation,' he says of the project, meaning that precious little about the home's original layout was changed.

While the couple is known for their shop's minimalist Scandinavian aesthetic, for their country home they chose objects and furniture that they felt would blend in well with the historic property's rustic aura. 'We tried to make it feel like these things could have been here all along,' John explains. Among the pieces that now occupy the space are a sheepskin-upholstered Poet sofa designed in 1941 by mid-century Danish master Finn Juhl, a 200-year-old Carrara marble soaking tub, vintage Ercol dining chairs sourced in England, a Shaker-inspired kitchen table in blond wood that the couple designed and produced themselves for their shop, and an antique Japanese screen depicting a forest scene that, they say, reminds them of the deer that pass by the window and which brightens up one of the stone house's dark and draughty corners.

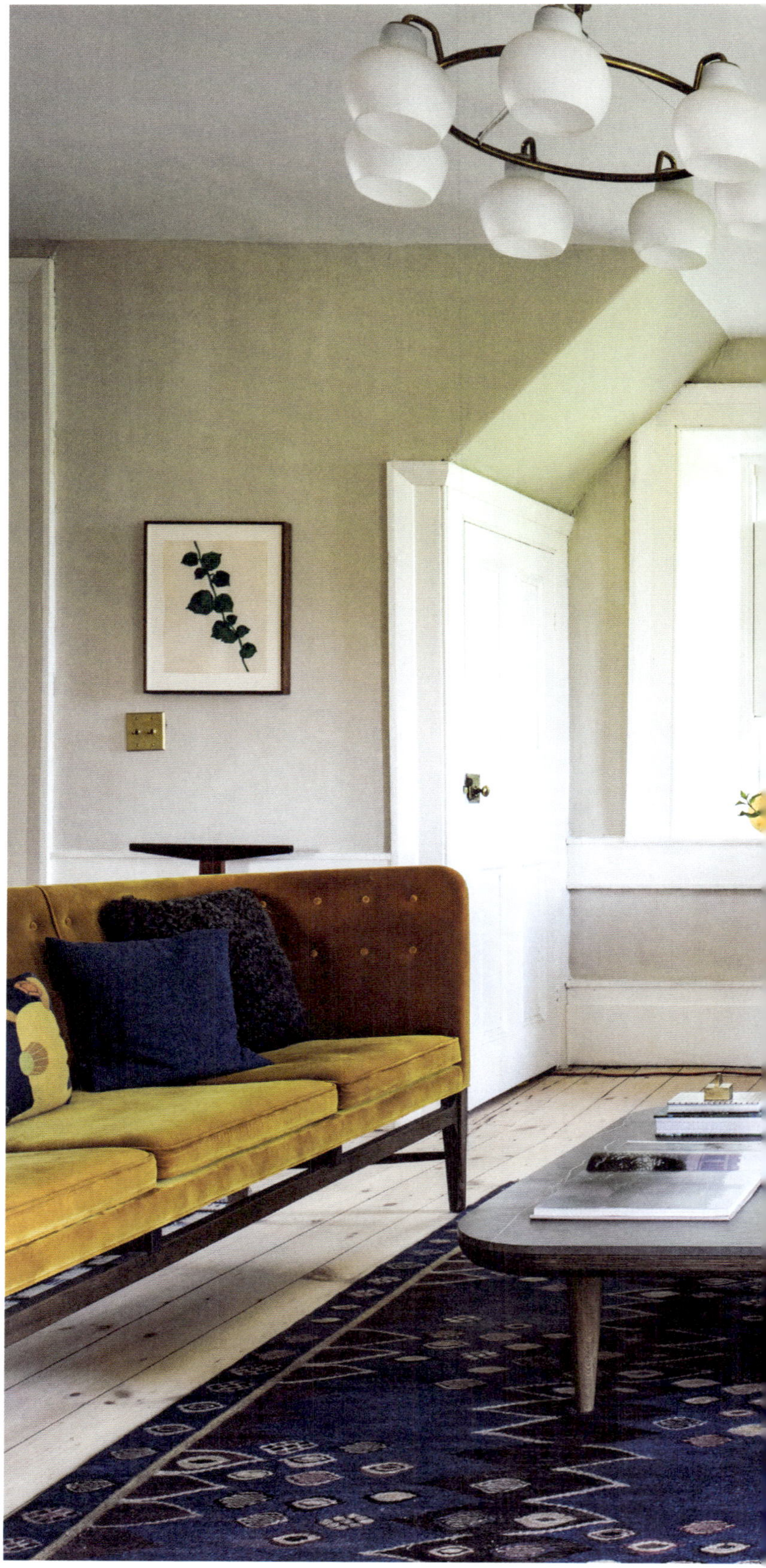

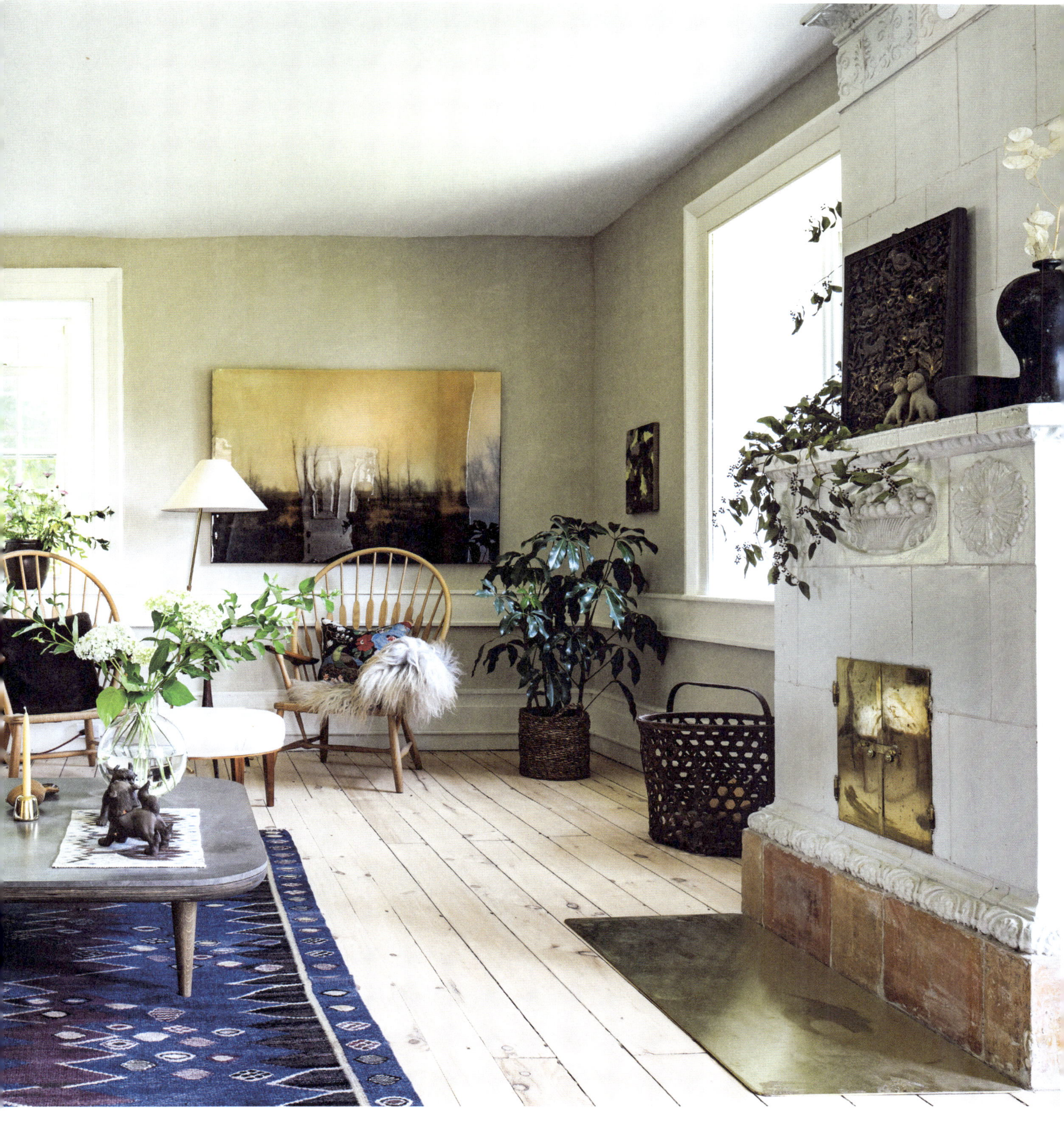

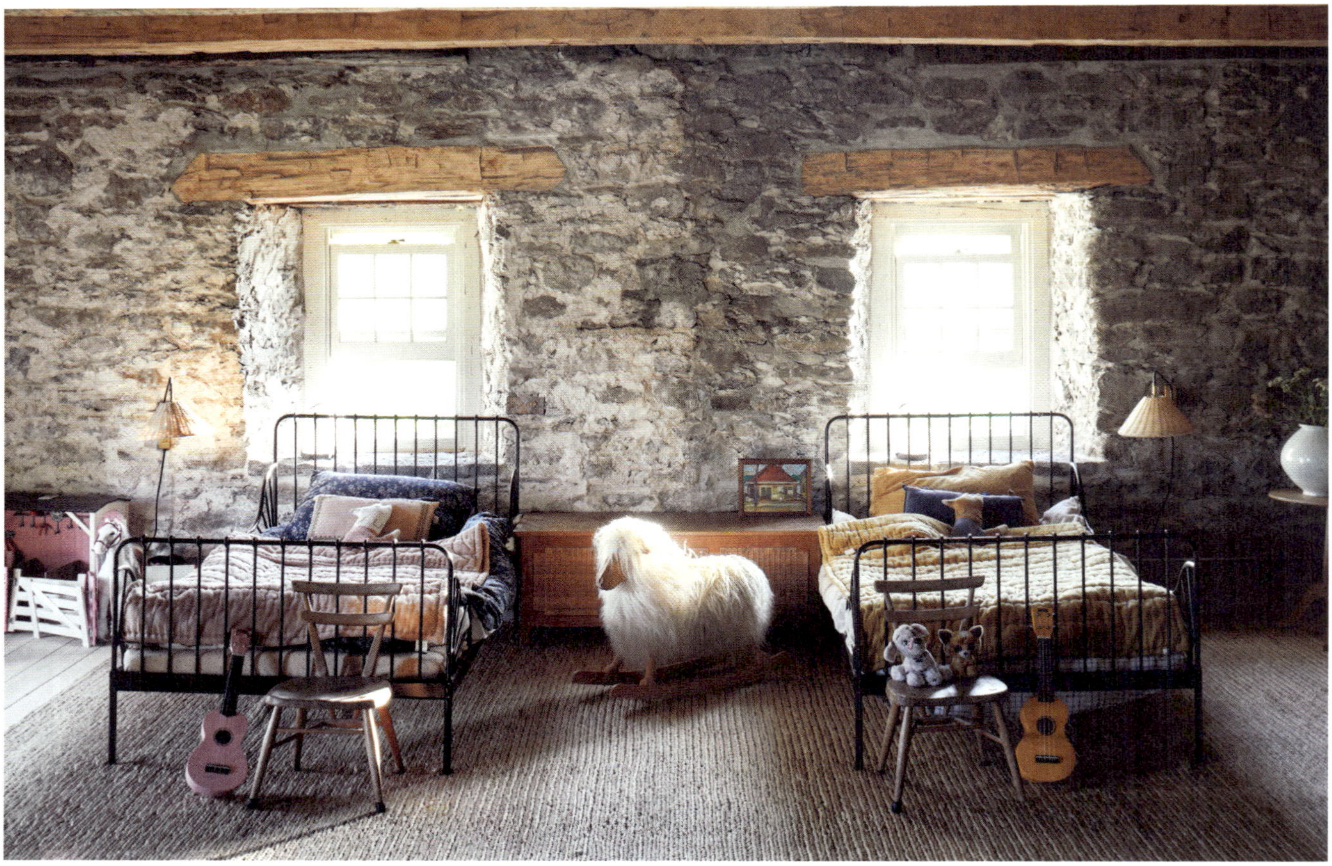

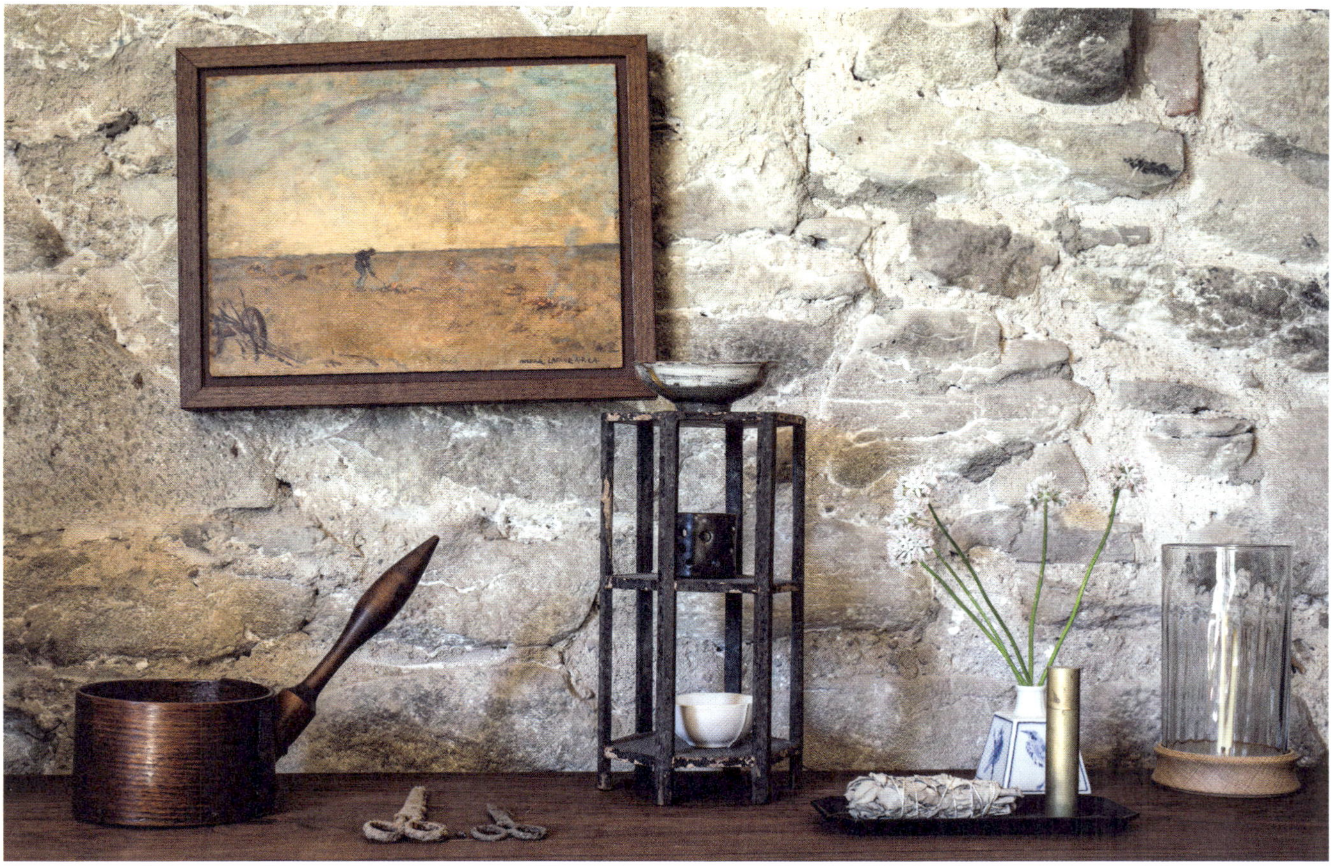

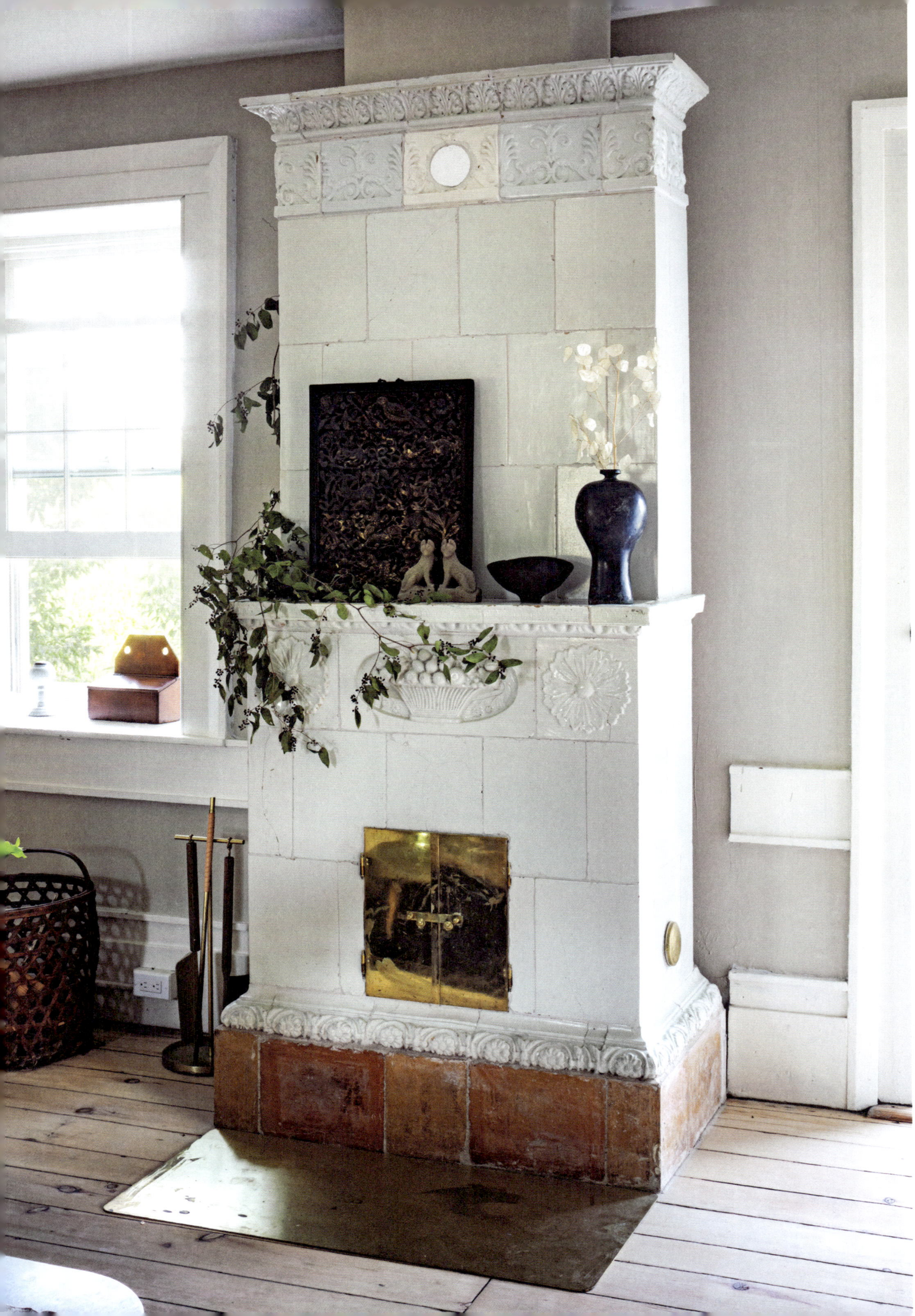

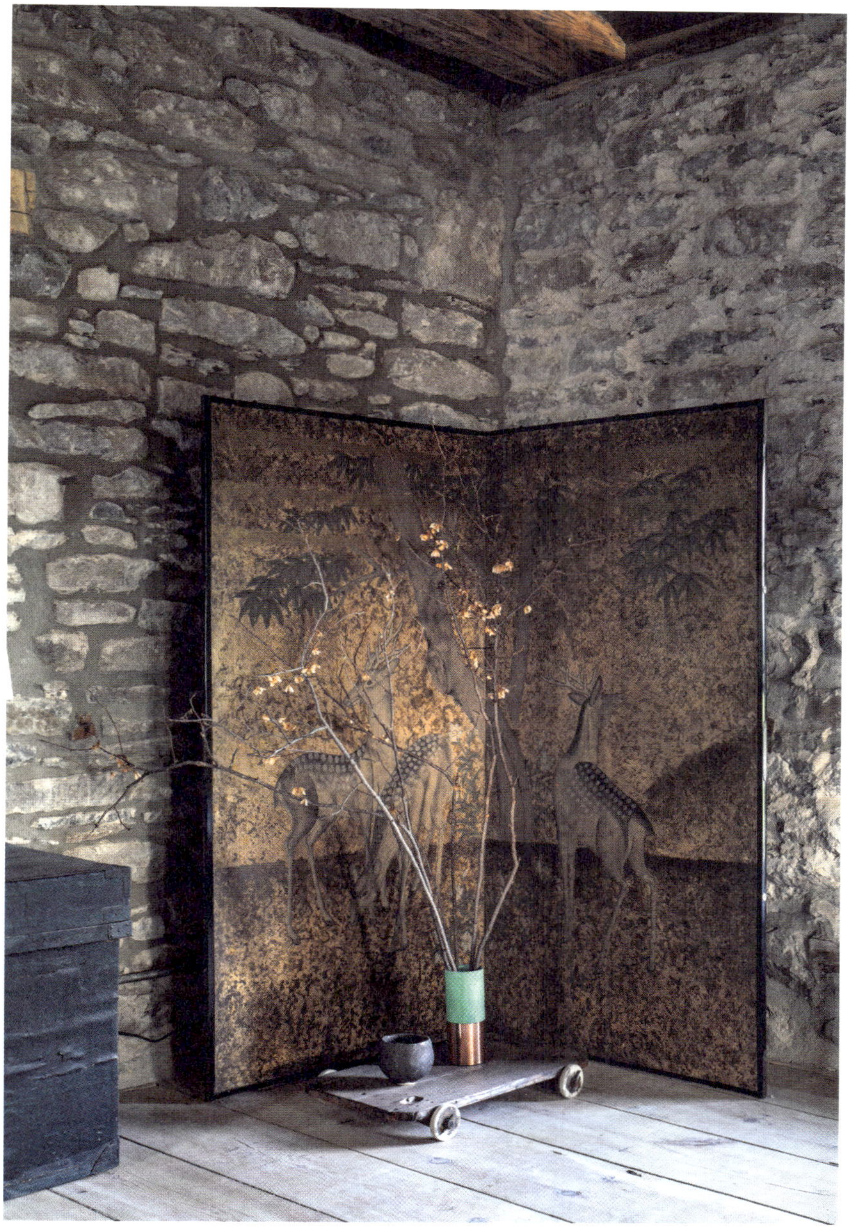

Sitting at the head of the kitchen table is one of the couple's most treasured pieces: a 1700s Windsor chair that once belonged to the erstwhile head of the Montreal ballet. 'It's super strong, but it leans to one side because the person who sat on it previously always crossed his legs,' John says of the seat, which they found at a nearby antique store. 'It's one of our favourites. We always love to find objects that come with a story.'

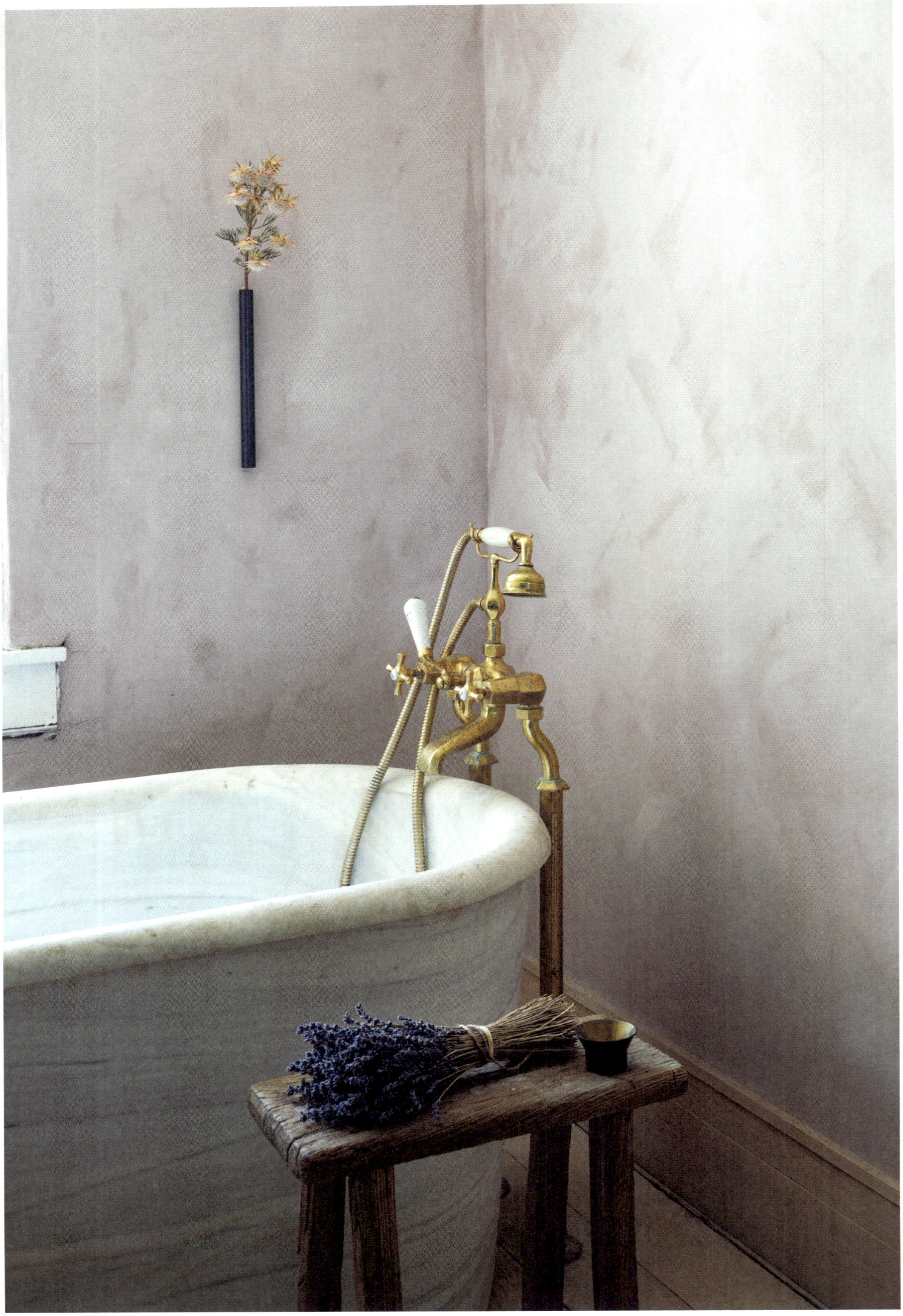

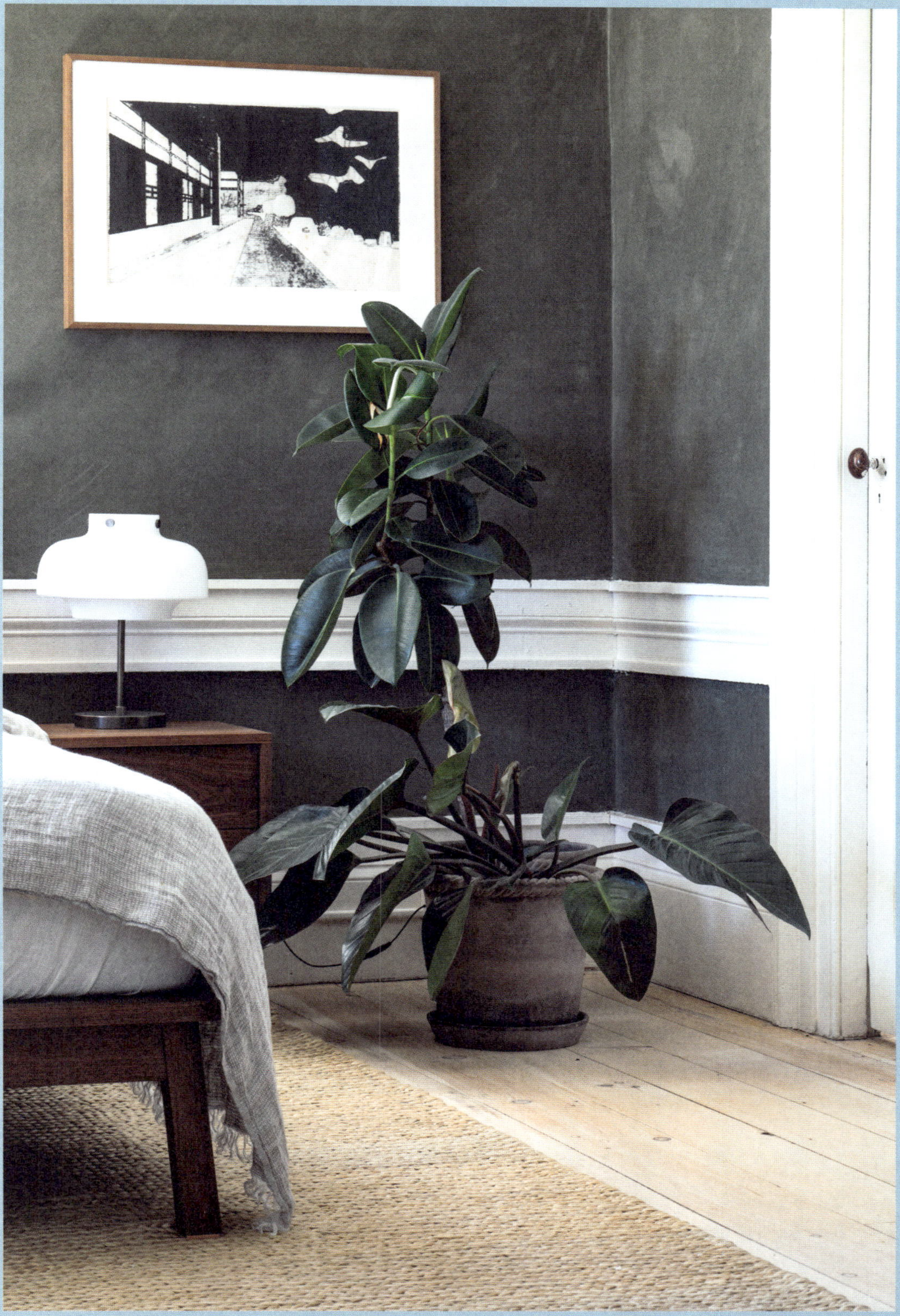

Interview

Curators, designers and shopkeepers John Baker and Juli Daoust Baker founded their cult design store and gallery Mjölk in the west end of Toronto in 2009. Over the past decade, it has become a pilgrimage place for Scandinavian and Japanese design in Canada's largest city. They purchased their nearly 200-year-old stone barn in 2018 as a retreat from the city for themselves and their young children, Elodie and Howell.

John Baker & Juli Dasoust Baker

What is the home's history?

JB: It's an old stone house originally built between 1840 and 1860 by a Scottish family. Most of the stone used to build the structure was actually collected when they were clearing the land for the first time. It's made almost entirely of fieldstone, so it feels quite natural and part of the landscape. It had been abandoned for well over 10 years when we saw it for the first time, and was very much inhabited by creatures – definitely not very hospitable. But there was something interesting about it.

What are the surroundings like?

JB: It's a very, very pretty area of eastern Ontario. The rolling hills just keep on going. We're actually in a very strange, wonderful spot within this hill. We're at the bottom of the valley so when you look at the landscape it just goes up and up and up. You can't see beyond it, which gives it a very reassuring feeling. It's very bucolic.

What sort of renovations did you need to do?

JB: It wasn't as extensive as you might think. One of the things we did that I thought turned out well was that we worked within the pre-existing layout. We didn't really add walls; instead, we worked within the parameters of what was there already. Upstairs, which is where the sleeping area is now, there were false walls made of pine board that were put up very haphazardly. You could literally push them over. So we opened up that whole space. We found out later from one of the sons who grew up there in the 1950s that that upstairs space was completely open originally. He told us that back in the early 1900s they would even have dances up there. So we brought that back to what was originally there.

In the parlour, which is the more finished part of the house, we hired a plasterer to restore the walls. Where the bathroom is now, there used to be a pantry, so we had to totally remake that, but the kitchen and living area was probably the biggest work. It was, in a way, an indoor – outdoor space – kind of like a garage. The window was originally a big door where they would bring the horse and buggy into the building and unload it. So we had to put some extra love into that one.

Your shop and gallery, Mjölk, is very much influenced by Scandinavian modernism. How much aesthetic crossover is there between this house and the gallery?

JB: I think the cool thing about a lot of the Scandinavian designs that we carry is that from the 1930s all the way to contemporary design it's a big spectrum of styles. I find that with Scandinavian furniture, you can always dress it differently to make it feel like it's from a different era. We have a gold velvet sofa in the parlour that is by Arne Jacobsen – a super-modern Mid-Century designer who did the famous Egg chair and Swan chair – but when you pair that with gold velvet, which is very luxurious, it feels period-appropriate for the house. We definitely have a lot of Scandinavian design objects and furniture, but the way we upholstered them or chose darker woods lends itself to the environment. We like to mash a bunch of things together from different periods and create something new.

What would you say is one of your favourite features of the house?

JB: The fireplace is probably one of the most important features of the home. It is shocking how appropriate it looks – like it's always been there. The ceramic tiles are actually reclaimed from a farmhouse on Gotland in Sweden dating back to the 1700s. We brought all the tiles here, and it came with instructions on how to lay them out. We had a masonry builder reconstruct the stove, then we clad the outside in the antique tiles. It's the heart of the home in many ways. It's decorated with these beautiful roses and baskets of flowers and vegetables – all symbolism tied to a rural property.

It sounds like you have taken a very back-to-basics approach with the restoration of the home.

JB: It's true – the only means of cooking is a wood oven. It heats the kitchen, you can bake with it, you can cook with it on the top. We don't have a shower, only a tub, and there's only one bathroom. We come from the stimulation of the city with all its conveniences, and when we are there we slow down in all senses. Everything takes a lot longer, and you have to find joy in that. We joke that it's like Oz in *The Wizard of Oz*. And that when we go back to the city, we're going back to Kansas.

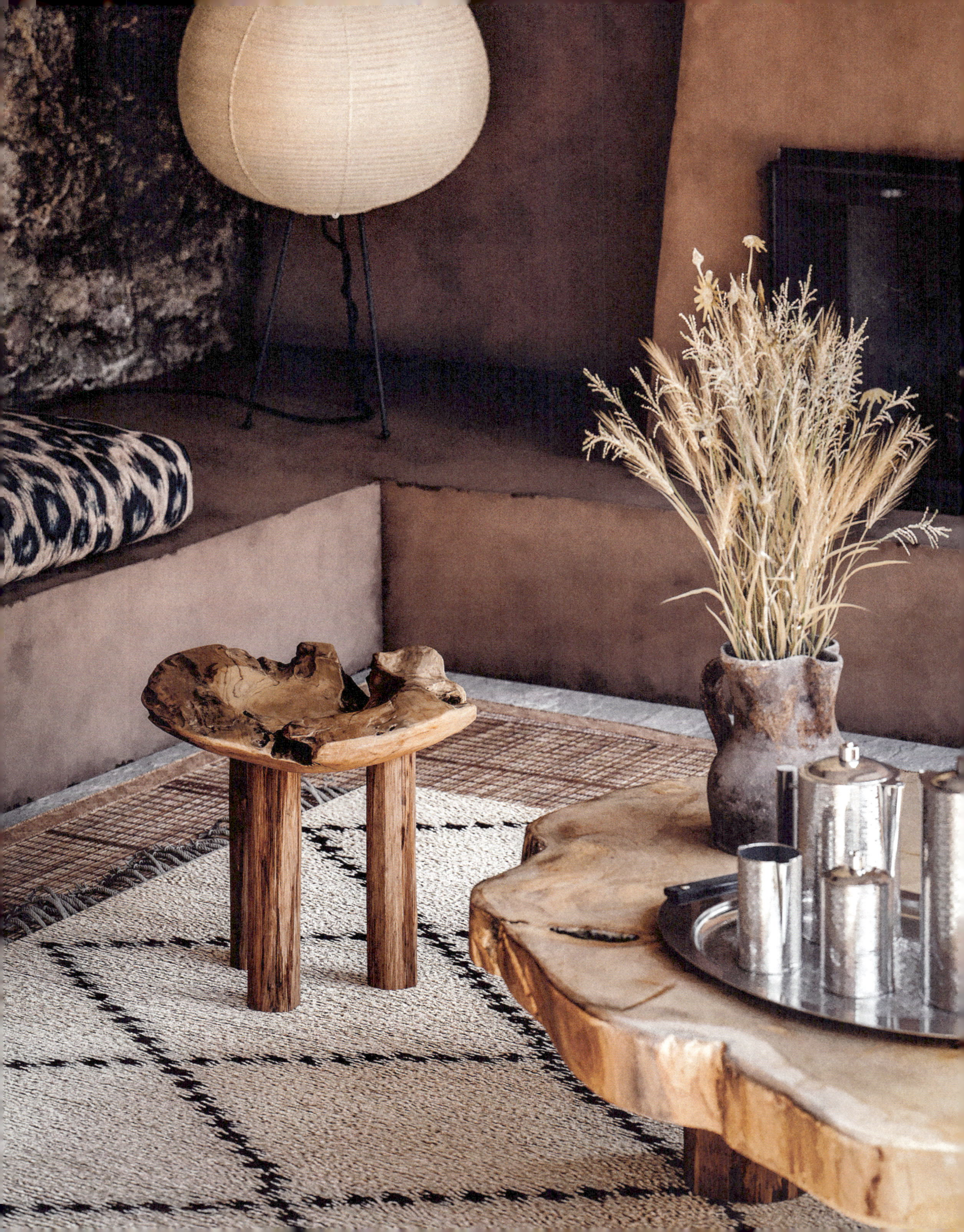

CHAPTER 04

Sand & Stone

Even in the most unforgiving of landscapes, one can still find refuge. From the arid deserts of the American West to the rocky ridges of a Lebanese mountain chain, these architects and designers have created inviting oases that brilliantly incorporate their often hostile surroundings.

A Stone Guesthouse Hidden within a Mountain

BHAMDOUN, LAMARTINE VALLEY (LB)

CARL GERGES ARCHITECTS

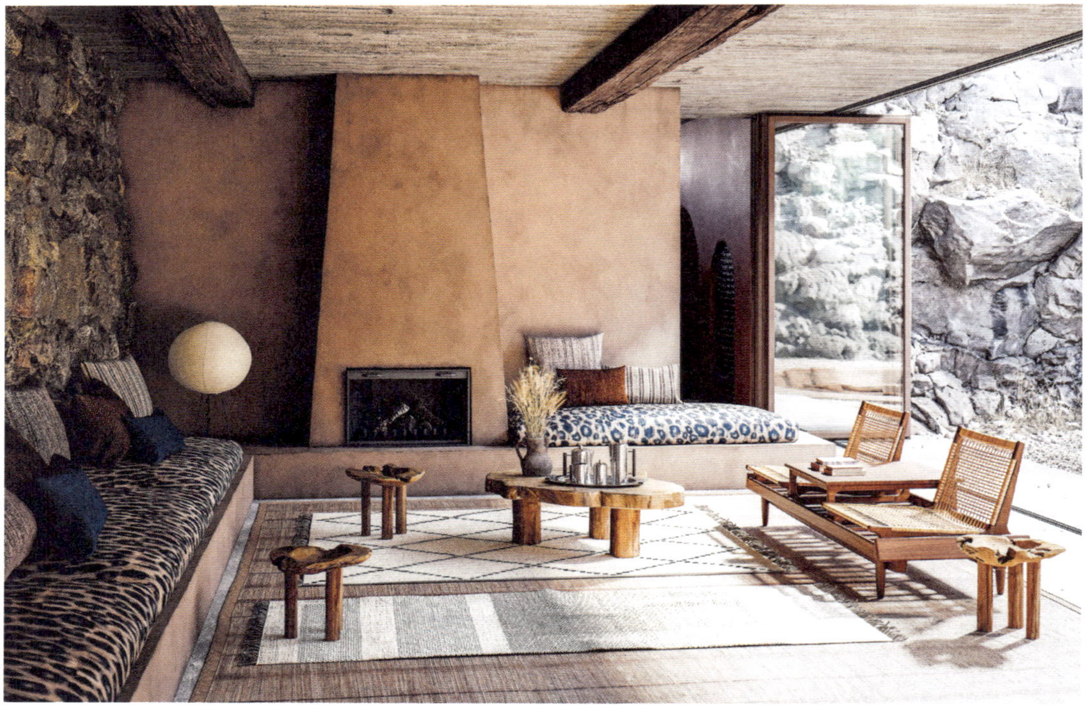

Hidden in the rugged peaks overlooking Lebanon's Lamartine Valley, a vast and remote region straddling the main road to Damascus where Phoenician tombs and ancient rock formations have sat undisturbed for millennia, is this monolithic stone guest house designed by Beirut's Carl Gerges Architects. Created as a mountain retreat within an area known for its fertile vineyards, the house has an imposing facade that gives way to a bright and inviting sanctuary.

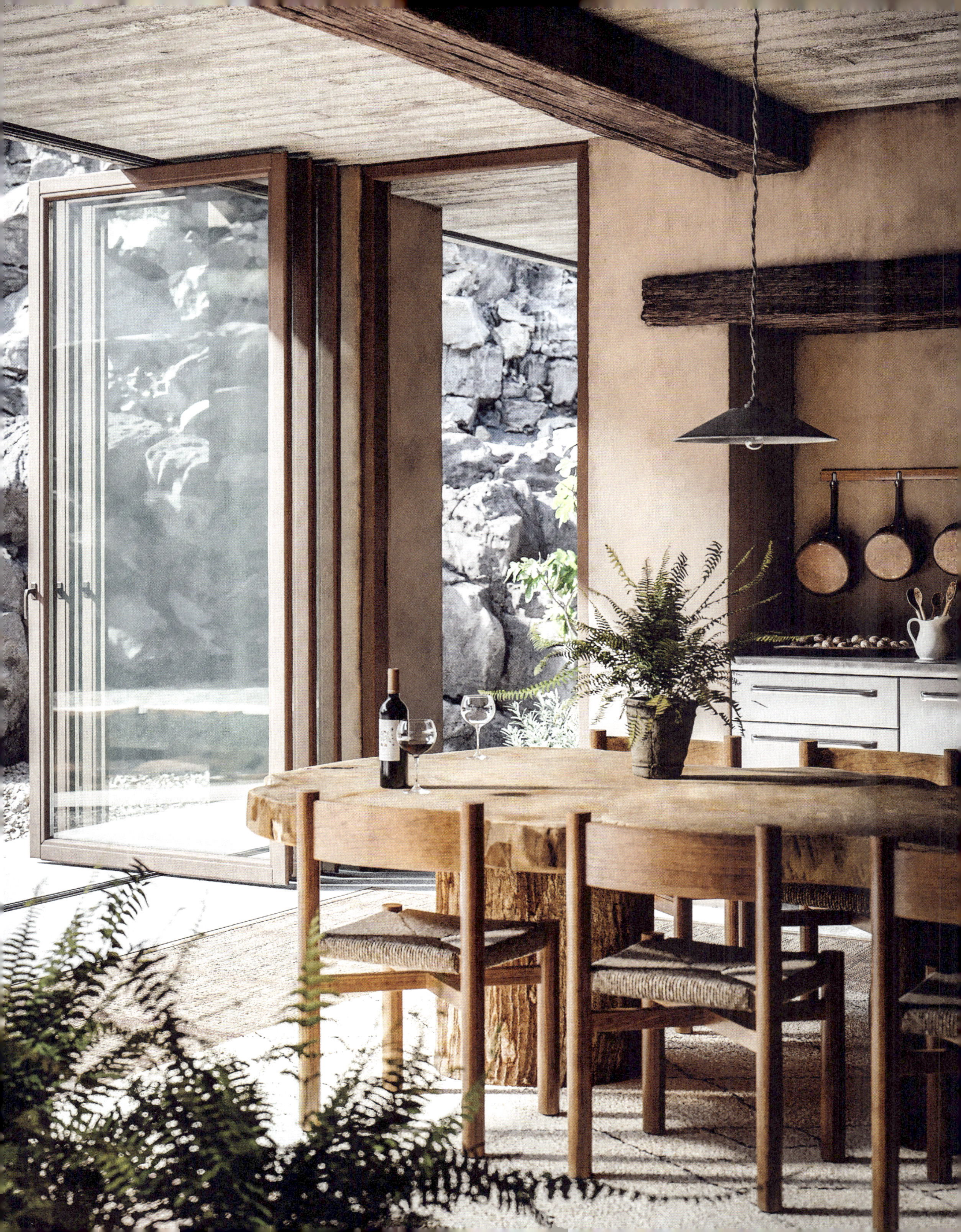

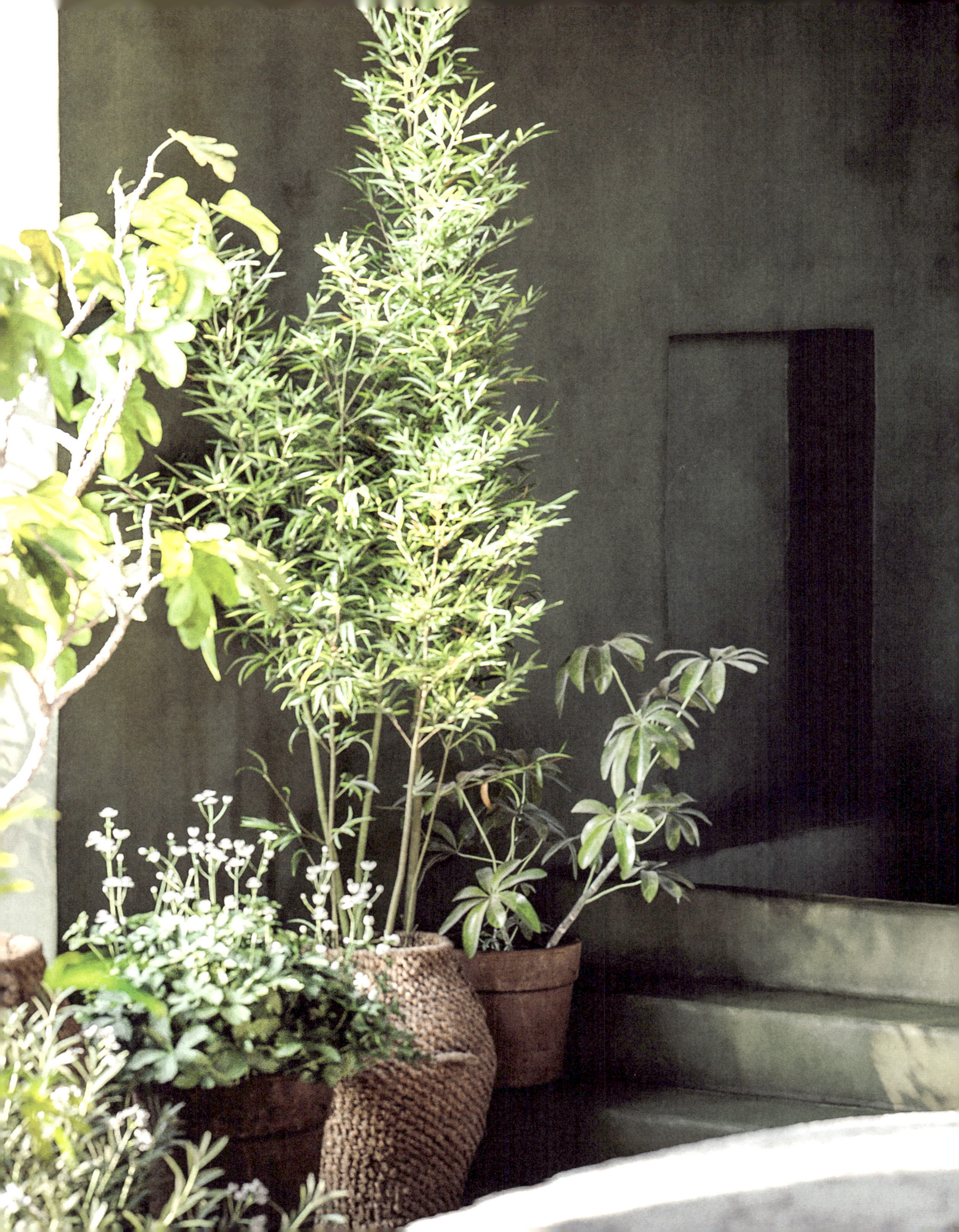

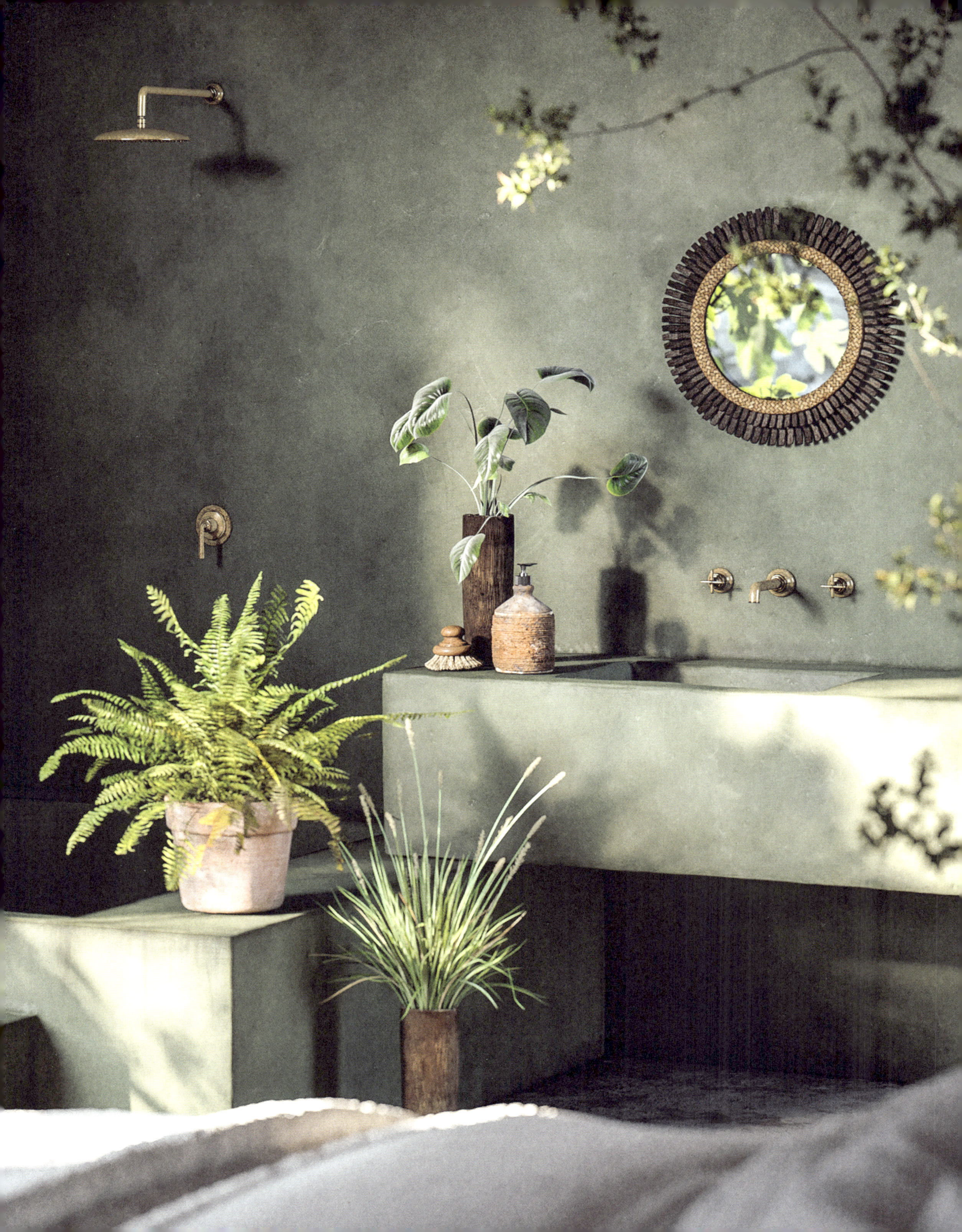

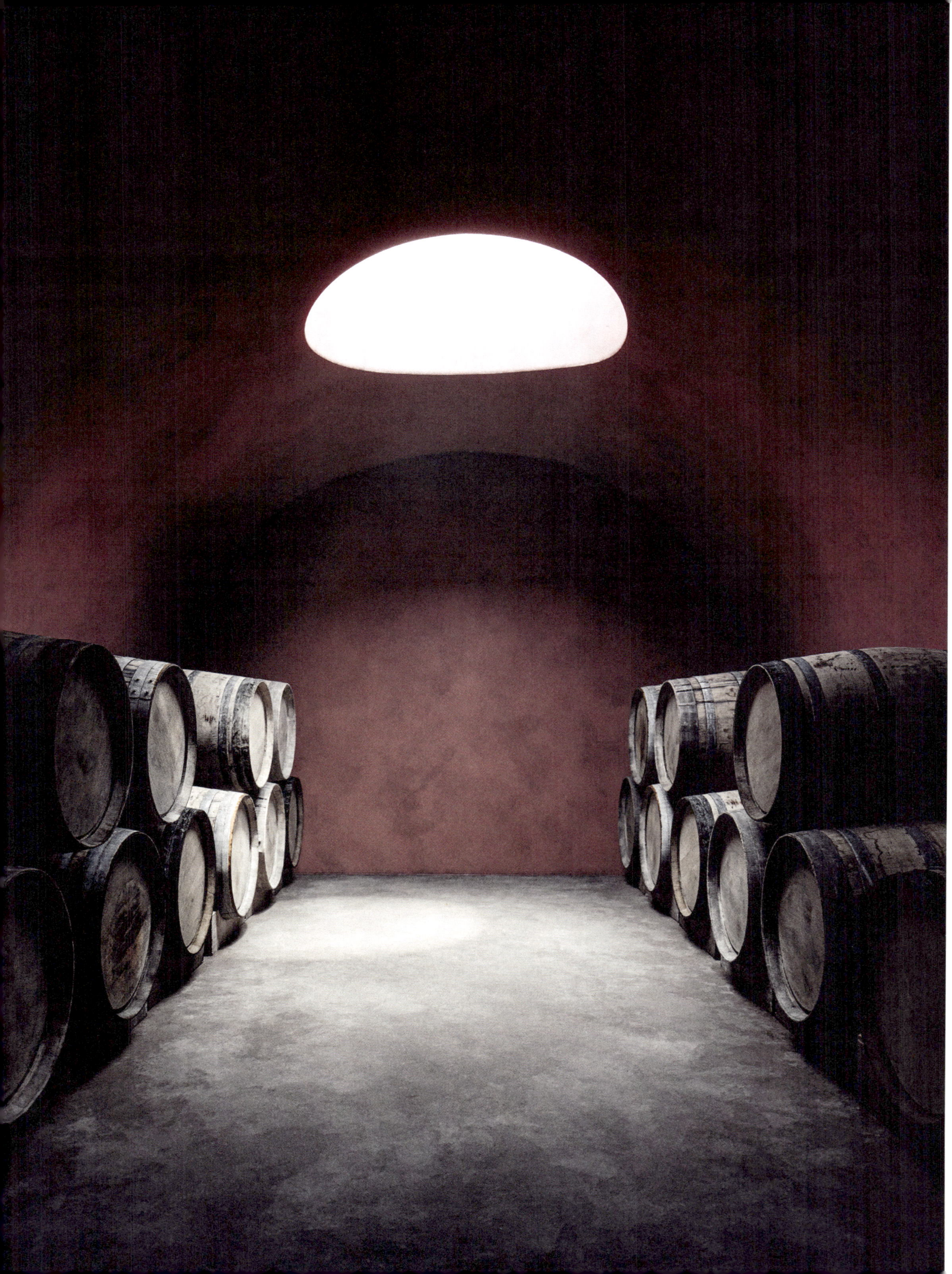

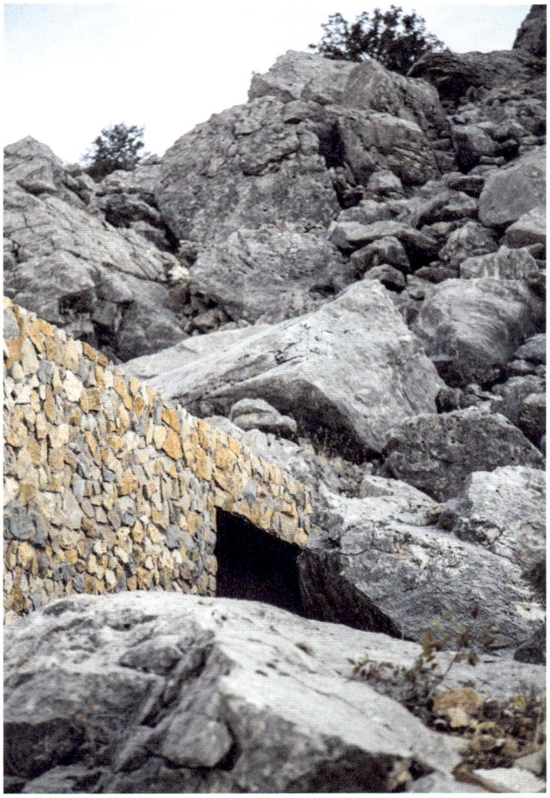

Beyond the seemingly severe exterior of roughly hewn grey and yellow limestone boulders is a home perfectly suited for entertaining. Warm natural materials such as reclaimed timber ceiling beams, organically shaped wooden furniture and textiles in the form of thickly woven Berber rugs provide a gentle foil to the harsh surroundings, which are integrated into the design in the form of natural stone interior walls – rendering the structure almost indistinguishable from its landscape.

Gerges turned to traditional North African building techniques for the design of the primary bedroom and bathroom. The cloudy olive-green walls are finished in *tadelakt*, a form of waterproof plaster first used in Morocco over 2,000 years ago that is still common in vernacular building today. The fully glazed wall that extends along the building's perimeter, coupled with the addition of abundant lush greenery within the space, engenders a feeling one is sleeping, bathing and living outdoors.

In a home so geared towards entertaining, the exterior living spaces were naturally given equal attention. A circular sunken fire pit sits at the base of a natural rock formation, creating a dramatic focal point against the backdrop of stone. But the real secret weapon in this home's arsenal of features perfectly envisioned for entertaining is the underground tunnel that leads to a cavernous wine cellar, moodily lit from above by a single skylight, and holding barrel upon barrel of locally harvested wine.

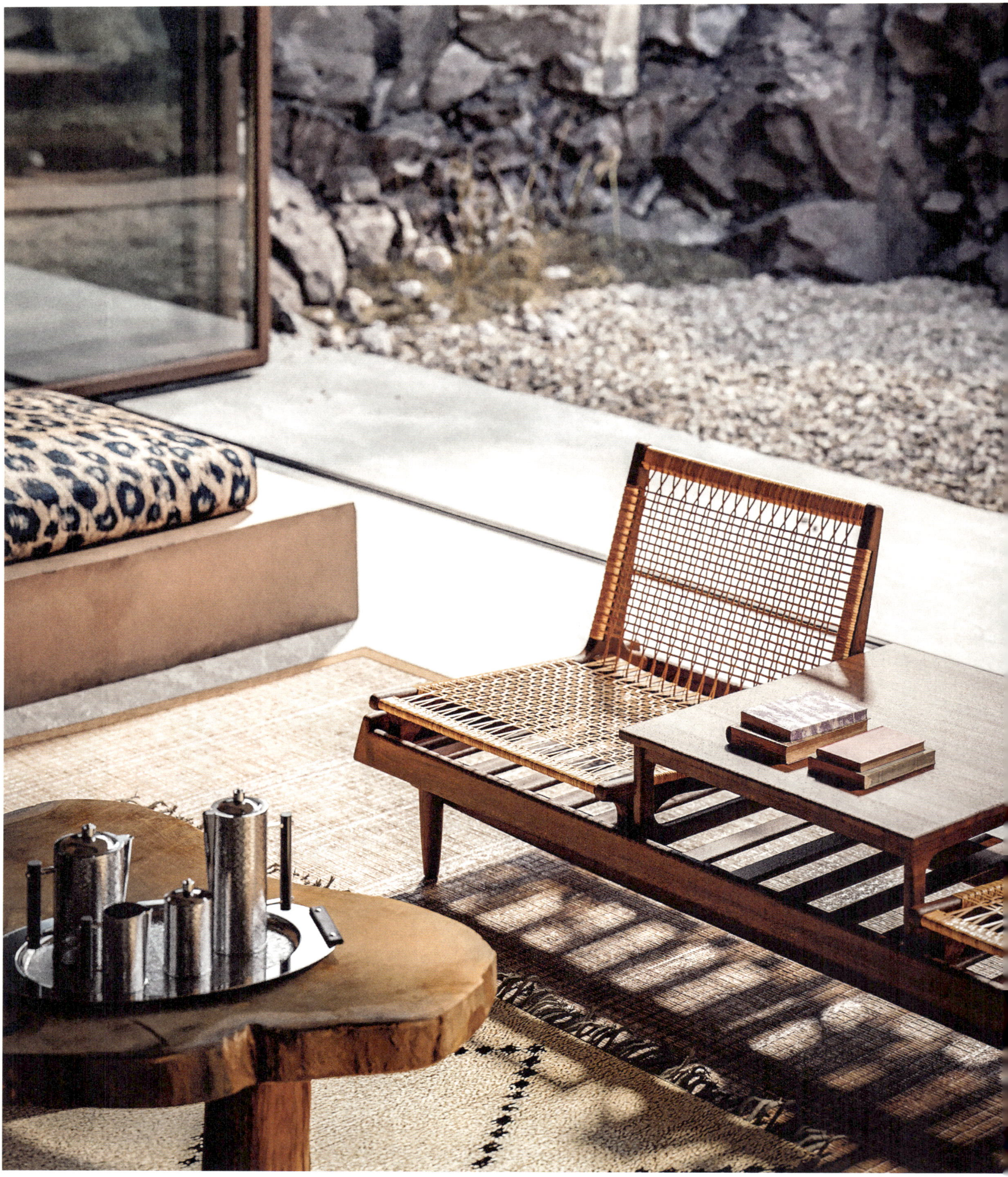

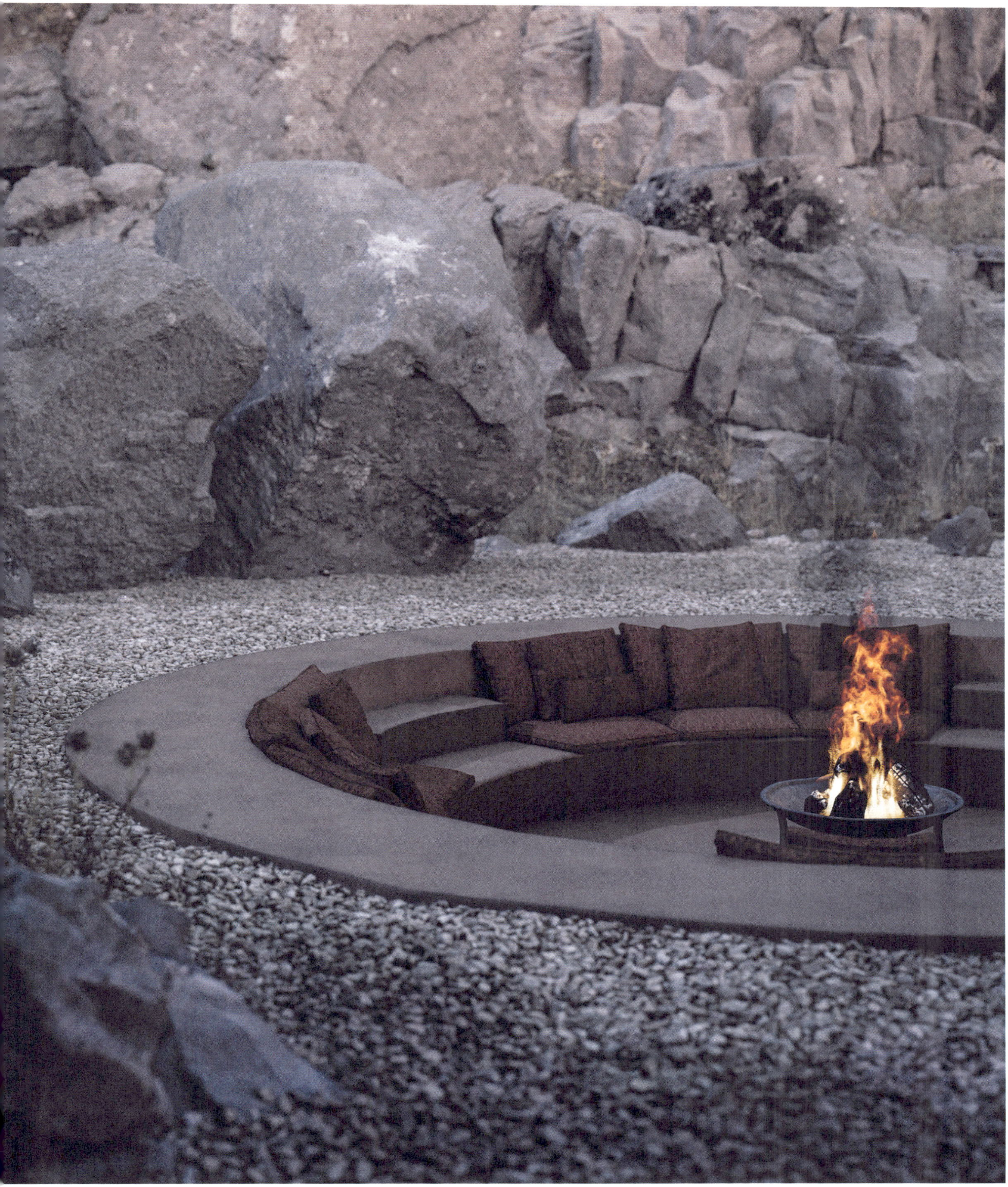

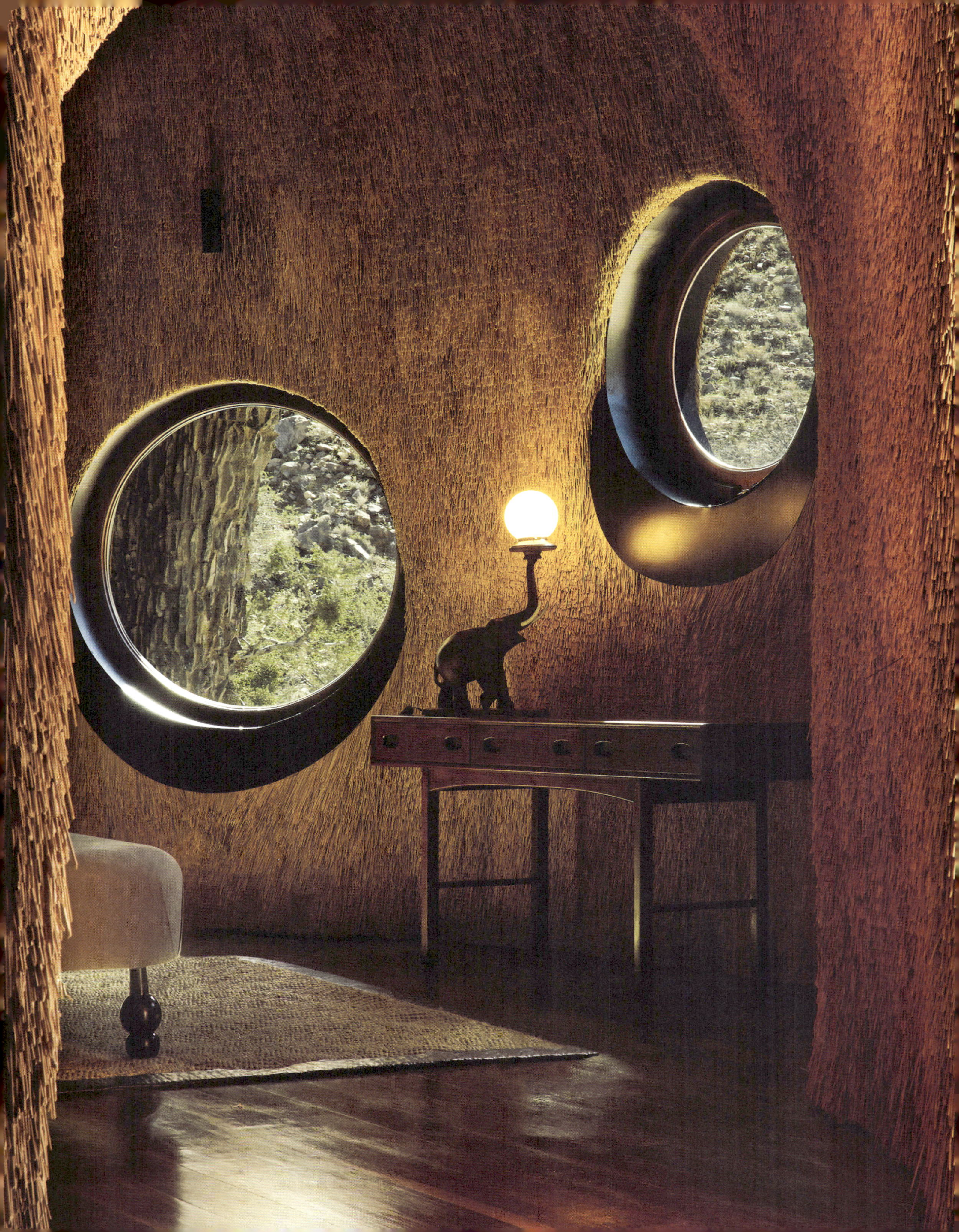

An Organic Nest Deep in the Desert

NAMIB TSARIS CONSERVANCY, NAMIB DESERT (NA)

PORKY HEFER DESIGN

Nearly 400 kilometres of dirt roads away from the nearest city, deep into the arid stretches of a 247,000-acre nature reserve in the Namibian Desert, is this unconventional home created by South African artist and designer Porky Hefer. Hefer's inspiration for the elaborate structure, known as The Nest, came from observing the sociable weaver (*Philetairus socius*), a small but industrious finch-like bird capable of building sprawling, multilevel nests that can house multiple generations of a single lineage. The resulting house represents the ultimate experimentation in biomimicry.

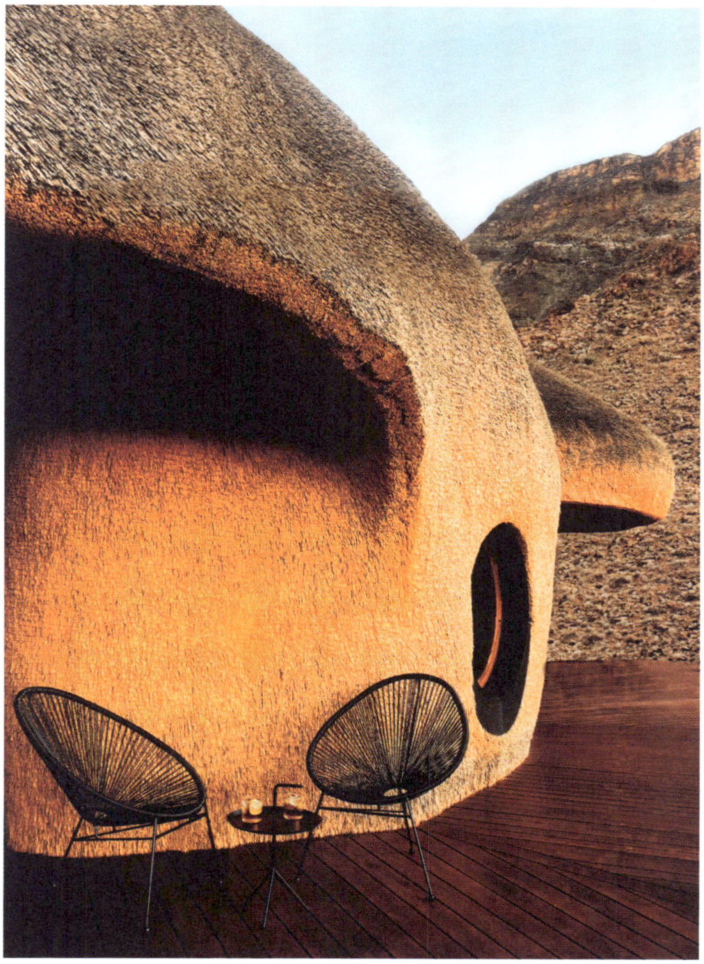

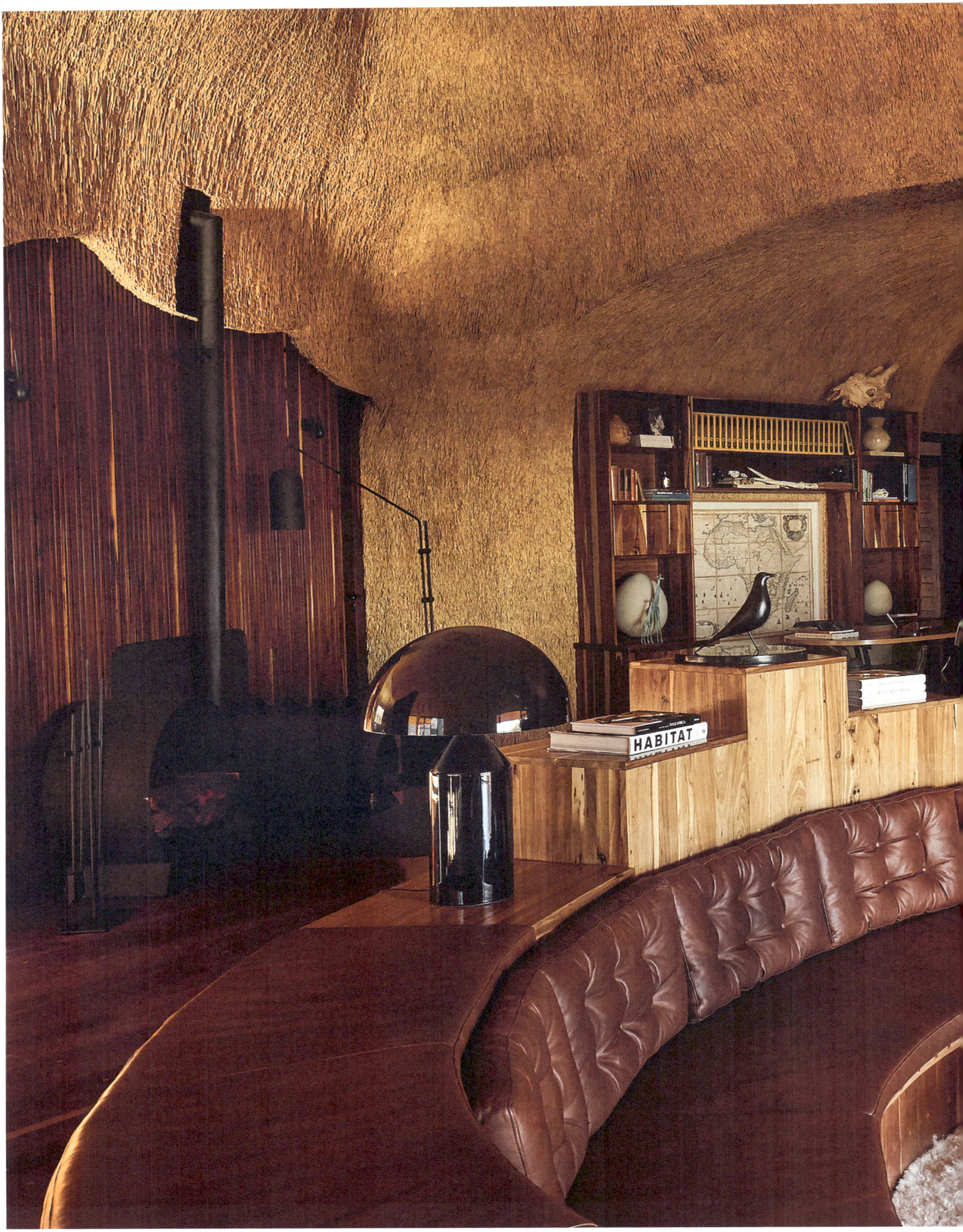
HABITAT

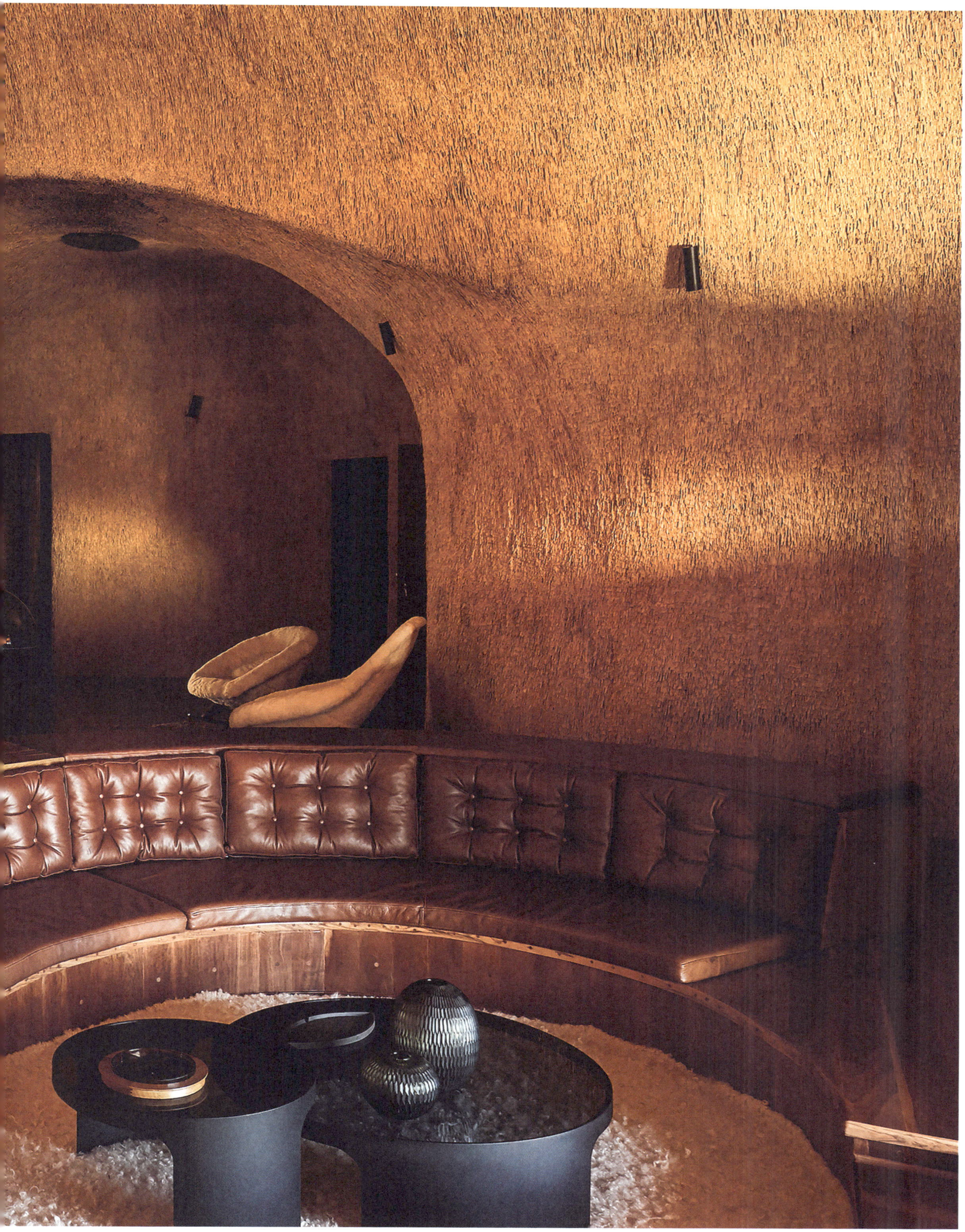

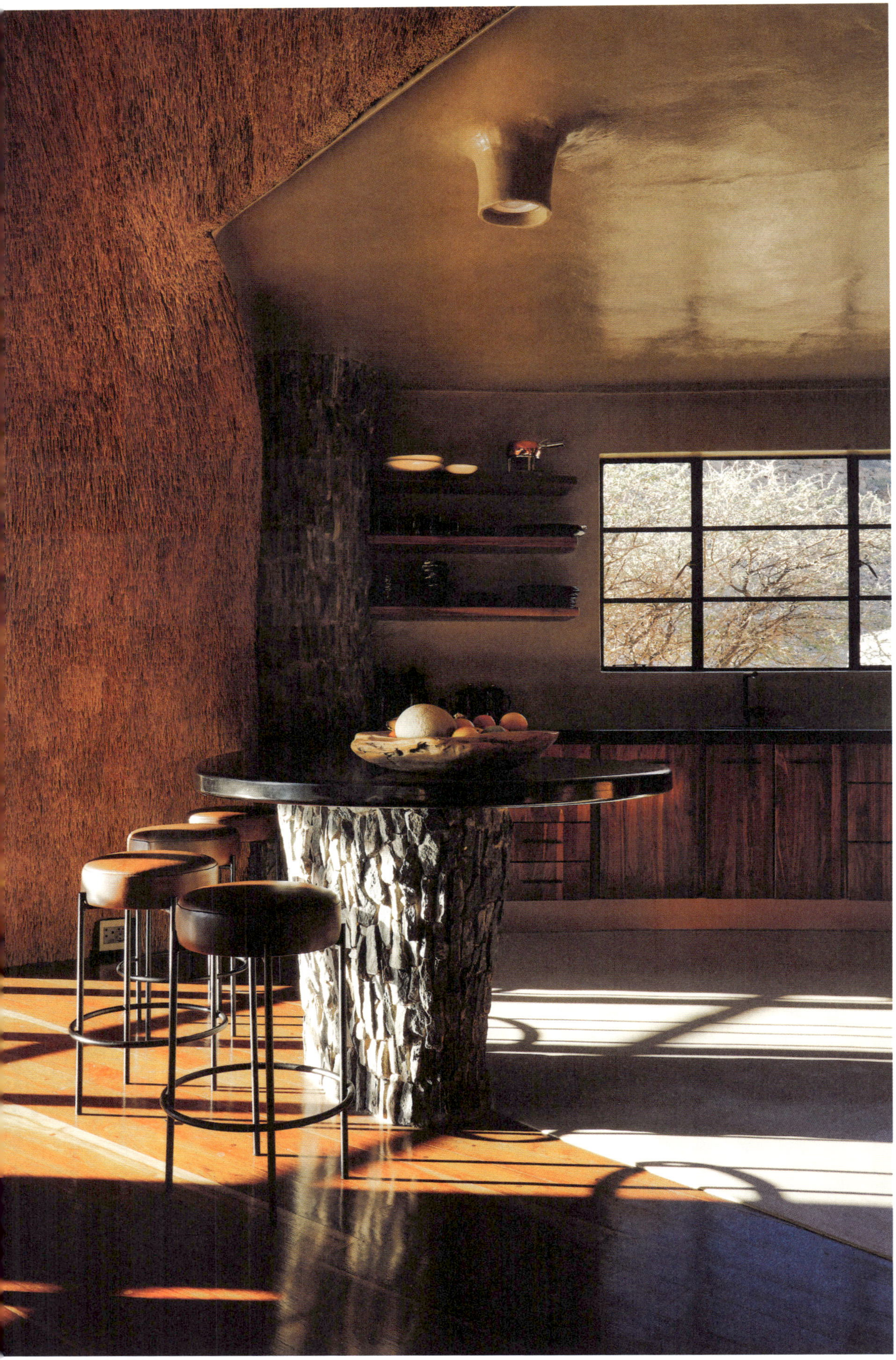

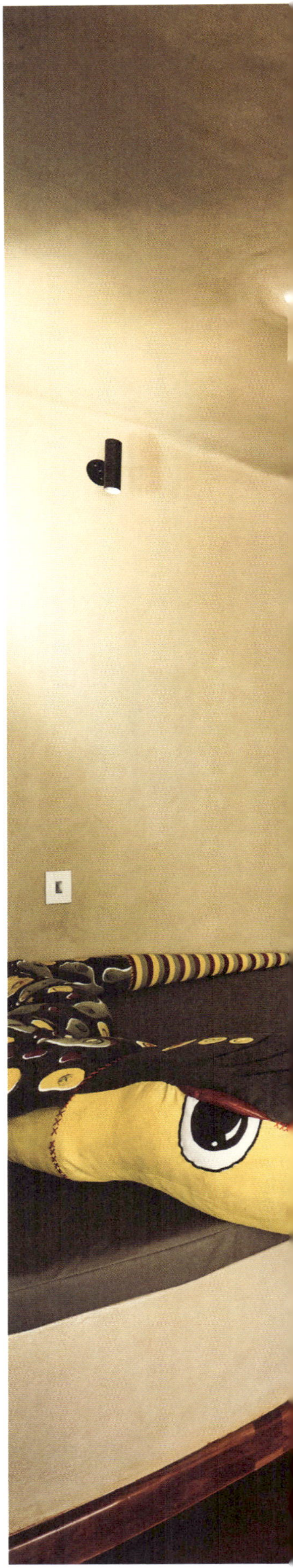

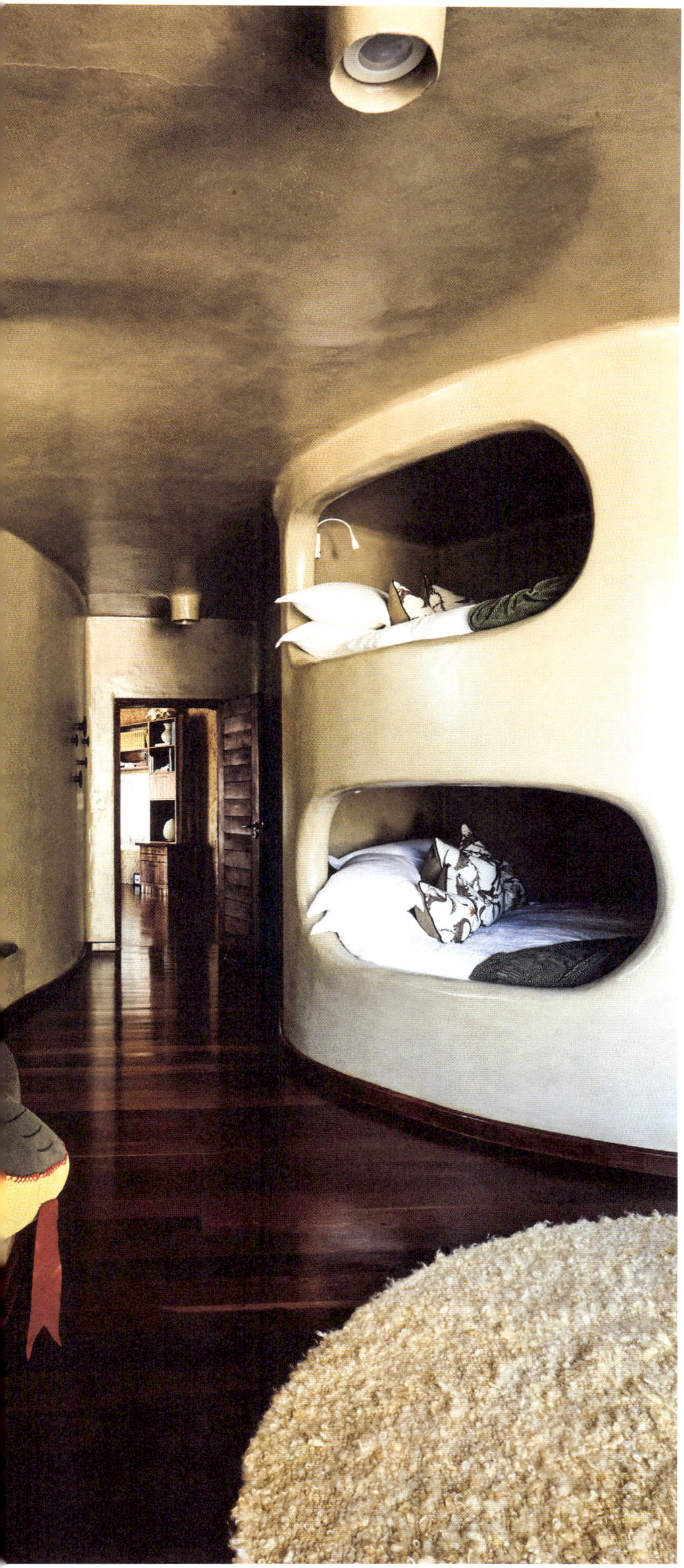

To create the peaked dome shape of the two-storey, four-bedroom villa, Hefer used river grass harvested from the Zambezi River in northern Namibia thatched atop a steel rebar frame, while local granite was chosen to clad sections of the exterior. Layered vertically rather than using a typical horizontal construction, the stone facade was designed to recall the bark of the camel thorn tree, where social weavers often build their homes.

Inside, Hefer carried through the same concept, building much of the furniture in situ – just like a nest. A grand conversation pit defines the living room upholstered in gleaming, mahogany-coloured leather. In the sleeping quarters, beds are burrowed into the walls bunk-style or constructed from glossy, locally sourced kiaat and Rhodesian teak, conjuring the feeling of a cosy escape in every sense of the word. As a clever juxtaposition to the otherwise earthy home, pieces brought in to furnish the space were chosen to channel the luxe glamour of mid-century Italian design.

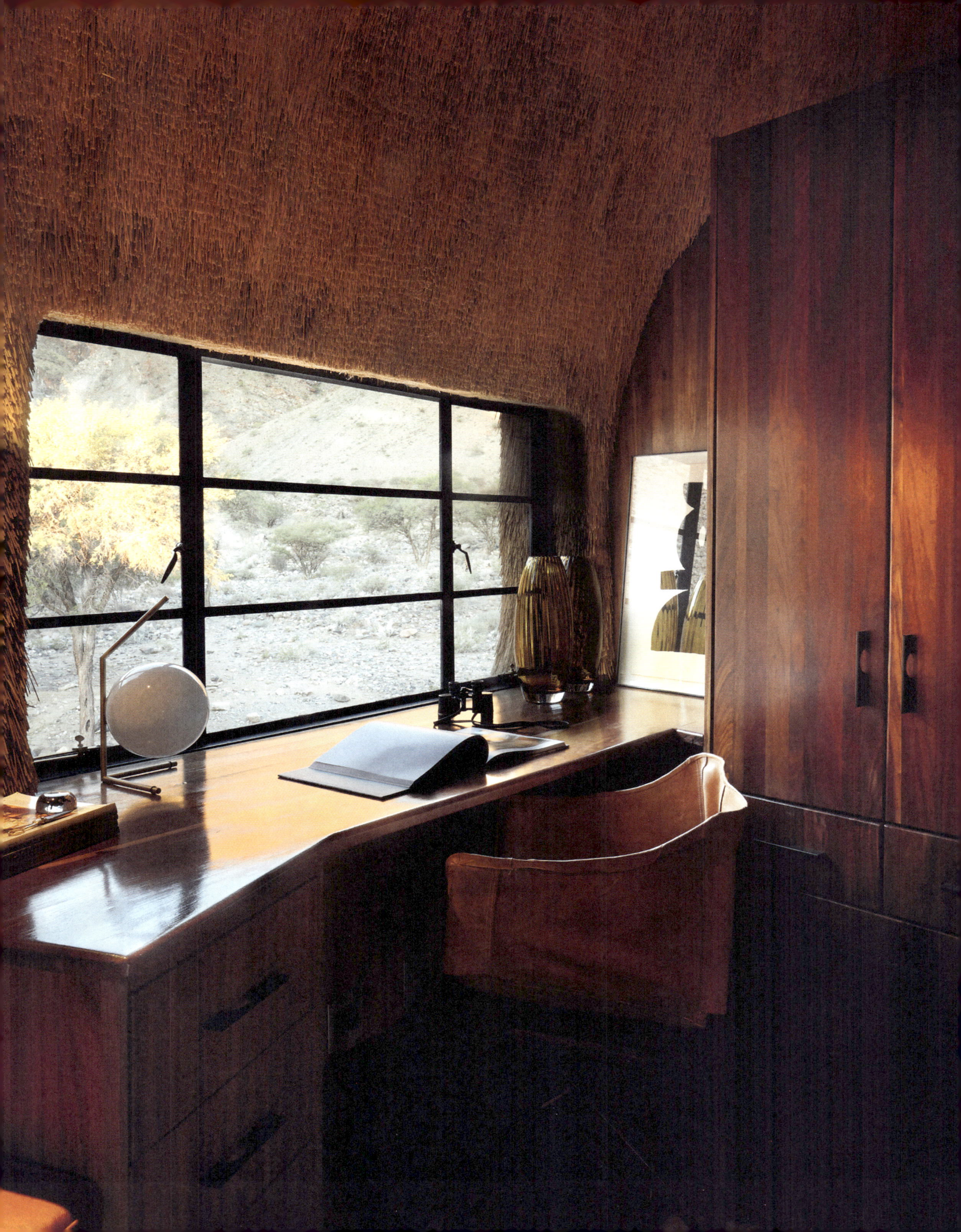

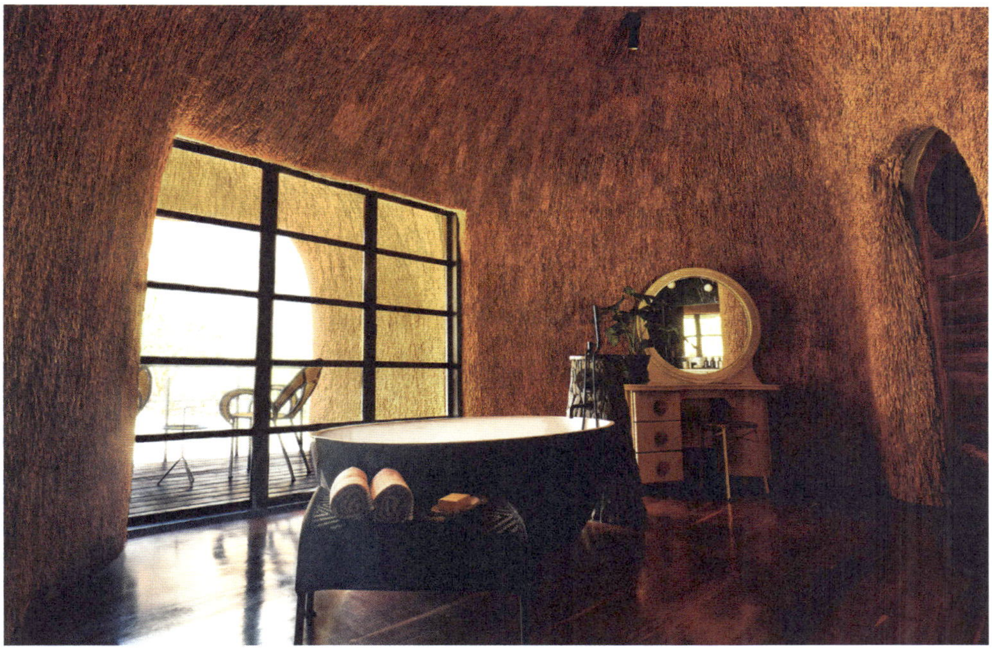

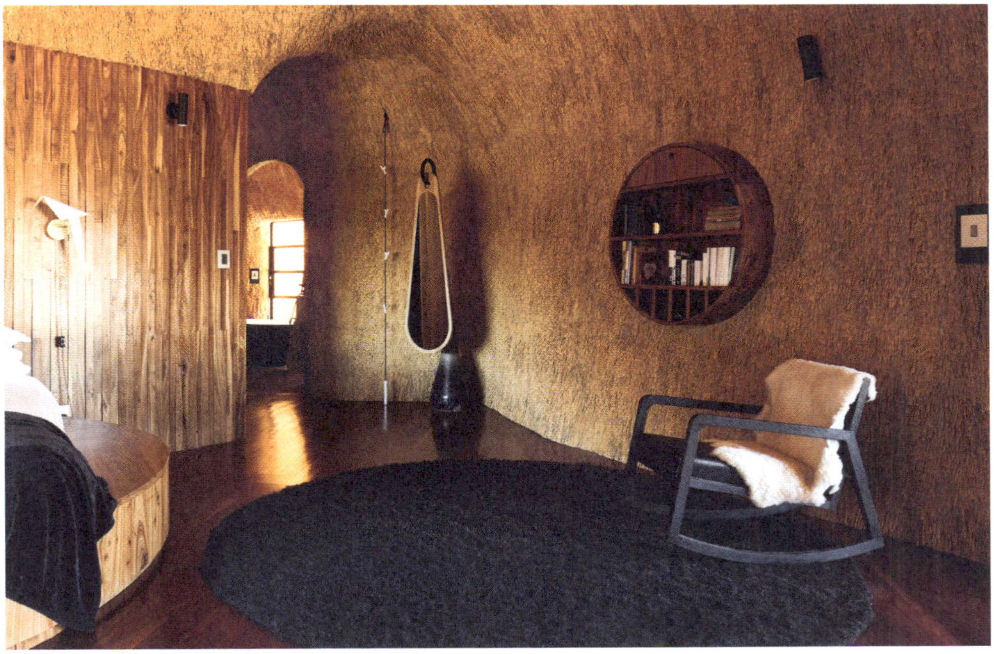

Blending so seamlessly with its surroundings – the orange-brown hues of its dried grass facade seemingly melting into the desert – The Nest has become a prime location to spot the wildlife that calls the nature reserve home. Zebras and baboons have been known to stop by and peek in the windows, just as curious about this monumental architectural experiment as their human neighbours would be. If, of course, there were any.

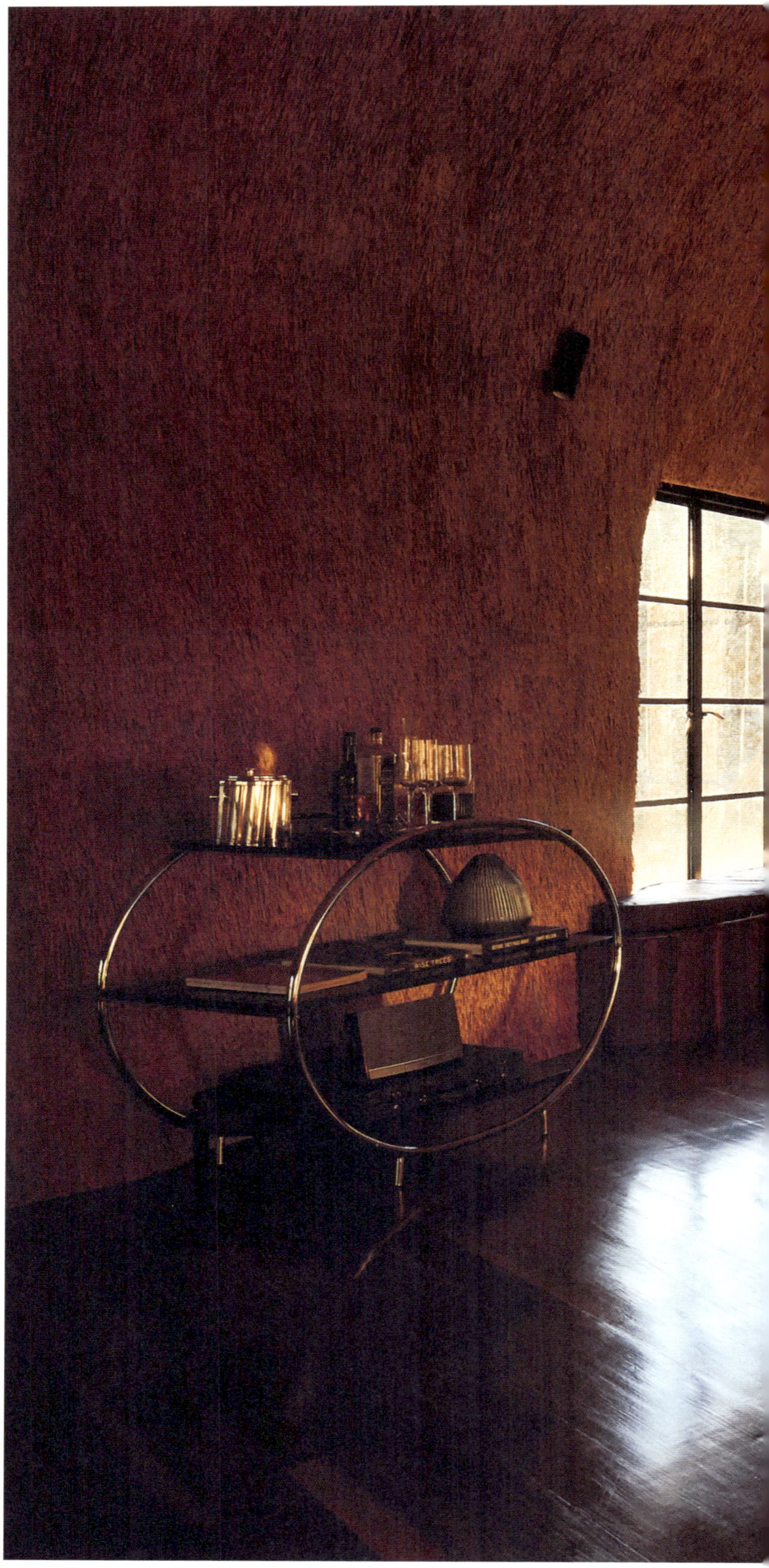

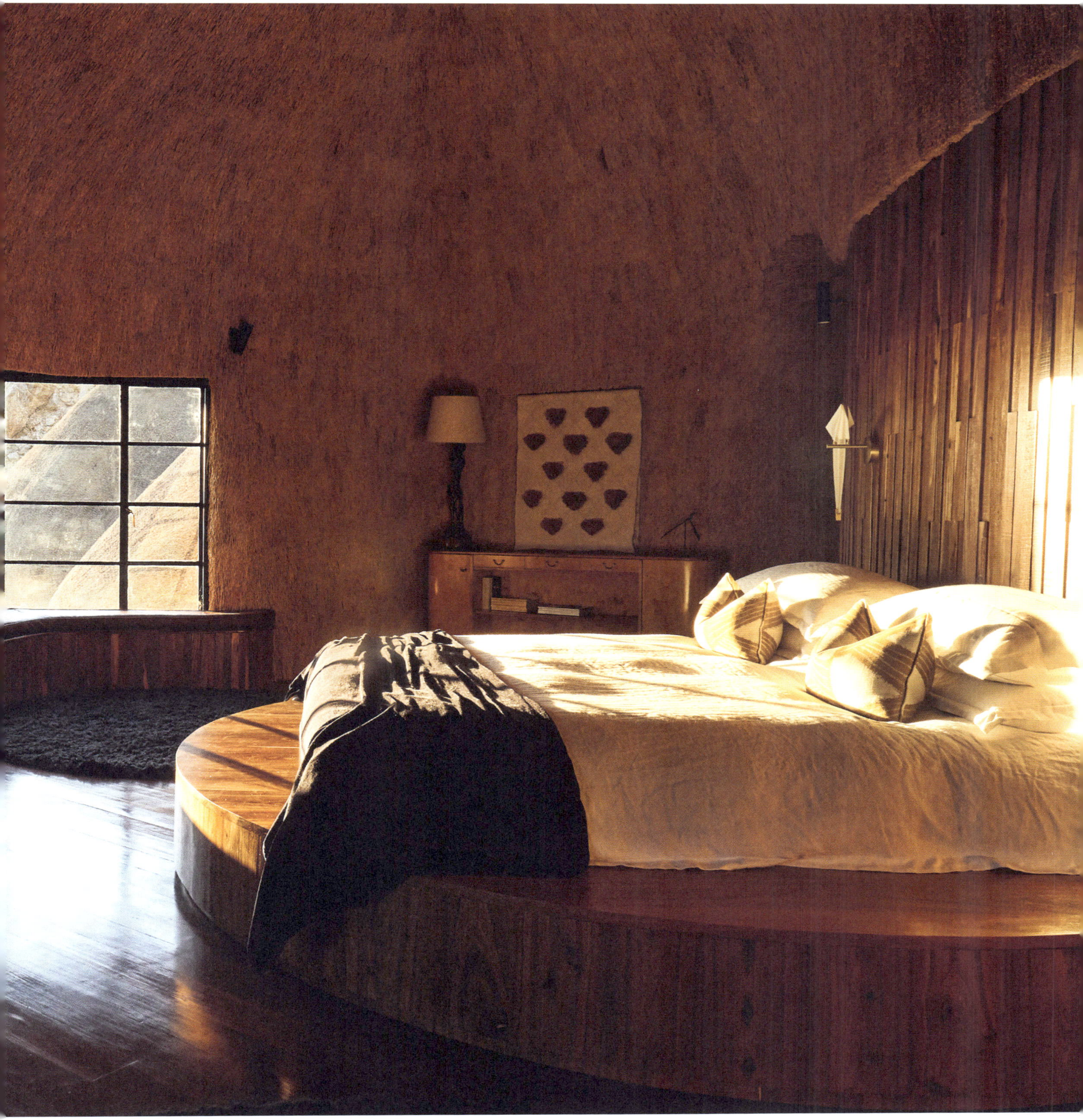

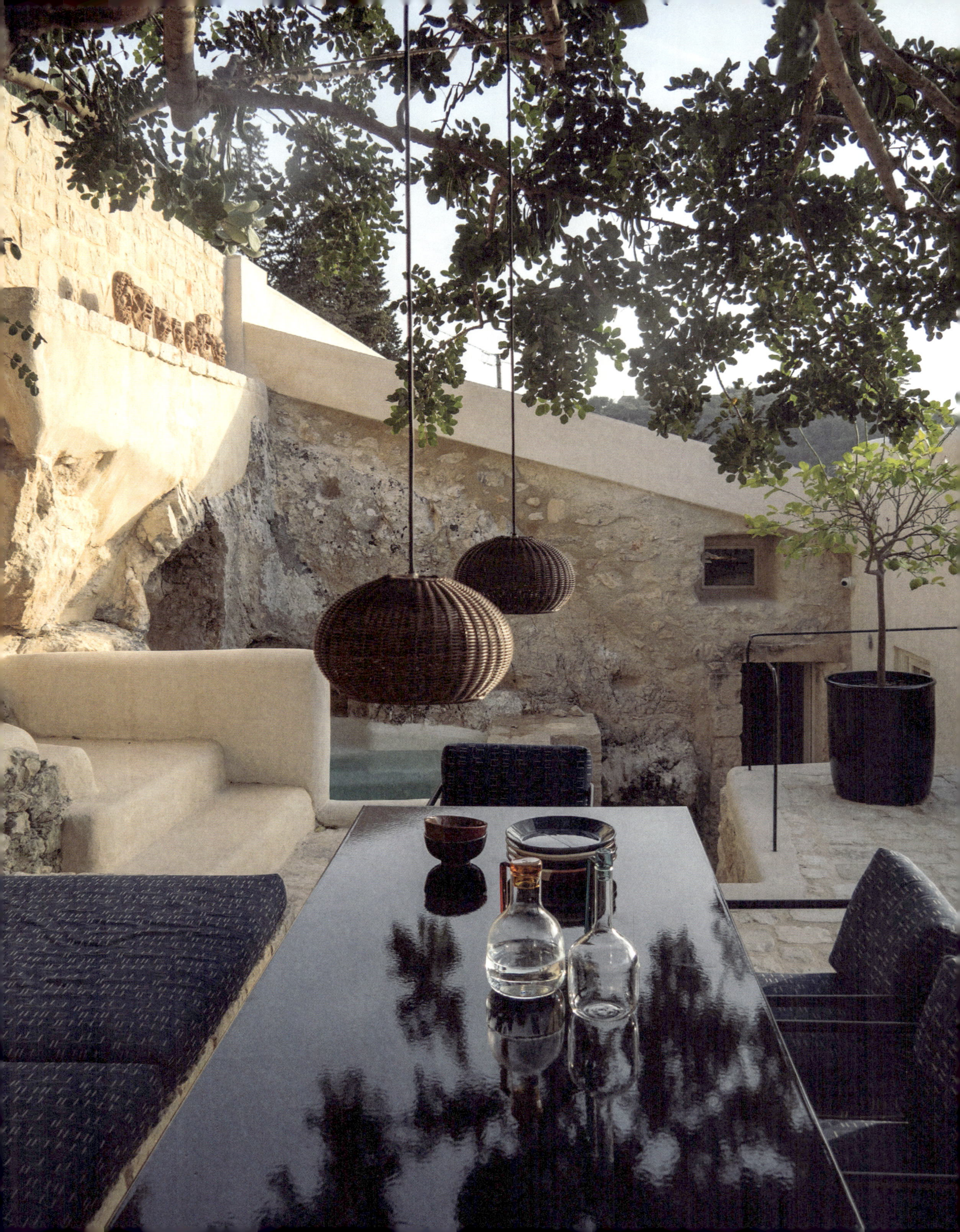

A Playful Family Escape Built into the Rocks

SCICLI, SICILY (IT) **MARGHERITA RUI**

The ancient town of Scicli, near Ragusa on Sicily's southern coast, was first founded in the Bronze Age, and remained an important agricultural hub throughout the following millennia. But a devastating earthquake in 1693 forced inhabitants to completely rebuild the city, which now reflects the extravagant Baroque architecture of the time. 'For three years, my husband and I spent our holidays in Sicily,' says designer Margherita Rui. 'We fell in love with the area of Ragusa, and then we decided to find a place in Scicli because of its UNESCO heritage.' Visiting the town, packed tight with elaborately decorated churches and stunningly ornate palazzos, is like stepping into another century.

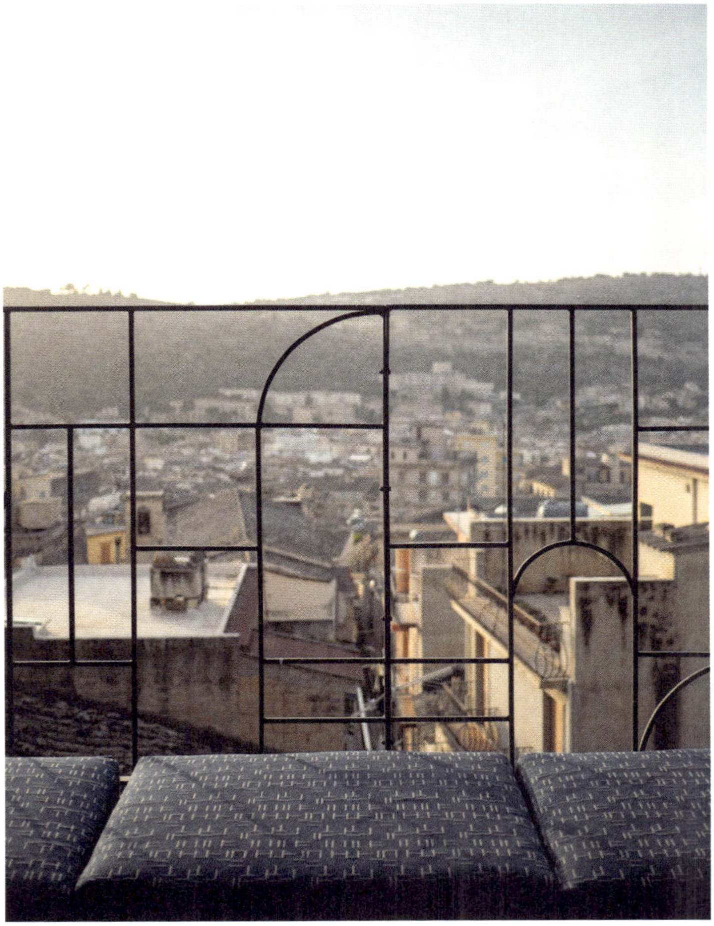

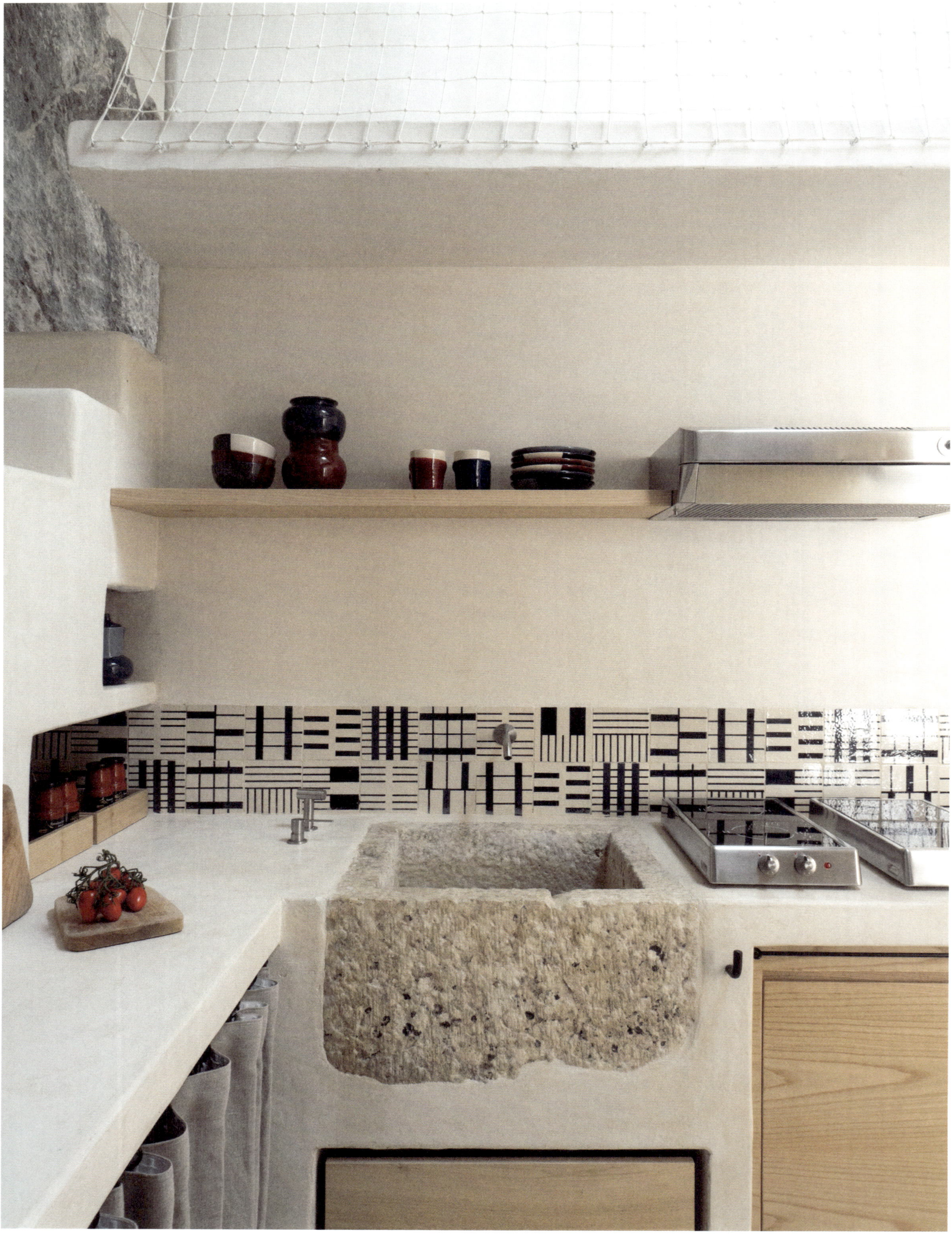

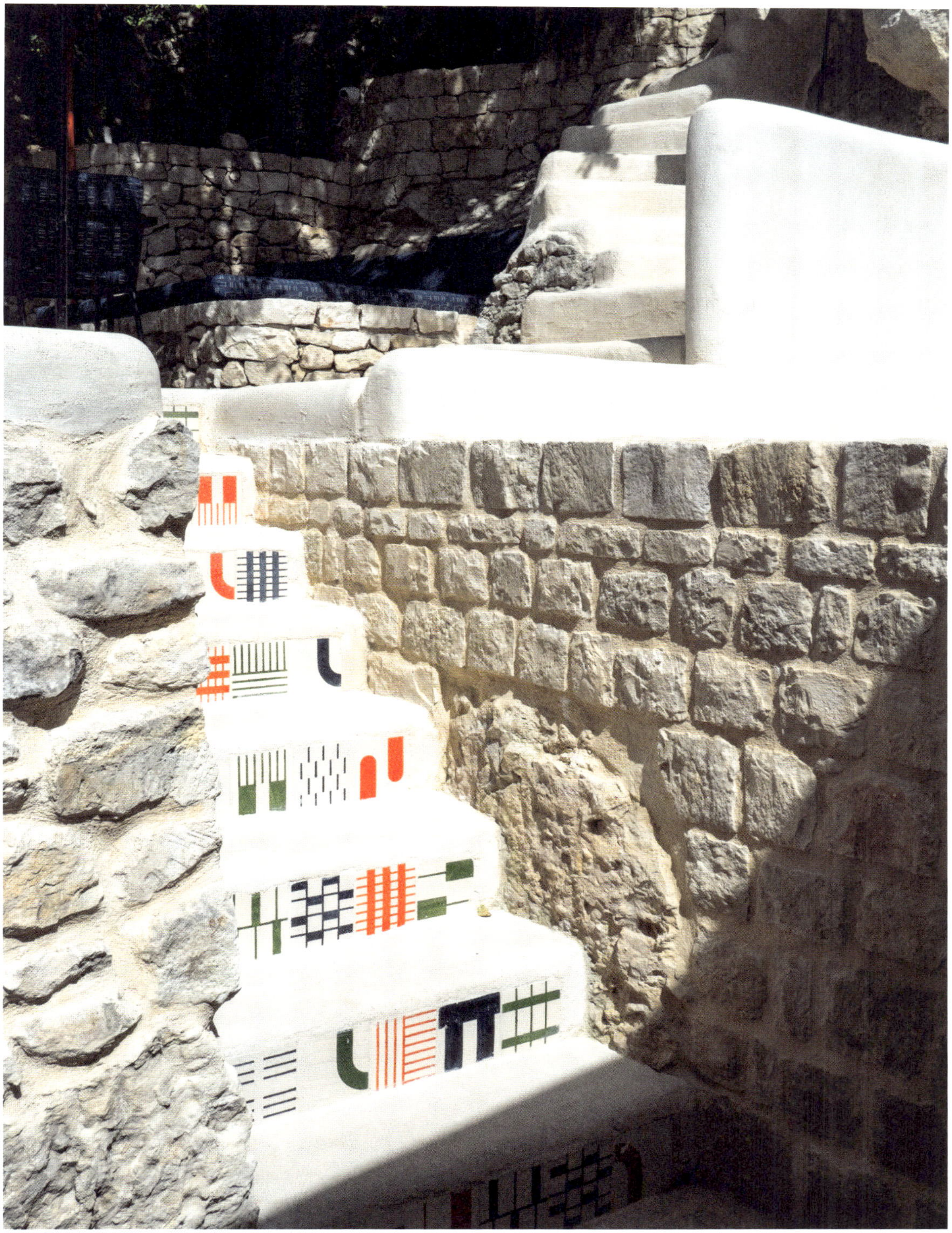

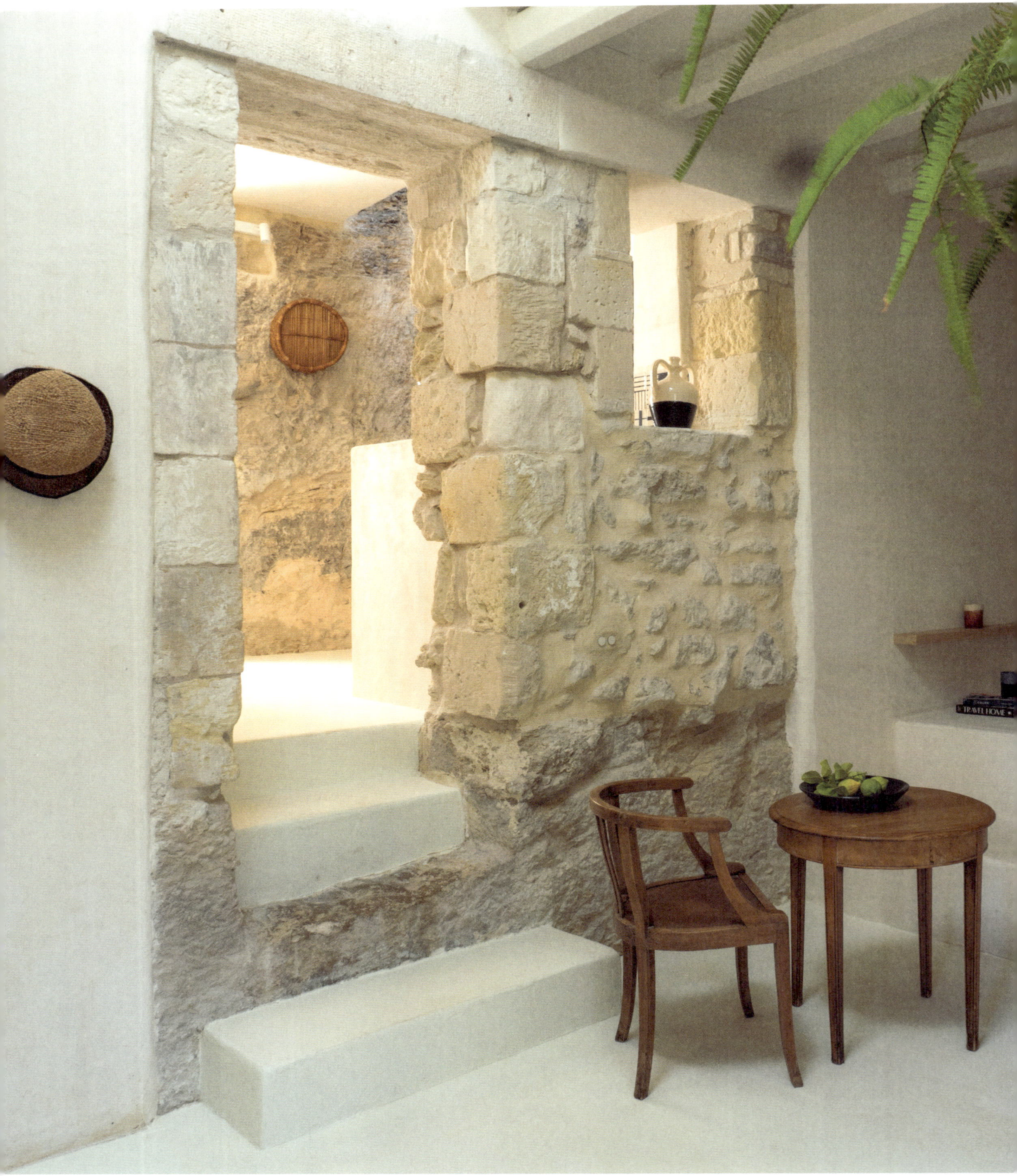
TRAVEL HOME

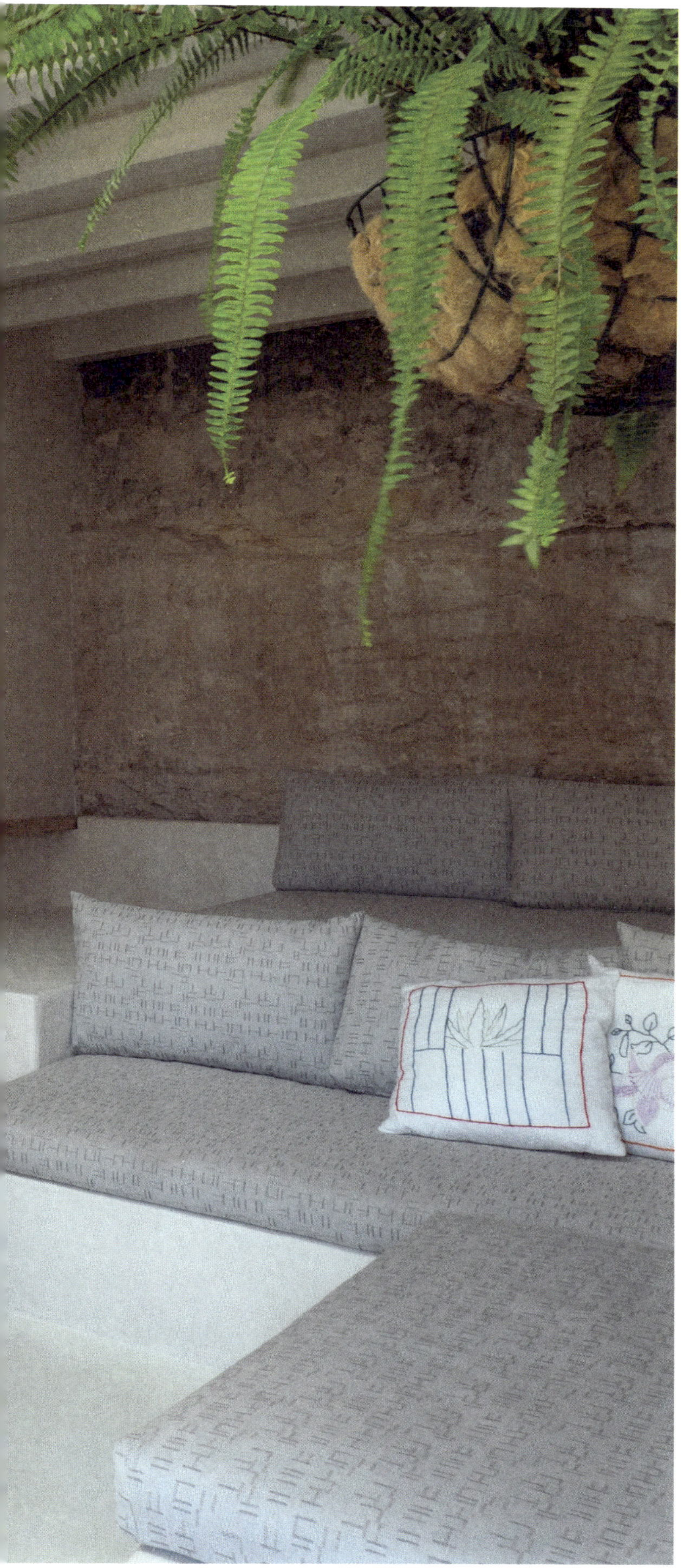

Their hillside hideaway in Scicli's Old City, named Grotta e Carrubo for the caves and carob trees that define the grounds, was carved into the rough crevices of a rockface overlooking the jumble of rooftops that rise and fall in sand-coloured waves in the town below. The house was built to cascade down the steep cliff over five levels connected by an exterior staircase, which is decorated with colourful graphic tiles that Rui hand-makes for her ceramics brand, Ninefifty. Comprising two bedrooms, a simple kitchen, sitting area and netted loft for Rui's two sons, the home sits just below the town's church of San Matteo and incorporates the UNESCO-listed dry-stone walls that have delineated the property for centuries.

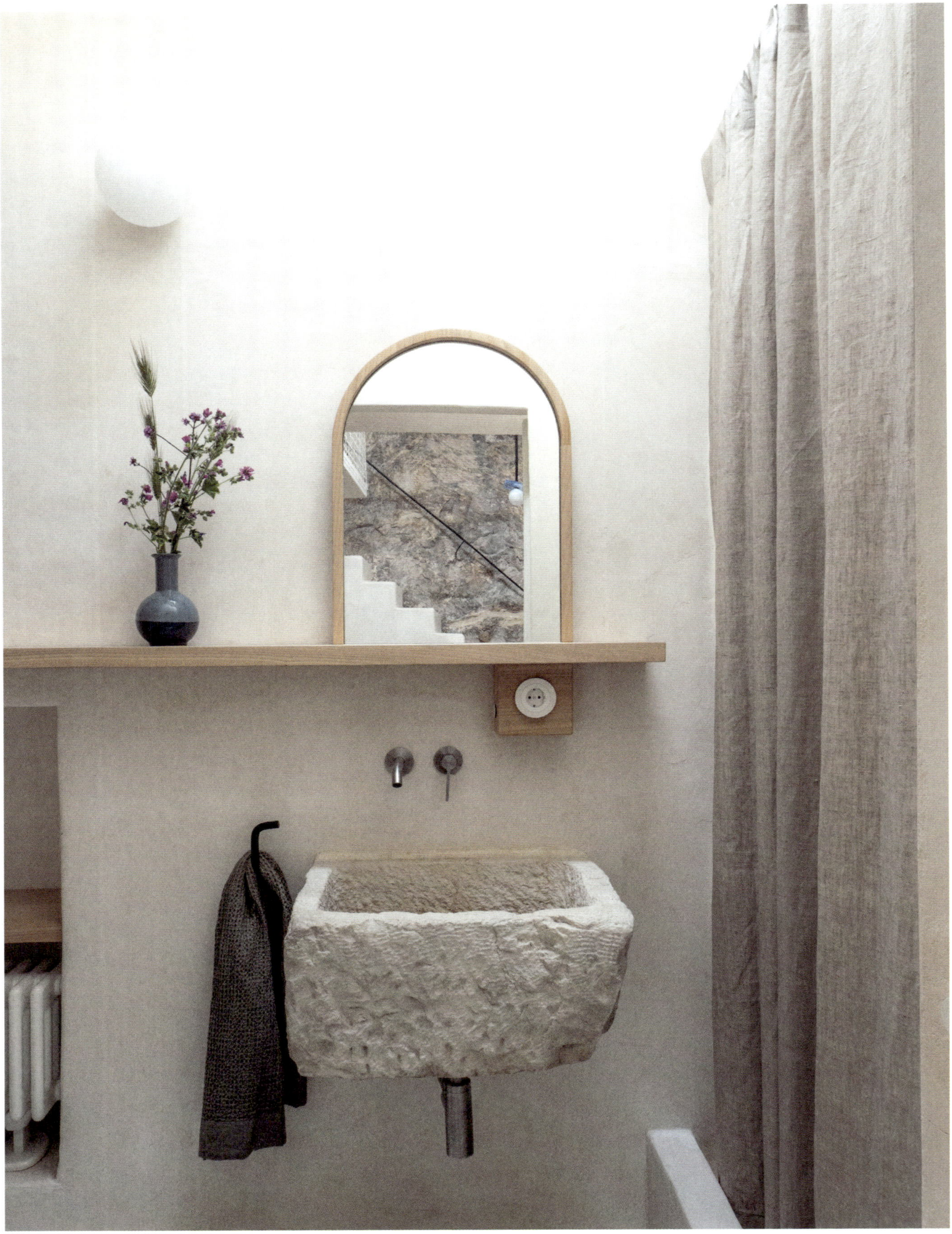

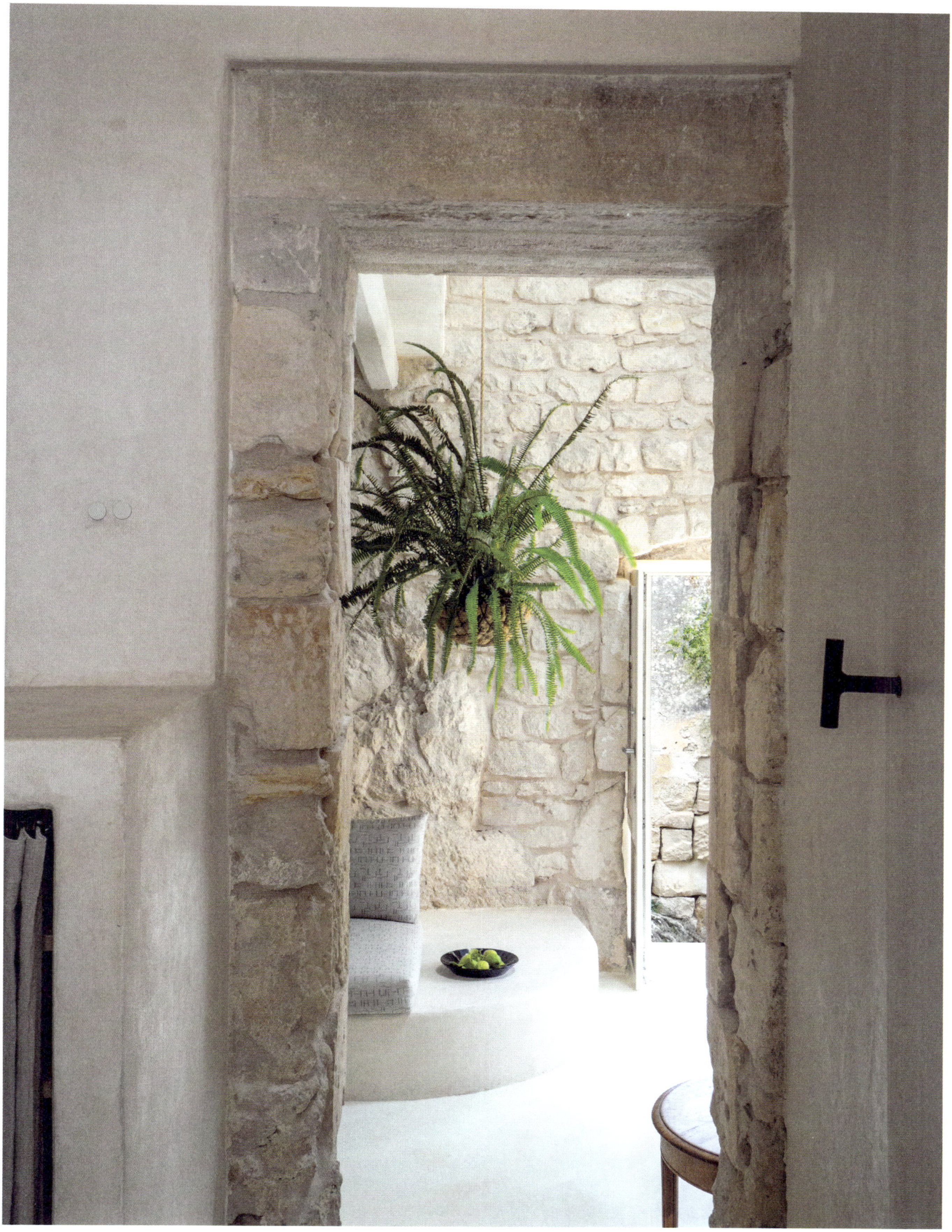

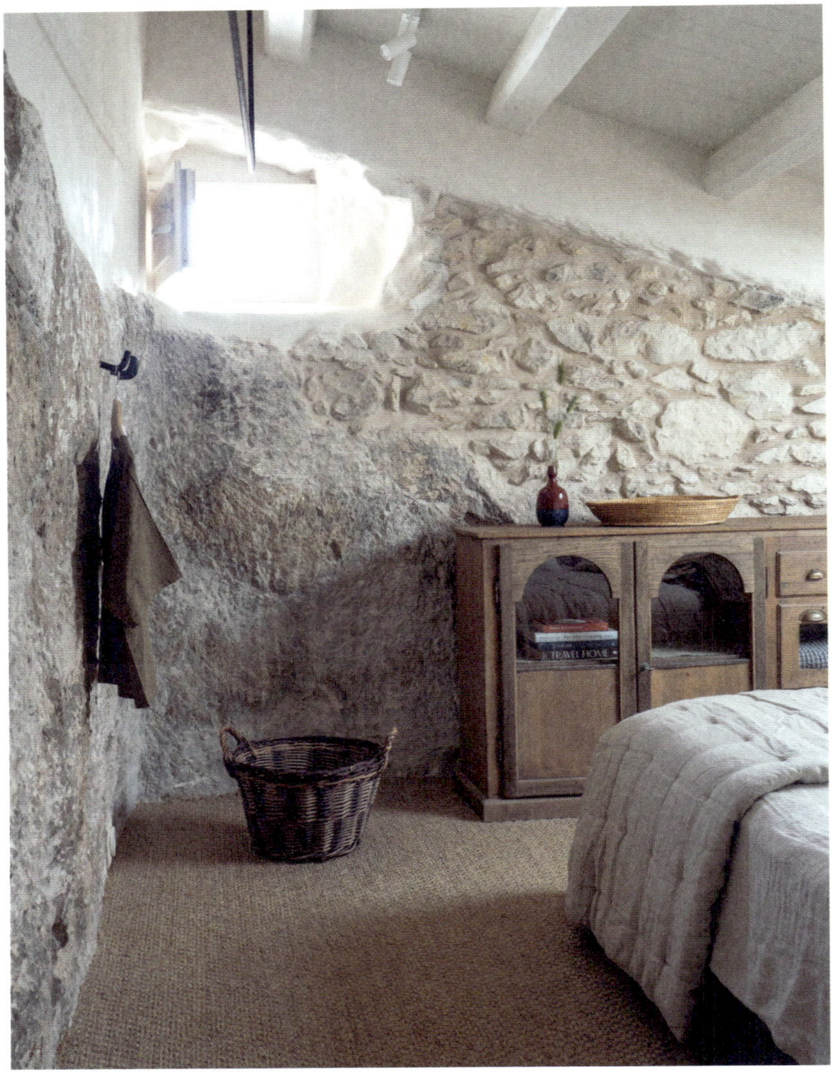

'I'm a designer and creative director, and in my work I'm driven by the desire to experiment with materials, paying attention to the know-how and culture of different locations,' she says of the design, which she called on architects Cristiano Urban and Rachele Sebellin to realise. Indeed, the elements that decorate the space were heavily informed by the region's craft history. Rui pulled from traditional Sicilian building techniques to create the home's bespoke features, collaborating with local metalworkers to render the graphic, wrought-iron fencing and forming the roughly hewn walls out of pale Modica stone, natural lime and timber from local chestnut trees – an effect that feels simultaneously contemporary, thoughtfully handmade and true to the area's long history of settlement.

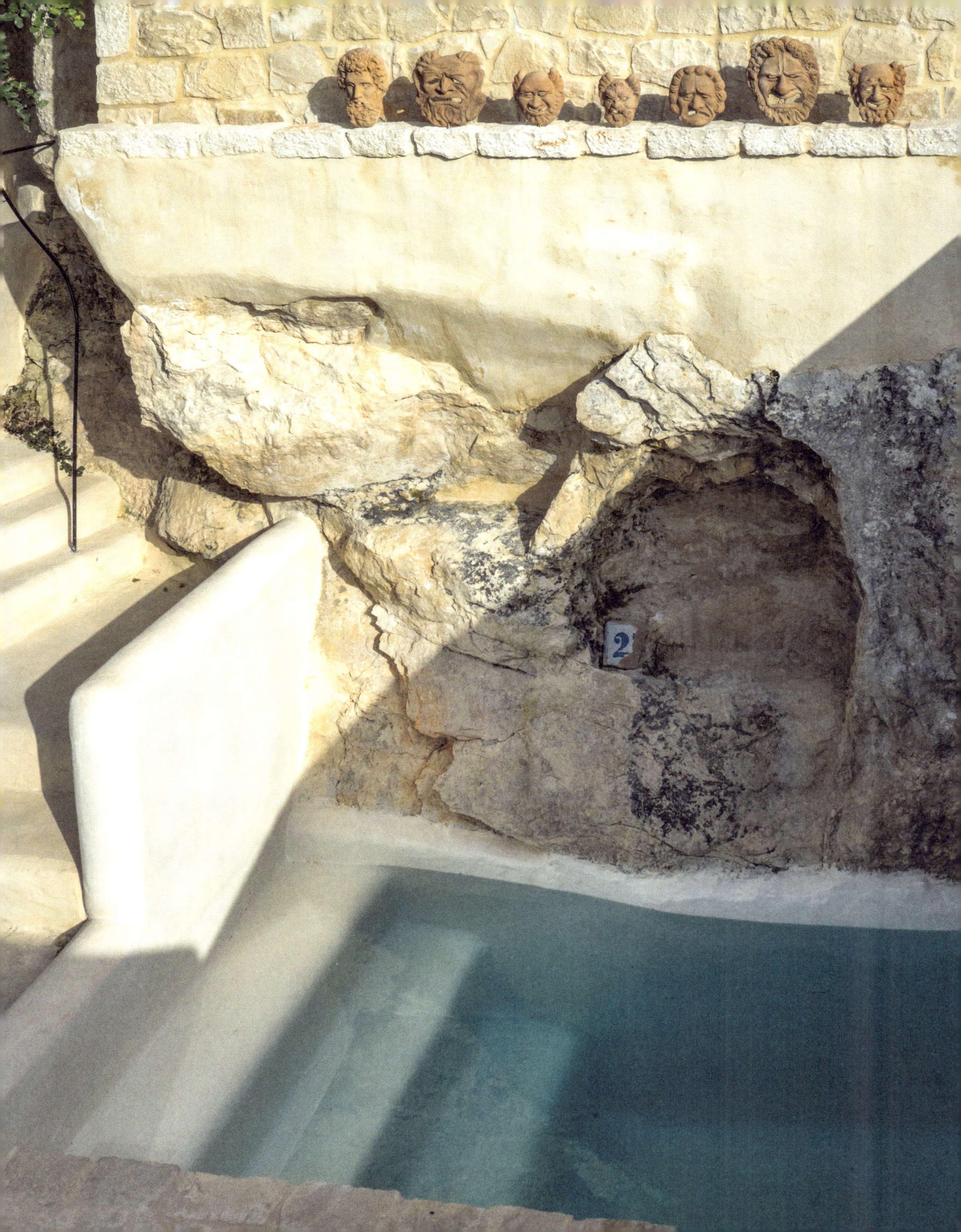
2

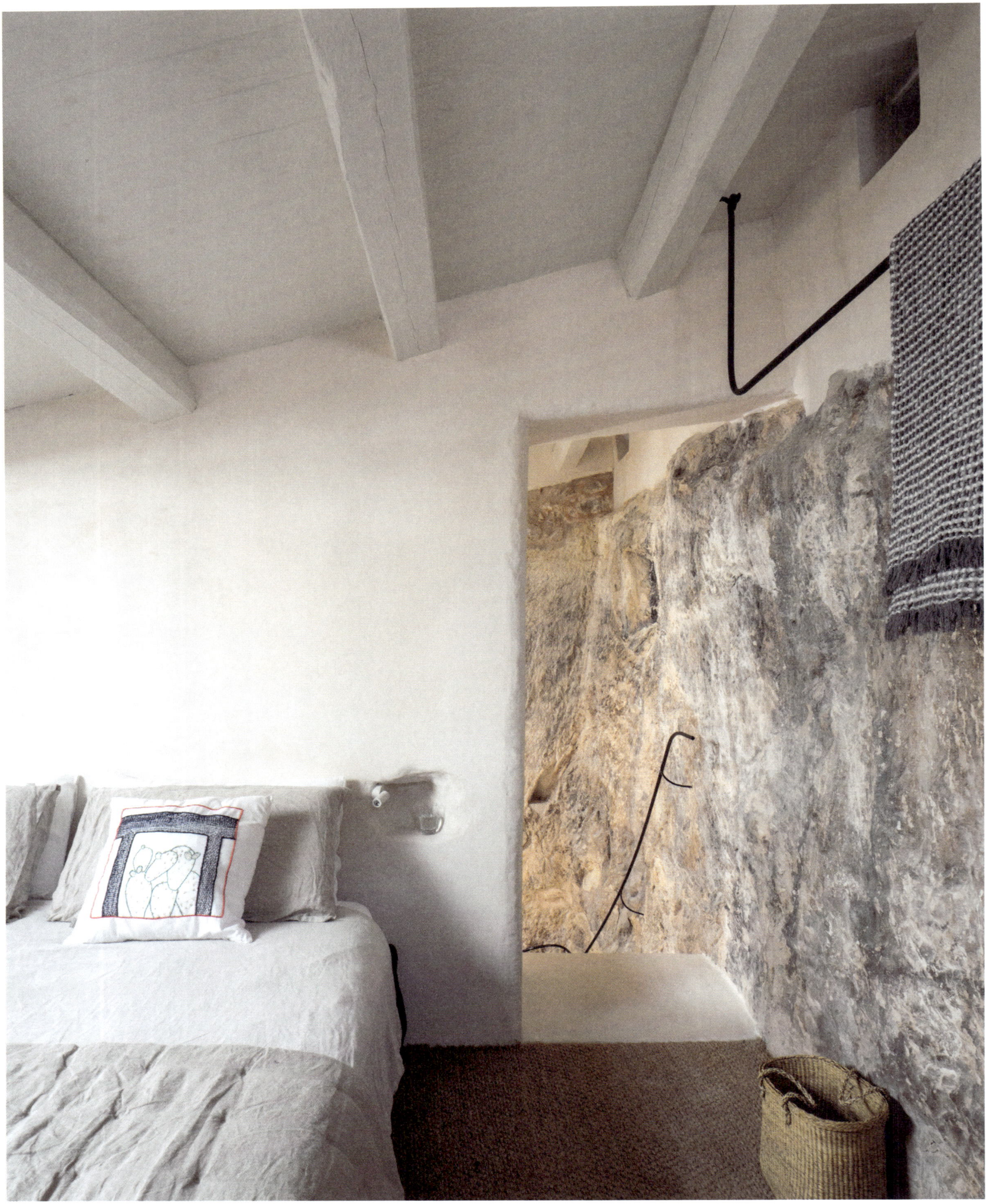

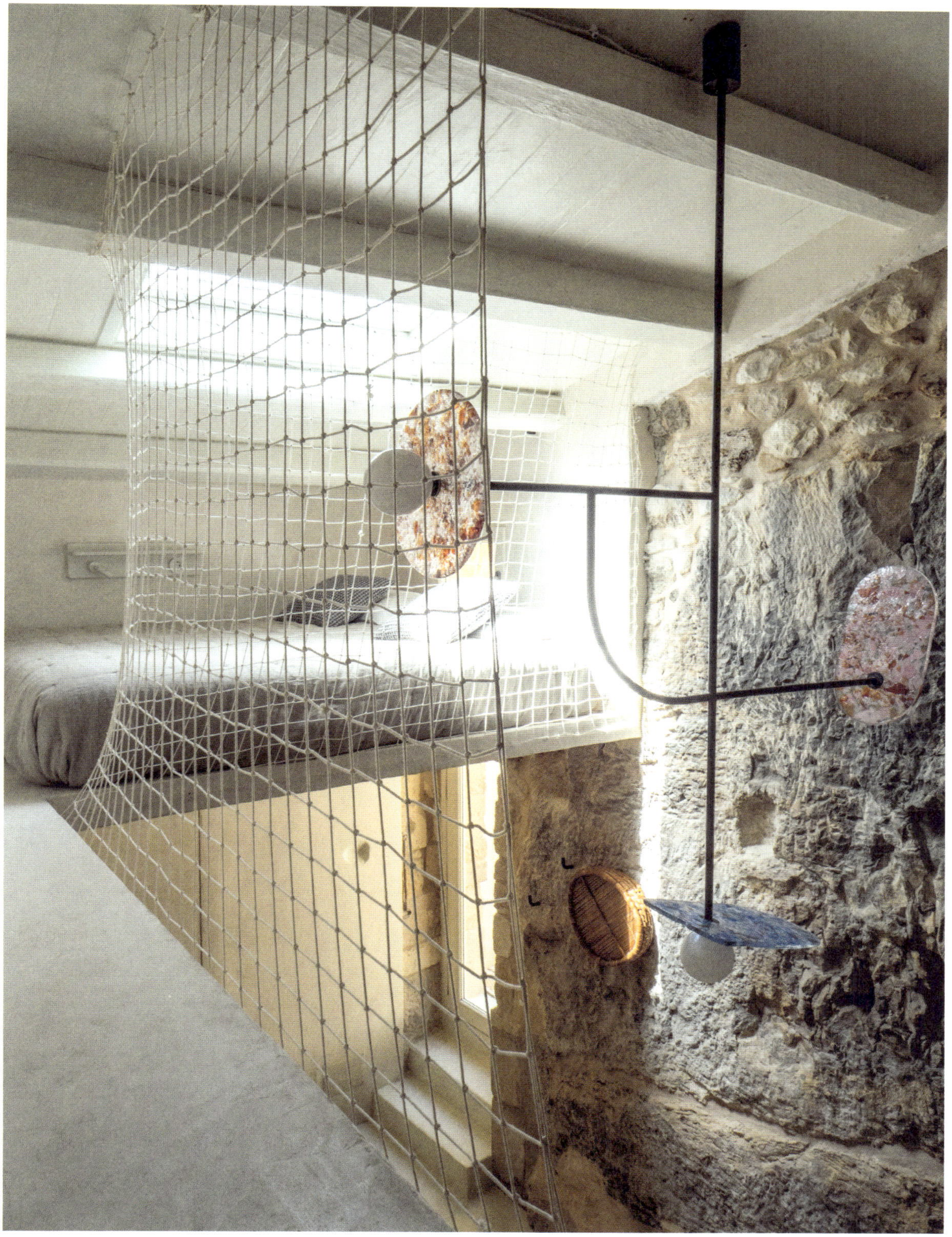

A Spiritual Retreat in the American West

JOSHUA TREE, CALIFORNIA (US) **PETRONIO STUDIO**

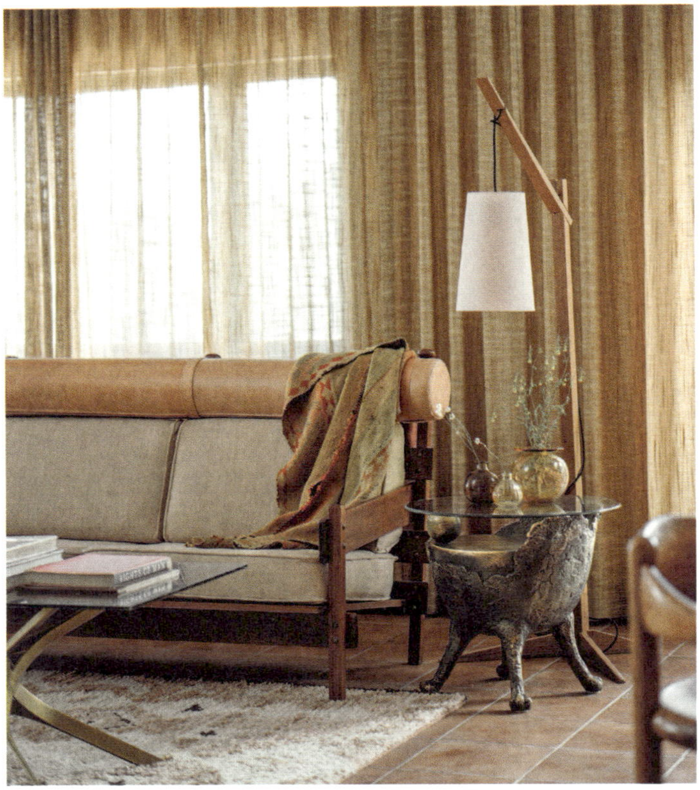

Joshua Tree National Park, a stretch of arid desert in Southern California that is home to the spiky, alien-like shrub that gives the region its name, has long been a pilgrimage place for artists. From the 1960s architects who populated nearby Palm Springs with buildings designed in their iconic space-age style, to the musicians in the 1980s and 1990s who turned to the desert's mystic aura for inspiration, Joshua Tree has a reputation for being a hotbed of creativity. This artist's retreat designed by Los Angeles–based Petronio Studio perfectly channels that vibe.

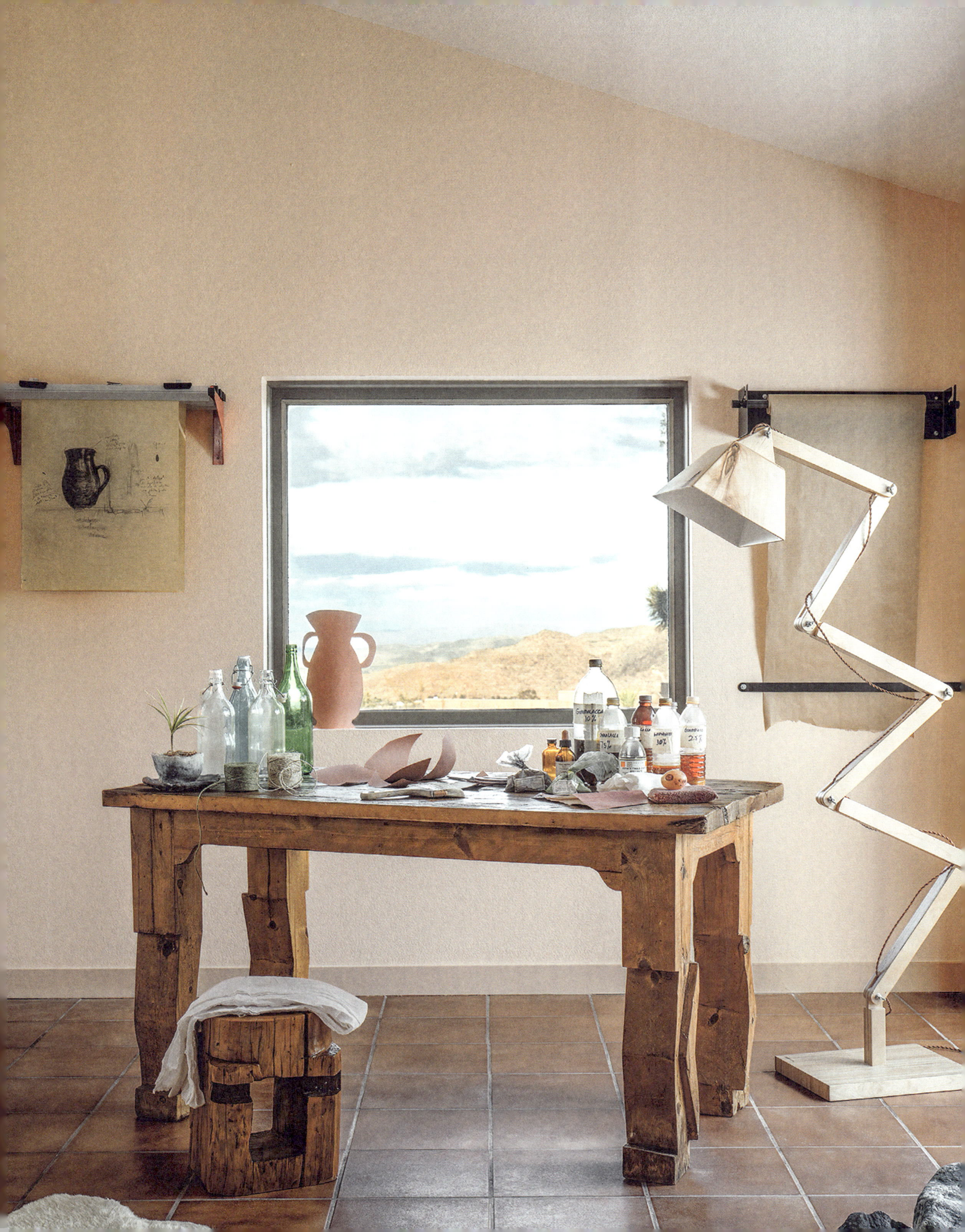

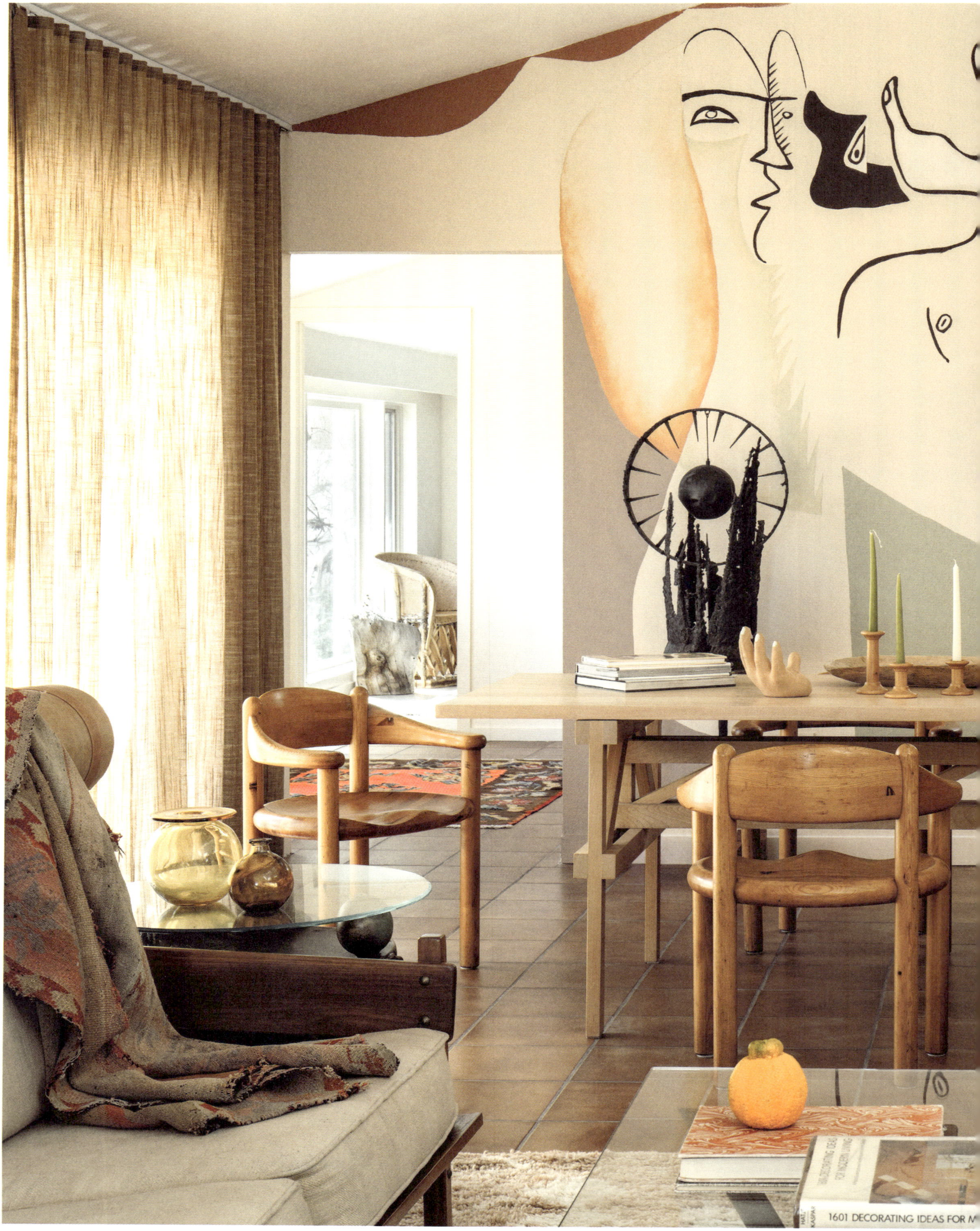
1601 DECORATING IDEAS FOR M

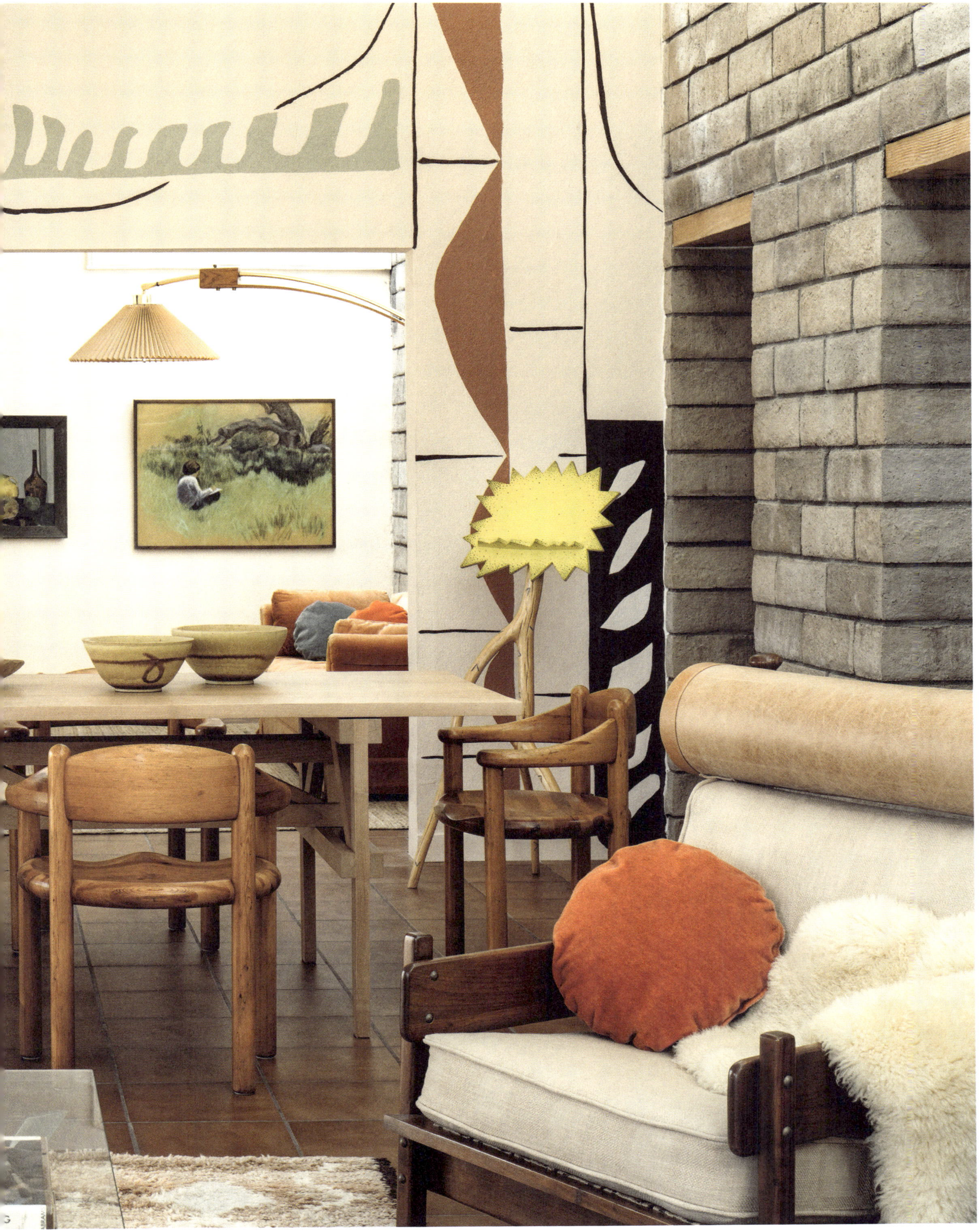

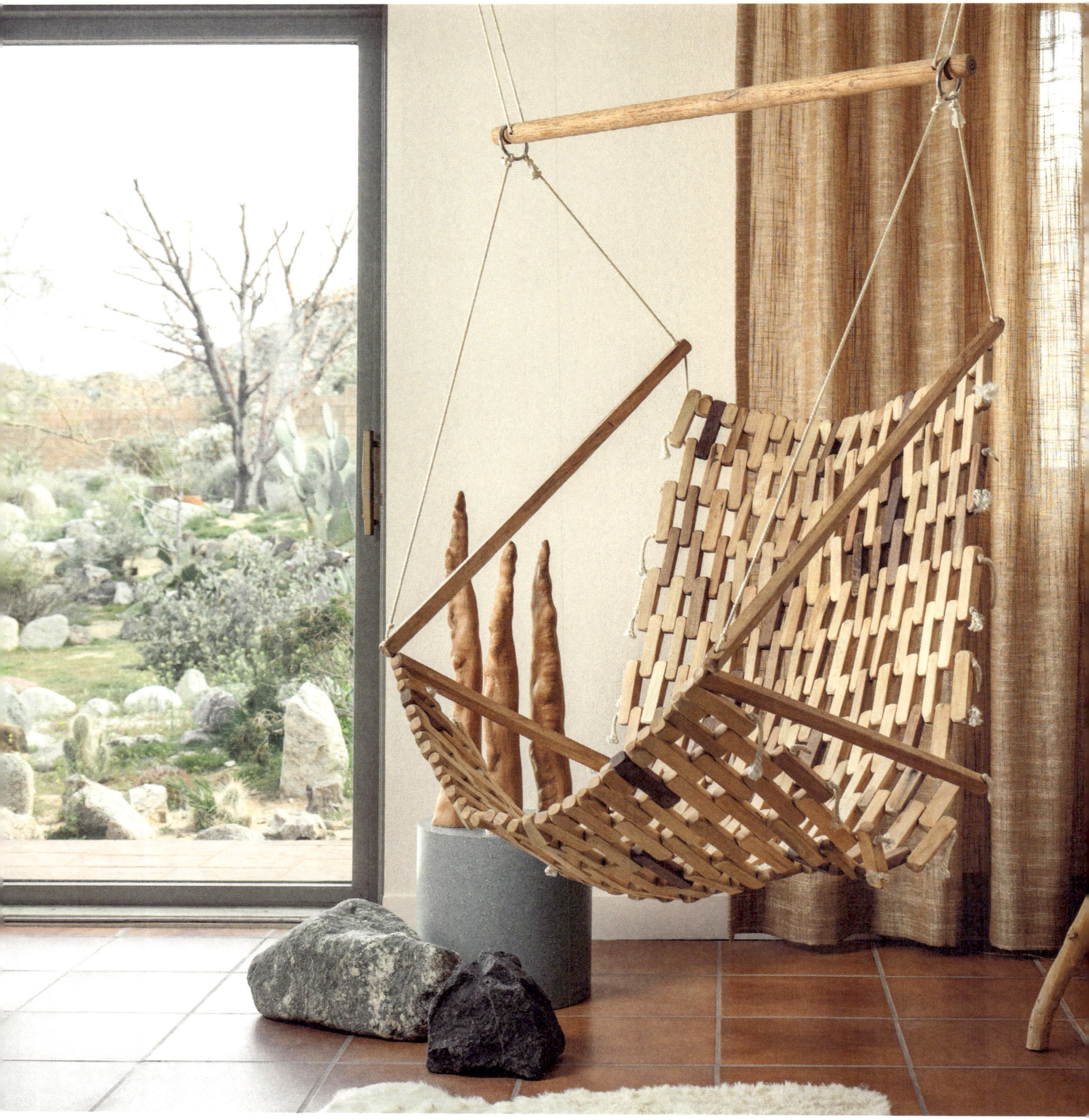

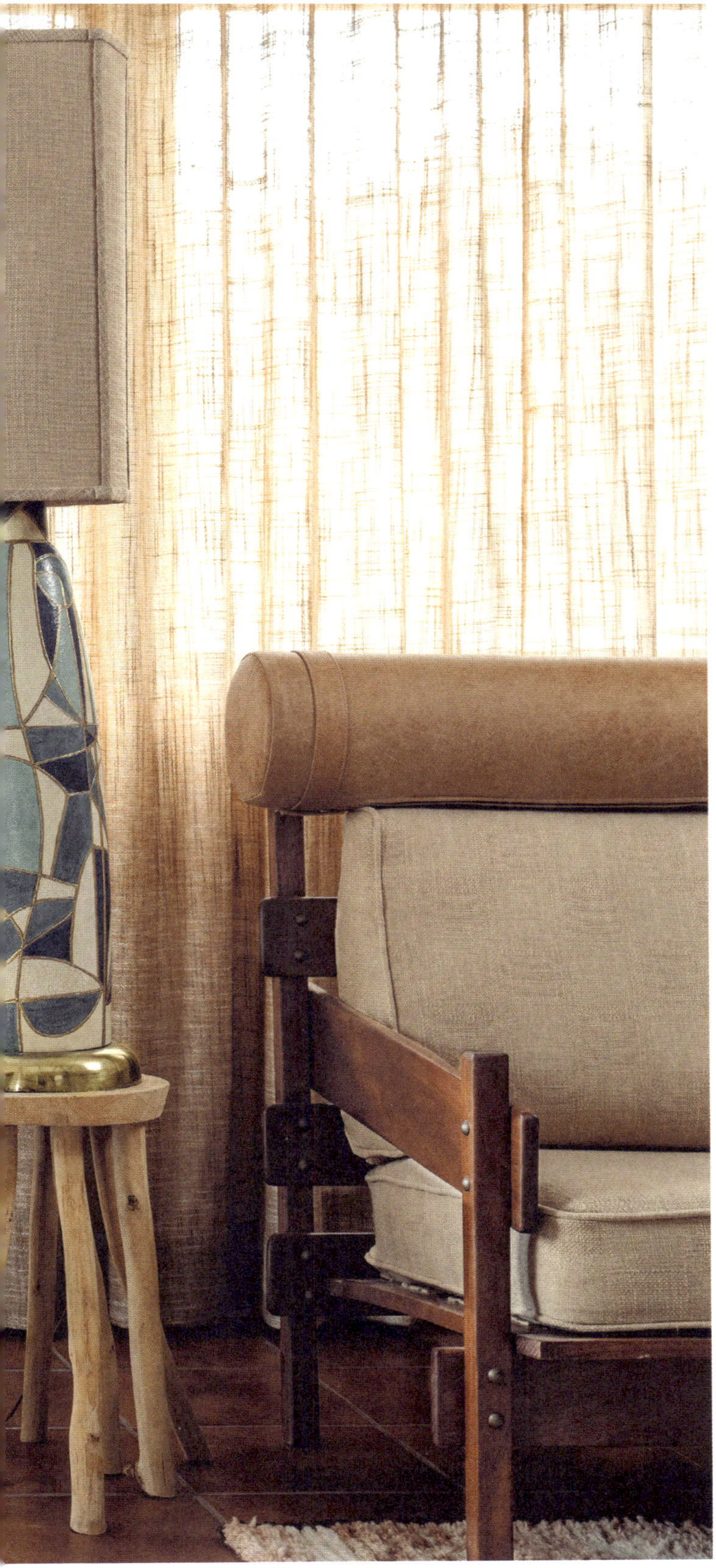

'In approaching this project, we tried to strike a balance between the existing architecture and the exterior landscape,' say the architects of the renovation, which spills out into a verdant garden of desert succulents, cacti, sand, turquoise stones and lava rocks. A 1960s A-frame cottage provided the structural backbone for the project, which Petronio Studio left mostly intact. Instead, with help from local artist Violet Hopkins, the architects poured their creative energy onto the interior surfaces, painting an expansive floor-to-ceiling mural inspired by the designs and drawings of mid-century architect Le Corbusier. 'We adopted some of the colours that thrived in the surrounding desert including turquoise, pink and gold sand to form our palette for the interiors,' they say.

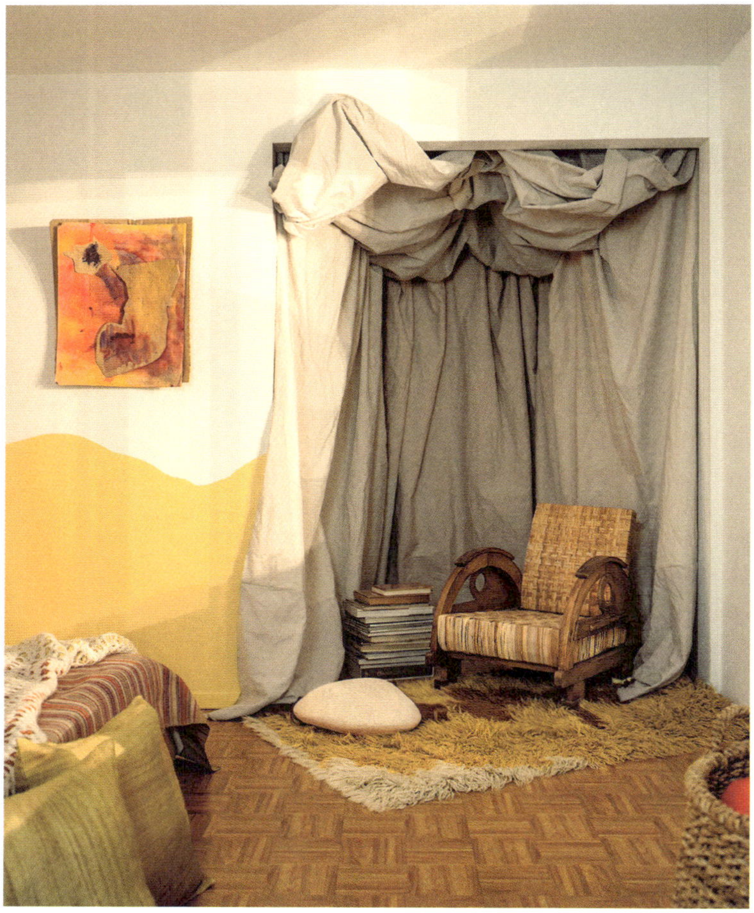

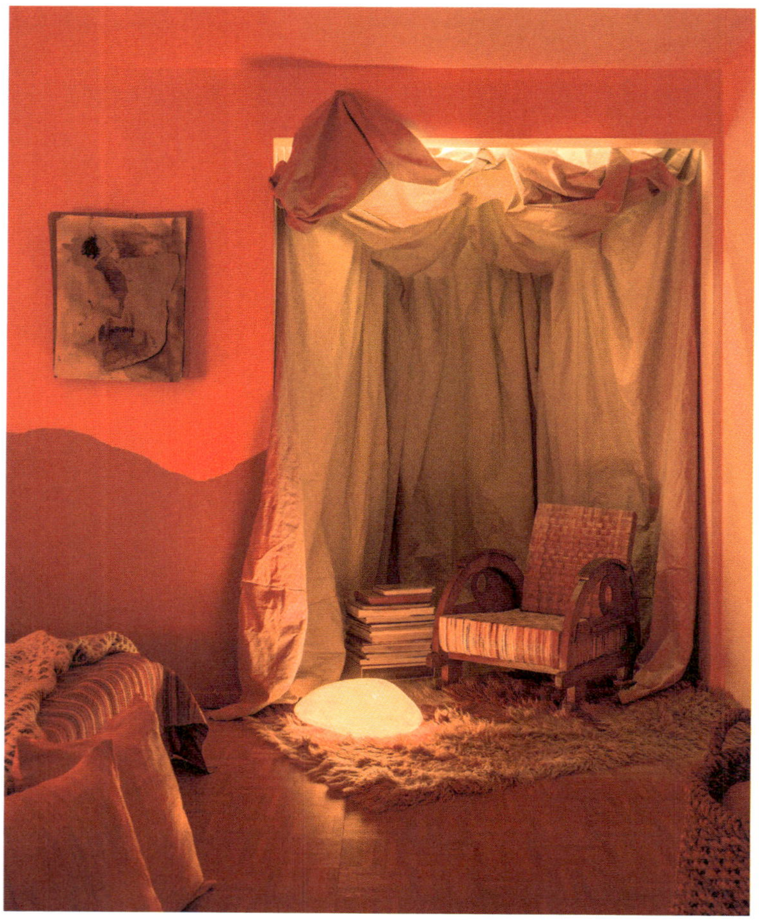

Throughout the house, thoughtful touches based on the owner's personality were incorporated into the design: 'He works in the tech industry but has a secret passion for art. His work combines craft paper, natural pigments, precious stones, and fabric into raw and suggestive two- and three-dimensional collages.' Indeed, the entire house channels the spirit of a creative workshop, with arts and crafts details – such as a contemplation corner draped in voluminous textiles – as well as ample space to work, dream and relax. 'The atmosphere is calm and flows slowly,' posit the architects, 'offering different opportunities for isolation and meditation.'

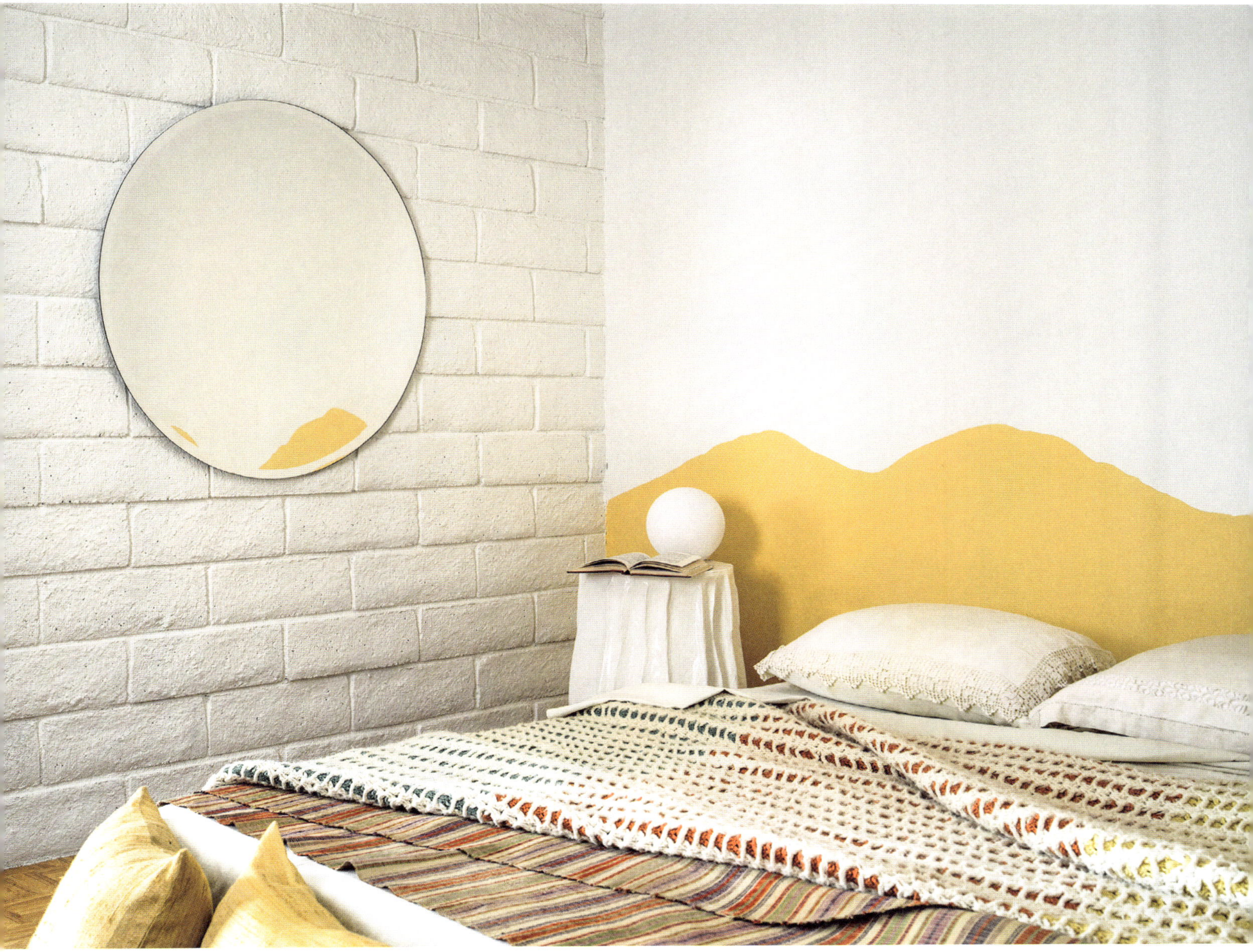

An Off-the-Grid Escape in the Moroccan Hinterlands

NEAR MARRAKECH, MARRAKECH PREFECTURE (MA) **STUDIO KO**

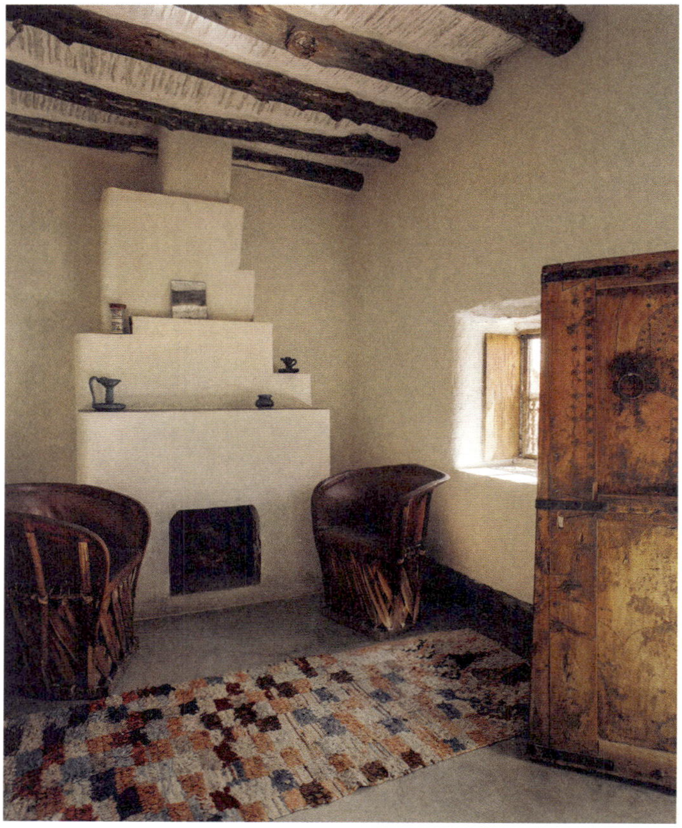

The arid topography surrounding the Moroccan city of Marrakech is nothing short of a visual feast. Gently undulating hills of red earth, carpeted with rows of cacti and scrubby desert bushes, dominate the panorama, occasionally punctuated by a solitary rammed-earth home or rural village. Studio KO's Karl Fournier and Olivier Marty have long been enamoured with this land, which is why they chose a sprawling compound 20 miles from the city as their place of retreat.

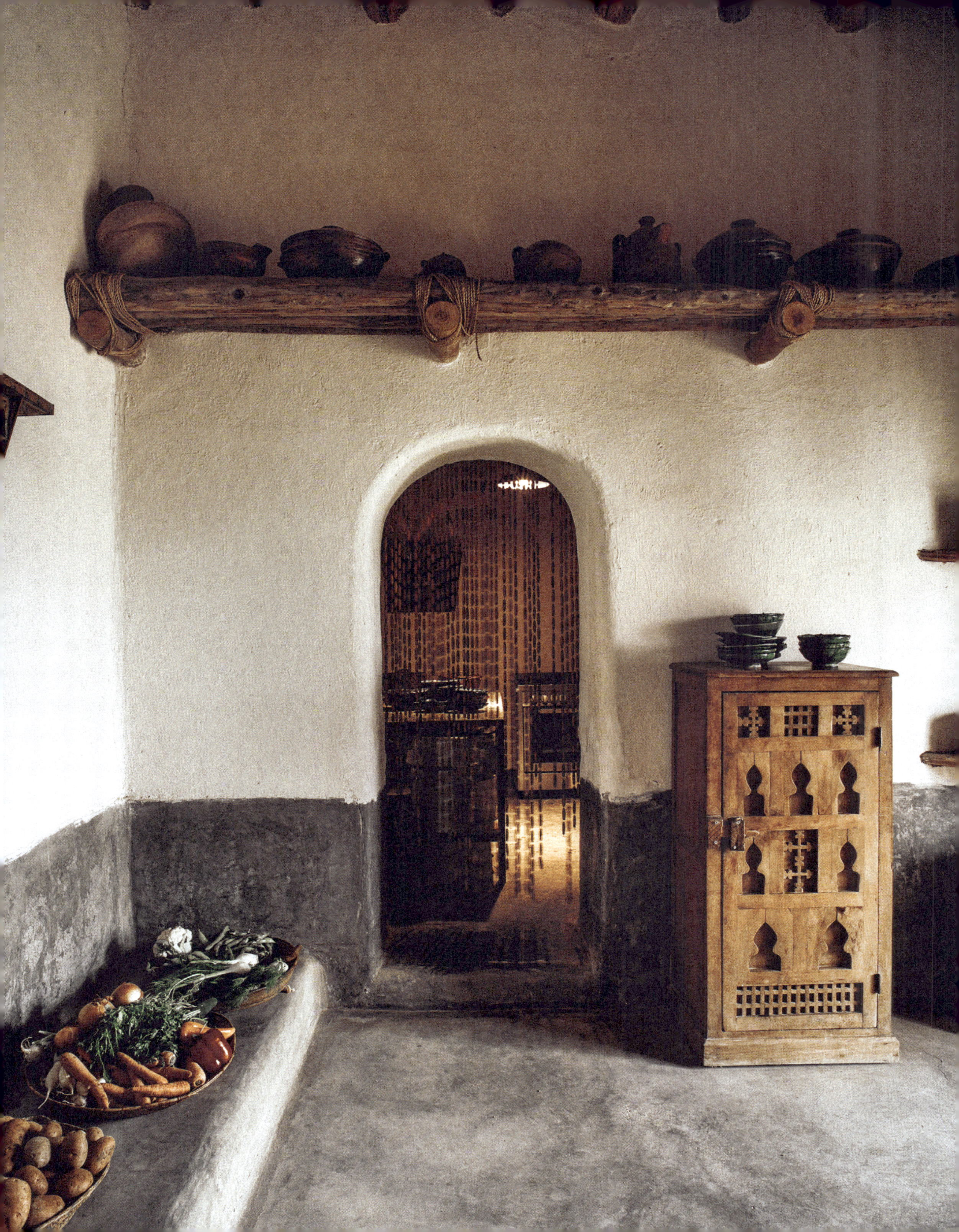

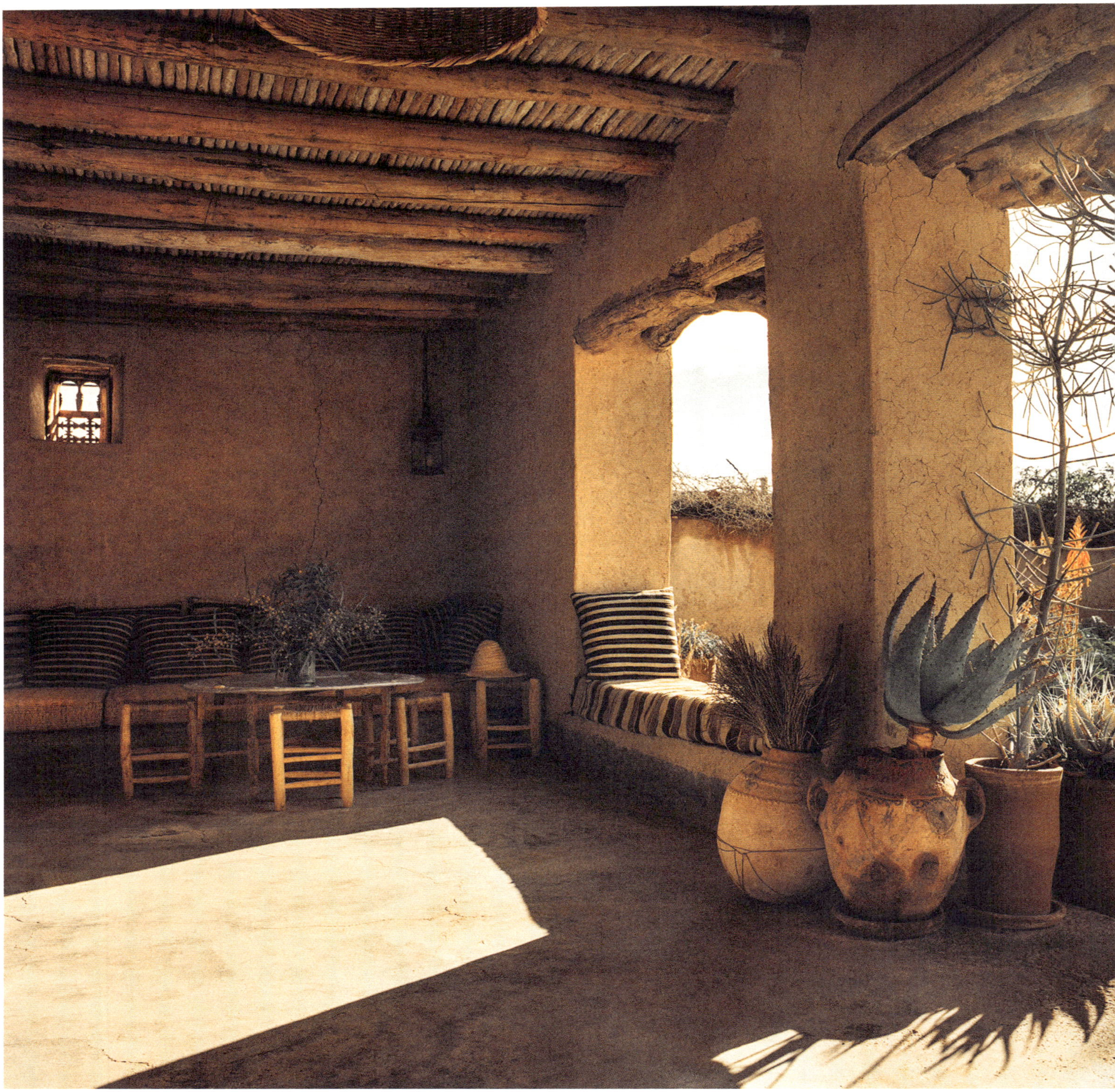

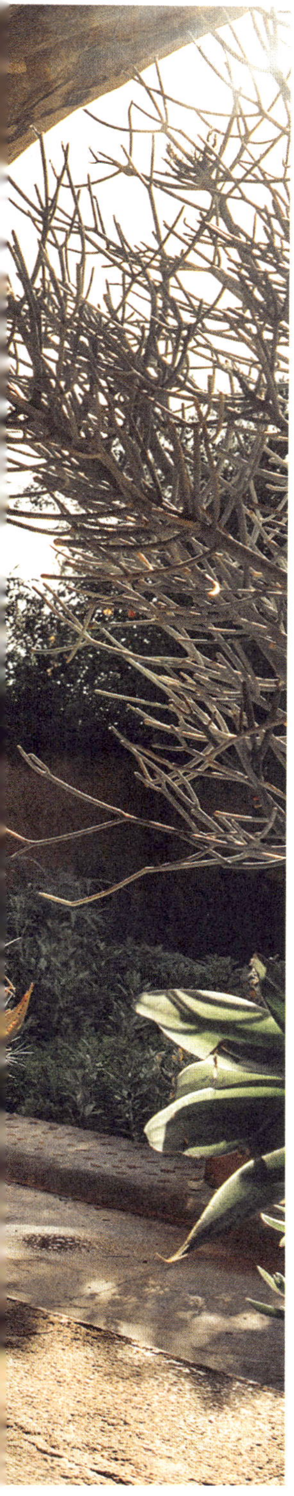

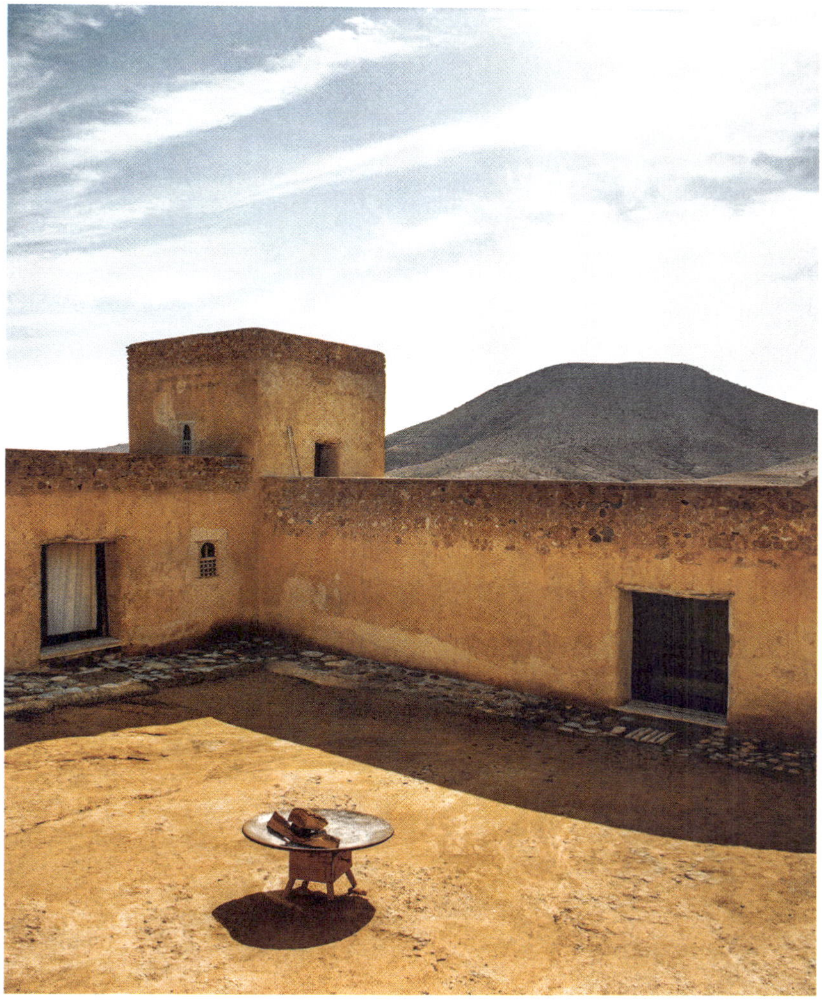

What was once a farmhouse owned by a Sahrawi family, a people native to this region of North Africa, had fallen into disrepair by the time Fournier and Marty were introduced to the former owners through a mutual friend. After acquiring a 99-year lease for the adobe-walled structure, they went to work restoring and rearranging the rooms while keeping many of the vernacular architectural elements intact. 'The home is entered through a very large, long room that serves the main courtyard,' they explain, referring to the traditional entranceway where arrivals to the house are first greeted, a rectangular volume with staggered entranceways that obscures views to the private areas. 'This is an area dedicated to guests.' Beyond this formal greeting room is a 'large courtyard with four bedrooms, the hammam, the kitchen and the winter lounge,' they add. 'This is truly the heart of the house.

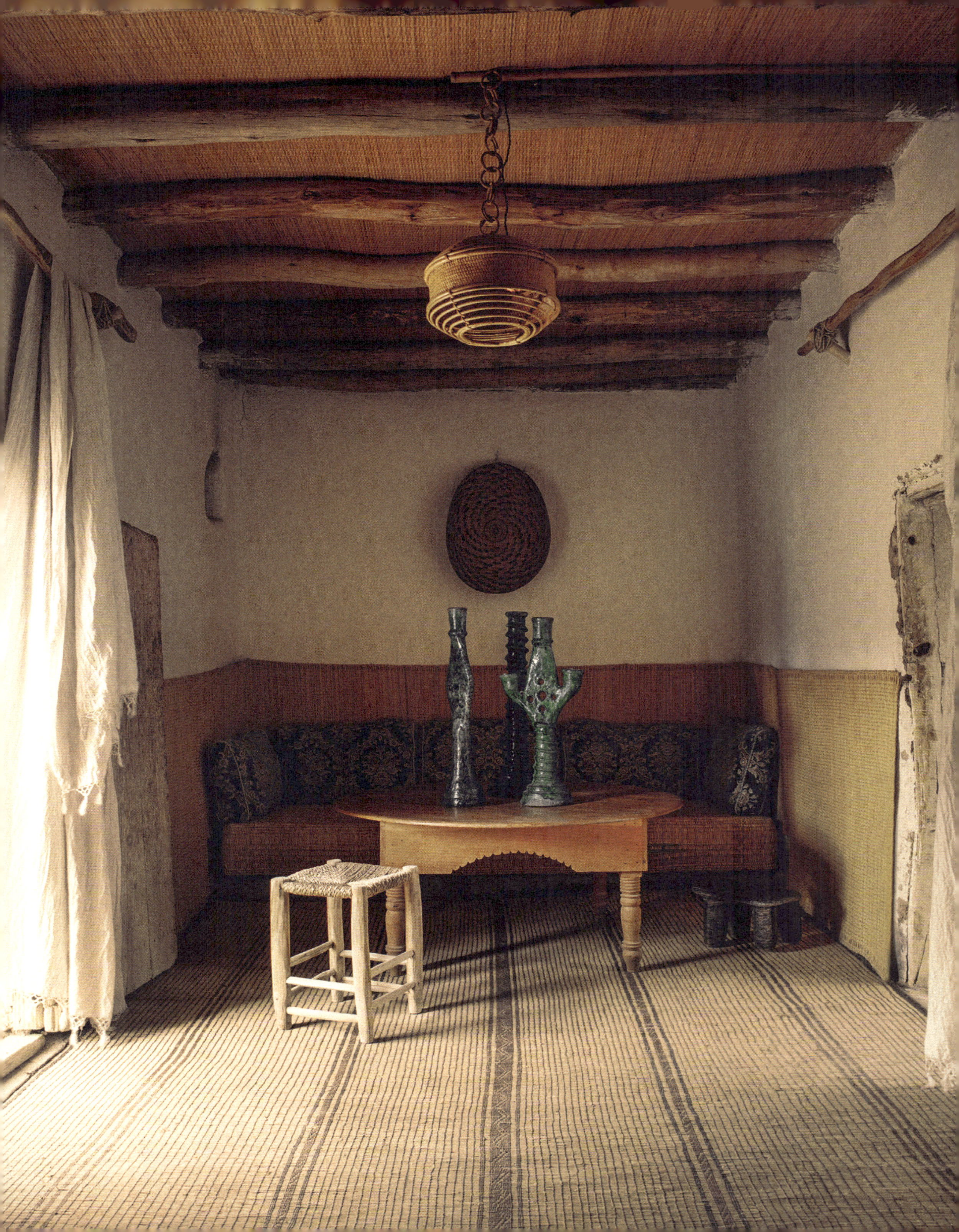

Throughout the dwelling, they've kept the furnishing and decoration intentionally spare – a far cry from the opulent hotels and luxurious, art-filled villas they are best known for. 'We don't have clients who would ask us for such a simple, authentic and pared-down place. People don't call on architects for that,' they explain. Instead, they chose pieces that would echo the traditional Berber homes that populate the region. 'We designed some things like the beds inspired by Moroccan *koursi*, which are small stools made of laurel wood and straw. Others have been found locally, like the chests of drawers and the desks.'

Both Karl and Olivier point to different places in the home that they best connect with. For Karl, it's 'the tower and the terrace. I can spend hours there, the view on the landscape is always changing.' While Olivier claims the hammam and the kitchen are his most treasured spaces. 'I like watching our housekeeper Fatima preparing meals,' he says. Each sojourn to the remote house is often accompanied by family and friends, both old and new. 'Once a year, for a month, we welcome an artist in residence; a writer, filmmaker, photographer, designer,' they say. 'We didn't want a selfish place that exists only for our personal pleasure.'

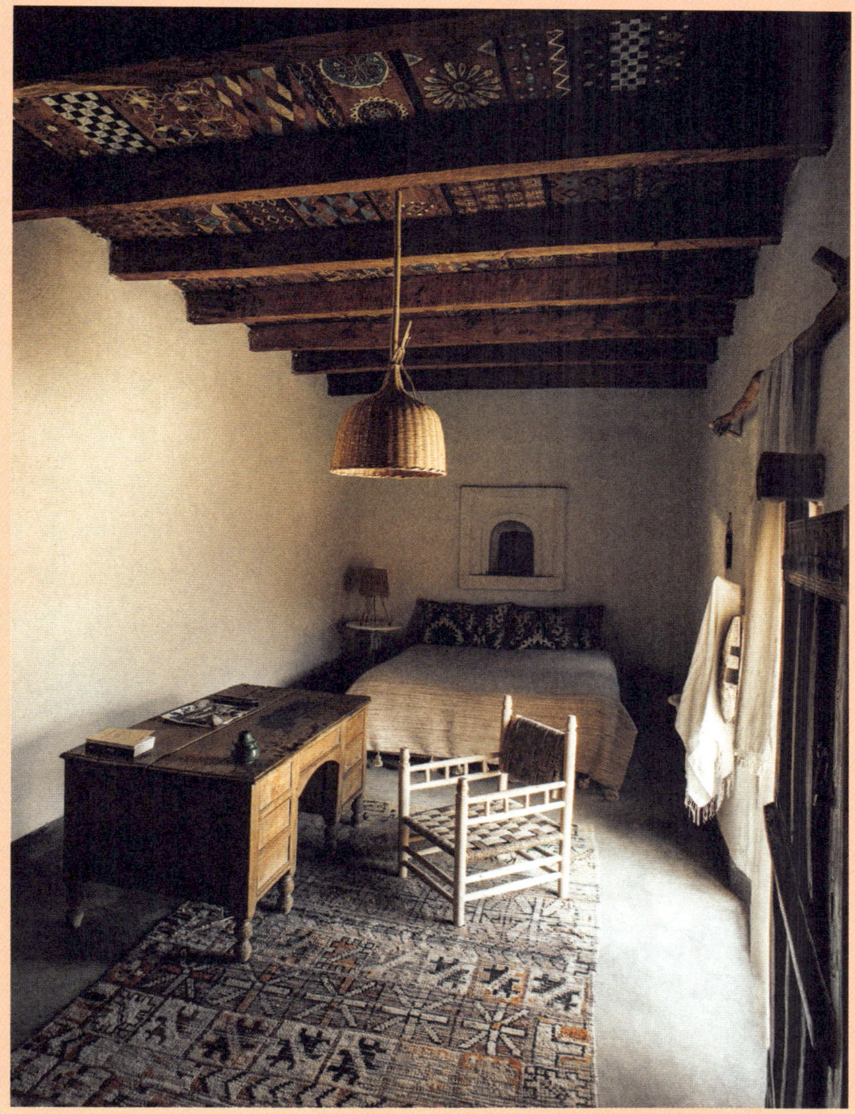

Interview

Karl Fournier and Olivier Marty first met as students studying architecture at the École des Beaux-Arts in Paris. Partners in life and work, since founding their studio in 2000 they have realised projects across the globe, from luxurious hotels in London to Marrakech's Musée Yves Saint Laurent. With offices in France and Marrakech, they, along with their son, Chrismaël, split their time between their home in Paris and their Moroccan retreat.

Studio KO

Why did you choose Morocco?

KO: We would say that it is Morocco that chose us, offering us so many wonderful opportunities to meet people and work. We have known Morocco since we were students; we often stayed there and have long felt at home there.

Where in Morocco is it? Why did you choose this particular spot?

KO: It is located 33 kilometres from Marrakech, hence its name: KM33. Places there are often named for their distance in relation to a 'main' point. We have known this place since it was a farm inhabited by a Sahrawi family whom our friend Jean-Noël, who opened so many doors in Morocco for us, had known well. When they left the region to return to the Sahara, we offered to take over the farm. We did not want it to fall into ruin; we had already been in love with the place for a long time.

What was the overall concept for the house?

KO: The idea was to respect as much as possible the typical habits and customs of the Berber way of life. The heart of the house is reserved for close friends and relatives, whereas, strangers and passers-by are received in the summer living room via the vegetable garden and do not penetrate the intimacy of the house.

What was this space like when you originally found it? What kind of interventions needed to be done?

KO: Everything has been completely redone, but it all looks original because everything was done following the rules of the art and by hand. Some parts were about to collapse; some areas had already completely collapsed. It was necessary to rethink everything, to reallocate everything for a new use, it was like a new page in the life of the house.

The house is quite cut off from the world, without a phone or internet connection. Why was it important to you to be able to totally disconnect?

KO: In the beginning, it was by chance; we did not choose it for that. But it turns out that with time we realised that being cut off from the world, far from being an inconvenience, was a real opportunity. It became a real retreat thanks to the disconnection. A friend once told us that it's not a house, but a prayer to God, and in a way he was right; it's a very meditative place that doesn't aspire to connect to the world, but calls on you to refocus on the self.

You have said before that you designed the home with respect for 'ancestral Berber techniques'. Could you go into detail about that element of the design?

KO: Even if we had to save this house from the ruin that threatened it, we wanted to do it according to the traditional crafts and techniques that prevailed at the time of its creation. We therefore began by scrupulously respecting the footprint – nothing was removed or added. The narrow rooms have remained so because they usually measure only the maximum length of the tree trunks available thereabouts, palm, olive and, more rarely, eucalyptus. Then we had to rebuild the whole house because the original walls were no longer stable, apart from one or two exceptions; but we did it in *pisé*, a technique that utilises a concrete made of rammed earth. The interior walls are coated with lime, as was originally done.

Do you keep any collections here?

KO: We have a large variety of peppers in the garden to please Karl who is a great fan and loves to eat them but, apart from that, there is no particular collection, except perhaps the Berber dishes that we can track down quite enthusiastically with Jean-Noël and also the carpets of the High or Middle Atlas.

What do you love about this area?

KO: Its authenticity. Here there is only the essential. We return to a form of archaism in the art of living and inhabiting a place. We once made an inventory of the objects that populate the whole house and there were fewer, much fewer, than in our son's room in Paris. Here he plays for hours with a piece of wood, an old bottle; he makes things, he collects what he finds, he manages to keep himself busy sometimes with nothing. Usually, he is surrounded by so many things, toys and objects, that he doesn't really play with anything.

Can you describe your day-to-day life while you are staying there?

KO: In the morning it's breakfast, everyone taking it at his own pace, either in the vegetable garden or in the summer living room, sometimes in small groups directly in the kitchen, especially in winter, because it's the warmest room and we make big fires there. Then everyone does what he wants: reading, writing, walking or sunbathing on the terrace. Then the hammam with the wood fire is lit again and we spend some time in there in turn according to our mood – some prefer the morning, others the evening before going to sleep, as it is a beautiful way to relax. Then we all meet for lunch and Jean-Noël, our friend with whom we began the renovation of the house, rings the bell when everything is ready. The meals are delicious and last until nap time. The afternoon is filled with simple tasks like gardening or other pursuits, again everyone is busy. In the evening, we meet for an aperitif on the high terrace to admire the sunset. Then we go down to dinner at nightfall. There are always calm or passionate discussions, according to who the current guests are, which sometimes last late into the night. The more nocturnal of our guests extend the evening outside so they can admire the incredible starry sky, free of any light pollution. And we count the shooting stars!

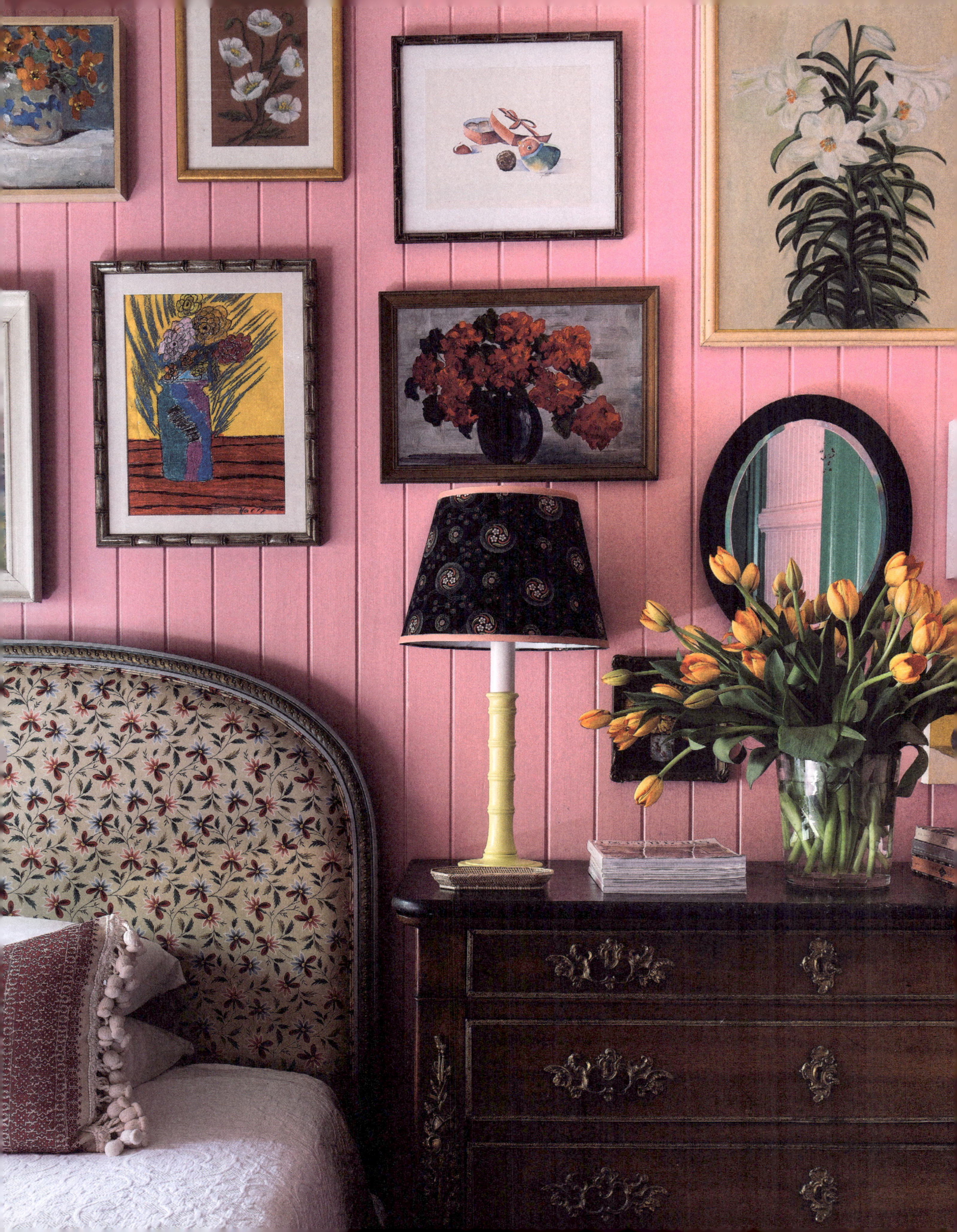

CHAPTER 05

Decorated Dens

What does a unique retreat look like for some of the world's most creative artists and designers? Colourful, art-filled castles, guest cottages turned into design laboratories and a jewel-box Sicilian escape illustrate the decorative potential of the modern getaway home.

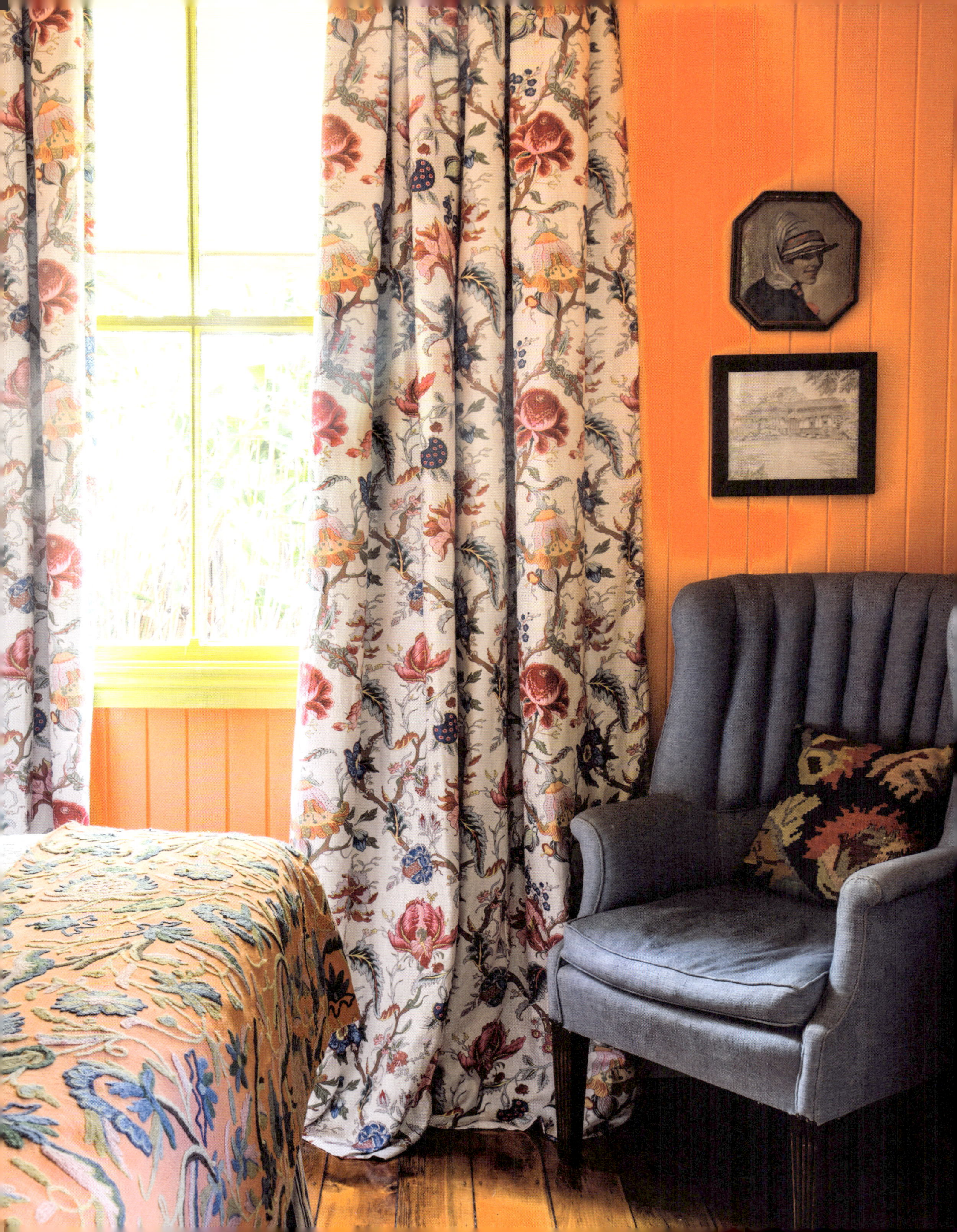

A Colour-forward Guest House in Brisbane

BIRKDALE, QUEENSLAND (AU) **ANNA SPIRO**

There's no hard and fast rule that says your getaway home has to be a simple cottage on some far-flung beach or an isolated cabin in the depths of a forest; your retreat can be as close as your own backyard. Such is the case for Australian decorator and textile designer Anna Spiro, who has put her masterful spin on a dreamy guest house behind her home in Birkdale, a quiet coastal suburb in Redlands Shire, outside of Brisbane.

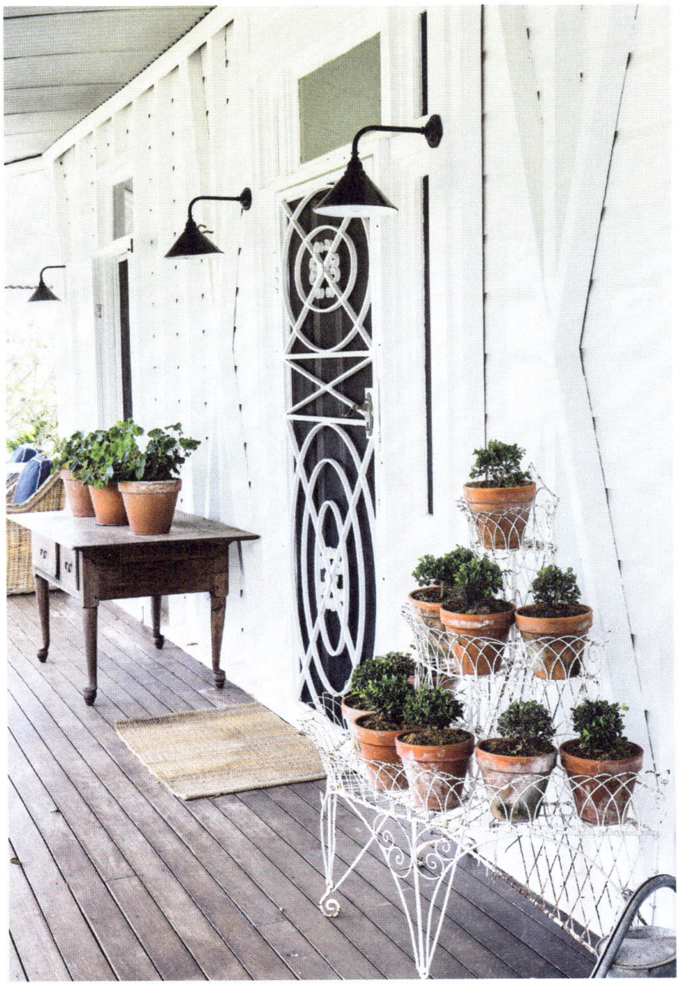

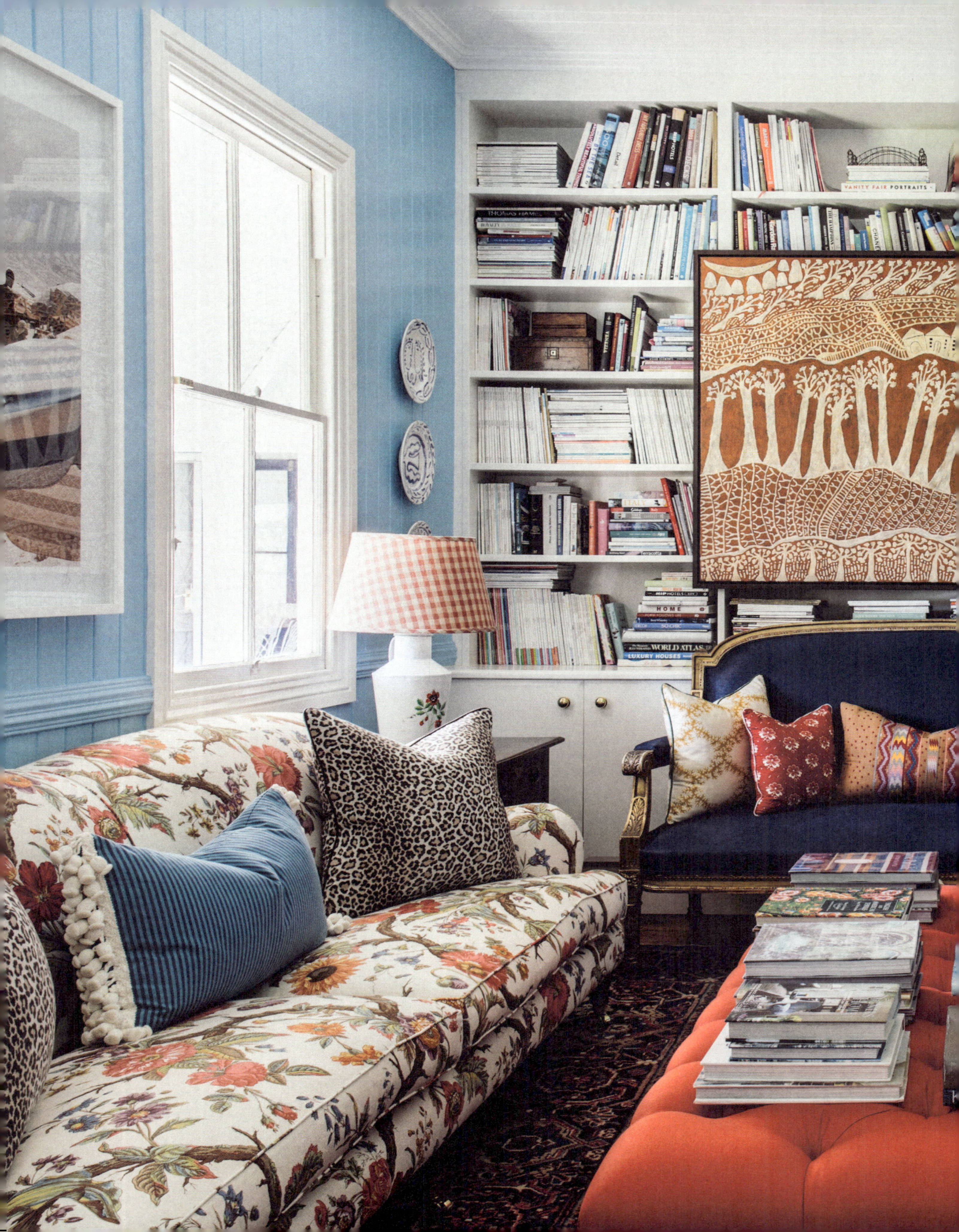
VANITY FAIR PORTRAITS
HOME
WORLD ATLAS
LUXURY HOUSES
Terracotta

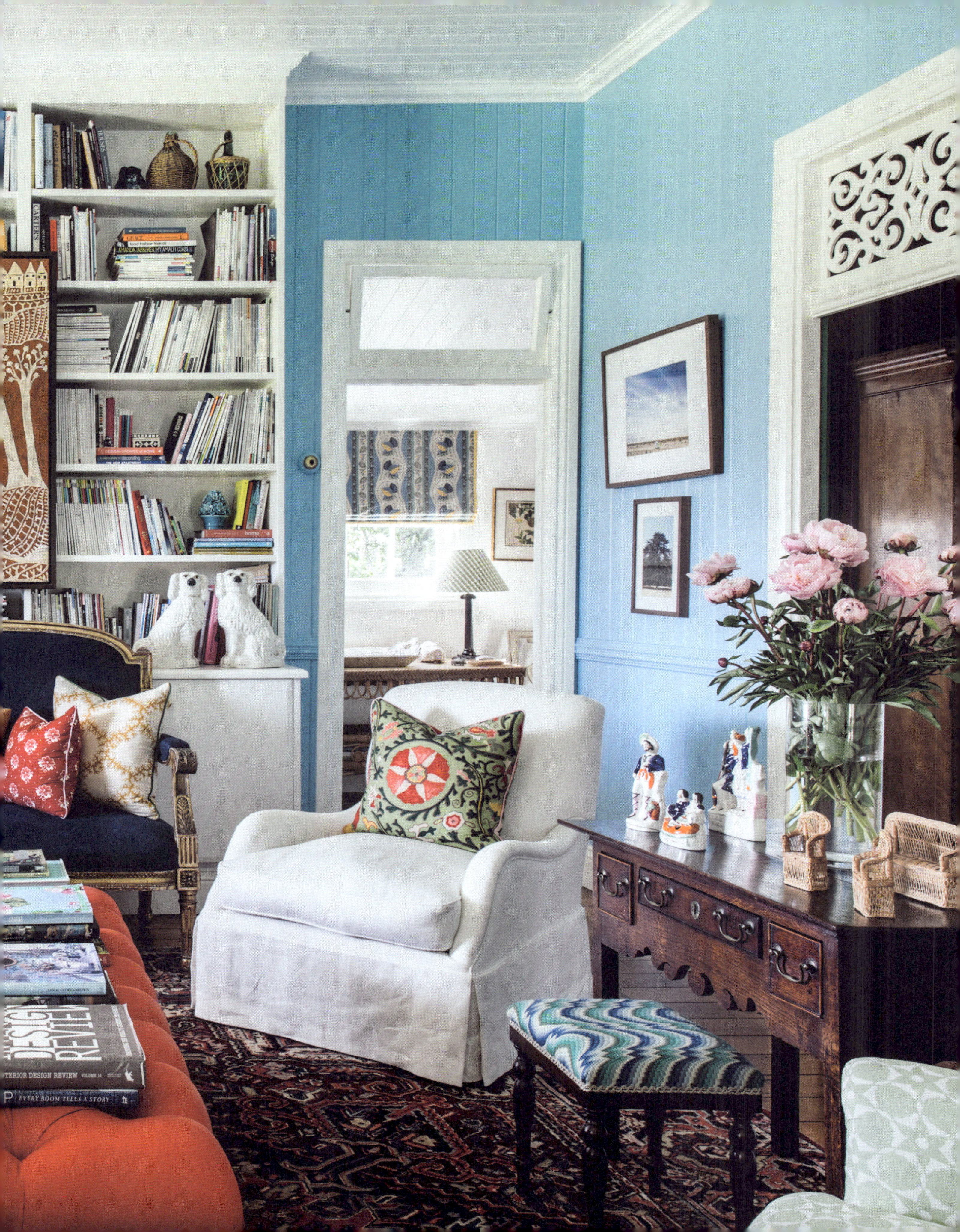
DESIGN REVIEW
EVERY ROOM TELLS A STORY

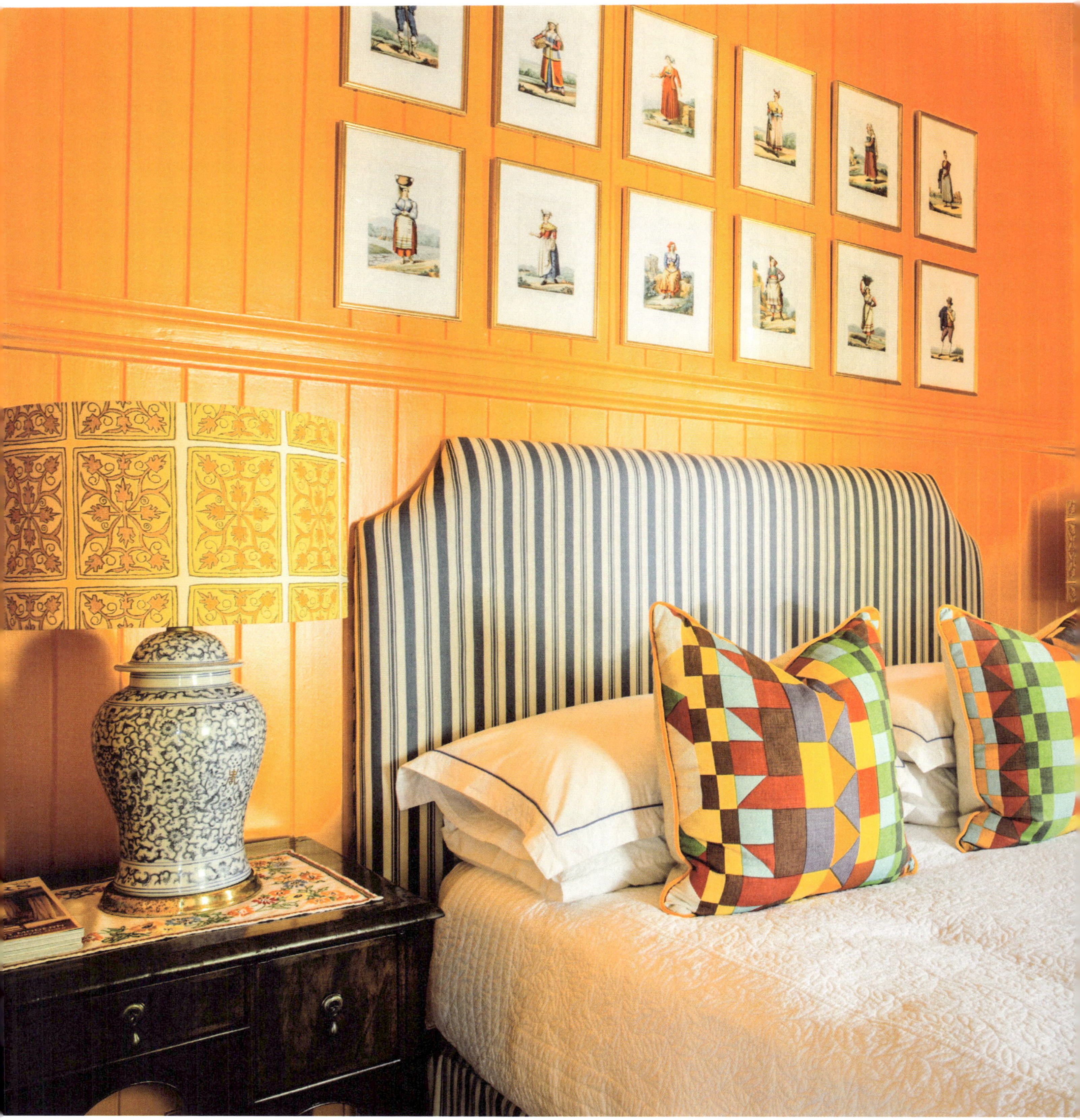

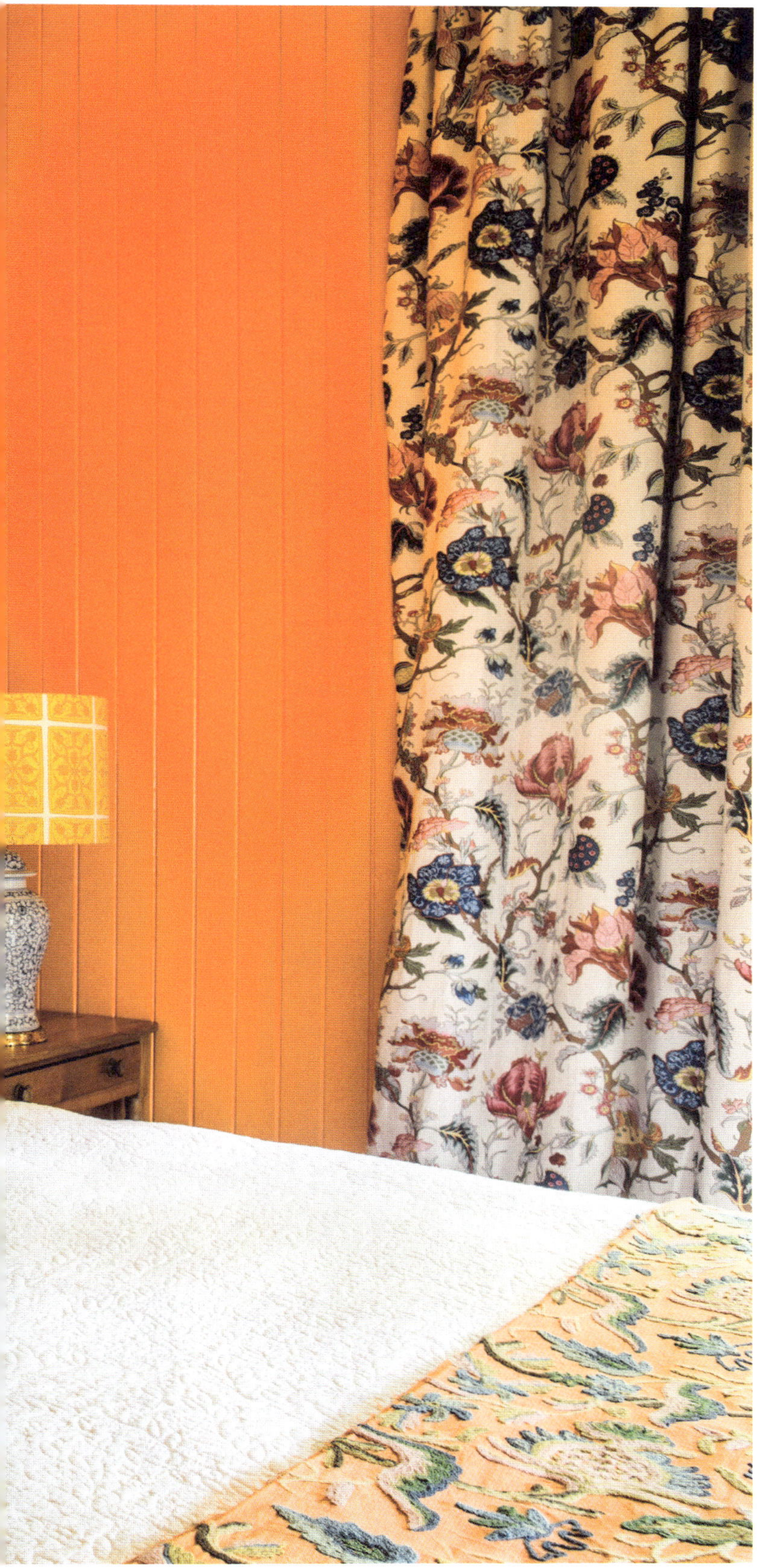

Once an old workers cottage nestled within the verdant lawns, ancient palms and towering gum trees of Spiro and her family's nineteenth-century homestead, the petite bungalow has become a laboratory for Spiro's colour-forward maximalist design sense. 'It is somewhere to play around with interesting paint colours and layers of fabrics,' she says. 'I could have some fun, unrestricted by the tastes and needs of my husband and the boys.'

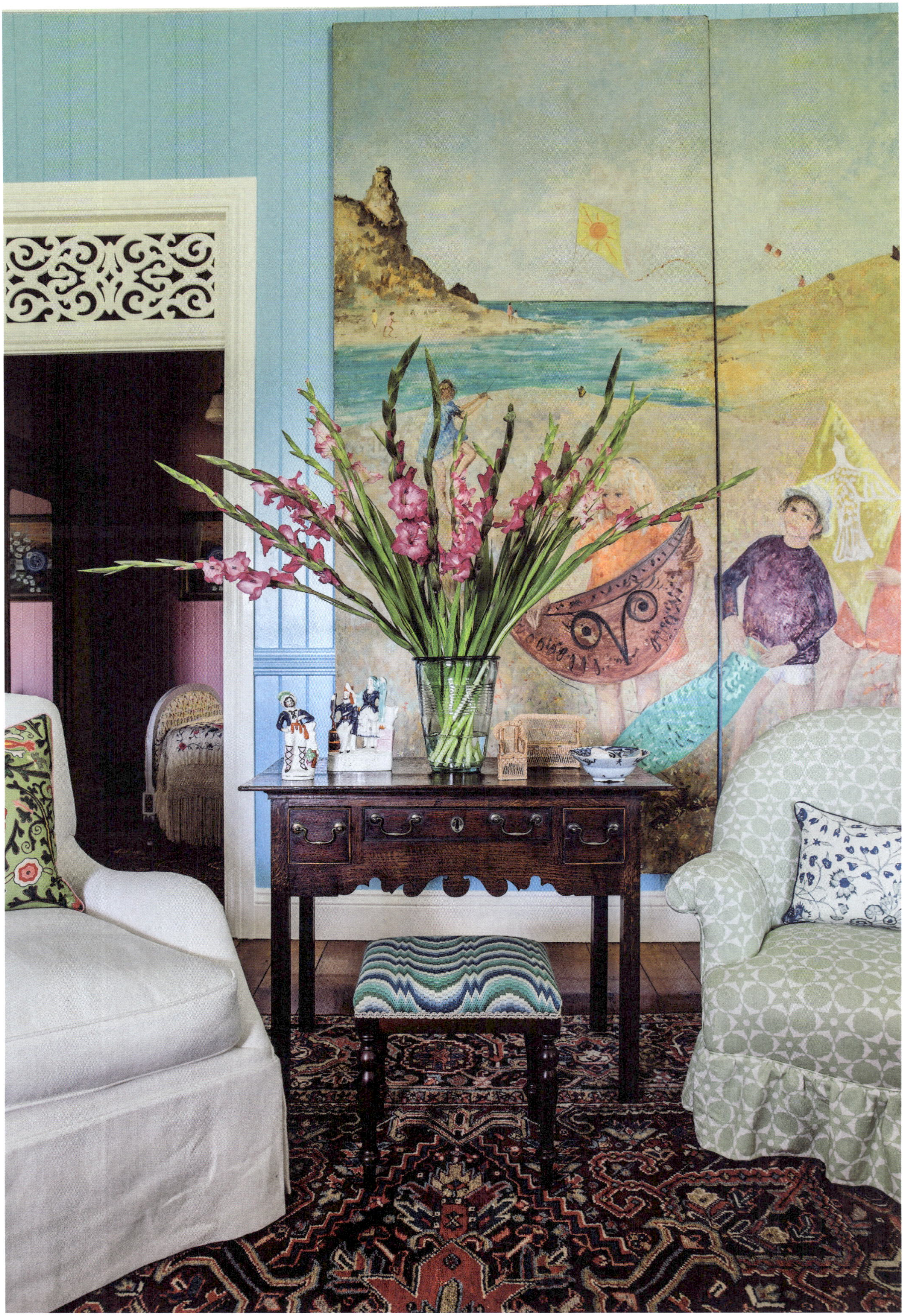

Each room of the quaint clapboard cottage feels like a separate, colour-soaked world: bubblegum pink and a mish-mash of floral still lifes in the main bedroom, traffic-cone orange and layers of geometric and foliage prints in the guest suite and a bright shade of teal in the salon, chosen to match a triptych painting of seaside frolickers that dominates the back wall. Though the home hosts so many wildly disparate palettes, there is a certain sense of cohesion in the chaos. Under Spiro's expert eye, the eclectic mix of objects, textiles and hues all work together to create a charming *mise-en-scène* as bright and cheerful as a Brisbane summer's day.

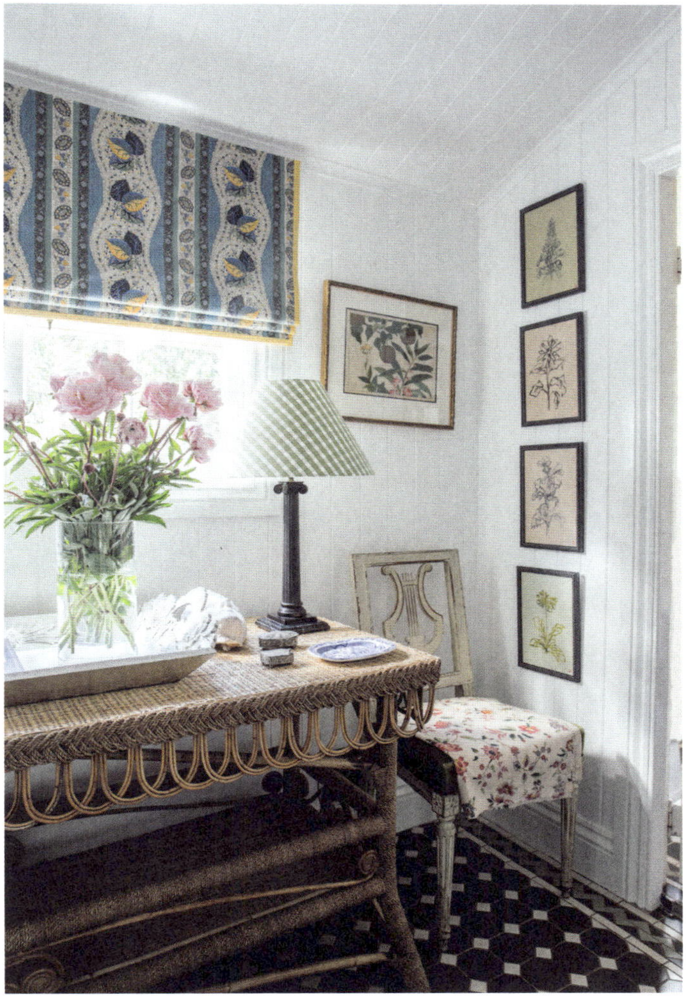

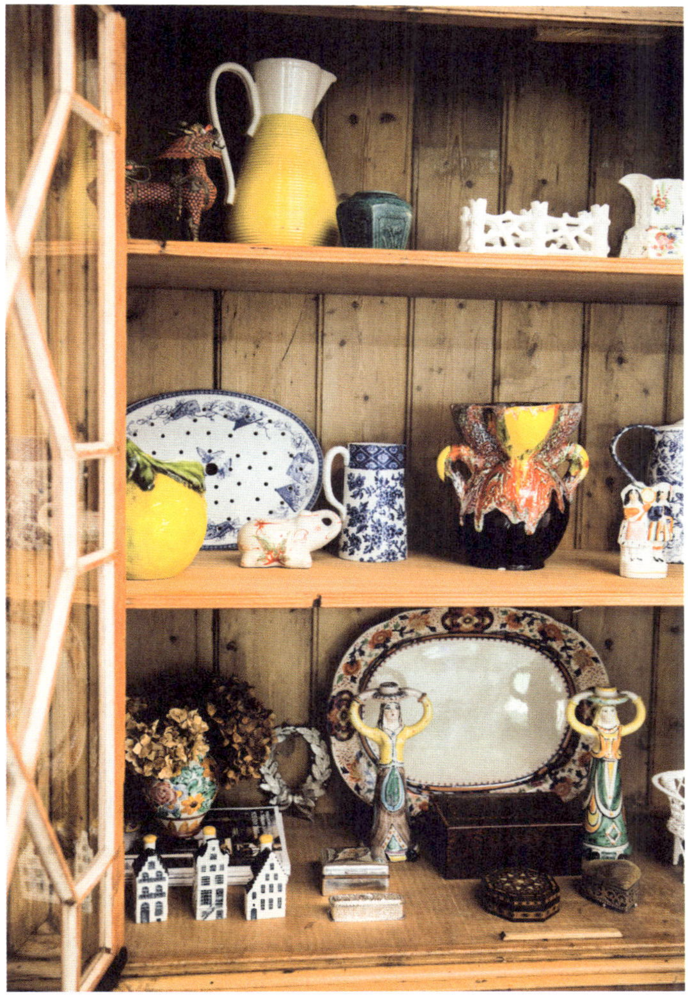

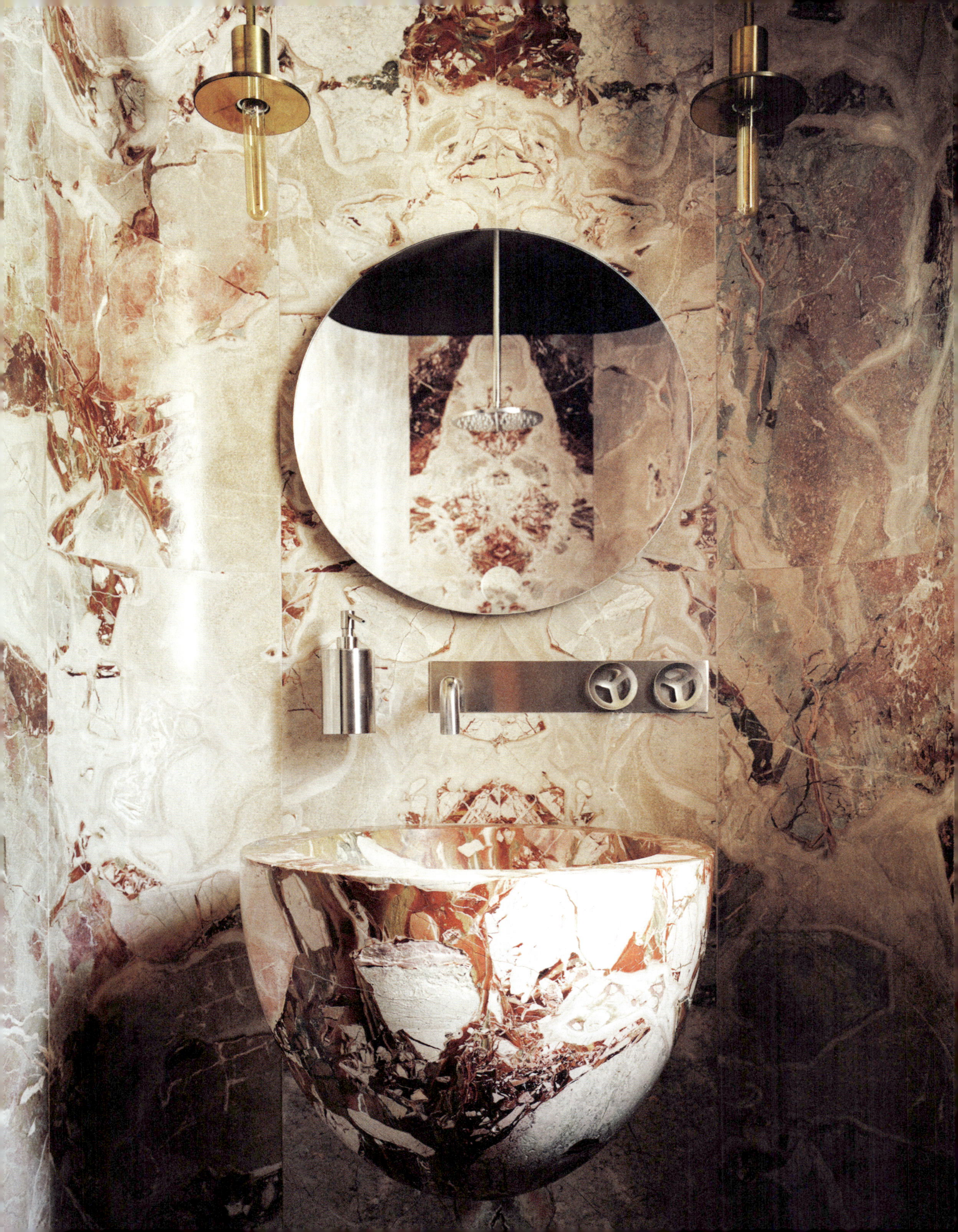

A Simple Stone House Hiding a Jewel-Box Interior

GULF OF MACARI, SICILY (IT) **JEAN-PASCAL LÉVY TRUMET**

The Gulf of Macari in Sicily's Trapani province occupies nearly the westernmost point of the Italian island that sits at the junction of the Ionian, Mediterranean and Tyrrhenian seas. Overlooking an expanse of shimmering water, this area has seen the rise and fall of countless civilisations – the Phoenicians, Greeks, Normans and Spanish have each claimed Sicily for their own at various points in history – all of which have left their marks in the form of ruins and artefacts that can now be found scatted across its arid terrain.

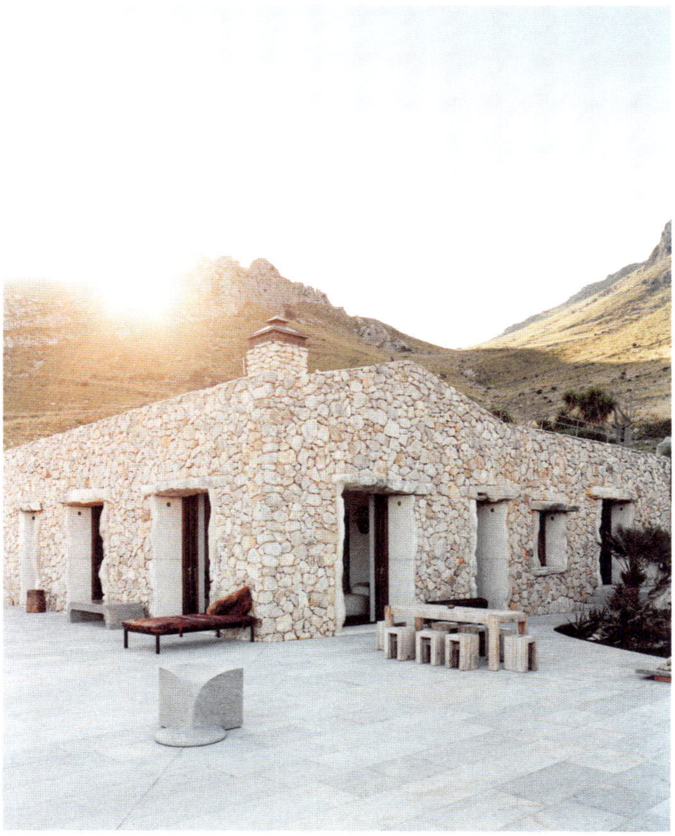

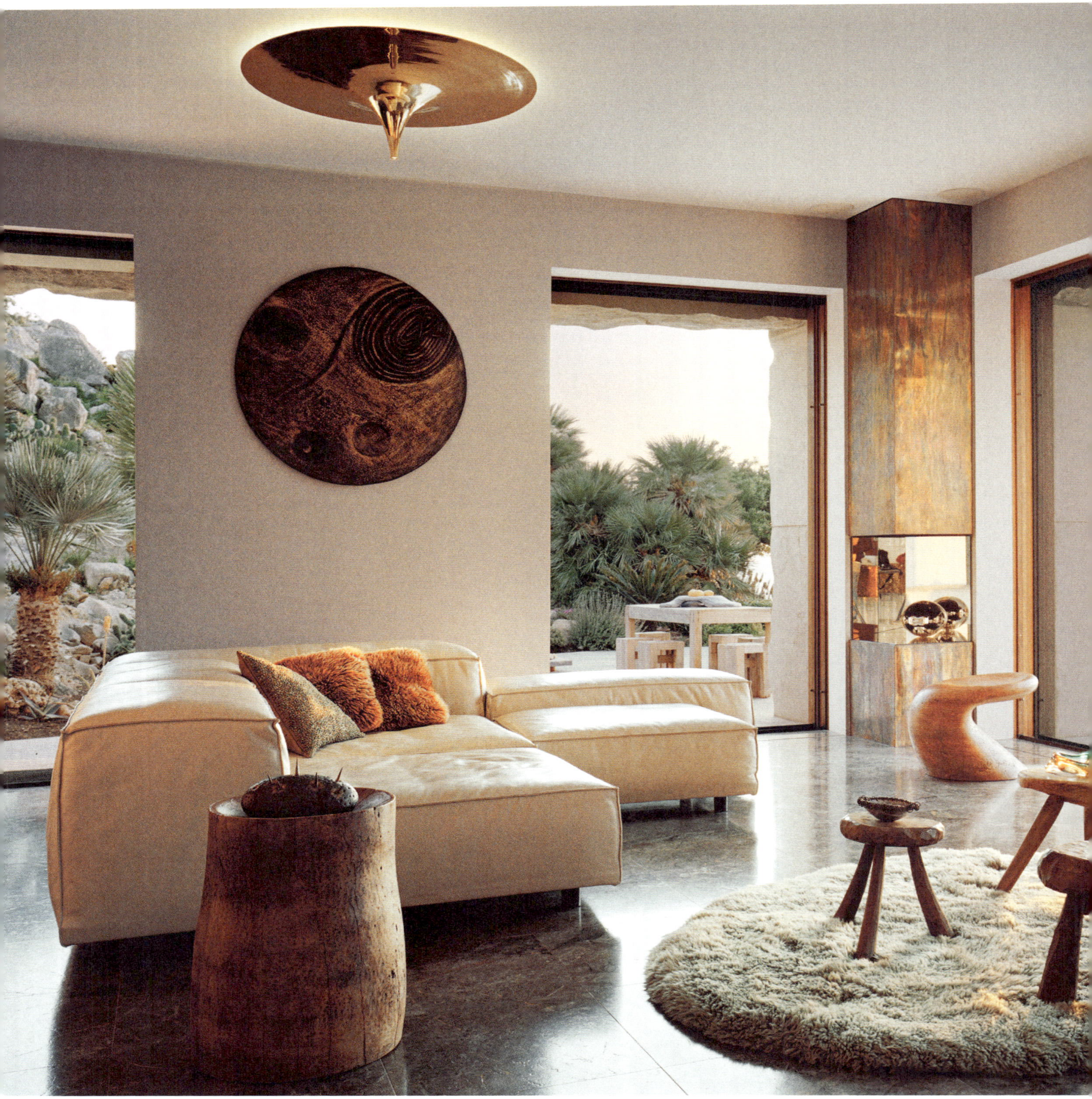

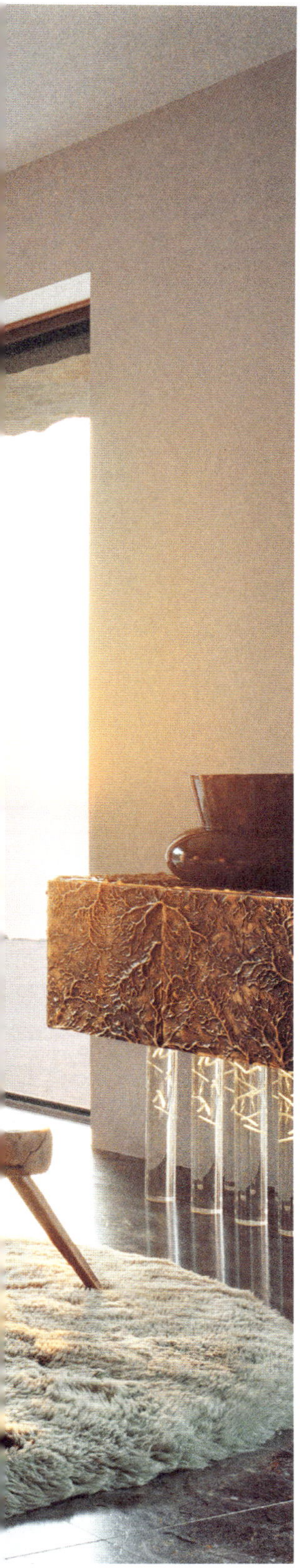

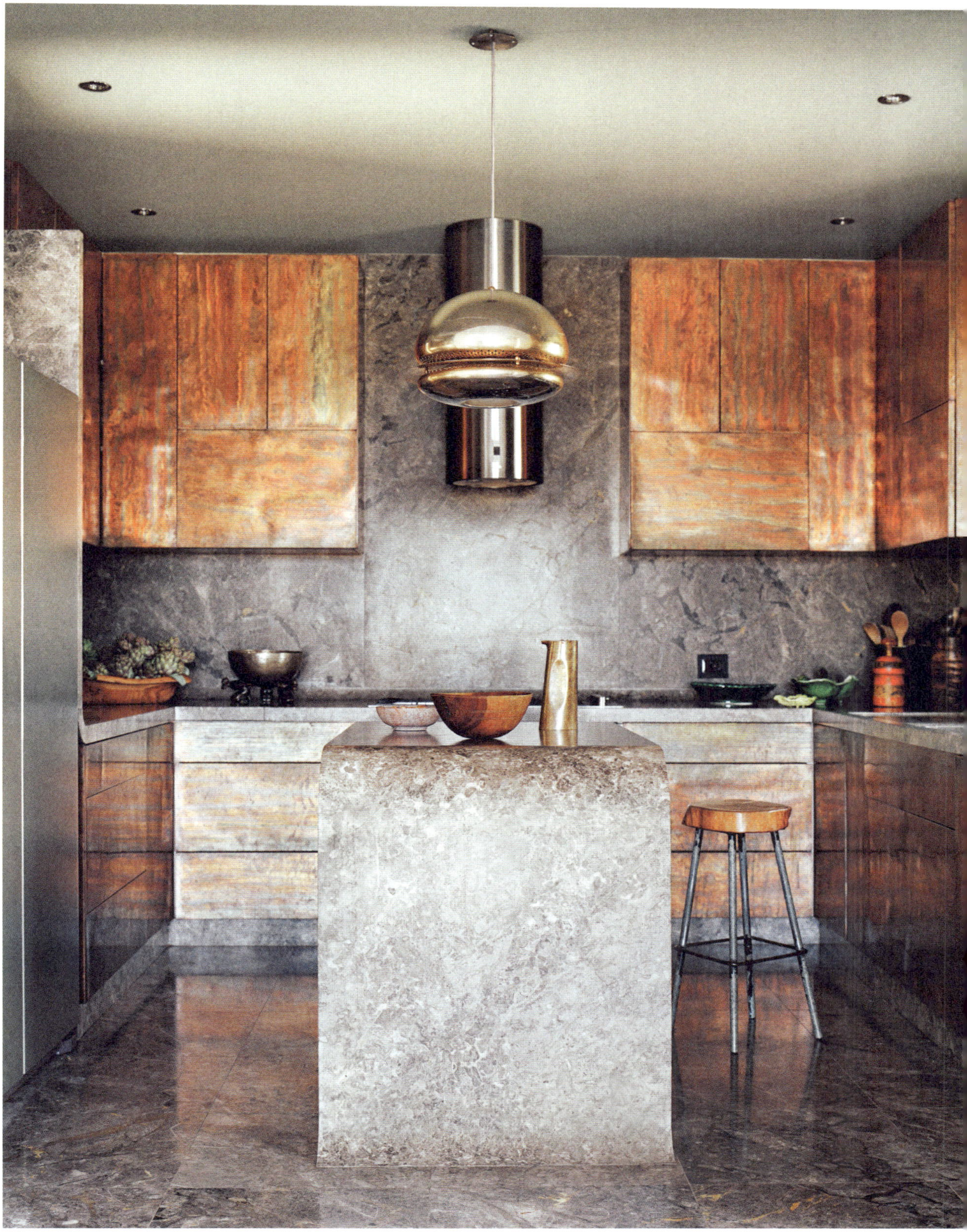

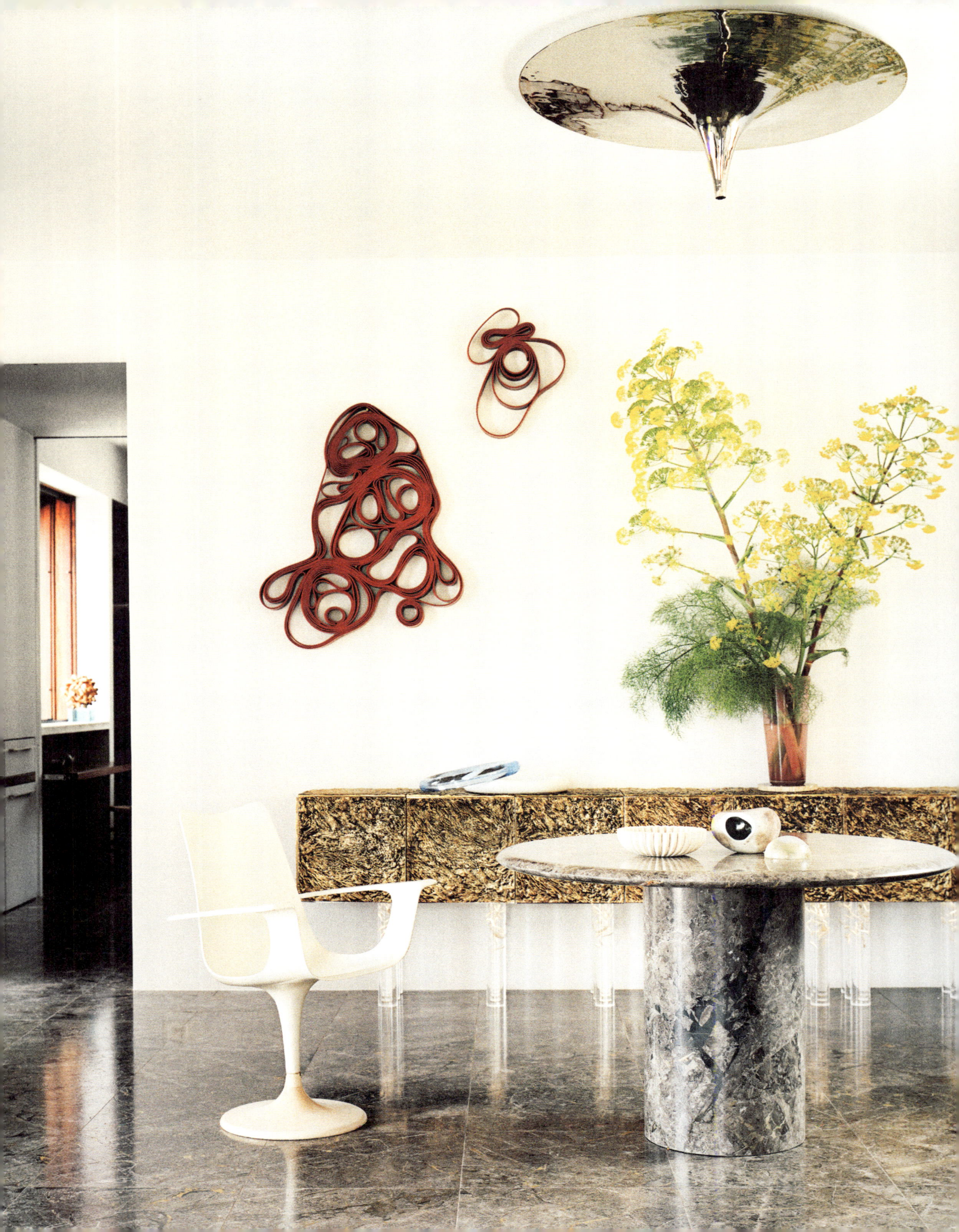

One of these long-abandoned ruins — a simple stone house overlooking the bay set in a hollow between rocky hilltops — caught the eye of French artist and scenographer Jean-Pascal Lévy Trumet on one of his many sojourns to the region, prized for its golden sand beaches and charming rural villages. Following a 30-year career as a set designer for contemporary dance and performing arts companies, he channelled a similar sense of theatricality into the design of his home. Using the ancient stones retrieved on site, he rebuilt the house's walls in the style of a traditional rural dwelling. Meanwhile, on the inside, he devised a thoroughly contemporary aesthetic – in sharp juxtaposition to the deceivingly humble facade.

Striking contrasts and luxurious materials define the home's interior, from the red-and-white veined Libeccio Antico marble that envelops the bathroom, to the torch-scarred copper used to cover kitchen cabinetry, to the deep-grey Billiemi floors – a type of marble quarried in Siciliy and prized for its intricate veining and streaks of fossilised sedimentary rock – which sweeps across the living room floor. Much of the furniture in the house was designed bespoke by Lévy Trumet himself, exactingly realised to complement the bold interior.

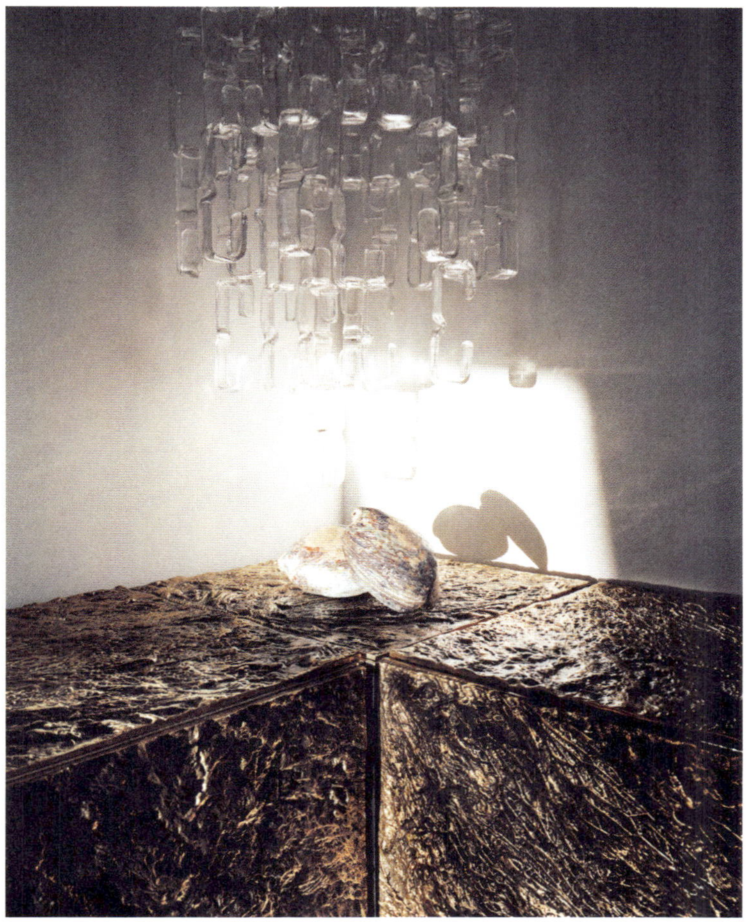

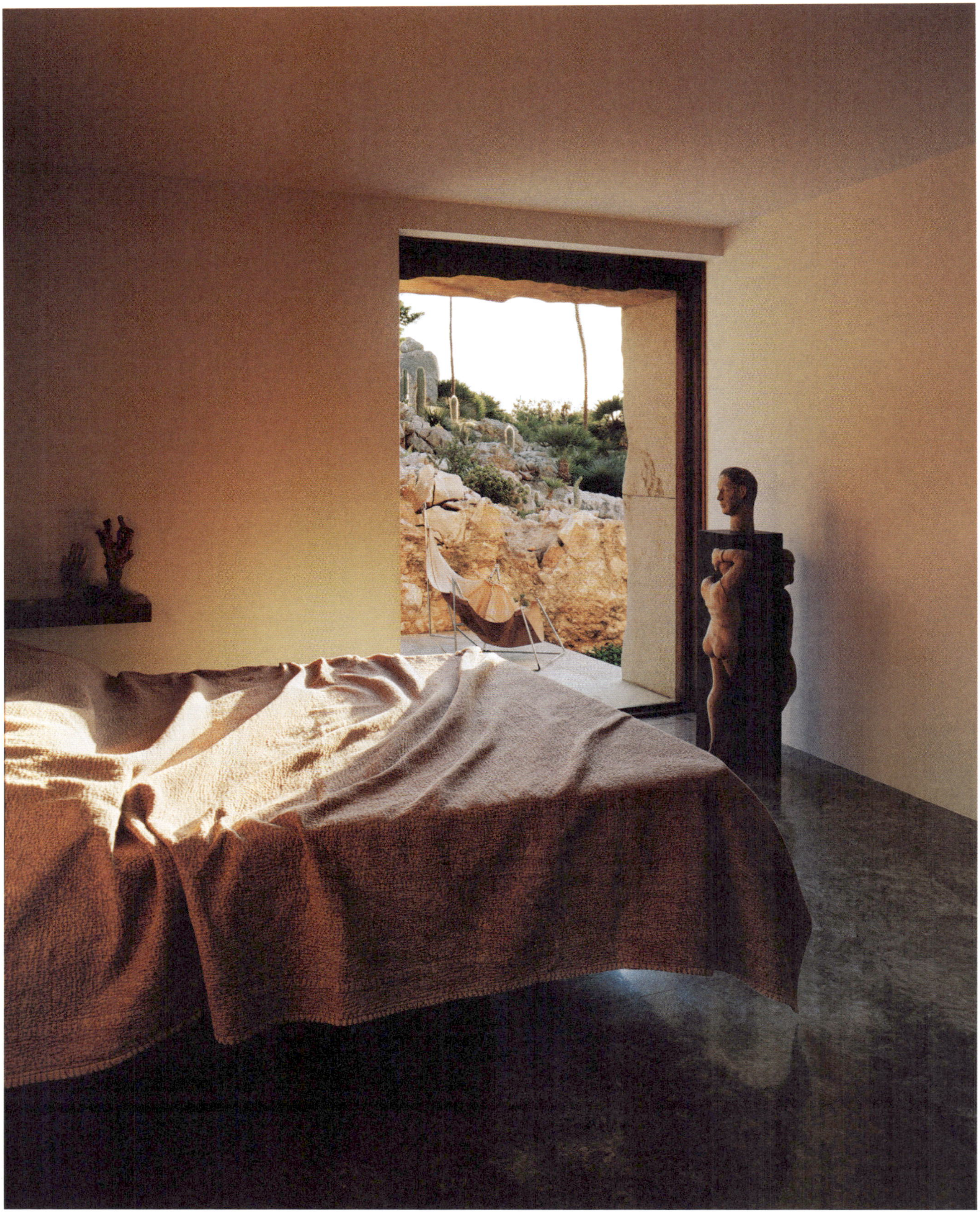

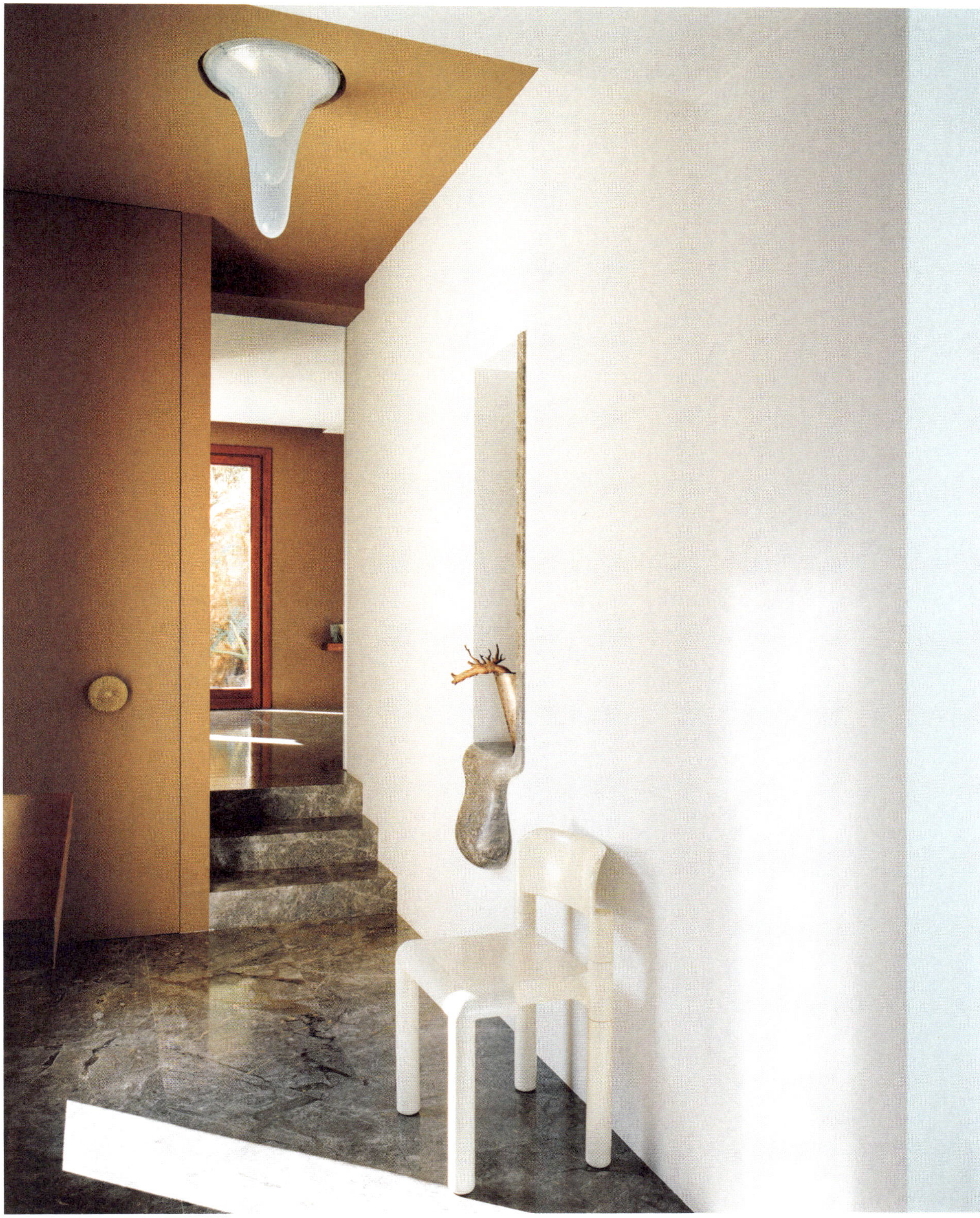

In organising the 1,000-square-foot home, Lévy Trumet carefully oriented the layout based on the surrounding views. The private areas, such as the bedroom and bathroom, face inwards towards the craggy peaks of the hills above. By contrast, the west-facing open-plan living room's windows afford sweeping views over the coastline beyond, catching the orange glow of the sunset and its fading evening light.

A Swiss Castle for a Nomadic Artist

TARASP, GRAUBÜNDEN (CH) **NOT VITAL**

Nomadism has always defined the practice of Swiss artist Not Vital. Known for his architectural installations set in some of the world's most remote locations, from an uninhabited island in Patagonia to the foot of a volcanic in Indonesia to the Mongolian hinterlands, the conceptual artist's peripatetic tendencies have made him a genuine citizen of the world. But even the most well-travelled of characters hail from somewhere, and the idyllic, mountain-ringed valley of Engadine is where his story starts.

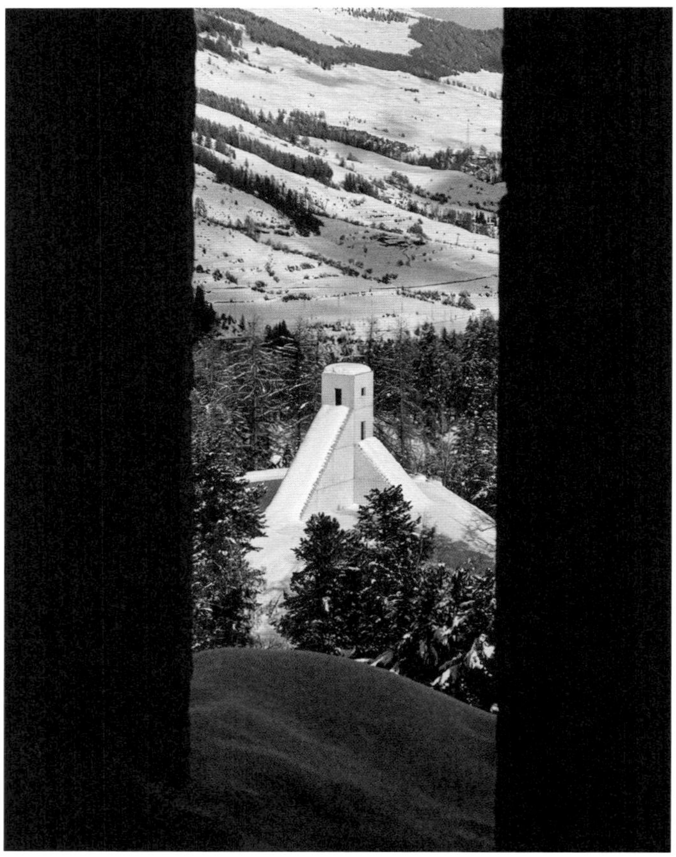

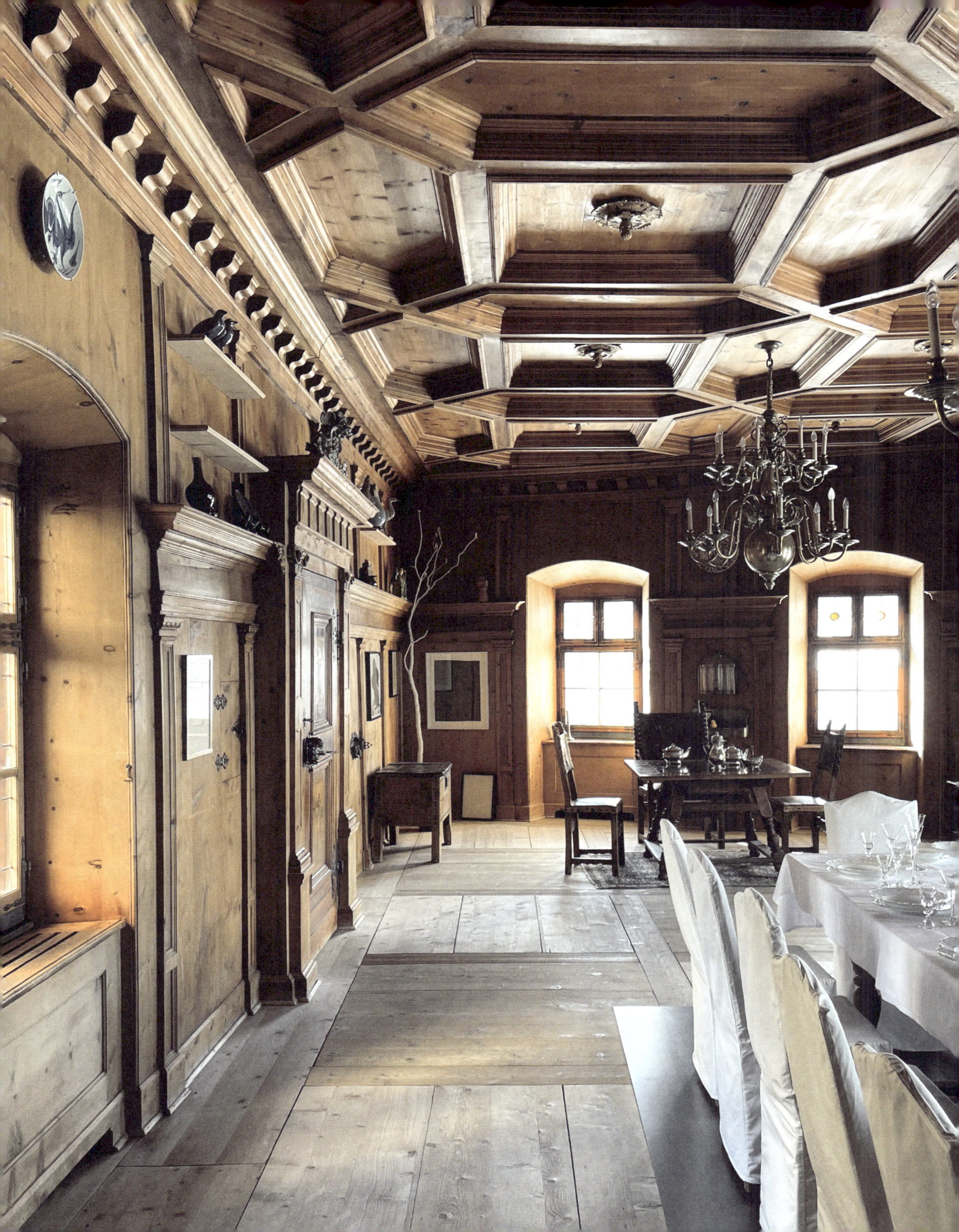

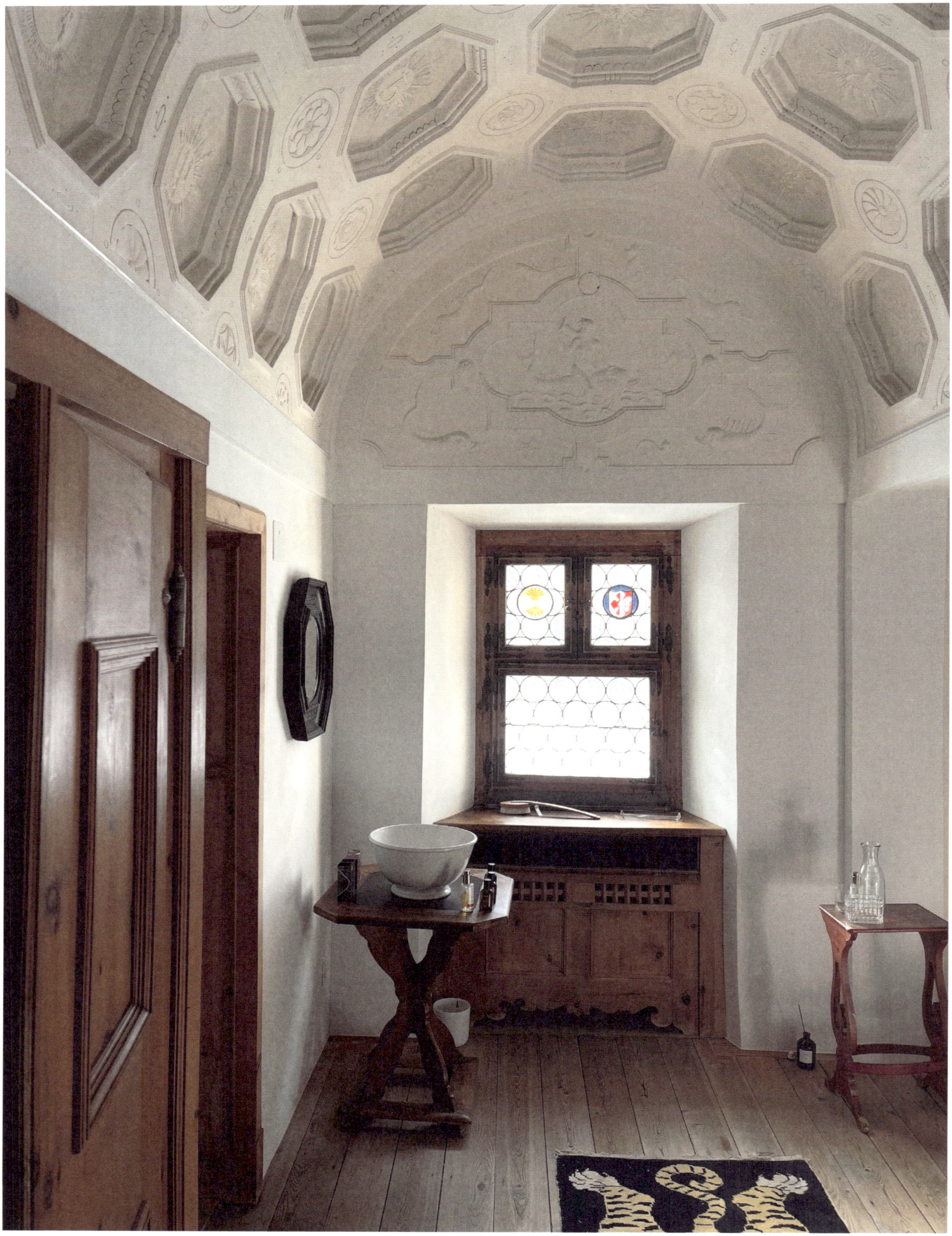

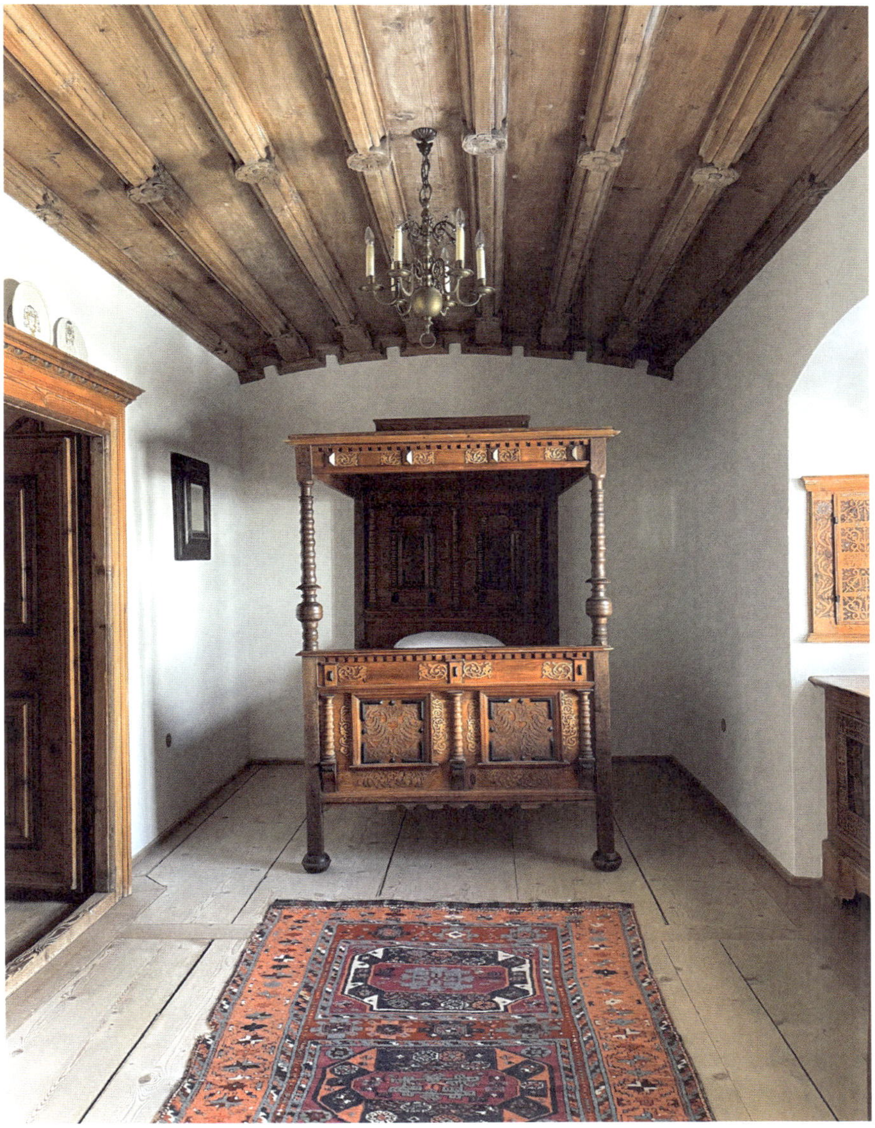

In 2016 Vital transformed the medieval castle of Tarasp – last restored nearly a century prior – into an art foundation and occasional residence. The sprawling fortress was first built in 1040, but over the centuries changed hands between the Austrians, Napoleonic armies and the Swiss Republic until 1900 when it was acquired by German industrialist Dr Karl August Lingner and renovated to its current state.

Inside the castle, the ingenuity of the Swiss woodworking tradition is on full display. Wooden boiserie arranged in complex geometric patterns line the walls and ceiling – an architectural feature that both speaks to the status and wealth of the original builder and creates a sense of warmth in the draughty stone mansion. When it was brought back to life by Lingner, he sourced precious antiques from the surrounding valley: carved wooden four-poster beds, traditional Stabelle chairs and long tables purpose-built for feasting, many of which were still in situ when Vital took possession.

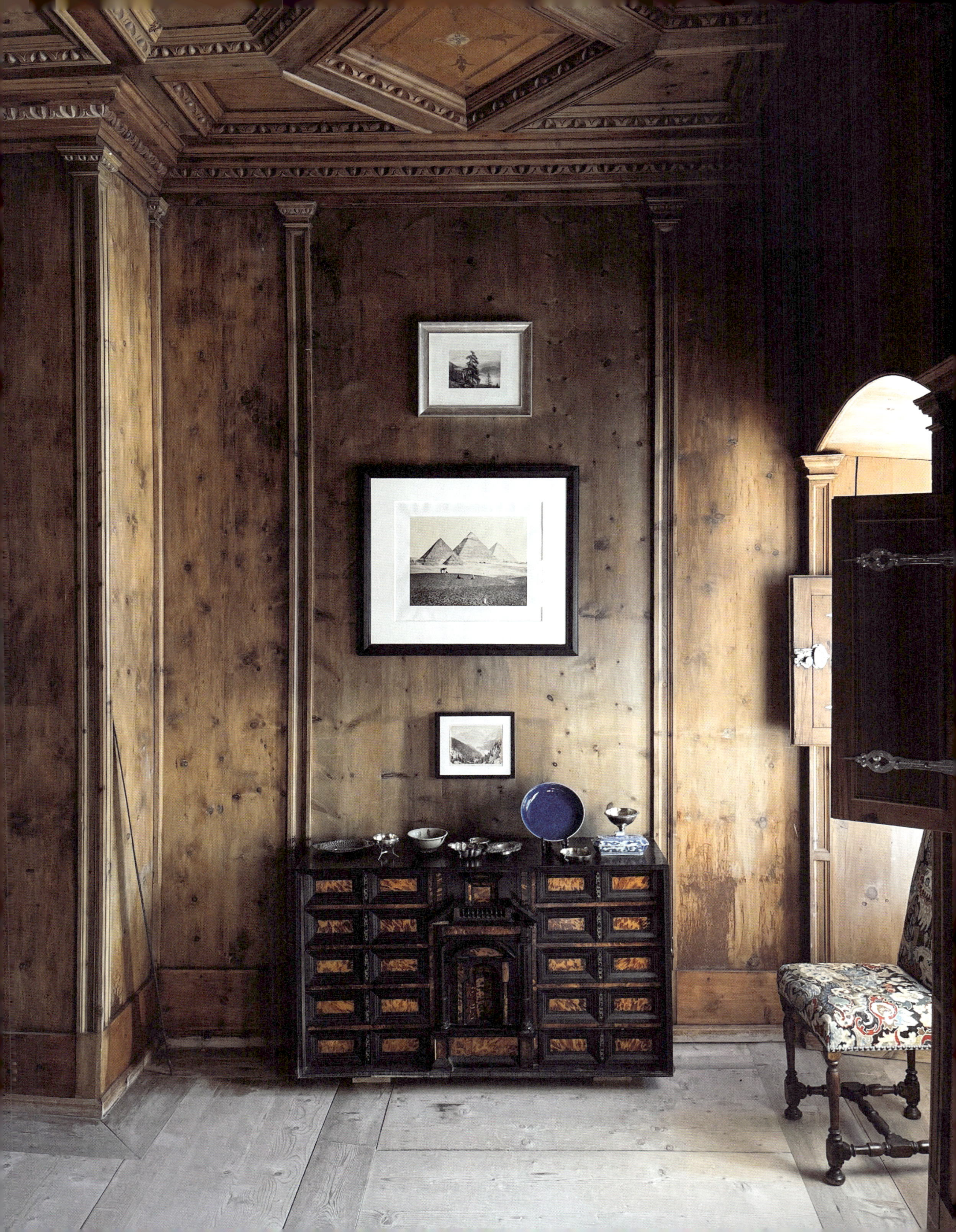

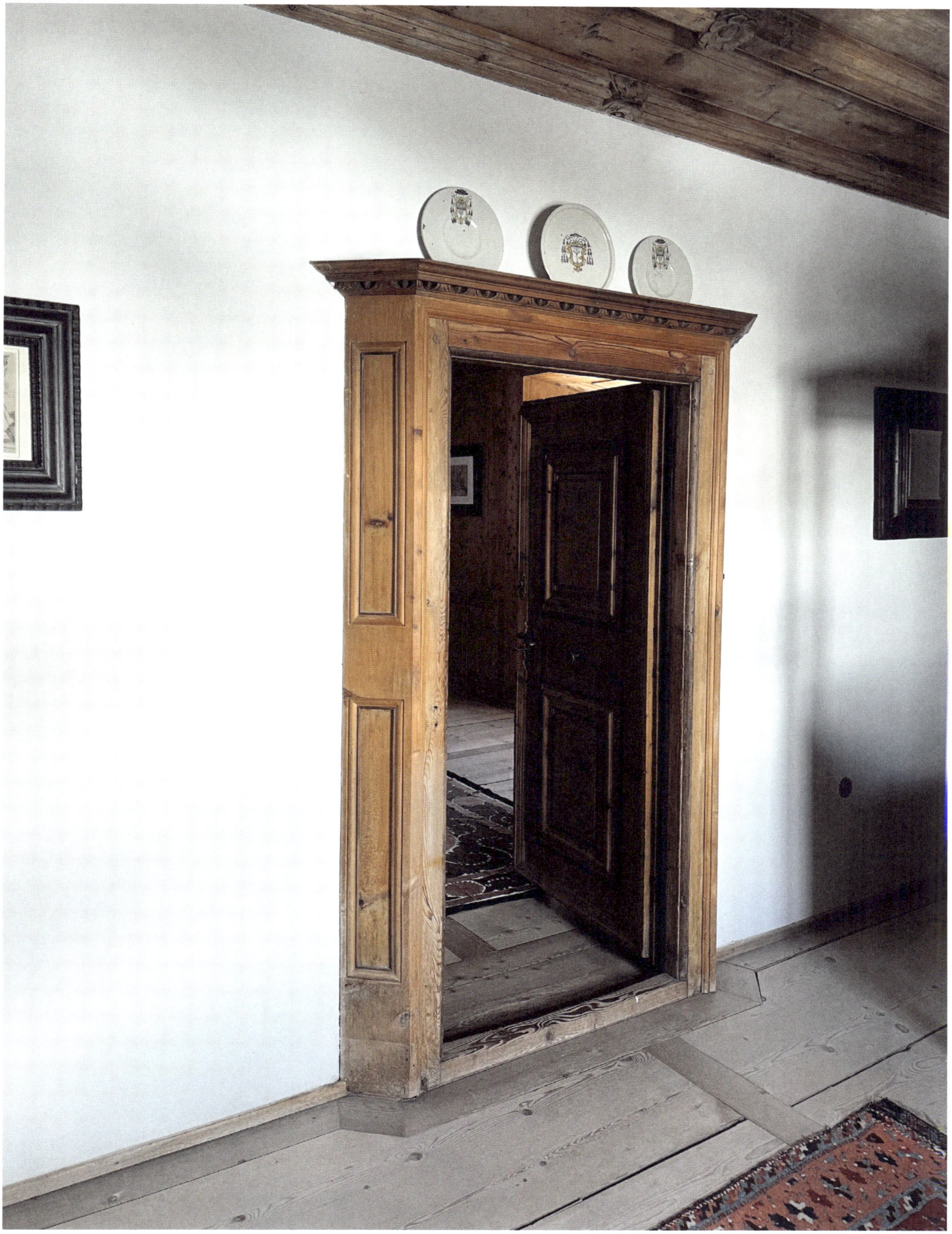

As dramatic and imposing as the castle may be, it merely acts as a backdrop for Vital's extensive collection of antique, modern and contemporary art. Even the sight lines from the castle's windows, originally organised to frame the monumental Graubünden Alps across the valley, provide views onto the impressive sculpture park that now occupies the property's grounds, the highlight of which is Vital's own 'House to Watch the Sunset', a monumental tower he describes as 'Scarch' – a portmanteau of sculpture and architecture – which raises visitors skywards, allowing them to reach that much closer to the heavens above.

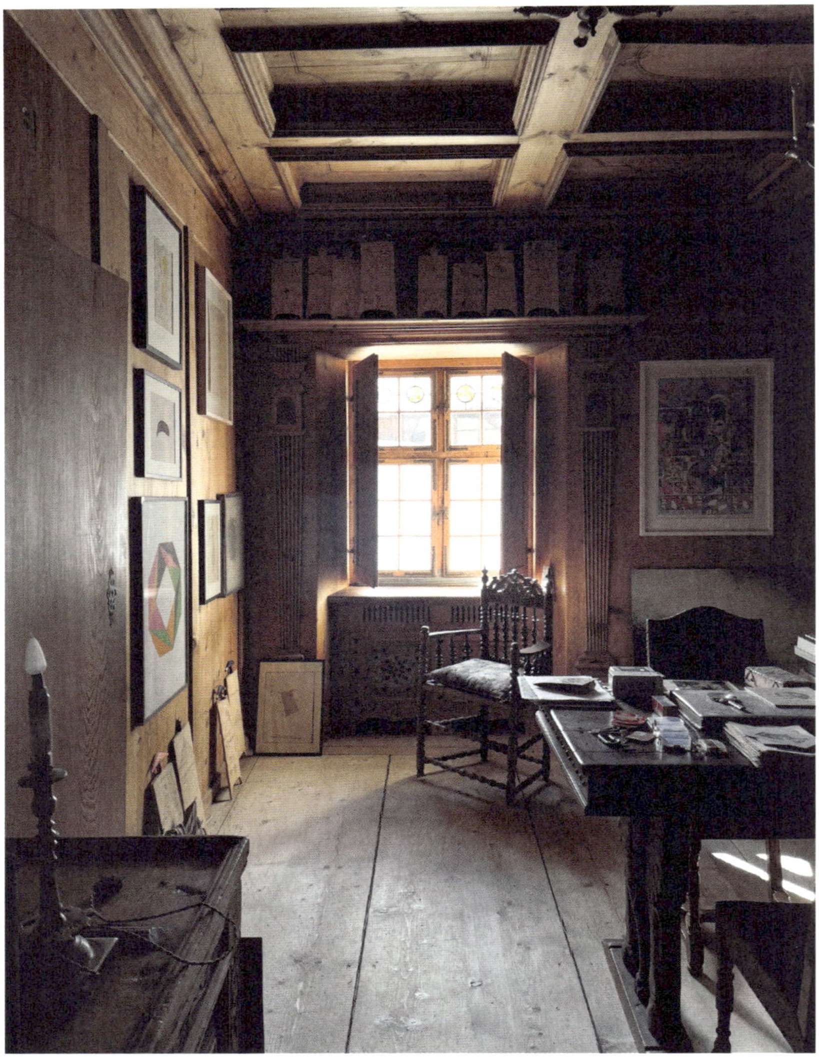

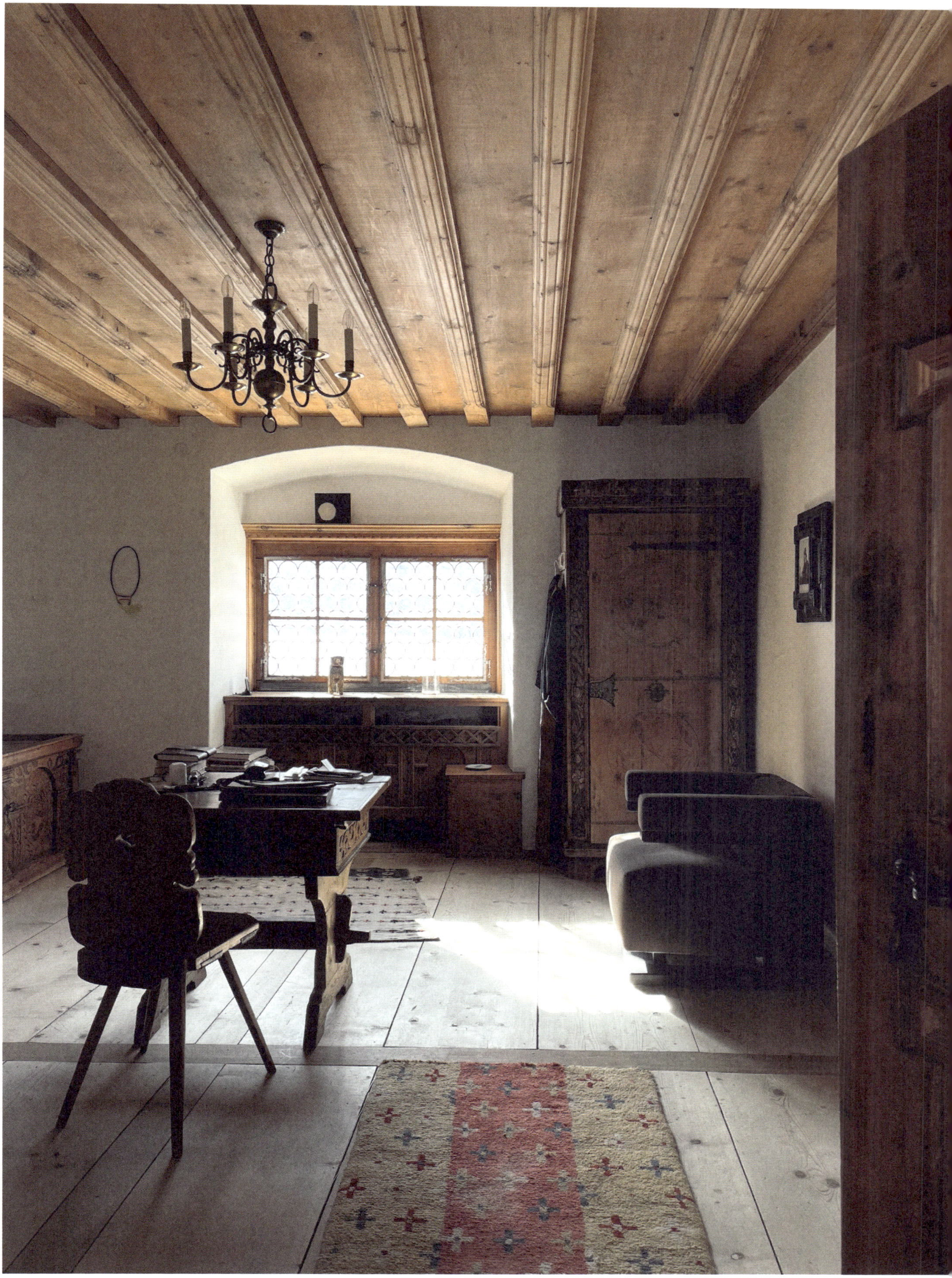

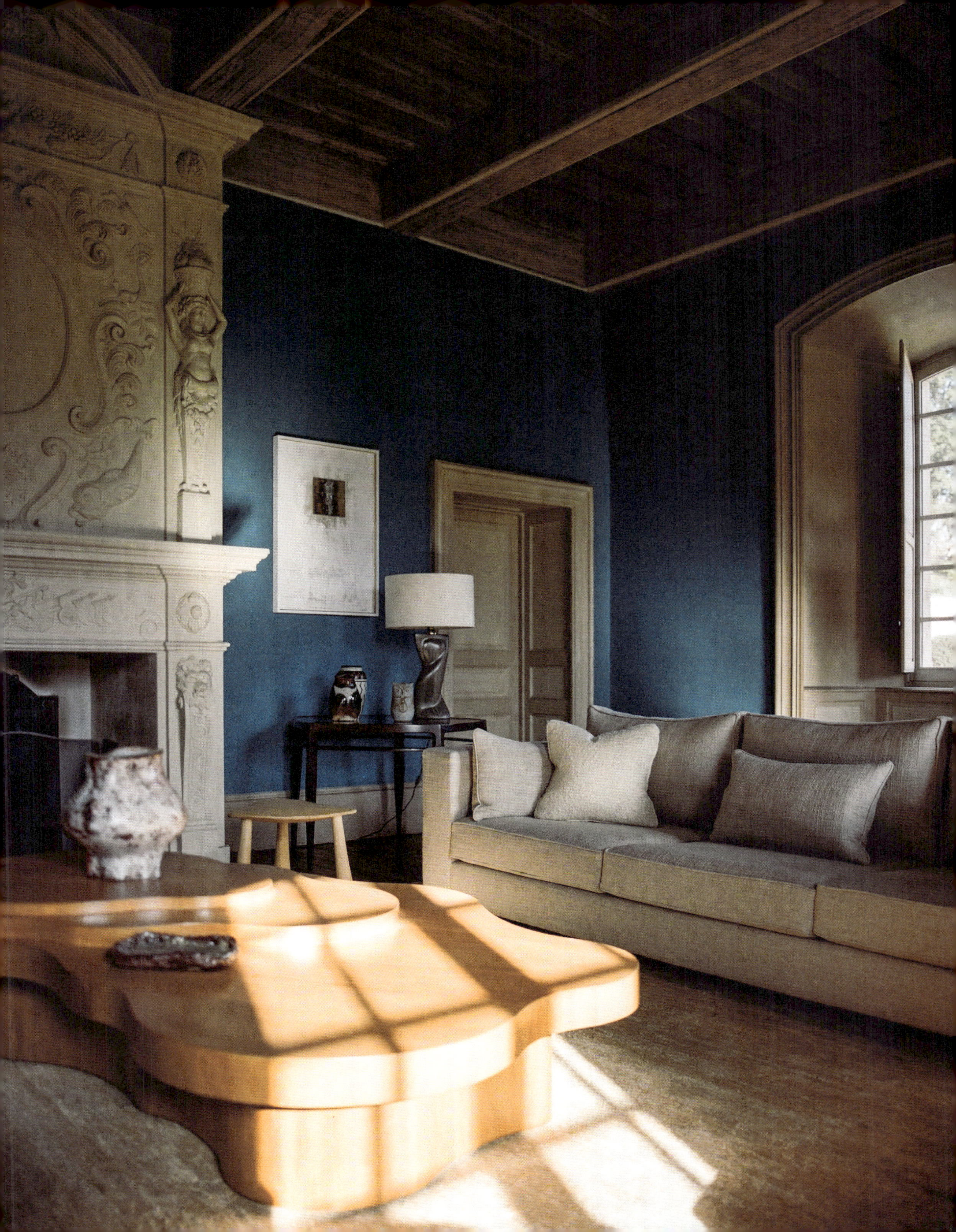

A 17th-Century Chateau with Art around Every Corner

HAUT-VAR, PROVENCE (FR) **PIERRE YOVANOVITCH**

France's Provence region is one of the most bountiful and varied in all of the country – spanning the turquoise waters of the Côte d'Azur in the south and the rugged foothills of the French Alps in the north, passing olive groves, lavender fields and vineyards on the way. This is the landscape that provides the backdrop for the weekend getaway of interior designer Pierre Yovanovitch.

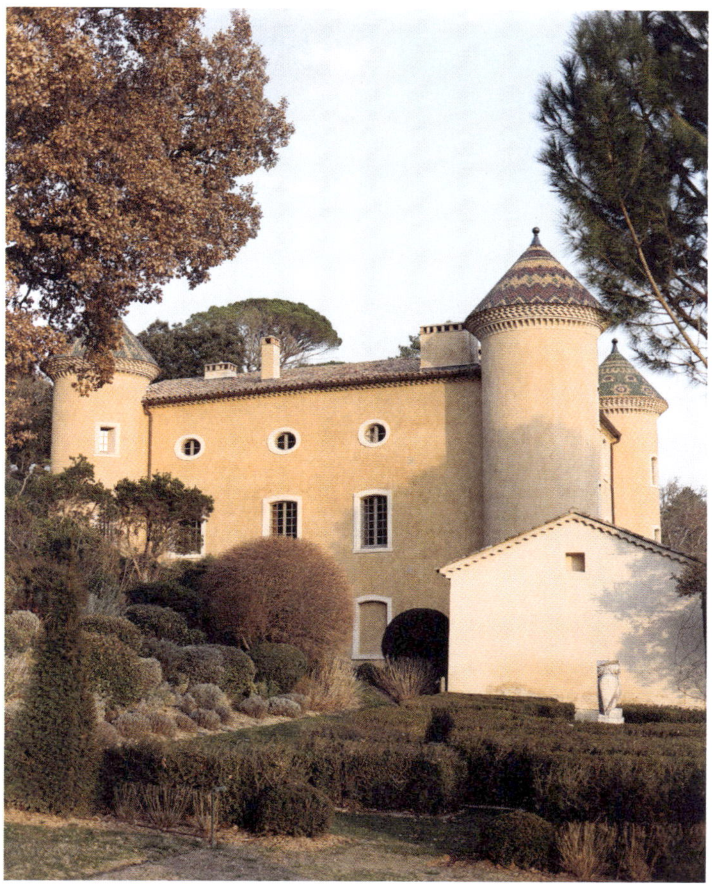

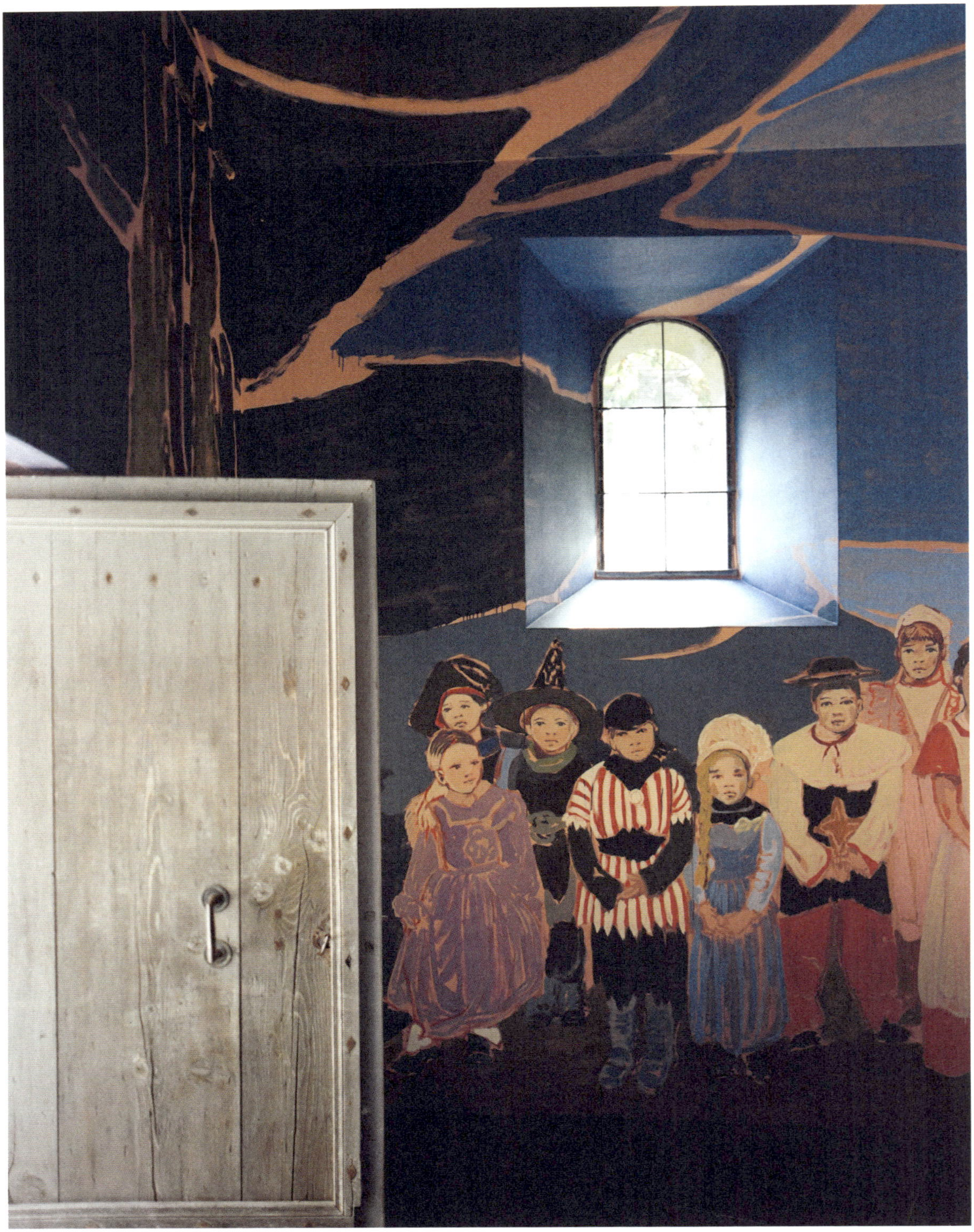

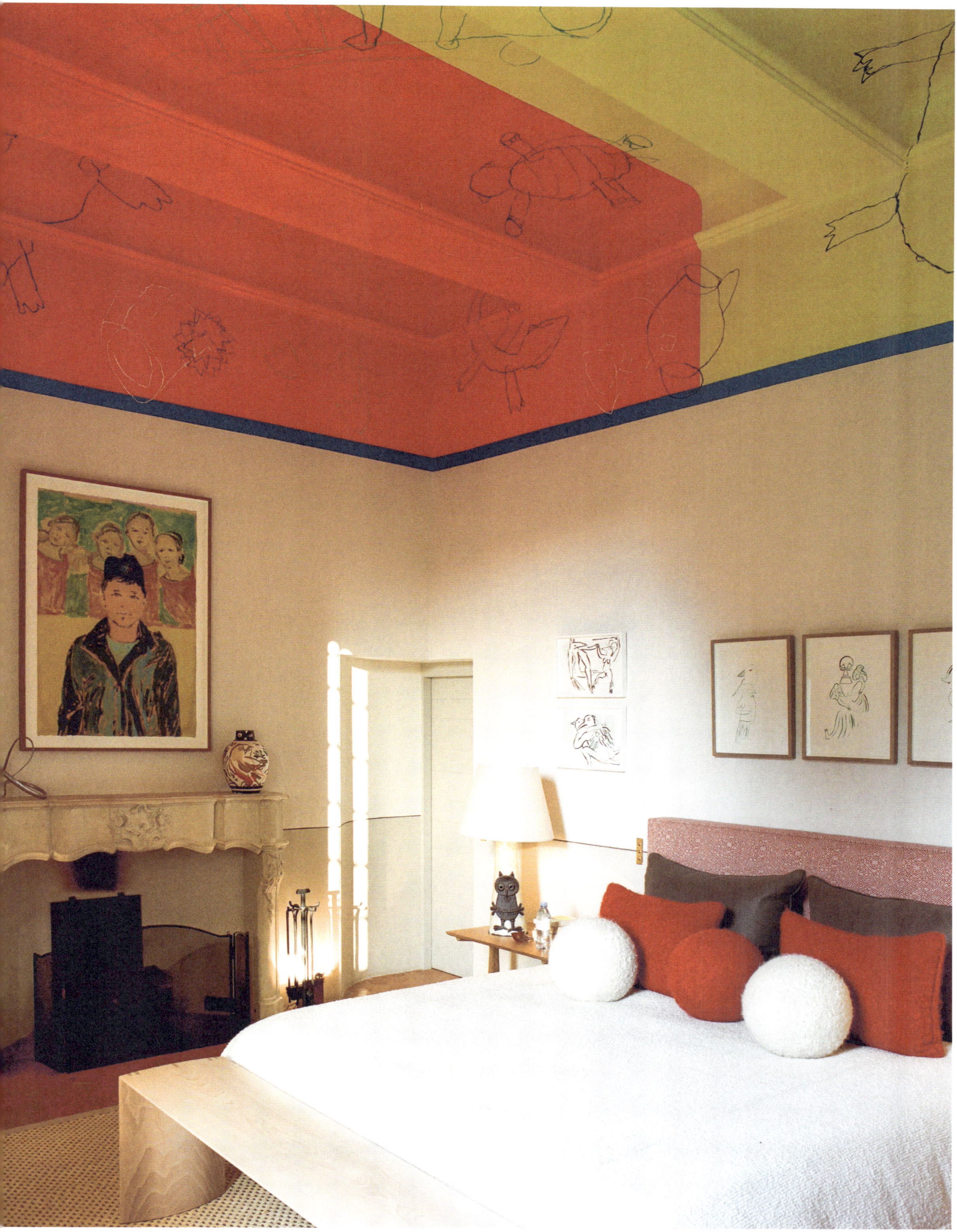

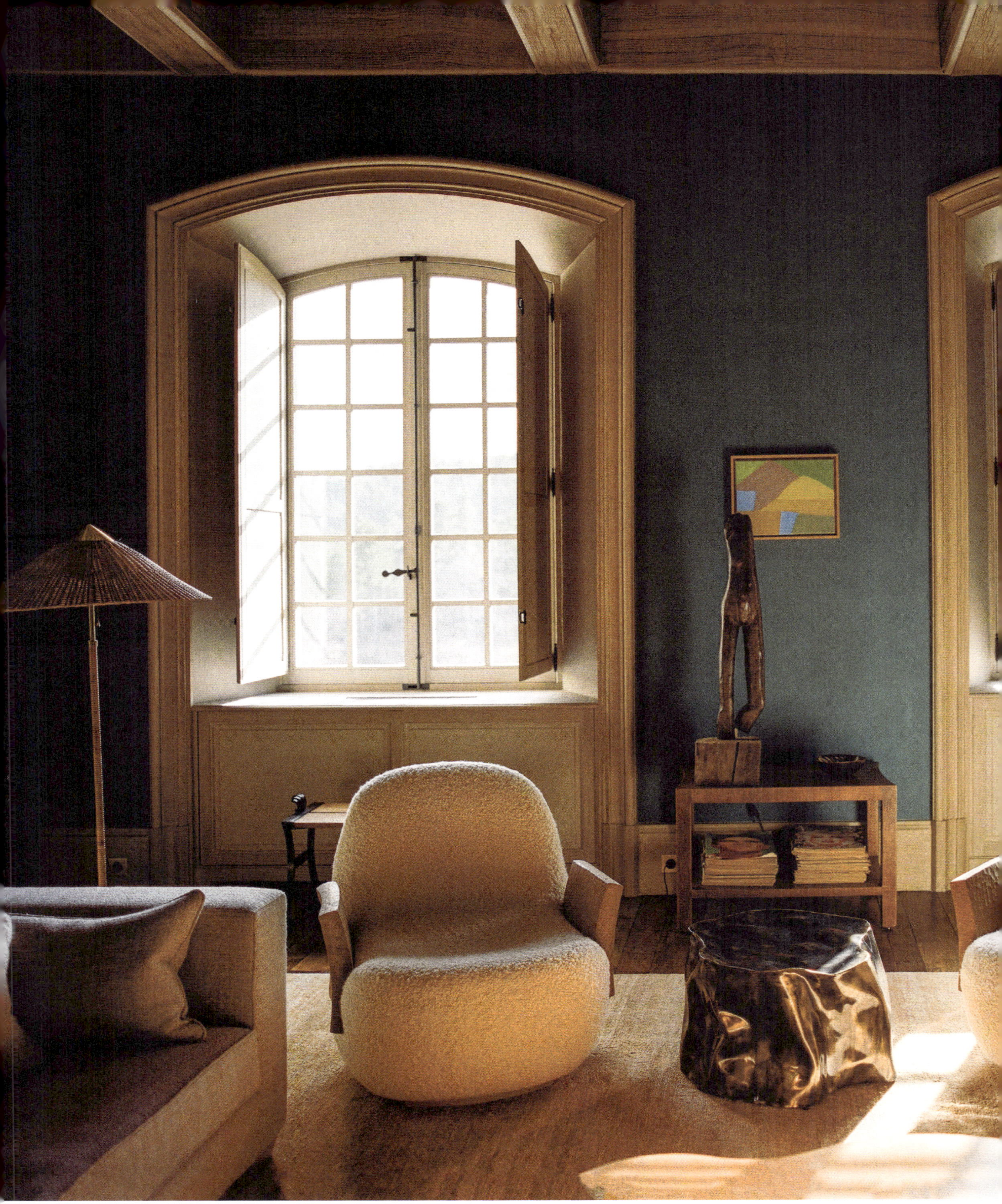

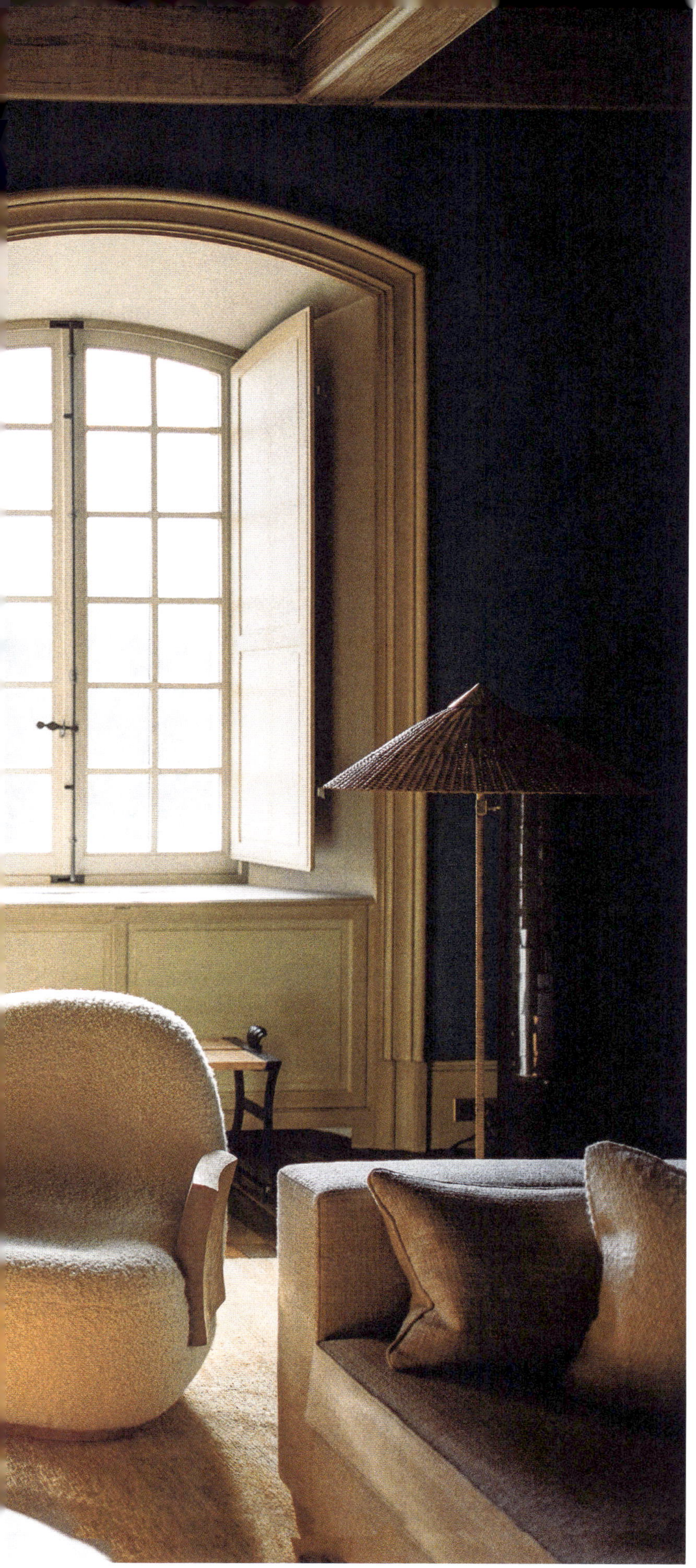

'When we first encountered the chateau, it was a run-down 17th-century wonder,' Yovanovitch says of the estate, nestled within 400 acres of fallow land and forest. The property had been owned by the same family, the Fabrègues, since the 10th century, until he and partner Matthieu Cussac purchased it in 2009. 'The structure was beautiful and had a lot of potential, but needed work,' he says.

To make it fit for habitation, Yovanovitch had to completely reinforce the structure but was able to leave much of the original decoration intact, including the coffered ceilings, elaborate plasterwork and colourful glazed tiles, adorned with motifs based on the changing seasons, that clad the castle-like mansion's soaring turrets.

In each of the stately rooms, Yovanovitch deftly mixed his quietly refined approach with the chateau's opulent original features. In the main living room, he left the timber beam ceiling untouched but painted the walls a deep shade of petrol blue. The contrast highlights the elaborately carved gypsum mantle by artisan Joël Puisais and sophisticated collection of furniture – a mid-century mahogany table by T.H. Robsjohn-Gibbings, a hemp rug hand-knotted in Nepal and a cream-coloured sofa designed by Yovanovitch himself – both of which conform to a more neutral palette.

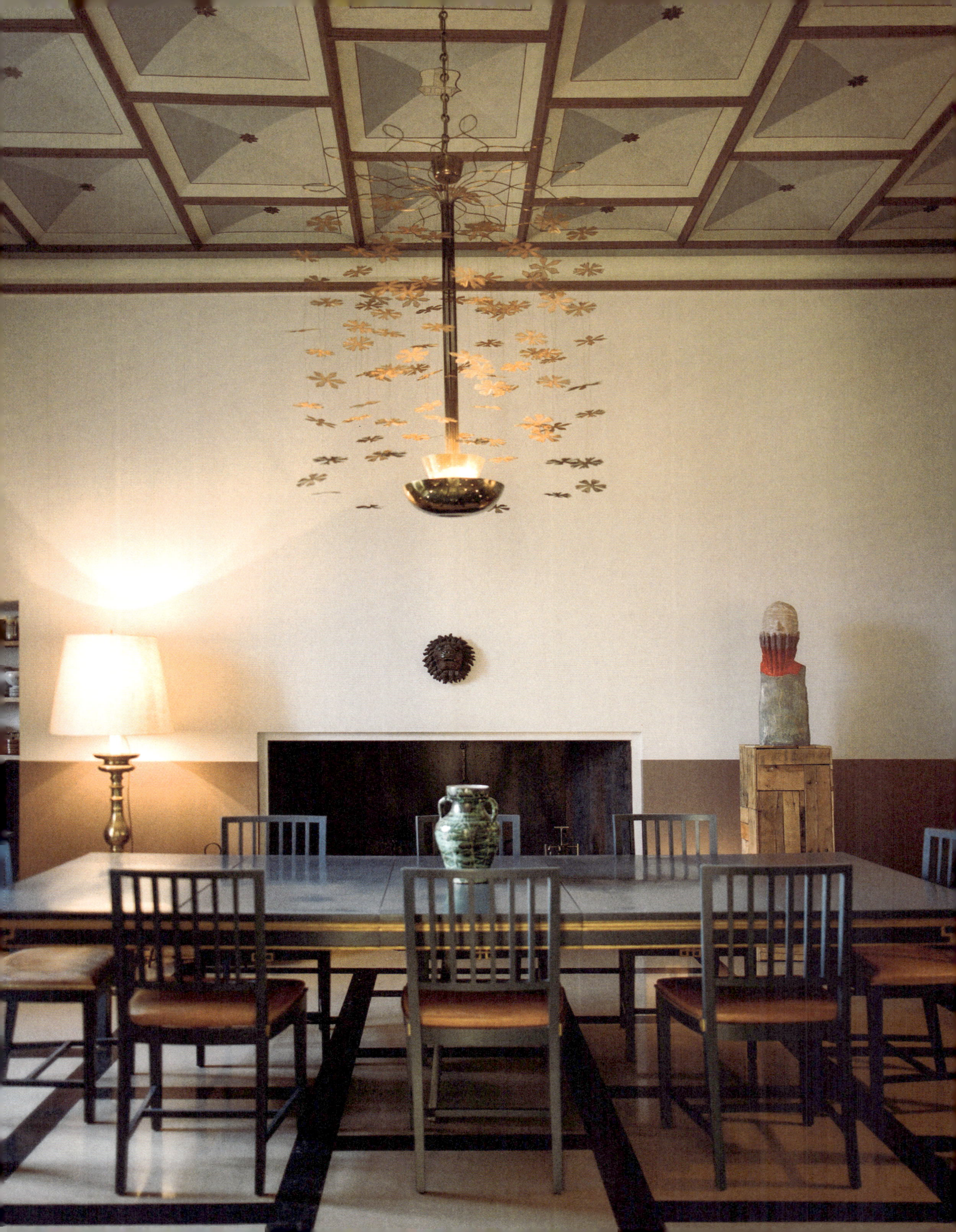

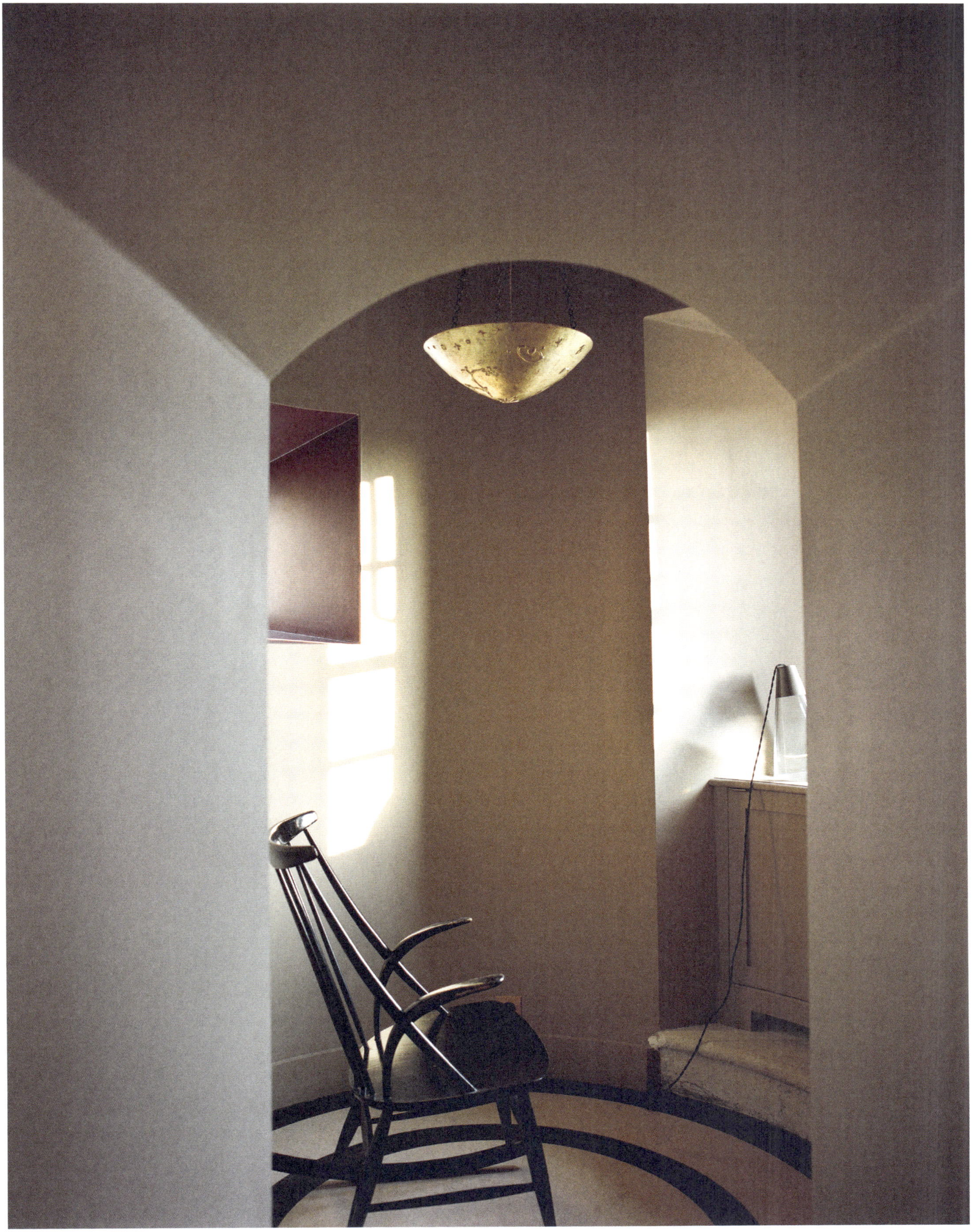

Site-specific artworks define many of the chateau's rooms and outbuildings. In a small, previously abandoned chapel on the grounds, Yovanovitch commissioned contemporary artist Claire Tabouret to paint a haunting mural, *Les Enfants de la chapelle*, on the walls and ceiling, while in one of the numerous bedrooms painter Alexandre Rochegaussen devised a fresco of naively drawn figures on the ceiling in acid shades of yellow and orange.

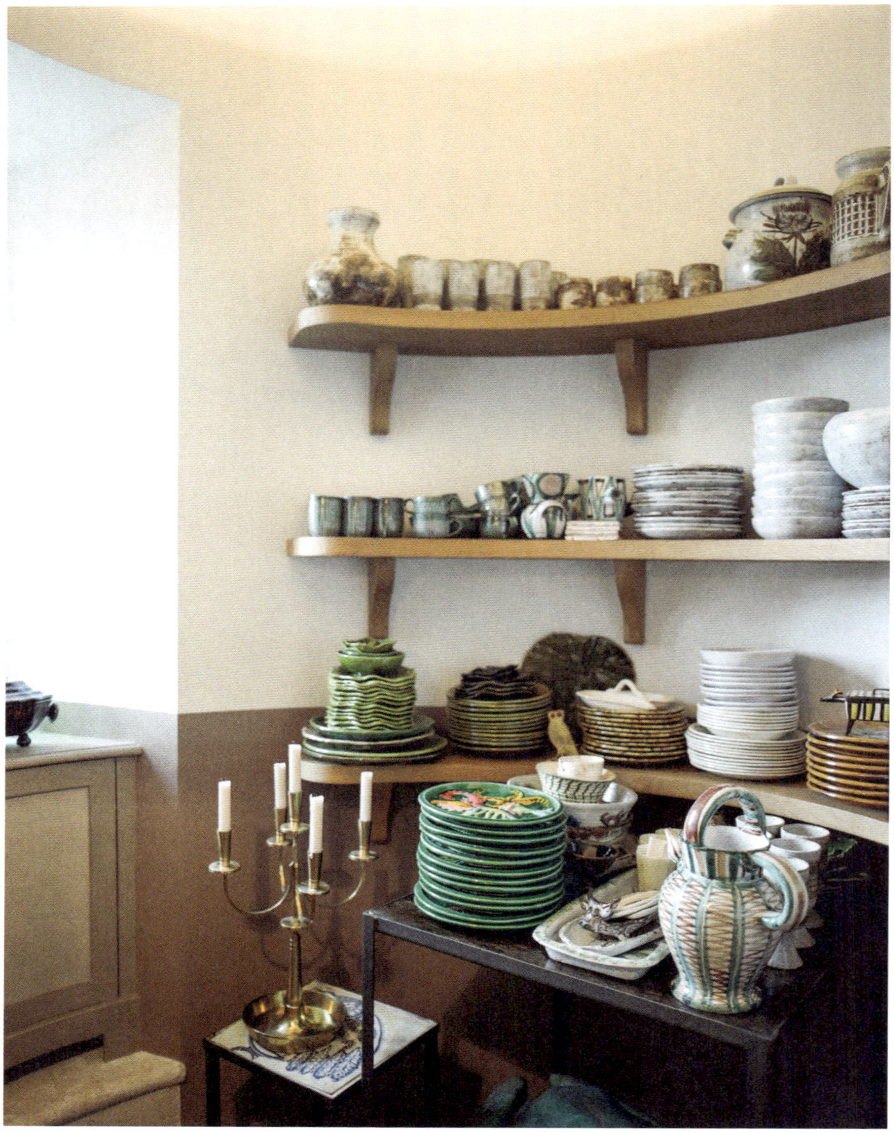

To reimagine the expansive grounds, Yovanovitch called on renowned landscape designer Louis Benech, who created a yew tree maze that snakes across the lawn. 'The surrounding land had no garden, no path, nothing but pine trees,' Yovanovitch says of the isolated location. 'It was certainly an ambitious undertaking, but there was a magic to the property. I was entranced.'

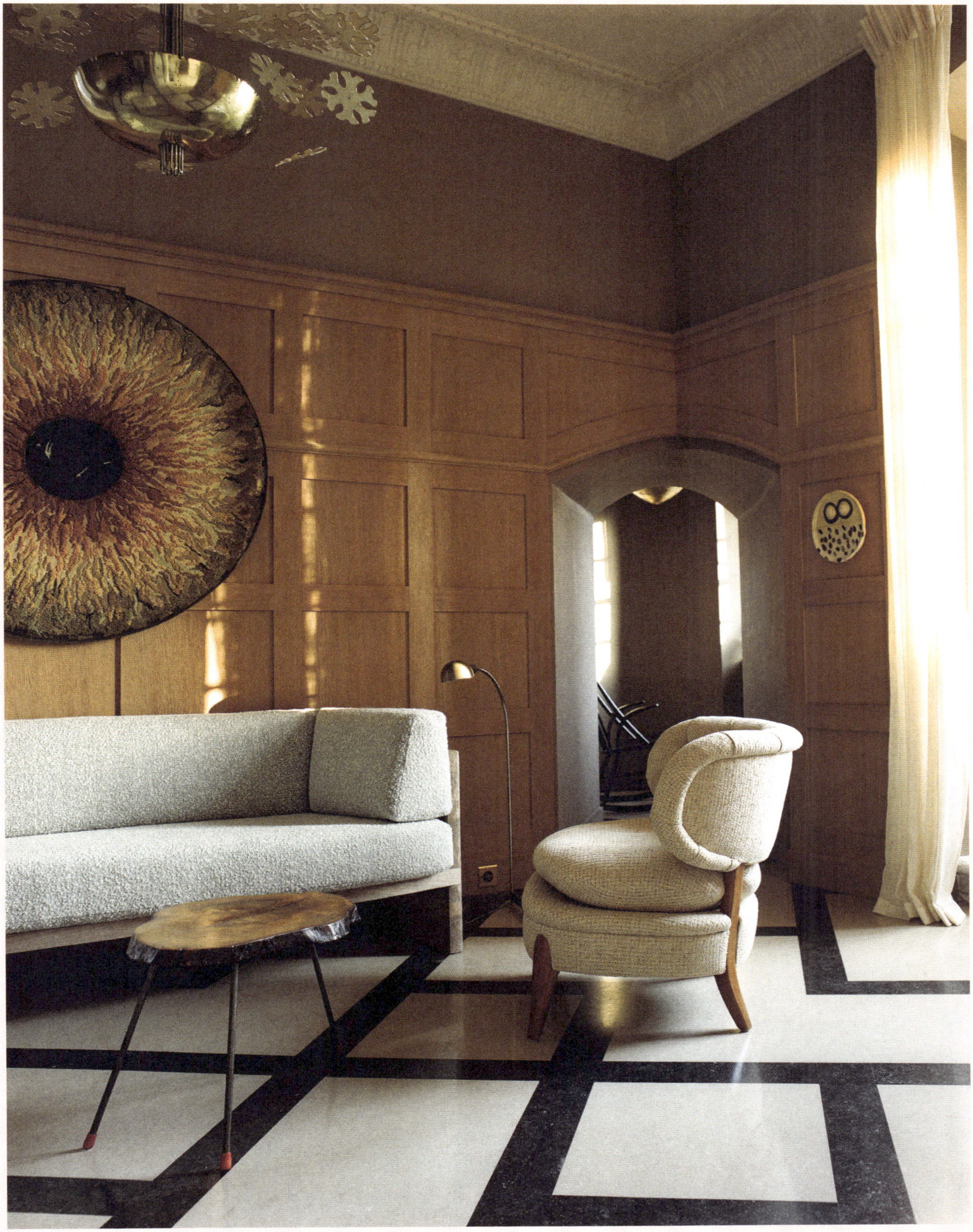

Interview

Pierre Yovanovitch is one of Europe's most sought-after interior designers. He started in fashion, working for acclaimed French designer Pierre Cardin, but left in 2001 to open his own interiors studio. Known for his refined yet unpretentious interiors, he has designed countless spaces for prestigious private and commercial clients from New York to Tel Aviv and beyond. In 2021 he launched his own furniture line and showroom in Paris, where he spends his time when not at his Provencal estate.

Pierre Yovanovitch

What is the history of the chateau?

PY: It was constructed in the early 17th century. The property had belonged to the Fabrègues family, Provençal artisans who were made nobles in the 1400s. It did not leave the Fabrègues family until my partner and I purchased it in 2009. The property is located on the northern edge of the Var region in Provence. There is not another structure in sight. The space, the silence and the smell of the forest are magnificent.

How did you originally find the property?

PY: I wasn't necessarily looking for a country home; I thought it would be too much upkeep. In 2009, however, I was flipping through the real estate pages of a magazine and spotted the listing for the chateau and had to go see it for myself. The rest is history. I know the region well as I grew up in Nice, so the estate ended up being a very natural fit.

What state was the building in when you first found it? What were some of the major interventions made?

PY: Initially, I planned a modest renovation, but when I realised the roof needed extensive repair, I decided to examine the entire structure. I learned that it had no foundations aside from under one of the four towers – the only part of the chateau with a cellar. Except for that it was built directly on clay, to the extent that the facade tended to tilt forward. To reinforce it, foot-thick metal beams were installed behind the walls. We ended up having to renovate almost everything. One of my favourite features that we preserved were the coloured tiles depicting the different seasons, which were installed in the 19th century atop the chateau's four towers.

How do you approach designing for yourself differently from designing for a client?

PY: In many ways, it can be more of an involved process because designing for oneself is open-ended, and I love to constantly evolve the design of my home and take it in new directions. That said, I try to lead all of my design work with my intuition, even with client work – with my own home it's particularly personal and exciting for this reason.

What was the primary concept behind the design?

PY: I typically work to restore the historical integrity of a building to the best of my ability. I love the minimalist spirit of the 17th-century architecture of the chateau, though structural issues with the building made it impossible to preserve everything. In this way, it was about preserving the original essence of the property while infusing it with some new life and contemporary elements. I often update the interior of the space and work with artists to create site-specific works.

Each room is defined by a different bold colour or pattern – petrol blue in the sitting room, neon orange, yellow and teal in the bedroom, a trompe-l'oeil ceiling in the dining room. What is your process in discerning these bold elements?

PY: I like to distinguish the spaces of the home with different colours. It brings a different energy to each area of the house which can help set the tone for different facets of the day. I also work to change the wall colours every so often to keep things interesting. I've worked with a handful of painters I admire, Matthieu Cossé, Rochegaussen, Claire Tabouret, to create site-specific frescos on my property. I love how these interventions tell a story and incorporate an age-old form of painting as a tie-in with the historic nature of the property.

You're known for being a prolific collector of contemporary art. Did your collection help shape the design of the space?

PY: Definitely. Art is a central part of my design work and something I use to help bring a unique character to any space and really set the tone for the property. With my own home, I love this idea of inviting contemporary artists I admire to stay on the property while they create a commissioned piece as it fully immerses them in the space and, in my opinion, can provide a much richer story to the work.

The chapel on your property was painted by the French artist Claire Tabouret. Can you explain the concept behind the project? How do you normally use the chapel?

PY: Yes, the fresco Claire created reflects the subject of childhood, a theme that is central to her work. The painting is composed of 85 children. It unveils her own image of childhood and also ties into the reflective nature of the building as a former 17th-century chapel. I continue to use the chapel as a place of solace and reflection.

The property hosts a Louis Benech–designed yew maze. Do your guests ever get lost in it?

PY: Ah, not yet! The environment of the region is quite finicky. It can get very cold at night and hot during the day, so we really wanted to work with someone who understood the region and there is no greater mastermind than Louis. In terms of a brief, I really let Louis lead the charge and he did a brilliant job of using the landscape to frame the home. I did request a maze, which Louis, begrudgingly, created for me.

How do you spend a typical day there?

PY: I spend a lot of time gardening. Spending time in nature grounds me, and I've learned a lot from working with Louis. With interior architecture, you can create the design and the space will more or less look the same way over the years to come. With a landscape, you have to constantly work with the plant life. It's amazing how different the gardens can look after a month of growth – it's a constant effort to maintain, but I love doing it!

Credits

INTRODUCTION

p. 6 – 12 M. Thomas Arch. Photo courtesy of Bohlin Cywinski Jackson

CABINS & COTTAGES

p. 14 James Perkins Studio; photography Ngoc Minh Ngo
p. 16 – 23 Kevin Rylan & Rob Ashford; photography Chris Mottalini
p. 24 – 33 Ido Yoshimoto; photography Alanna Hale
p. 34 – 45 Workstead; photography Matthew Williams
p. 46 – 53 Christian & Ruxandra Halleröd; photography Erik Undehn
p. 54 – 65 Ionna Vautrin; photography Gianni Basso
p. 66 – 73 James Perkins Studio; photography Ngoc Minh Ngo

COASTAL HIDEOUTS

p. 76 Photography Andrea Wyner
p. 78 – 89 Wilbert Das, D.A.S. Atelier
P. 90 – 99 Photography Andrea Wyner
p. 100 – 107 Hauvette & Madani; photography Luca Madani
p. 108 – 115 Daniel Mitchell & Hilda Sembiring; photography Tommaso Riva

REIMAGINED FARMHOUSES

p. 118 General Assembly; photography Matthew Williams
p. 120 – 127 Practice Architecture; photography Oskar Proctor
p. 128 – 135 General Assembly; photography Matthew Williams
p. 136 – 143 Timothee Mercier, Studio XM; photography Simone Bossi
p. 144 – 153 Atelier Rua; theAdresses; photography Francisco Nogueira
p. 154 – 165 John & Juli Daoust Baker, Mjölk; photography Andrew Rowat

SAND & STONE

p. 168 – 177 Carl Gerges Architects
p. 178 – 187 Porky Hefer; photography Katinka Bester
p. 188 – 199 Margherita Rui; photography Giulio Ghirardi
p. 200 – 207 Petronio Studio; photography Lance Gerber
p. 208 – 213 Studio KO; photography Matthieu Salvaing

DECORATED DENS

p. 216 – 225 Anna Spiro Design; photography Timothy Salisbury
p. 226 – 233 Jean-Pascal Lévy-Trumet www.jplt.net; photography Aurélien Chauvaud
p. 234 – 241 Fundaziun Not Vital; photography Paolo Abate
p. 242 – 251 Pierre Yovanovitch; photography Mary Gaudin

CONCEPT & TEXTS LAURA MAY TODD
EDITING LÉA TEUSCHER
BOOK DESIGN ELISE CASTRODALE

Sign up for our newsletter with news about new and forthcoming publications on art, interior design, food & travel, photography and fashion as well as exclusive offers and events.

If you have any questions or comments about the material in this book, please do not hesitate to contact our editorial team: art@lannoo.com

D/2021/45/267 – NUR 450/454
ISBN: 9789401478328
www.lannoo.com